FEUDAL BRITAIN

To R. G. C.

FEUDAL BRITAIN

The Completion of the Medieval Kingdoms
1066-1314

BY

G. W. S. BARROW

Professor of Medieval History University of Newcastle-upon-Tyne

EDWARD ARNOLD

Printed in Great Britain by
Whitstable Litho Ltd., Whitstable, Kent

AUTHOR'S PREFACE

No-one attempting a survey of British history from 1066 to 1314 can complain of any lack of expert guidance. The richness of recent original work on this period is indeed embarrassing. It is not only that articles on specialised topics, large-scale monographs, and good editions of original documents exist in abundance, and that in the main they are characterised by the highest standards of scholarship. The history of these centuries is also illuminated for the student by a number of outstandingly good general works, some of which, such as Pollock and Maitland's *History of English Law* or, in our own time, Sir Frank Stenton's *Anglo-Saxon England* and Sir Maurice Powicke's *King Henry III and the Lord Edward*, have become classics of historical literature. Nevertheless, modern historical scholarship is so penetrating, and advances so rapidly on so wide a front, that even general surveys of the type of the *Oxford History of England* may be too congested with detail to make the best introduction to the serious study of our history. For example, in the latest Oxford volume to appear, *The Thirteenth Century*, Sir Maurice Powicke treats of ninety-one years of English history in 778 pages.

There may, therefore, be a place for another kind of general survey which, while based as closely as possible on the original sources together with the best from past research, and using a representative portion of the huge mass of current research, nevertheless attempts to cover a longer period in smaller compass and with greater emphasis on the most important themes. *Feudal Britain* is intended to be a survey of this sort. Its very considerable indebtedness both to specialised studies and to a number of general works will, I hope, be made clear both in the course of the text and in the footnotes. At the same time, the book stands as an independent essay on the history of Britain between the two decisive battles of Hastings and Bannockburn. At a number of points where the interpretation of the evidence is controversial, I have put forward what seems to me to be the historically preferable view even where the controversy has been between scholars of equal eminence and repute. Here and there, as in the case of Becket, disagreement runs too deep to be resolved, while elsewhere, as with the death of Arthur of Brittany, the essential facts cannot be ascertained.

5

Author's Preface

It should be emphasised that this book is not a history of England, with a few chapters on the Celtic fringe thrown in for completeness' sake. It is a serious attempt to trace the medieval ancestry of modern Britain, to narrate the development of England from 1066 to 1307, of Scotland from 1058 to 1314, and of Wales in the thirteenth century, in as full a manner as possible and in relative proportion.

I am happy to acknowledge my personal indebtedness to a number of friends who have helped me in the writing of this book. In particular, I should like to thank Miss Kathleen Major, Principal of St. Hilda's College, Oxford, and Mr. R. G. Cant, of St. Salvator's College, St. Andrews, who read the work in typescript, corrected many faults and suggested several improvements. I am grateful to Dr. A. MacPhee, of the University of London, who read part of the typescript and offered some useful criticisms ; and to Mrs. A. Munro, for typing almost the entire text. Finally, I wish to thank my wife, whose interest in the book and encouragement while it was being written have been unfailing.

G. W. S. B.

University College London,
1956.

CONTENTS

7

Contents

PART III

The Channel State

PART IV

Wales and Scotland

PART V

England in the Thirteenth Century

Contents

PART VI

The Long War

9

MAPS AND DIAGRAMS

MAP I. THE DIVISIONS OF ENGLAND AND WALES AT THE TIME OF
THE NORMAN CONQUEST

The names of shires derived from their shire towns are not shown
separately. Stippling indicates land over 1,200 feet

PART I : INTRODUCTION

CHAPTER I

THE MEDIEVAL SETTING

THE patient work of scholars has succeeded in breaking down much of the rigid barrier which in our historical thinking used to divide the " middle ages " from the " modern world ". There is always a danger that a term coined at first for convenience, to enable the mind to grasp the unity of vast periods of time, may assume a deeper and more categorical meaning. The constant use of the phrase " middle ages " has encouraged, at least half-consciously, a belief that the whole range of human life in Europe before A.D. 1500 possessed qualities, " medieval " qualities, which marked it off sharply from the modern age that has succeeded it. As we are now slowly coming to realise, for many important aspects of civilisation this division is either too sharp, or made at the wrong point in time, or even quite meaningless. Nevertheless, when a wider knowledge and deeper insight have shown that the clear-cut demarcation between medieval and modern is an illusion, it will always be necessary, in any study of European history, to propound—and to criticise —generalisations about the period and people normally comprehended in the terms " middle ages ", " medieval society ". And in any such judgments passed on the epoch as a whole, the character and achievement of " medieval Europe " will stand or fall on the history of roughly two hundred years, from the end of the eleventh to the beginning of the fourteenth century. If there was ever a truly medieval Europe, capable of being studied as a whole, worth contemplating for its own sake, it reached its highest achievement and built up its most characteristic institutions within these approximate limits of time.

Merely to reflect on the quality of this achievement is to grasp the truth of the statement. The range and inventiveness of these profoundly creative centuries is astonishing. The most sustained and thoroughgoing attempt to give a framework of law and discipline to the community of Christian folk, under the admonishing direction

13

of a reformed (and highly bureaucratised) Papacy; the nearest approach to the notion of one central secular rule and headship over western Europe which the consistent policy of emperors supported by the massive propaganda of theorists could bring about; the apogee of secular and Christian monarchies in the reigns of Frederick II in Sicily and Louis IX in France; the sermons of St. Bernard; the *Summa Theologica* of Thomas Aquinas; the exemplification of modern scientific method in Robert Grosseteste's and Theodoric of Freiberg's work on optics; the *Divine Comedy* of Dante; the " description of all England " in the Domesday Book; the universities; the building of the great cathedral and monastic churches of north-west Europe—all these things, many of which we think of as characteristically medieval, were the products of this age.

We shall be concerned in this book with an account of the nations and kingdoms forming what is now Britain, during these centuries, and within the context of this frequently creative and always restless activity. It would be surprising if this brilliant flowering of European life had not been reflected in the remote, yet rich and busy island of Britain. In Roman times she had experienced close integration in a Mediterranean culture. Since the sixth century, she had been drawn more and more effectively into the orbit of the continental society which slowly grew from the interaction of barbarian peoples with classical civilisation. In fact, Britain was affected deeply by the " renaissance of the twelfth century ",[1] by the tremendous expansion of human energy in greatly diverse pursuits, military, commercial, industrial, and intellectual, which made possible, though it does not explain, the greatness of the age. Britain drew inspiration and confidence from the fresh thought and experiment and new institutions of the continent; but also, in turn, she herself contributed much to the enduring work of medieval Europe, and for herself devised institutions that have lasted to the present day. The geologist's dictum that " the present is the key to the past " may here be applied to human history. The British Parliament, the Common Law, much of the pattern and structure of local government, the preservation of the separate identities of England, Scotland, and Wales, the organisation of the Church of England, even in a sense the concept of limited monarchy in Britain,

---

[1] An expression familiarised by C. H. Haskins's admirable book of which it forms the title (Harvard, 1927).

all these stand today as monuments to the genius or tenacity of the twelfth and thirteenth centuries. They are not mere relics or antiques from the past, nor are they like piles of ancient documents, unaltered save for layers of grime. Rather do they resemble some old country house, which may have had something added or taken away by each successive generation, but which preserves for all that the spirit and some of the form of the original structure.

At the date at which our account opens, about the middle of the eleventh century, much of this development lay far in the future. It has been said that a mainspring of the age was an expansion of human energy. A feature of this expansion, in its simplest physical sense, was already showing itself before the end of the century. The hundred years before 1150 were, above all, years of *movement*: not the blind, instinctive migration of whole peoples, but the purposeful journeying of individuals and small groups. Many different sorts of traveller persevered in the face of obstacles to communication which were often fearsome. Merchants, for example, from northern Italy or the Rhineland, penetrated to every part of Europe exposing new wares for sale and seeking new sources of raw materials. Professional soldiers offered their services in foreign lands, and found an unequalled arena for their prowess, once the attempted recovery of the Holy Land had been proclaimed, either in the Near East itself or in countries such as Sicily, Greece, and southern Italy which lay temptingly in their path. Men of religion were stirred to send themselves into a double exile, both from the world and far from their own homes, and to carry the witness of their strict and ordered Christian life to areas where the teaching of the Church pulsed feebly or not at all. Most striking of all these examples of movement, the ruling aristocracy of Normandy and northern France, with a self-confidence that was irresistible, seized power in many parts of the world known to the west and proceeded to exercise their undoubted ability in the art of government.

This book begins at the most famous date in English history, and closes at the date best known in the history of Scotland. During the intervening two hundred and fifty years, the two kingdoms which together form modern Britain took on their final shape. At the start of this period, the geographical kingdom of England meant in practice the country south of the River Tees and east of Offa's Dyke; and in this area itself the separatism of local culture and local custom meant that though a single king might rule, he ruled nevertheless over a divided people. The Scottish monarchy had barely begun the laborious process of bringing under its sole governance the diverse and often mutually hostile peoples dwelling in what is now called Scotland. Wales the English had not succeeded in subduing, but at the same time no Welsh dynasty had accomplished the unifying work which in England had been carried out long before by the West Saxon ruling house, and which was shortly to be achieved in Scotland by Malcolm Canmore and his sons.

The contrast between this state of affairs and that prevailing in 1314 could not be more striking. The English nation had recently lived through a reign of thirty-five years which had demonstrated unmistakably that it was a united, self-conscious, homogeneous kingdom, ruled by a powerful and centralised monarchical government. The English king had brought under his direct control that part of Wales not already distributed among landowners of Anglo-Norman origin. He had followed this up by an attempt, more ambitious and more nearly successful than any between the Roman occupation and the eighteenth century, to give political reality to the idea, long grounded in history and literature, that Britain formed a single country. The failure of this attempt, which brings our period to an end, meant that development was arrested in the condition reached at the opening of the fourteenth century. For the next 400 years, England and Scotland developed not only along separate courses but actually in mutual antagonism.

A word should be said here about the title of this book, which is intended to express the dominant theme of the period. It was not chosen without hesitation. The period is, indeed, characterised by several different motifs, all of them prominent and formative. At no time in our history has foreign, especially continental, western European, influence been so pervasive in every field of life. At no time has the Church, taken as an institution set within and over the whole body of the faithful, played so masterful a role in social, political, and even economic affairs. At no time since the classical age has nationality counted for less, or the belief been more widely accepted that England, like the other states of western Europe, was a member of a single Christian society. Despite all this, the history of England, Wales, and Scotland in this period is best regarded as the history of an essay in government, whose basic principles were those usually summed up in the term " feudalism ". It is not here suggested that the effective unity of the English or of the Scottish kingdoms could have been achieved only by applying feudal ideas. The fact with which we are concerned is that that was how it was achieved. The adoption and adaptation by the monarchy of the principles and practice of feudalism set the course for the momentous developments here described.

Our story properly commences with the most famous of all ebullitions of Norman power-mania, the conquest of England in 1066 by the Duke of the Normans himself. But first it will be as well for us to follow the Conqueror's example, and to find out something of the nature of his new kingdom as it was (to use the phrase of the compilers of Domesday Book) " in the time of King Edward ", that is, at the death in 1066 of the last ruler of the ancient House of Wessex, Edward the Confessor, whose heir Duke William claimed to be.

CHAPTER II

IN THE TIME OF KING EDWARD

1. *The countryside and the peasants*

NEAR the beginning of his account of English law, a writer of the early twelfth century declared : " The kingdom of England is divided into three parts : Wessex, Mercia, and the land of the Danes." The fact that this writer was ignoring altogether Northumbria beyond the River Tees only serves to emphasise the extremely provincial quality of the country which William of Normandy conquered. Between Wessex, the region south of the Thames, and Mercia, between Thames and Mersey, provincial differences were not fundamental. But these two provinces together were sharply marked off, in custom and social structure, from the territory known as the " Danelaw ", which comprised about fifteen counties on the east side of England, reaching from Thames to Tees, and bounded on the west roughly by the line of the Roman road called Watling Street. At the two extremities of Wessex, the counties of Cornwall and Kent, neither of which had formed part of the original West Saxon kingdom, exhibited highly individual features. Similarly, within the Danelaw itself, there were four distinct territories, Yorkshire, the shires between Humber and Welland, those between the latter river and the region of London, and East Anglia (Norfolk and Suffolk). By 1066, all these districts, divergent as they might be in character, had been brought within one system of administrative divisions, or " shires ", corresponding almost exactly to the counties of the present day. There were also smaller divisions, known as " hundreds " in the south and midlands, " wapentakes " in the northern Danelaw, which were of particular importance for taxation, keeping the peace, and dispensing justice. The extreme north of England, " Norteisa " (" north of Tees ") as the Normans afterwards called it, was neither shired nor divided into hundreds. It consisted of a number of semi-independent lordships, of which the largest were the earldom of Northumberland (between the Tyne and Holy Island) and the lands and people known as "Haliweresfolc" (literally, "saint's folk") subject to the church of St. Cuthbert at Durham.

If a modern traveller, however, could undertake a journey across eleventh-century England, it would not be these local distinctions which would impress him first, but the one common feature presenting a fundamental contrast with the country today. A population of not more than a million and a half dwelt almost entirely in small villages and hamlets, and earned its living by working the land. Much of the countryside was heavily wooded, and elsewhere a vast acreage was undrained swamp or unworkable peat-bog. The woodland provided the essential cover for the game animals which it was a chief occupation of kings and other great lords (openly) and of the rest of the population (surreptitiously) to pursue. But the proximity of this wild country to nearly all inhabited places had its disadvantages. Both forest and swamp made excellent hiding for the outlaw and breaker of the peace, as well as other undesirable creatures. A Northamptonshire squire of the mid-twelfth century could speak quite casually of the possibility of his livestock being carried off by wild beasts.[1]

In most of Wessex and the midlands, the ground that could be worked by village communities stretched around their dwelling-houses in a great unfenced plain of arable. This plain was divided in two ways, first agriculturally, secondly according to its ownership or tenure. For farming purposes, all the ploughed ground was distributed either in two or in three big fields, each one of which in turn lay fallow for a year to allow the soil to recover its fertility. The remaining field or fields would be put down partly to winter-sown, partly to spring-sown corn. From sowing till harvest a fence round the whole field kept out the villagers' animals, who found their feeding either on the permanent pasture common to the whole village, or (after haymaking and harvest respectively) in the hay-meadows and on the corn-stubble. The great fields, several hundred acres in extent, were far too big to be ploughed in a single operation; so, according to the lie of the land and the limitations of ploughman and plough-beast, they were sub-divided into

---

[1] Osbert de Wanci, *c.* 1150, referring to Astwell in the south of Northamptonshire; cited by Sir Frank Stenton, in *The First Century of English Feudalism* (Oxford, 1932), 246-7.

" furlongs " (literally, " lengths of a furrow "), which could be ploughed in one piece.

The tenurial division had come about originally from a distribution of the ploughable ground among the first village settlers. Each man was allotted a number of acre or half-acre strips, distributed equally among the big fields and scattered here and there in the various furlongs. At first the intention may have been that each head of a household should have roughly the same amount of land, and the dispersal of strips made sure that everyone had his share of good and bad. The degree of equality among the peasant farmers which this system implied no longer existed by the time our period begins. The strip-holdings, and the number of beasts allowed to pasture on the common (which was strictly proportionate to the acreage of arable held), might differ in quantity, and descended by inheritance or sale in the families of the more substantial peasants. While arable and stock were owned individually, the crops to be grown, the dates of ploughing, sowing and reaping, and the periods during which animals might graze in the different fields, were subject to the decision of the village. The necessity for common action which this practice entailed can hardly have been a tiresome burden of responsibility, for these farming operations were rooted in longstanding custom which it would have been impossible for an ordinary villager to override.[1]

Geography determined the range of the " open field " system ; it did not find a place either in the really hilly regions of north and west,[2] or in the densely wooded areas, such as Essex, Kent, and Sussex. In these parts the average peasant's holding was more compact, and might be an isolated clearing, a " denn " or " fold " in the south-east, a " thwait " in the north country. In Kent and Sussex the inhabitants of many villages had pasture rights in the Wealden forest or in salt-marshes which might be many miles distant. Likewise, in the moorland areas of the north, the dale villagers held stretches of rough upland grazing, called " shielings ", to which in the early summer they moved themselves with their sheep and cattle, remaining there until the pasture was exhausted.

In most of England outside Kent and parts of the Danelaw the

[1] See Map III, p. 95.
[2] H. P. R. Finberg (in *Devonshire Studies* (1952), 265-88) has shown that contrary to accepted belief many Devon villages used the open field system.

free peasant farmer, the *ceorl* (churl), was obliged to perform labour service for a lord. The inhabited land was largely composed of landlords' estates, known to us by the Norman name of " manors ". It is essential for an understanding of medieval economic history to grasp that the agricultural population and its holdings lay inside the manors. Briefly, the manorial system meant that practically every peasant holding land for his own support was also bound to contribute labour to keep his lord's estate in cultivation. In return, he looked to the lord for protection, for the security he might give in hard times, and in some cases for supplying him, at the start of his tenure, with the necessary implements and stock. The lord's own land, his " demesne ",[1] was not always distinct agriculturally from that of the peasants ; his arable, like theirs, might be dispersed in strips (or at least in furlongs) in the open fields—he simply had more of it. But he usually had a larger area of ground enclosed for his own sole use, where perhaps his hall would be built. In addition, his rights in and control over the uncultivated wood or heath might be extensive, and there was little to prevent an influential lord carving out a park for his deer in such territory. If, under the system of communal agriculture described above, there was an increase of population, the best outlet for a land-hungry peasant lay in this " waste " ground ; often, only a lord could give him permission to make a new clearing, or " assart " as it was called, and only from a lord could he obtain the necessary capital assistance. This assarting of fresh ground was going on throughout our period, and is one of the most notable features of medieval English agriculture.[2]

We may with reasonable accuracy divide the midland and south-country peasant hierarchy on the eve of the Conquest into three grades. The most substantial peasants, the *geneatas*, were unquestionably free men. They were nevertheless subject to a lord, and paid rent in recognition of his lordship, but the labour services which were performed, e.g. haymaking and reaping, were mainly seasonal and seldom burdensome. There is little contemporary evidence as to the amount of land held by individual members of this peasant aristocracy. To judge from later evidence, there was

[1] This word, like manor, is Norman-French, and is merely a variant of domain, derived, as are several medieval words, e.g. dungeon, from the Latin *dominium*, " lordship ".

[2] For an example of this process, see below, p. 108.

much variety in the size of their holdings, though it was probably uncommon for them to consist of less than one virgate or yardland (about thirty acres). In some parts of England, particularly the western shires, men of this class were known in the twelfth century and later as " radmen " or " radknights ", in reference to their ancient duty of riding in their lord's escort.

The peasant in the second grade was called a *gebur* (" farmer "). He was the indispensable peasant tenant of a manorial estate, and to that extent may be regarded as typical. His usual holding was one virgate, in return for which he performed heavy labour services. These might be two days' work each week throughout the year, increased to three during harvest and the spring ploughing. Over and above the week-work, the *gebur* might owe a variety of payments in cash and kind. The fact that on taking up his holding he received stock and implements from the lord of the manor placed him in definite economic and social dependence, and his position tended to set the standard for the whole class of village dwellers or " villeins". Moreover, there was below the class of the *gebur* the third and lowest stratum of peasant society. This was composed of men and women who possessed at most a few acres of arable, and whose humble dwelling-place—*cot, borda*, or cottage—was sufficiently characteristic for a member of this class to be given both before the Conquest and for centuries after it the name *kotsetla, bordarius*, " cotter ", in other words, one who lives in a cottage. The cotter paid little or no rent, and his programme of week-work was considerably lighter than the *gebur's*. In many districts, he was a " Monday man ", owing labour only on the second day of the week, though doubtless ready to offer it for a wage on the remaining five or six.

In Old English law, the peasants of all three grades were freemen. But in the midlands and the south, men of the quality of the *geneat* or radman formed a decided minority, and the economic dependence of the ordinary *gebur* or villein and of the cotter made it easy for foreign lords after the Conquest, accustomed as they were to regard their peasantry as servile, to treat as unfree or at best semi-free the English tenants of their manors. Hence, though in 1066 there were very many small peasants who were legally free men, by the close of our period " villein " had become a technical term to denote peasants (and they were the majority) who were not free at law but were both tied to the manor on which they had been born and subject to the

will of its lord. Their holdings were protected by custom, later to
be symbolised by the record of their entry into their lands, payments
of rent, etc., copied into the manor court roll (" copyhold tenure ") ;
they were said to be " free towards everyone but their lord " ; but
in all other respects their position was subordinate.

While, in the generations following the Norman Conquest, many
formerly free peasants were depressed into the general class of unfree
villeins, this class also received entrants from below. In most parts
of Anglo-Saxon England there were slaves who were legally chattels
of the lords on whose estates they worked. Considerable numbers
of slaves had been made legally free by their masters ; but these
freedmen stayed on their native manors, and while continuing to
work for the lord, often for a wage, they also cultivated the small
plots of land which the lord had assigned to them. The coming of
the Normans and the more effective teaching of the Church gave a
great impetus to the emancipation of slaves, who either as small-
holders or wage-labourers began to swell the ranks of the villeinage.
The villein himself, in our period, might gain emancipation from his
degree of servitude by entering the Church, or, more commonly, by
finding employment in a town and living there without being claimed
by his lord for a year and a day. The air of a medieval town might
be insanitary, but (as the saying went) it made a man free.[1]

In East Anglia and the Danelaw the manorial system was not
characteristic of the countryside as a whole, and the dominant
feature of the village communities was not the presence of lords,
though these certainly existed, but of large numbers of peasants who
were both legally free and economically independent. It has been
convincingly demonstrated by Sir Frank Stenton,[2] that in the
northern Danelaw this phenomenon was due chiefly to colonisation
of the area by the invading Danish armies at the close of the ninth
century. The decision of thousands of socially equal Danish
soldiers to turn their swords into ploughshares for the tilling of
English soil not only made for a more independent peasantry in
East Yorkshire, Lincolnshire, Nottinghamshire, and Leicestershire ; it
also imparted a strongly Scandinavian character to the legal customs,
the land-divisions, and the place-names of this part of England.[3]

[1] Best known as the German proverb *Stadtluft macht frei*.

[2] *Anglo-Saxon England* (2nd edn., 1947), 250-5 ; see also the same
author's lecture, *The Danes in England* (British Academy, 1927).

[3] Among other Scandinavian customs persisting in the Danelaw was

Many of these free peasants of the Danelaw were described in Domesday Book and later documents as " sokemen ". They formed an upper stratum of agrarian society, subject to lords but, in East Anglia at least, they were free to choose what lords they wished. Even in the northern Danelaw, where the place in which their holdings lay invariably determined the particular lordship to which they were subject, the sokemen nonetheless enjoyed a remarkably independent status. The payments and services they rendered were neither burdensome nor of a kind associated with servility.

The word " soke " is usually translated by " jurisdiction ". The modern term is almost certainly too precise and too exclusively connected with the holding of courts of law to convey the fuller and vaguer meaning of the Anglo-Saxon original. It has been suggested that " soke " in fact represented all that was owed to the king from a given area of land, payable by the free men settled upon it.[1] Of course this would include the obligation of attending the king's court, but it would involve various payments and services in addition, such as guarding the king whenever he stayed in the district, carrying food renders to the royal manor, mowing hay for the royal horses' fodder and so forth. The Old English kings had often granted away to bishops and thanes the right to receive these essentially royal dues. Hence the sokeman might be directly subject either to the king or to a great territorial lord. In both cases, the relationship had little to do with agriculture. It was, to use terms which may be too modern for what was after all a primitive society, a political and administrative relationship. Its most prominent feature was, without doubt, the compulsory attendance by the sokeman at the court to which his village was assigned. It was this feature which characterised the northern Danelaw and East Anglia. In this region there were many groups of villages which looked to the lords of certain especially great estates for the exercise of justice. It was, for example, the wide jurisdiction of the great Benedictine abbey of St. Peter of Medeshamstede that gave rise to the " Soke of Peterborough ", which survives as an administrative unit to the present day.

---

the use of a duodecimal system of counting, producing the so-called " long hundred " equal to a hundred and twenty.

[1] R. H. C. Davis, *Kalendar of Abbot Samson of Bury St. Edmunds* (Camden Soc., 1954), p. xl.

It would be easy to draw too simple a picture of the structure of Old English peasant society. Between different regions there were many variations in such matters as labour service or the amount of one family's holding ; within any one region there were numerous gradations of status among the peasants themselves. Variety, in short, was the keynote of social relations on the eve of the Conquest.

2. *Lords and Local Government*

In 1066, the identity of the lesser kingdoms which had formerly composed Anglo-Saxon England was still preserved to some extent by the existence of a number of large provinces ruled by earls. The Northumbrian earldom has been mentioned already. It was divided into two, the name " Northumberland " being reserved for the northern half, lying between St. Cuthbert's Land and the River Tweed, which already formed the border with Scottish territory. Yorkshire, with parts of modern north Lancashire and Westmorland, formed the southern half of the earldom.[1] Southward lay the earldom of Mercia, and less important earldoms, such as East Anglia, while the whole of southern England might be comprehended within the earldom of Wessex. The earl was a royal officer, responsible for the maintenance of the peace within his earldom, and, jointly with the local bishop, for the proper holding of the shire courts, of whose profits he was entitled to a third share. It was his duty to call out and lead the local militia, the *fyrd*, in time of war. It is clear that the king regarded the earldoms primarily as groupings of shires for administrative purposes, to be formed or redivided or suppressed as the need arose. But it is equally clear that among the small class of men who held earl's rank there was a powerful tendency to treat an earldom as an hereditary dignity and source of wealth, and to exploit its local loyalties. From the standpoint of national unity, the earldoms of Wessex and Northumbria were dangerously independent ; and it was natural that on Edward the Confessor's death one of these earls, Harold of Wessex, should in fact be chosen king.

Few earldoms consisted of as little as a single shire, and to carry on the detailed work of local government the king had in every

---

[1] A contemporary inscription in the porch of the tiny church of St. Gregory, Kirkdale (Yorkshire, North Riding) says that the building was " made anew from the ground " in the days of King Edward and Earl Tostig (of Northumbria).

county an officer of lower rank, the " shire reeve " or sheriff. This office was fraught with enormous possibilities. The history of English local government for the next four and a half centuries is a commentary on the position and functions of the sheriff. In King Edward's time he had already begun to assume some of the functions of the earl, even occasionally the military one of leading the *fyrd*. If he did not preside over the shire court, he played nonetheless a central part in its deliberations, for he attended to watch over the king's interests, and it was through him that the king's will was made known to the county. First and foremost, he had the task of collecting every year the rents in money or kind that were due to the king, chiefly from the royal manors. In earlier times these had consisted largely of the food-renders, called the *feorm* or " farm ", which the king's tenants and subjects owed him by immemorial custom. In many counties these dues were probably compounded in a fixed sum of silver, still known as the " farm ", which the sheriff paid into the king's treasury.

While the sheriffs were socially inferior to the earls, they might well be drawn from among the large class of thanes who formed the bulk of the Old English aristocracy. Originally, the word thane (*thegn*) meant " servant ", and the wide variety in wealth and position to be found in the pre-conquest thanage may be explained by the fact that the thanes of a king or an earl would naturally be men of more substance than those of lesser lords. But although some thanes might be lords of many manors while others owned scarcely more than did a prosperous villager, every thane was distinguished from the class of free peasants by his rank and his higher " wergild ".[1] The almost unbridgeable gulf between thane and churl, between *twelfhynde* and *twyhynde*, reveals the intensely aristocratic stamp of Old English society. The thane was normally the holder of land which had been given to him or to his ancestors as a reward for honourable service to the king or some other great lord. In Anglo-Saxon terminology of more primitive times, he belonged to the class described as " companions " (*gesithas*) of a lord, worthy to hold this rank through nobility of birth and, perhaps, proven service in war.

---

[1] This was the compensation which must be paid in law by a murderer and his kinsmen to the relatives of his victim. In most of England, a thane's wergild was 1,200s. (shortened to *twelfhynde*), a churl's 200 (*twyhynde*).

Owing, however, to the absence in Anglo-Saxon England of the rule that a man's estate must be inherited only by his eldest son (primogeniture), the landed estate considered a decent reward for a thane might be sub-divided among his sons and grandsons until the individual holdings of the third generation had become very small. To offset this tendency, it was always open to an able young man of thanely rank to earn some addition to his shrunken patrimony by service with king or earl. Moreover, aristocratic as they were, the English recognised that mere agricultural and commercial prosperity could admit a man into the governing class : a churl who throve so well that he owned five " hides " [1] of land, and a merchant who made three voyages at his own expense, were held to be worthy of " thane-right ".

Of much more recent origin than the thanely class, but equally noble in rank, were the " house-carles ", or military household retainers, introduced by the Scandinavian King Cnut (1016-35), groups of whom seem to have been granted landed estates in various parts of the country. The house-carles were a *corps d'élite* of specialists in warfare, the nearest approach in Anglo-Saxon England to the professional cavalry soldiers, the knights, retained in the household of the Norman kings.

3. *The King*

A deep-rooted strength resided in the monarchy of which Edward the Confessor had, personally, so feeble a grasp. The passing of six hundred years since the Anglo-Saxon settlement of south Britain had not altogether effaced the tribal veneration for the king as descendant of the gods, warrior-leader, law-giver to the folk, and symbol of its unity. Moreover, since pagan times the monarchy had received an enormous accretion of authority first from the close association of early kings with the Christian Church, so that, for example, the kingship had not a little of a priestly character, and secondly, from the prestige which the West-Saxon dynasty had acquired in the ninth and tenth centuries by preventing a Danish conquest of the whole country, and by accomplishing in the process a constructive measure of unification, so that all English peoples and provinces readily acknowledged a single ruling house.

[1] A unit of land varying in area in different parts of the country from forty to one hundred and twenty acres.

In addition to this moral and spiritual prestige, the monarchy's power rested on a material basis that was substantial. There was hardly a county in England in which the king was not a landowner on the largest scale. As he moved about the country with his retinue of priests and officials, thanes and house-carles, he could receive enough revenue from his manors in any one district to enable him to live and to dispense hospitality—in the true tradition of a barbarian leader—on a lavish scale. This direct income was augmented from at least two important sources. First, the king was entitled to a share in the profits of justice done in the " popular " courts of shire and hundred ; moreover, the fines for certain serious crimes were due to the king. Secondly, since at latest the time of Ethelred II (979-1016) Englishmen had been familiar with a system of national taxation, assessed on land, and called, from its originally humiliating purpose of buying off Scandinavian marauders, " Danegeld ". A prescribed sum was levied from each of the recognised units of cultivated land, from the " hides " of the south and parts of the midlands, from the " carucates " or " ploughlands " of the north and east. Each village, hundred and shire was rated, somewhat arbitrarily, at a certain number of these units, and so long as the king's reeve collected the proper amount of geld from every village and larger district it mattered little to the king how the burden of payment was shared out among the local landowners. Some of the greatest of these (unfairly, as it seems to us) obtained exemption from the geld ; but scarcely anybody was exempt from the three duties, much more ancient than Danegeld, of serving in the *fyrd*, and of helping to repair bridges and the king's fortified strongpoints, or boroughs. Altogether, the array of obligations which bound the free subject to the king in Anglo-Saxon England made its monarchy, at least potentially, the strongest in Western Europe.

Something has been said of the local agents, the earls and sheriffs through whom the king made his authority felt. The king was served more directly by a private household, which by 1066 included some men whose tasks were appreciably specialised. The most important were the chamberlains [1] who had charge of the king's " hoard " of jewels and cash and fine robes, and the chaplains who beside their religious duties carried on the work of an official

[1] The English word was *hraegl-thegn*, " servant in charge of clothing ".

writing office, and had developed a formal means of expressing the royal will, both in the solemn " diplomas ", written in Latin and religious in tone, by which extensive and permanent privileges were granted, and in the sharply contrasting vernacular " writ ", which was brief and peremptory, although it was authenticated in a solemn enough manner by having attached to it a big wax seal, showing the king seated " in majesty ". One of Edward the Confessor's chaplains, Regenbald, had an exalted rank equal to that of a diocesan bishop, and may justifiably be regarded as the immediate forerunner of the line of royal chancellors.[1]

To support and advise the king on high affairs of state, or to lead the nation during a minority or vacancy of the Crown, there existed a large but ill-defined council of the greatest of the king's subjects, the *Witan* or *Witena Gemot*, literally, " council of wise men ". All the bishops, the abbots of the greater monasteries, the earls, and the king's thanes, would normally be expected to attend the meetings of this body. The ecclesiastical members, for whom the Archbishop of Canterbury was the natural spokesman, wielded very great influence. Because of its widely representative character, the *Witan's* unanimous opinion would be decisive ; but the occasions when its opinion was likely to be unanimous were rare ; it did not meet with any regularity, and it was in no sense an organised, regulated institution. The last major act of the *Witan* was to precipitate the Norman Conquest : on the death of Edward the Confessor early in 1066, its leading members chose Earl Harold of Wessex as king, and so forced the Duke of Normandy, if he were serious in his claim to the English Crown, to

" put it to the touch,
To win or lose it all."

[1] F. E. Harmer, *Anglo-Saxon Writs* (1952), 59-60.

CHAPTER III

THE CONQUEST OF ENGLAND

FROM 1016 to 1035, England had been ruled in right of conquest by a Danish king. Between 1035 and 1066, the country was threatened seriously and frequently by other Scandinavians intent on conquest. Against this background, the invasion of the Normans seems neither sudden nor unprecedented. And, when all has been said regarding its good and bad effects, it must be borne in mind that England, once conquered by the Normans, was at least never conquered by anyone else. When Duke William had the crown placed on his head on Christmas Day, 1066, he—and his dynasty—had come to stay.

Historians are generally agreed that until shortly before his death the childless Edward the Confessor, who was educated in Normandy and had personal leanings towards French men and manners, wished his successor to be William the Bastard,[1] Duke of the Normans since 1035. Nominally, the Duke of Normandy, ruler of a rich and compact region from the Côtentin peninsula to the mouth of the River Somme, was the subject of the King of France. But ever since the early tenth century, when the Scandinavian pirates had become permanent settlers and had founded the duchy, Normandy had maintained a much greater degree of independence towards the French kingdom than normal feudal custom would have permitted, and no Duke of Normandy would have regarded the possible acquisition of the English throne as dependent on his nominal overlord's consent.

King Edward's intention and the duke's acceptance were probably signalised as early as 1051, when William paid a personal visit to the English court. But between that date and Edward's death English politics had become dominated by the family of the earls of Wessex, who stood for a powerful and growing anti-foreign reaction among the English governing class. Their head until his death in 1053 was Earl Godwine, and he was succeeded by his son Harold, a man of

---

[1] He was the son of Duke Robert I of Normandy by his mistress Arlette, daughter of Fulbert, a tanner of Falaise.

much courage and some ability, free, moreover, from the treacherousness and excessive ambition which characterised his father. Harold established his reputation in English eyes in a brilliant campaign in 1062-3 by which he destroyed the power of the Welsh ruler, Gruffydd ap Llywelyn. By 1065 Earl Harold and his brothers held through their earldoms a political command of the country that was, under the Crown, decidedly monopolistic. Mercia was the only earldom not in their hands. But before King Edward died, the Northumbrians had revolted against Tostig, the particular son of Godwine whom they had for earl, and Morcar, the brother of Earl Edwin of Mercia, was confirmed in his stead. Tostig took refuge in Flanders, determined, however, to regain his rank and position in England.

Duke William cannot have viewed the rise of the House of Godwine with indifference. It seems that at some date in the 1060s a fortunate accident had placed Harold in his power, and that he took advantage of this not only to confer on him the continental honour of knighthood, but to extract in return a promise, sworn on holy relics, that Harold would support the duke's claim to the English Crown. This famous incident is historically extremely obscure ; but there is hardly any doubt that Harold was bound by some allegiance to William, even if it was exacted under what amounted to duress. When the duke began his campaign of invasion, he could portray King Harold not only as a usurper but also as a flagrant breaker of his oath.

The Norman venture was anticipated by an equally-feared attempt at conquest by the King of Norway, Harold " Hardrada " (" the Severe ") who, like his predecessors since 1042, looked upon the English kingdom as his legitimate prize.[1] What made the Norwegian threat in 1066 especially dangerous was that Harold Hardrada was supported in force by the exiled Tostig, who was perfectly willing to attack his brother, and that Tostig had an ally in the King of Scots, against whom there had been since 1055 no effective defender of the northern border. Clearly, an invasion by Tostig, with the troops he could raise in Flanders, and able to use Scotland as a friendly base, would be serious enough. Collaboration

---

[1] *Circa* 1038, the kings of Norway and England had agreed that the first of them to die without heirs should be succeeded by the other ; the King of England, Harthacnut, died first, in 1042.

between him and the Norwegian king, sailing without hindrance from Orkney with a great fleet, produced a situation that could be met only by a resolute national effort of defence. This effort was forthcoming, but unhappily it was divided into two phases, between which there was little co-ordination. In the summer months of 1066, King Harold of England had no means of knowing at which end of his kingdom a major invasion would first be launched ; but a preliminary repulse of Tostig in May, coupled with the knowledge that Duke William's preparations were far advanced, kept Harold in the south, where in September many of his ships guarding the coast were sunk in bad weather. Harold was still in the area of London when it was reported that Tostig and the King of Norway were bringing a fleet of over three hundred ships up the River Humber, into the heart of Yorkshire. The defence of the north lay with the brothers Edwin and Morcar, the earls respectively of Mercia and Northumbria. They did not wait for possible help from the king, but there is no reason to think that their army was not in good heart when it took its stand by the River Ouse at Fulford, south of York, on September 20th. But the fierce and sustained onslaught of the Norsemen proved too much for it, and by the end of the day many of the Englishmen had perished, and York and Northumbria lay at the mercy of the invaders. Before pushing further into England, Harold Hardrada halted his army some miles east of York, at Stamford Bridge on the Derwent. In the meantime Harold of England, moving with great despatch, had gathered an army of considerable size and within four days of the defeat at Fulford had brought it to Yorkshire. The next day (September 25th) Harold's army attacked the Norwegians before they even knew he was on his way. The battle was hard-fought, but the King of Norway and Earl Tostig were killed, and it was a mere remnant of their forces which made peace with Harold and sailed for home. For the English, Stamford Bridge had been a triumph of speed and surprise. But it was the irony of this battle that in overwhelming the Norwegian host King Harold had in fact secured the kingdom not for himself but for the Duke of Normandy.

The north wind that had blown Harold Hardrada's fleet from Orkney to the Humber had kept William on the French side of the channel. To carry out his project, the duke had amassed in the previous months a fleet of warships and transports and an army of some thousands of men, not only his Norman lieges from the duchy but adventurers from Flanders, Brittany and even further afield, lured by the prospect of military glory and the cash and land with which William, if victorious, might be expected to reward them. The bulk of this army consisted of men heavily armed and armoured, and trained, as had become the custom on the continent, to fight on horseback. This cavalry was dominant, but a body of lightly-protected archers provided it with essential support, and there were some infantry. In addition to assembling this force and organising it into a disciplined unit, William successfully sought the most exalted patronage for his expedition. The leaders of the Church thought it a scandal that the Archbishop of Canterbury, Stigand, had been intruded into the primacy while its rightful holder Robert of Jumièges [1] was living in exile, and to this injury Stigand had in their view added the insult of being consecrated by a Pope (Benedict X) generally regarded as uncanonical. The influential Archdeacon of Rome, afterwards Pope Gregory VII, urged the righteousness of William's cause at the papal court, and the duke was sent a banner of Saint Peter beneath which his men could believe that they fought with the blessing of the western Church.

As if to confirm this benediction, the wind began to blow from the south on September 27th, while Harold and the English army were 250 miles from the Channel coast. The Norman fleet sailed from St. Valery-sur-Somme, and by the next day the entire force of knights and archers, with their horses and arms and equipment, and all their attendant paraphernalia,[2] had been brought ashore. The Normans, as an obvious precaution, " dug in ", first at Pevensey, then in a stronger position at Hastings. There was no defending army in the south, but for all that William knew he might be facing a victorious Harold Hardrada, with a fleet of 300 ships which could easily be brought to the channel, and, if the Normans were to ride too far inland from their bridgehead, completely block their line of retreat. But such a move, which could hardly have escaped a viking like Harold Hardrada, was apparently not contemplated by Harold of England, though he had some ships at London. Instead, as soon

---

[1] A Norman protégé of Edward the Confessor, exiled by the Godwine family.

[2] The Bayeux Tapestry makes it clear that while the Normans were ready to rely on foraging for their food, they had to bring their own supplies of wine, in great hogsheads, with them.

as he received news of William's landing (about October 1st), he set off from Yorkshire with the mounted sections of his army, sending out a hurried summons for reinforcements to the men of distant shires. Without waiting for a response to this call, or for Edwin and Morcar to recoup their losses at Fulford, Harold pressed on impulsively to Hastings with his own house-carles and those of his brothers Gyrth and Leofwine who accompanied him. With them was a body of perhaps 5,000 or 6,000 men, ranging from mounted thanes and peasants to rustics armed with primitive stone-slings made out of split sticks. The rapidity of Harold's southward march is astonishing. On the morning of October 14th he had already arrived at a halting place on some uninhabited rising ground a few miles north-west of Hastings,[1] and there William, coming upon him by surprise, gave him battle.

The most vivid representation of the battle of Hastings is given by the wonderful piece of English embroidery, some eighty yards long, known as the Bayeux Tapestry. The artist was obviously prevented by his medium (which was precisely that of a modern strip-cartoon) from depicting a large-scale battle in detail. But a dominant impression is conveyed of the irresistible weight and uniformity of equipment of the mounted Norman *milites* (knights), contrasting with the variously armed Englishmen, among whom, once battle has been joined, there is not shown a single horse. That Hastings was a decisive defeat of infantry by cavalry-with-archers is, of course, a commonplace of history. Its truth is not affected by a recent attempt [2] to prove that the English, contrary to accepted modern belief, were accustomed to fight on horseback themselves. But although it is probable that, in the words of Sir Frank Stenton,[3] " the art of fighting on horseback, if not entirely unknown, was little practised in England ", it does not follow that Harold's defeat at Hastings was inevitable. The more up-to-date tactics and weapons do not automatically win victories. A competent contemporary judge, indeed, advised the Conqueror that his smaller force would be engulfed by English numbers ; moreover, the native army had just defeated the Norwegians, and their morale

---

[1] The lack of habitation is borne out by the earliest accounts, which speak of a battle at the grey apple tree, or at " Senlac ", that is, Sandlake, the name of a small stream within the boundaries of modern Battle.

[2] By R. Glover, *E.H.R.*, lxvii (1952), 1-18.

[3] *Anglo-Saxon England*, 576.

must have been high. The fact was that Harold, through his very energy in taking a large force to the north to deal with Hardrada, and then through his impetuosity in returning to meet William before he could deploy all the resources undoubtedly available to him, had greatly weakened his chances of success. As it was, the Normans found it difficult for some hours to pierce the ranks of the English, and gained the upper hand only when the defenders broke their own ranks to pursue Normans whom they thought (mistakenly) to be in retreat. After this, they were unable to re-form into a solid phalanx and the knights—whether they had deliberately feigned flight, or merely retired to have a better second charge is not certain—rode unchecked among the scattered foot soldiers, hacking and slaying. The gallant resistance of the king and his brothers, who were all killed on the field, could make no difference to the outcome. By nightfall the English army was destroyed beyond hope of recovery.

The rest of the country could not at once admit that Hastings had been decisive. There was still one representative left in England of the House of Wessex, the young prince (*Atheling*) Edgar, grandson of Edmund " Ironside " who had ruled briefly in 1016, and he was in fact elected king. But to much of England Edgar the Atheling could have been only a name, while those who did know him must have realised that he could never provide the leadership necessary at this crisis. As William of Normandy slowly advanced through Kent and Surrey to encircle London, first Archbishop Stigand, and then the other English leaders, among them Earls Edwin and Morcar, abandoned their resistance and submitted to the duke. To charge them with a spineless lack of patriotism would be anachronistic. They could not possibly have foreseen that within twenty years the Old English ruling class would have virtually ceased to exist, that their land would have passed to French-speaking foreigners and that a new direction, harsh and strongly military in character, would have been given to English government. The Duke of Normandy himself did not have this in mind. He took pains to remind them that he had come as the lawful successor to King Edward. He was duly crowned,[1] December 25th, 1066, in King

[1] Because William did not recognise Stigand as rightful Archbishop of Canterbury, he was crowned by the Archbishop of York, Ealdred. Otherwise, the crowning followed the established custom of the land.

Edward's new abbey church, the " West Minster " on the isle of thorns, and after his coronation he issued a writ in English, informing the Bishop and citizens of London that he greeted them as a friend, that he wished them to have the same status in law as they had enjoyed in King Edward's day, and that he would protect them from injury.

William the Conqueror had been extremely lucky. Although before 1066 his own campaigning had brought Brittany into submission, it was not the result of any diplomacy on his part that the Count of Flanders was friendly disposed and was moreover regent for a child king of France, or that the Angevins, the Normans' traditional enemies, were at this juncture incapable of hostile action. William's powers of leadership were immense, but unless he had been able to sail across the channel at the end of September, it is highly doubtful how much longer he could have kept his army together. When the opportunity did come, it was not through the duke's good management that Harold was over 200 miles away, at grips with a rival invader. Finally, when we reflect that the Normans depended on cavalry, and that horses suffer acutely from sea-sickness, we can only marvel at William's good fortune in having a wind that was not merely favourable in direction, but gentle enough not to incapacitate his main fighting arm. From the start the conquest of England had been a fearful gamble ; but few gambles have ever paid so handsome a dividend.

PART II : NORMAN BRITAIN

CHAPTER IV

ENGLAND AFTER THE CONQUEST, 1066-87

1. *The Conquest underlined*

AFTER the submission of the English magnates, and his acclamation and crowning at Westminster, William of Normandy was master of England. The fact that hardly a year passed between 1066 and his death in which the king was not in his saddle directing the suppression of some rebellion should not mislead us into any notion that the conquest of England occupied William for the whole of his reign. Rebellion was endemic in the eleventh-century state. But historians have usually recognised that, by reason of their wide extent and national character, and because of the ferocity of their suppression, the revolts of the years 1068-71 mark a watershed in William's government. The famous nineteenth-century history of J. R. Green goes so far as to say,[1] " It was in fact only the national revolt of 1068 that transformed the King into a conqueror ". To understand why the country did not settle down peacefully after Hastings we must consider first the nature of the Conqueror's early rule, secondly the survival of the threat from Scandinavia.

William took over in its entirety the English administrative and judicial system, and left its operation very largely in the hands of the native magnates, officials and clerks who had served the Confessor. He naturally retained his own household and his own *Curia*, or Council ; but though several of its members, e.g. the two Norman bishops Geoffrey of Coutances and the king's half-brother Odo of Bayeux, and the king's steward William fitz (" son of ") Osbern, were given very great authority in England, the number of Normans entrusted with rule was at first surprisingly small. They were intended to co-operate with the surviving English bishops, abbots and sheriffs, by whom they were greatly outnumbered. Even though

---

[1] *History of the English People* (1878), i. 116.

the king evidently mistrusted the greater English nobles, the Atheling and the earls, Edwin and Morcar and Waltheof of Huntingdon, he did not deprive them of their rank or diminish their honour. On the military side, however, William made a clean break with the past. For him, adequate defence meant castles on the continental model and disciplined bodies of mounted knights under more or less permanent training and ready for immediate action. Hereford, one of the very few castles of the new type which existed in England,[1] was assigned to William fitz Osbern as the headquarters of a new earldom specifically for defence against the Welsh, while at the opposite end of the country the same man was given command of Norwich to guard East Anglia from Danish attack. For the defence of the Narrow Seas, Odo of Bayeux—a bishop in scarcely more than tonsure—was made Earl of Kent, with a new castle at Dover. The two new earls quickly made themselves hated for the harshness of their rule, and after the king had felt it safe to return to his duchy (March, 1067) the men of Kent appealed to the Count of Boulogne to help them get rid of Odo, while the men of Norfolk and the Severn valley rose against William fitz Osbern. In the south-west, the citizens of Exeter ejected the king's agents. On his return, William had little difficulty in putting down these sporadic risings. But within a year, the Atheling had fled to Scotland, giving his sister Margaret in marriage to the King of Scots, and a succession of much graver insurrections forced William to reverse his policy of keeping native leaders in positions of authority, and led directly to the normalisation of England.

There was some half-hearted insubordination from Edwin and Morcar in 1068, but the real trouble began early in 1069 with the burning to death at Durham of Robert of Comines, a Norman placed by the king as earl over Northumbria beyond Tees. This deed, like a beacon, signalled the Yorkshiremen to rise in revolt. In the previous year, however, the Conqueror had constructed a network of castles at strategic centres in the midlands and the north, and the wisdom of this act was proved by the insurgents' failure to capture the castle at York itself. At this point, the Atheling's English supporters might have given up the struggle, but fresh heart was put into them by the appearance of another Scandinavian fleet in the

---

[1] It had been built probably by one of a small group of Normans settled in Herefordshire by the favour of Edward the Confessor.

Humber, this time sent by the King of Denmark, Swein Estrithson. York castle could not stand against the combined forces of Danes and Englishmen, and the news of their success incited the natives of western Wessex and Mercia to rebellion. King William himself led the counter-attack against the Mercians, and after defeating them at Stafford was able to recapture York through the defection of the Danes, who accepted a bribe to retire from the conflict.

In grim contrast with the Danes, who received a price for their part in the rebellion, the English were made to pay heavily. In the winter of 1069-70 the king set about the deliberate devastation of the most fertile and populous areas of Yorkshire. Not only was the livestock slaughtered and the stores of corn and other food burnt ; the implements with which the survivors of this visitation might have hoped to make some recovery in the spring were also systematically destroyed. The Conqueror's whole policy towards the north was negative, but this was destruction of so thorough-going a nature that the king must have rejected all idea of the north forming a useful and valuable part of his kingdom for years to come, and must have viewed it simply as a field for possible military activity. After making a desert of the Vale of York, William took his army across the Pennines in appalling conditions and laid waste, with only slightly less intensity, the shires of north-western Mercia.

Although neither Edwin nor his brother Morcar had joined the rebels in 1069, the leaders included several men powerful in the north, among them one former Earl of Northumberland, Cospatric, and the son of another, Waltheof of Huntingdon. It is an indication of the barrenness of the king's policy towards the north that while he destroyed southern Northumbria he left Cospatric in power beyond the Tees and restored Waltheof to his earldom in the eastern midlands. No sooner had these men been reprieved than Edwin and Morcar came out in revolt. Edwin was soon slain, but Morcar made his way to Ely, where a rich monastery had been built on an island of firm ground in the fens, then so wide and deep that the only practicable means of transport was by boat. A highly miscellaneous collection of men were defying the Normans there. They included viking plunderers, a Danish bishop, and a band of the Abbot of Peterborough's English tenants, who bereaved his church of all its treasures out of pure patriotism because he was a Norman ! Like many other forlorn hopes, the leader of this desperate group, a thane named Hereward, became a popular hero. The Ely rebellion could have been serious only if the Danish king, who brought a fleet to England early in 1070, had persevered with his invasion. But William bought him off, and the Ely resistance was short-lived. The king blocked the escape routes with ships, and had a causeway built across the fen, whereupon all surrendered save Hereward and a few followers, who escaped.

The great insurrection of 1069-70 was the last national rising of the English against their French conquerors. Soon after he had crushed it, the king was employing English soldiers in increasing numbers on expeditions to Wales or across the Channel. It is in fact a sign of the completeness of the conquest that the last really serious revolt of his reign, in 1075, was instigated by a Breton, Ralf, Earl of East Anglia, in conjunction with one of the king's own Norman barons, Roger, Earl of Hereford,[1] and the English Waltheof, who since 1072 had been Earl of Northumberland in addition to Huntingdon. In general, the English gave their support to the king in putting down this feudal rebellion. Ralf of East Anglia escaped to Brittany, but the king dealt drastically with the other two chief offenders, imprisoning Earl Roger for life and having Earl Waltheof beheaded.

If the conquest of England had been sufficiently underlined by 1075, the problem of what were the geographical limits of conquered England still remained. King William was not the man to leave any task half-finished, but he had commitments and ambitions in so many directions that the accomplishing of some tasks might be beyond his powers. We must remember that for William, Normandy, his ancestral inheritance, enjoyed a priority of regard. We should bear this in mind when we consider the king's policy towards the Welsh and Scottish borders. William was clearly concerned about the defence of England against incursions from Wales and Scotland. But he gave a much freer hand to the men entrusted with this defence than to any other of his barons, and he evidently looked on their territories as military " buffer states " rather than as integral parts of his kingdom. Only thus can we explain why Hugh of Avranches was given (1071) the earldom of Chester, together with possession of nearly all the land in his earldom, with " palatine " or semi-regal powers and jurisdiction. This new earldom bordered the province of North Wales (Gwynedd), but Hugh of Avranches

[1] The son of Earl William fitz Osbern, who was killed in 1071.

obviously did not regard his position in Cheshire merely as one of defence. He placed his cousin Robert in a new outpost castle at Rhuddlan, far into Gwynedd at the mouth of the River Clwyd, and anticipated a total conquest of North Wales.

To guard the march against mid-Wales (Powys), the king (c. 1075) established Roger de Montgomery, another of his great barons, with almost equally extensive powers, as Earl of Shrewsbury. The earl erected the castle named after him some twenty miles south-west of the English shire town, on the very edge of purely Welsh territory. Three routes of possible advance into Wales—the northern coastal strip, and the upper valleys of Dee and Severn—were thus given bases. The aggressiveness of these earls in building Rhuddlan and Montgomery was enhanced by the ineptitude of Gruffydd ap Cynan, the only Welsh ruler in the north who might have stemmed the Norman advance, in allowing himself to be captured by them in 1081.

The symmetry of King William's feudal defence against Wales broke down in the southern march after the fall of Earl Roger of Hereford. The king did not put another earl in his place, and the control which had been gained by William fitz Osbern and his son over the district of modern Monmouthshire (Gwent) was offset after 1081 by the rise to power of an able native ruler, Rhys ap Tewdwr (Tudor) in the " southern part " (Deheubarth) of Wales. It is true that in 1081 the king brought an army as far as St. Davids, but after thus employing the method of a " show of strength " customary at this period when nothing more definitive was intended, he acquiesced in the rule of Rhys, though he regularised it by making the Welsh prince's relation with himself a feudal one, equating his position with that of Robert of Rhuddlan in the north.

The problem of the Scottish border was vexed by the militantly anti-Norman feeling of many Northumbrians. In this matter, William not only showed a less constructive approach than in Wales, he also had much less success. Scotland resembled the Scandinavian kingdoms in providing refuge for political malcontents and in being too remote for easy punitive action. A protracted struggle was just beginning between the rulers of England and Scotland for the control of the extreme north of England. The Conqueror's reign saw the first phase of this struggle, and it was indecisive. No fewer than six men, natives and Normans, appointed by William to govern Northumberland, all failed in turn to fulfil their commissions. In

1072, having at last deposed Earl Cospatric, who fled across the border, the king organised a large-scale expedition into Scottish territory, in which the land forces were supported by a fleet. King Malcolm of Scotland decided prudently not to risk a Scottish version of Hastings, and at Abernethy, in the heart of his kingdom, he became William's vassal and gave him as a hostage his eldest son, Duncan.

Later generations of Englishmen and Scotsmen, whose attitude was coloured by the warfare between the two countries, read into this event a declaration that the Scottish kingdom had been brought into formal subjection to England. We should be guilty of anachronism if we followed them in this belief. The notion of sovereignty in any modern sense was not then developed, and we should remember that while today all states are in theory independent, though many are not so in practice, exactly the reverse was true in the eleventh century. Then hardly any state was independent in theory, but in practice nearly all were. It is certain that Malcolm was following precedents in acknowledging the superiority of the English king; but equally certainly he would not have felt that these precedents threatened his independence. The only practical result for William of the submission of Abernethy was the removal of the Atheling from Scotland to the continent. Within a few years, a serious Scottish incursion prompted the English king to send another large force into Malcolm's land, led by his eldest son, Robert. No settled peace was obtained, and the border of England, militarily at least, was in effect withdrawn by the construction of the " New Castle " to guard the crossing of the River Tyne (1080-1). It was left to the Conqueror's other son, William Rufus, to take the problem of the Scottish frontier seriously, and to adopt a policy of treating both Northumberland on the east and the area of modern Cumberland on the west as integral parts of the English kingdom.

2. *The Feudal Settlement*

The social revolution which followed the introduction into England of Norman feudalism was brought about not through any deliberate intention on the Conqueror's part of replacing English by continental custom, but from his need for a large standing army of specially trained knights and a system of castles of a type unfamiliar north of the Channel. A factor of secondary, but not negligible, importance was that many of the leading men who fought for the duke at Hastings were at once rewarded, as they expected, by grants of landed estates which had belonged to King Harold and his followers. Thus, shortly after the conquest, there had been planted in many parts of southern and central England a foreign aristocracy imbued with the feudalism of Neustria (north-west France), the fitness of whose application to their newly won lands they took for granted. Since after the rebellions of 1068-70 the king granted away vastly more land to his Norman or other continental adherents, this application of feudal ideas became general throughout England, and a brief account of them will be necessary in order to understand the change which English society and government underwent.

It was implied rather than stated that the king was owner of all the land in the realm, and that even the greatest of his subjects held their estates by " enfeoffment ", that is, on condition, fixed after some contractual agreement had been reached between him and them. This agreement was symbolised by the ceremony of swearing *fealty*—fidelity—and doing *homage*. The tenant, or vassal, took an oath to support his lord in " life and limb and earthly honour ", and, placing his hands between those of his lord, bound himself to become his man, devoted from henceforth to his service and subject in many aspects of daily life to his will. It is important to understand that a tenant would swear fealty and render homage to a lord in respect of a particular estate. The service due to the lord from this estate, once agreed on, was regarded as fixed permanently, and the tenure of the estate normally became hereditary. It is from the word used to denote an estate of this sort (*feudum* in Latin, *fief* or *fee* in French and English) that our modern phrase, " the feudal system", is derived. Nothing precisely like the fief existed in pre-conquest England. There, land was usually held either by immemorial inheritance, without specific service, or by an outright grant from the Crown, or else under a lease which, while it would normally require some service from the lessee, did not, like the enfeoffment, burden the land itself with a fixed, permanent (and often military) service.

While the feudal lord was assured of the service he needed from the land he had granted out, he parted with direct control of the estate, which he could recover only if the tenant failed to perform his service adequately. The tenant, for his part, expected as his right that the lord should protect his interest, aid him in trouble, defend him in danger, and do him justice in his court. He required that the service due from his fief should not burden it excessively, and felt that he should be free to treat his own fief exactly as his lord had treated his, that is, that he could if need be create smaller fiefs himself in favour of his own retainers. In the ultimate resort, if the lord refused to meet his share of obligations, the tenant might renounce his allegiance by solemn " defiance " (literally, " removal of fealty "). If the lord refused to admit that he had wronged his vassal, defiance would in his eyes be rebellion or even treason ; but in either case it would not be regarded as a really heinous crime : defiance was, as it were, within the rules of the feudal compact. If, on the other hand, a vassal were to desert his lord in battle, or plot against him with his enemies, such conduct would be regarded as the blackest treachery, for which the term *felonia*, felony, was reserved.

Other consequences, " incidents " as they are called, followed from the feudal relationship. To underline the lord's perpetual ownership of his vassal's fief, he was entitled to take it into his own hands on his vassal's death, and to demand payment, a " relief ", from his vassal's heir before the latter could take possession. To ensure that the military service due from the fief could always be performed, the lord had the right to hold a fief in his own hands if the heir was under age and to have custody (" wardship ") of the heir in order to supervise his training and arrange his marriage. Similarly, if the heir were a woman, the lord could, and normally would, personally decide on a suitable husband for her who, after marriage, would himself become tenant in right of his wife and perform the service on her behalf. In the event of a complete failure of heirs, e.g. if the tenant's family died out or if the tenant had forfeited his land by committing a felony, the fief then reverted to the lord's direct possession. In technical language, it " escheated " to the lord (Latin, *excadere*, " fall back "). Finally, in addition to these incidents whose operation was more or less automatic, the lord was entitled to call upon his vassals for help in a dangerous emergency or on an important social occasion. It seems to have become customary before the middle of the twelfth century for a lord to expect an aid, without expressly consulting his vassals, on any of these occasions : (i) the knighting of his eldest son ; (ii) the first marriage of his eldest daughter ; (iii) the payment of his ransom if he should fall into the hands of his enemy.

From this it will be seen that the social structure whose keystone was the fief, permanently owned by the lord, yet as permanently held, in return for specified service, by his vassal, was characterised not merely by the dependence of many lesser men upon a few of the greater—such dependence had been a feature of Anglo-Saxon England—but more essentially by a vastly greater rigidity in the relationship between members of the ruling class, and also by a closer intimacy symbolised in the ritual of homage. The great lords, the " barons ", of the feudal state were bound to the king not only by the traditional allegiance of subject to monarch, but more concretely by the fact that every inch of ground they possessed was held by them as a conditional grant from the king. In like fashion, the lesser landowners held their estates neither independently, nor (save in a few instances) directly of the king ; they were themselves the vassals (" barons ", if the estate of their lord were large) of the greater lords, and were bound to them as intimately and definitely as their lords were to the king. Many of these lesser barons in turn might have feudal tenants of their own, usually trained knights, not men of great property or social standing, yet raised, by virtue of the intensely military cast which the Normans gave to society, above the level of the free peasant or even the thane inexpert in mounted warfare.

This preoccupation of the Normans with military service and skill formed the second feature distinguishing Norman from Anglo-Saxon England. It was a reflection of what amounted to a cult of soldiering on horseback which was far from peculiar to Normandy, but was general in north-west Europe. The concept of military prowess and honour found social expression in the notion forming in men's minds that there could and should be an " order " of knights and knighthood within society, to which young men who had proved themselves in battle or jousting might be admitted only by a solemn ceremony. It is significant for the discussion of how far Norman military feudalism was an innovation in England that the mystique of knighthood had not taken hold among the Anglo-Saxons. If it had done so, it is unthinkable that Earl Harold of Wessex, the greatest man in England under the king, should not have been a knight long before the Duke of Normandy made him one.

The force which King William reckoned necessary to secure his position in England and to defend the country against foreign invasion has been variously estimated to number 4,000 to 7,000 knights. It was quite beyond the Crown's resources to maintain so large a force directly, and, indeed, to have done so would have run counter to accepted feudal custom. Instead, the king established in every part of the country some scores of his most prominent followers (Normans for the most part, but including Bretons and men from Flanders) as holders of great estates, on the specific condition that they would provide the king with a fixed number of knights to serve in his army when required. We may envisage most of the country as divided up into rather less than two hundred estates of this kind, often called " honours " (later, " baronies "), each of which was burdened with a service of so many knights. Within each honour the lord would usually grant out on similar terms to his own tenants enough smaller estates (consisting of one or more " knight's fees ") to provide a fair proportion of the knights for which he was answerable to the king. The remainder of his knights he would keep about him as personal retainers and body-guard, feeding and clothing them from the proceeds of his demesne —that is, the portion of his honour which he had not granted out.

The complement of the field army of cavalry guaranteed in this way was a national system of castles, to which the greater military tenants of the king were bound to send fixed numbers of knights every year for a period of garrison duty. The biggest castles, in the shire towns or at other strategic points, were held in the main by the king himself, under a governor or constable. But he had no objection to the barons building their own castles, in accordance with feudal custom. The Normans had been brought up in a country in many respects more primitive and worse-governed than England, and they were, for example, used to private warfare among themselves, a custom which made the private castle a necessity. We should remember also that for many years after Hastings the Nor-mans were a tiny minority of foreigners among a potentially hostile population. The castle, which served as the home of a great baron and the administrative headquarters of his vast estates, was also the stronghold in which in time of revolt his household and chattels might find safety. It must be added that the private castle survived in England long after the post-conquest period of insecurity, and despite the monarchy's effective banning of private war. Its survival bears witness to the intensely military outlook of the Norman lord, and its multiplication before 1154 stood, as Sir Frank Stenton has written,[1] " for an organization of feudal service in which the defence of the private castle was at least as important as the provision of knights for the King's armies ".

A word should be said about the typical Norman castle, simple enough in our view, yet so novel and invincible for the English. Where no natural feature, such as a rocky outcrop, supplied a site, a mound of earth, a " motte ", was thrown up and compressed sufficiently to take the weight of a square tower or keep, usually made of timber, and surrounded by a wooden palisade. Later, such towers were built of stone. Adjacent to this tower was an enclosure, a " bailey ", palisaded (and perhaps moated) strongly enough to withstand sudden attack. Hundreds of these simple structures were built in the generations after the conquest. Many had only a brief existence, but others were strengthened and elaborated until eventually they became the massive and (until the invention of artillery) the virtually impregnable fortresses of the thirteenth and fourteenth centuries, like Kenilworth in Warwickshire or the huge castles built in Wales for Edward I. Some royal castles, however, must always have been impressive. To make room for Lincoln castle (*c.* 1068) 166 houses had to be pulled down ; and the extent to which the Conqueror's still existing White Tower of London must have dominated his chief city can easily be imagined.

The establishment of Norman barons with their castles and knights meant, by the end of the Conqueror's reign, the displacement of the Old English ruling class. Those native landowners who did survive, among whom the ancient cathedral and monastic churches were the most numerous and important, had to adjust themselves to a new order. A thane who could not provide the crown with knight-service was socially of no account among the feudal baronage. The estates of many thanes must have been embodied subordinately within the great feudal honours, since, in the king's view, all land must be held of him directly by military tenants—tenants-in-chief,

---

[1] *The First Century of English Feudalism,* 197.

47

as they were known—and if a thane could not adapt himself to such a position he had to move down a place in the social hierarchy. It is likely that the campaigns of 1066 and the subsequent rebellions had much reduced the number of thanes and house-carles. Many others are known to have gone into exile, to Scotland, Scandinavia, or even Byzantium. Otherwise, Englishmen of noble birth accommodated themselves as best they could to the needs of their Norman masters, serving the king or learning to become knightly tenants of a feudal honour. Many thanes of small substance may well have seen themselves and their sons sink, in the years after 1066, to a position in society indistinguishable from that of the free peasant, a process which the discontinuance of the wergild system must have hastened. Nevertheless, the replacement of English by foreign lords need not always have been drastic or violent. A number of Norman barons owed their estates to marriage with English heiresses, benefiting perhaps from the freedom of control over property which women enjoyed in the Old English state. There is no doubt that the status of women, which in Anglo-Saxon England had been a high one, was depressed by the introduction of military feudalism.[1]

With regard to justice, however, King William had to temper the Norman wind to the shorn English lamb. It would have been impossible for a few thousand French-speaking foreigners to impose at one stroke an alien law and entirely new courts on the native population. Here the king's policy was a statesmanlike compromise.

[1] For an interesting discussion of this neglected topic, see D. M. Whitelock, *The Beginnings of English Society* (1952), 93-5.

MAP II. THE DEVELOPMENT OF THE CASTLE (*see opposite page*)

A. Corfe, Dorset. A motte-and-bailey castle, using the natural advantages of the ground. The *motte* may be simply the adaptation of a natural hill-top. It and the western ward date from the twelfth century, the southern ward from the thirteenth. (Based upon Ella S. Armitage, *Early Norman Castles of the British Isles* (1912), Fig. 13, by permission of John Murray (Publishers) Ltd.).

B. Kenilworth, Warwickshire. A good example of a castle which has been developed from simple beginnings—an inner bailey with a keep (early twelfth century), and possibly a motte—into an extremely elaborate fortress protected by a long outer curtain wall with three towers, an artificial lake, and south of the lake a massive outwork. The parts emphasised in the diagram belong to the twelfth and thirteenth centuries. (Based upon G. T. Clark, *Mediaeval Military Architecture*, ii (1884), face p. 145, and P. K. Bailie Reynolds, *Kenilworth Castle* (Ministry of Works Guides to Ancient Monuments and Historic Buildings, 1948), by permission of the Controller, H.M.S.O.).

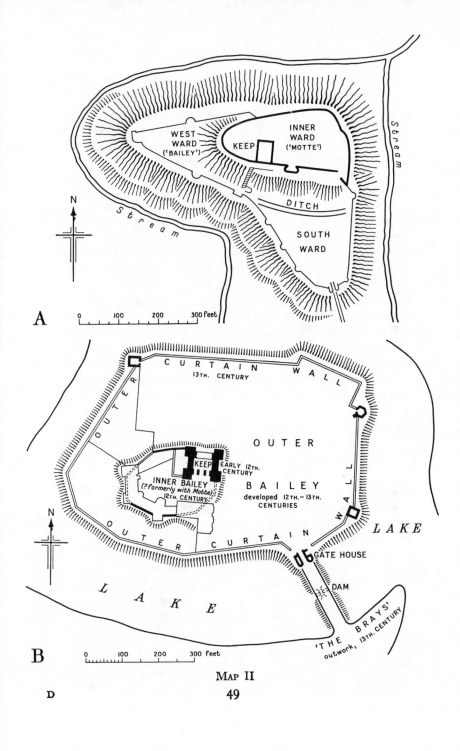

A

WEST
WARD
('BAILEY')

INNER
WARD
('MOTTE')

KEEP

Stream

Stream

DITCH

SOUTH
WARD

N

0   100   200   300 feet

B

CURTAIN   WALL
13TH. CENTURY

OUTER

OUTER

CURTAIN

KEEP   EARLY 12TH.
CENTURY

INNER BAILEY
(?formerly with Motte)
12TH. CENTURY

BAILEY
developed 12TH.–13TH.
CENTURIES

N

OUTER   CURTAIN   WALL   LAKE

GATE HOUSE

DAM

LAKE

'THE   BRAYS'
outwork, 13TH. CENTURY

0   100   200   300 feet

Map II

He retained the courts of shire and hundred which free men traditionally attended. While declaring generally that his continental followers should have his special protection, William decreed that all his subjects should enjoy and observe the law obtaining in King Edward's day. If a Norman accused a native of certain serious crimes, the Englishman might choose the method by which to prove his innocence—either the ordeal of the hot iron, familiar to his race, or the combat favoured by the Normans. Should a Norman fail in this proof, he must pay the fine due to the king under Anglo-Saxon law. By a provision even more strikingly in favour of the conquered, a Norman, accused by an Englishman who was unwilling for the charge to be proved either by ordeal or combat, was required to submit to the peculiarly Anglo-Saxon (or Anglo-Scandinavian) proof of " compurgation ", that is, the clearing of an accused man by oaths sworn collectively, according to complicated formulae, by himself and a body of trustworthy supporters or " oath-helpers ".

On the other hand, the king had to see that no conspiracy of silence on the part of the English should enable groups of natives to slay isolated Normans with impunity. If a man were found dead in suspicious circumstances, he was assumed to be a Norman unless the neighbourhood could prove he was English. If they could neither prove this nor produce the murderer, the whole hundred in which the body was found had to pay a fine to the king.[1] He insisted also, for the better keeping of the peace, that every free man for whose good behaviour a lord was not clearly responsible should belong to a group, known as a frank (" free ") pledge, or tithing,[2] collectively responsible for the peaceableness of its members. It was the duty of the tithing, if one of its members absconded suspiciously, to raise after him through hundred and shire the " hue and cry " (hornblowing and shouting).

The custom of feudal society required that every lord should have his court. Alongside the shire and hundred courts (from which they were not exempt), the greater Norman feudatories therefore had their own courts in which justice might be done among their feudal vassals. The importance of such an " honorial " court can be imagined on an estate of which one or two hundred knights

[1] This fine was called the " murdrum ", or murder fine, from the Old English word for a secret killing.
[2] So called because it had ten members, its head being known as the tithingman, or sometimes " headborough " (that is, " head of the pledge ").

were tenants. There is much evidence [1] that for a century or more after 1066 these courts played a substantial part in maintaining peace and securing justice among the landowning class. Those historians who have regretted the partial eclipse in this period of the Old English shire and hundred courts, and lauded every attempt by the monarchy to infringe the judicial rights of the baronage, have overlooked the fact that for some generations after the Conquest the honour courts of the great barons offered more chance than any English folk-moot of restraining a turbulent military aristocracy for whom only the sanctions of feudalism (apart, perhaps, from those of religion) were really compelling.

Early feudal England, whose ruling members formed, with the king, a closely integrated group, had little room for the great earldoms known before the conquest. But there were men of high rank in Normandy whose title of " count " (literally, " companion ", that is, of the ruler) set them above the ordinary baron. The Conqueror found a specialised employment in England for men whose responsibilities justified the importation of this exalted title, and both Normans and Englishmen found it easy to equate it with the native " earl ", of similar meaning. Nevertheless, the earls of Norman England did not resemble their Anglo-Saxon predecessors closely. The king reserved the rank for those barons to whom especially heavy military responsibility had been given, either in frontier districts (like Hugh of Avranches at Chester) or defending an important coast (like Odo of Bayeux in Kent). Such earls as there were, together with the prelates of the Church, would inevitably have held membership of the great councils which under William I stood in place of the Witan. But the essential character of these councils was feudal ; their members attended not because of any position they inherited from Anglo-Saxon England but because they were the direct tenants or vassals of a king who, like any other feudal lord, had his court. Moreover, the royal council was also attended by prominent servants of the king whose advice he found indispensable. Yet, as is clear from a famous passage in the Anglo-Saxon Chronicle,[2] William lifted this feudal court to the status of a solemn

---

[1] Most fully reviewed and analysed by Sir Frank Stenton in *The First Century of English Feudalism*.

[2] Now available in the excellent translation of G. N. Garmonsway (Everyman's Library, 1953). The passage referred to appears on pp. 219-20.

national assembly when, at the three great feasts of the year and at three chief centres of the Old English state, Winchester, Westminster and Gloucester, he wore his crown before " all the great men of England ".

The reduction of earls and earldoms meant a gain for the sheriffs. William I saw the value of these royal officials, and under him their powers and duties were augmented. In general, the king relinquished none of the rights that had belonged to Edward the Confessor. The *fyrd* was no exception, and for its summoning and leadership the sheriffs were now solely responsible. In addition to his military importance, the sheriff continued to exercise his judicial and fiscal duties, and his aggrandisement in these spheres was due first to the fact that the Conqueror and his sons insisted relentlessly on the full exploitation of royal rights, and secondly to the fact that the sheriffs of Norman England were appointed from among the great barons, and brought to their office a social and feudal influence which might well enable them to tyrannise the local inhabitants. It is ironical that the gravest abuse and exploitation by the Normans of their new power in England was through the Old English office of sheriff, which in the case of some unlucky counties, such as Worcestershire, became for a time hereditary. But the king might still come between a free man and the most powerful of his agents,[1] and in that safeguard, tenuous as it was, lies the explanation of the fact that for a century and a half after the Conquest the best king was the one who could be most ruthless and overbearing.

Twenty years after the battle of Hastings, and one year before his death, William the Conqueror sent his officials into every part of England south of the Tees to make a survey of all the estates in the country, with the names of the holders, their annual value and a list of their resources in agricultural tenants, livestock, and land. The commissioners travelled through an England whose partitioning into feudal honours had not eradicated—as it was never to eradicate—a community of villages grouped into hundreds and shires. In every shire juries of men, Normans and English, gave information on oath regarding the various hundreds, while each village was represented

---

[1] For example, the Norman baron, Nicholas de Tosny, who was sheriff of Staffordshire under William Rufus and Henry I, was ordered by the king (1087-1107) to do justice to Atsor the Englishman. (F. M. Stenton, " English Families and the Norman Conquest ", *Trans. R. Hist. Soc.* (1944), 9.)

by the priest, reeve and six villagers. The mass of information thus obtained was collected at a number of centres throughout the country, where it was edited and rearranged in such a way as to group the facts under the names of the holders of land, the tenants-in-chief of the Crown. In this form, the returns were sent to the king's clerks at Winchester, who digested them into an enormous and well-finished volume.[1]

Modern historians have given much thought to the problem of why Domesday Book (as the survey soon became known) was compiled.[2] In the ambitiousness of its design and the comprehensiveness and variety of its information, Domesday Book is altogether too extraordinary to be explained merely as the natural expedient of a government wishing to find the answer to one particular question. When all the analysis is done, there will still remain some extra, inexplicable quality about this monumental document. But if we turn from asking why Domesday was made to an appreciation of what in fact it is, we can see that first and foremost it provides a list, for every county, of the names and resources of the feudal landowners, from the king downward. Not only could Domesday settle the many disputes about landholding which must have arisen during the Norman acquisition of England ; it could tell the king in detail who paid the national tax, the Danegeld, and it could give him an accurate picture of the fiefs which he had created in the course of twenty years, the geographical [3] and economic background to the close relations established by William I with all his feudal tenants in England. In this sense, Domesday Book rounds off the period of feudalisation, and it is probably no coincidence that in the summer of 1086, while the survey itself was in progress, the king held an especially large Council at Salisbury, at which he made it clear that in England the entire feudal class was to be subordinated to the

---

[1] For some reason, the returns for Norfolk, Suffolk, and Essex were not carried to the stage reached in the finished volume which covers the rest of the country, but make up, in a much less abridged form, a separate volume on their own.

[2] The account given here, both of the method and purpose of the survey, follows V. H. Galbraith, " The Making of Domesday Book ", *E.H.R.*, lvii (1942), 161-77, and *Studies in the Public Records* (1948), Chapter IV.

[3] Most great fiefs were composed of estates scattered in many different counties. On the reasons for this, among which may be discounted any intention of the Conqueror to prevent a great baron having a compact holding, see Stenton, *Anglo-Saxon England*, 620 and n.

monarchy.   In this assembly, all the substantial tenants of the great feudatories, hitherto bound in direct allegiance to their immediate lords, swore fealty and did homage to the king "against all other men".

The "Oath of Salisbury" and the compilation of Domesday Book make a worthier end to the reign of William the Conqueror than the following year's indecisive campaign on the border of Normandy and France in which he was, by accident, mortally injured.   William died near Rouen, his ducal capital, on September 9th, 1087, having survived his injury long enough to indicate that while his eldest son Robert would, by the established feudal custom of primogeniture, succeed to the duchy of Normandy, the kingdom of England was to pass to his second son, William " Rufus " (" the Red "). The provision for Henry, his youngest son, somewhat curiously in a feudal society, yet no doubt shrewdly in view of his character, was a sum of 5,000 pounds of silver.

3. *The Church under Lanfranc, 1070-89*

The Norman conquest brought about changes in the English Church almost as profound as its consequences for English society in general.   Before we can appreciate these changes properly, it will be necessary to see something of the structure and character of the Church in England, an institution which had been of immense importance in the history of the Anglo-Saxons since the sixth century, and which was shortly to enter upon a phase in which its influence, failing the establishment of an outright theocracy, would be little short of dominant.

At the time of the Conquest, the church which sustained the Christianity of the English people was organised in a diocesan system of long standing.   The two provinces of Canterbury and York, each ruled by its respective archbishop, dated from the age of the conversion.   Subject to the metropolitan authority of the archbishops there were some fourteen subordinate or suffragan [1] bishops, most of whose dioceses bore a fairly close relation either to a shire or group of shires (e.g. Selsey for Sussex, Crediton for Devon-with-Cornwall), or to an historic region of England (e.g.

---

[1] In the medieval period, the term suffragan bishop was used of an ordinary diocesan bishop within a province ruled over by an archbishop as metropolitan.

Elmham for East Anglia). The archbishops themselves, in addition to their supervisory functions throughout their provinces, ruled as bishops over the dioceses of Canterbury and York, which corresponded very approximately to the secular divisions of Kent and Yorkshire. The bishop's throne (*cathedra*), the symbol of his public authority, was located in a church usually distinguished by its greater size and splendour from the ordinary parish churches of the diocese, and served by a considerable body of clergy, known as the "chapter", which might be either secular or monastic. In the former case, the clergy were canons, that is to say, priests intended to live communally, eating and sleeping under one roof, but maintained by incomes (later usually called " prebends ") derived from property held individually. Where the cathedral chapter was monastic, the serving clergy of the church were professed monks, confined to their church and its precincts, and living a wholly communal life in accordance with the Rule of St. Benedict.

The contact of ordinary men and women with the church came, however, only rarely through the bishop, and—unless they happened to live in a cathedral town—hardly ever through his capitular clergy. For the ministration of the sacraments and the performance of the perennial needs of the Christian life, baptism, marriage and burial, they were dependent on the local parish priest. The dioceses, much too large to be under the direct care of individual bishops, were subdivided into parishes which, ideally, were small enough to be served by a single priest. But the work of dividing the country into such parishes was far from complete in 1066, and especially in Mercia and parts of Northumbria parochial ministration was often carried out from large churches, known as " old minsters " or " mother churches ", which were staffed by communities of clergy and which served as the parish churches of sizeable districts. In outlying parts of these districts, there might be small chapels where people might hear Mass and where, under authority from the " mother church ", baptisms and burials might take place ; in time, if the population warranted it, such " chapels of ease " might be erected into full parish churches. The founding of parish churches was normally the work of local landowners, or the wealthier village communities. A lord whose ancestors had built and endowed a parish church, or who had himself done so, tended to look upon it as his private property. He was " patron " of the church, and reserved the right of appointing its officiating priest or " incumbent ", the right known later as the " advowson ". The late Anglo-Saxon or medieval parish was nearly always closely related either to the lord's estate or to the village, and the parish priest, though his social status might well be humble, was regarded as one of the leaders of the village community.

Besides the cathedrals, old minsters, and lesser parish churches, which were all concerned with ministering directly to the religious needs of the laity, there were in many parts of England south of the Humber communities of monks and nuns, men and women who had severed themselves almost entirely from the ordinary life of the world and spent their time performing the daily round of services in the churches to which their monasteries were attached. The influence of the monastic way of life had been of incalculable importance in the Christian society of the west from very early times, and in this respect England formed no exception. The great English church reformers of the tenth century, Oda and Dunstan of Canterbury, Aethelwold of Winchester, and Oswald of Worcester, had themselves been monks. They were convinced that in Benedictine monachism, characterised by its threefold vow of poverty, chastity and obedience, lay the highest exemplification of the Christian life. They believed that for the small minority fitted to undertake it, the life of a well-governed Benedictine monastery offered the surest hope of directing and maintaining individual fervour. In their view, the spiritual leadership of the Church would be drawn from this minority, and it should be borne in mind that in English eyes generally the monastery stood for the highest form of the spiritual life. Men and women thought it meritorious to found monasteries, and the granting of property to religious houses already established was one of the commonest forms of private charity. As a result, many monasteries became landowners on a large scale, with all the worldly responsibilities and ties that that involved. But it is probably true to say that in the latter part of the eleventh century the life of ordered calm offered to those who " entered religion " represented a tremendous liberation from the many kinds of economic and personal servitude unavoidable in the outside world.

The prominence of the monasteries in the ecclesiastical landscape of England found a parallel in Normandy. But whereas the English monastic revival had taken place in the tenth century, and monastic life was already showing some decline, its counterpart in Normandy was, in 1066, a phenomenon of recent growth, and was expanding with unabated vigour. The original inspiration had been the great abbey of Cluny in Burgundy ; but Norman monachism had acquired a strength and reputation of its own, largely derived from the sanctity or ability of the rulers of a few outstanding monasteries, of which the most notable were those of Fécamp and Bec. The prestige enjoyed by the Norman Church came almost entirely from its monasteries : there was nothing especially remarkable about the Norman episcopate or secular clergy. But the relations between the Duke of Normandy and his Church were marked by two distinctive features which were of the utmost importance for the future of the Church in England. First, the dukes exercised a most thoroughgoing control over the Church of their duchy in all its aspects : the appointment of bishops and abbots, the content of ecclesiastical ordinances, and relations with the Papacy, were all matters in which the duke's will would normally be decisive. Secondly, Duke William personally combined with this old-fashioned proprietary attitude towards the Church a keen desire for ecclesiastical reform. He encouraged the new religious houses, and himself founded one of the most famous of them, St. Stephen's at Caen. More generally, he was in sympathy with the first phase of the reform movement which was already beginning to dominate the western Church, which strove for the stricter control by the bishops over the clergy of their dioceses, and the freeing of ecclesiastical affairs and offices from the control of all laymen save rulers.

It was therefore a matter of concern for William the Conqueror that in 1066 there was no properly constituted head of the English Church. Robert of Jumièges was now dead, and Stigand at best only Bishop of Winchester, the see from which he had been raised to the primacy, and which, contrary to Canon Law, he still retained. The first object was to remove Stigand and appoint a new primate, lawfully consecrated in the eyes of the Church and personally suitable in the eyes of the king. It was four years before William could achieve this, but when at length in 1070 the deposition of Stigand was secured, it was the work of a council representing all the English clergy, sitting at Winchester under the presidency of fully-accredited papal legates, and capable of authorising the most solemn decisions. Two other bishops, Aethelmaer of Elmham and Aethelric of Selsey, were also deposed, and a fourth, Leofwine of Lichfield, resigned to forestall a like fate. When the legates left the country, nearly half the English dioceses, including the metropolitan sees of Canterbury and York, were vacant, and a new primate was urgently needed. The choice of Lanfranc was the work of the king assisted by the Pope, but for all Norman and English churchmen with any knowledge of affairs it must have been a foregone conclusion. Lanfranc, though so closely in the king's confidence, was not a Norman but a north Italian, from Pavia in Lombardy. Trained as a young man to the law (the fashionable career for young Lombards), he had been attracted to the study of theology, which brought him north, first to Tours, then to Avranches in Normandy. Eventually, in the early 1040s, he was converted to the life of a Benedictine monk, and joined the newly-founded community at Bec, not far from Rouen. He was soon made prior (that is, first in authority under the abbot), and during the next few years he gained a European reputation as a teacher and monastic administrator. In 1063 Duke William appointed him abbot of his new foundation at Caen. It was with reluctance that in 1070 he agreed to be consecrated Archbishop of Canterbury (August 29th) and to exchange the academic calm of his monastery for the heavy political and administrative duties which would fall to a conscientious head of the English Church.

The eighteen years during which Lanfranc was archbishop are rightly regarded as a period of reform within the English Church. But we must take care not to exaggerate the extent of this reform, and we cannot accept at its face value the reformers' own picture of the *status quo ante*. Only twenty years ago—not a long time in the growth of an historical judgment—it was generally agreed that the Church in pre-Conquest England had reached the advanced stages of decadence in morals and discipline. Its most exhaustive historian, Heinrich Böhmer, had written : " As the Norman Church was the most flourishing, so beyond doubt the English Church in 1066 was in gravest decline and most need of reform of all the older national churches of Europe." [1] Its bishops (so the view ran) were worldly men, immersed in secular business, who saw in their office merely the opportunity to acquire the incomes of several dioceses at once. In the monasteries the position was hardly any better. Abbots and monks were sunk in a torpor induced by the comforts of their well-

---

[1] *Kirche und Staat in England und in der Normandie* (1899), 79.

endowed convents, and lived out their days unembarrassed by the least trace of religious enthusiasm, occasionally composing gloomy chronicles whose pessimism reflected a nostalgia for a finer but long-vanished past. As for the parish clergy, the example which they set the laity was altogether lamentable. For the most part ignorant and unlettered, they were indistinguishable from the laymen among whom they lived, and might even be personally unfree.[1] They were often married men with families, though the law of the Church held that they should be celibate, and it was normal for benefices to pass from father to son. In contrast with this sombre picture, the coming of the Normans was seen as an infusion of vigour and light.

It may seem curious that historians were so ready to connect the reform of the English Church exclusively with the introduction of Norman churchmen by the Conqueror. The higher ranks of the Old English clergy (who already included several men of continental birth and training) contained no-one so utterly secular in life and character as William's half-brother Odo, who had been made Bishop of Bayeux at the age of fourteen, who had fought at Hastings in full knight's armour, and who held the military earldom of Kent from *c.* 1067 to 1082.[2] The first Norman Bishop of Durham, Walcher, was likewise an earl in the district north of the Tees (1075-80). Among the monks set by the Conqueror to rule English monasteries was Thurstan of Caen, who was made Abbot of Glastonbury. The monks of this famous church in Somerset were proud of its history and tenacious of its traditions. When Abbot Thurstan attempted to foist upon them, in place of their long-established Gregorian chant, the methods of singing practised at the abbey of Fécamp, they not unnaturally refused to accept them. Losing his temper, the abbot called in his Norman men-at-arms, who trapped the terrified monks in their own choir and killed and wounded several of them on the steps of the altar. Thurstan was banished for this outrage, but afterwards he is said to have been able to buy his return to office from William Rufus for five hundred pounds of silver. The fact that Böhmer could say of his act of barbarity that " it sprang only from an excess of reforming zeal " shows the absurdity to which a serious historian could commit himself through accepting too

[1] A. L. Poole, *The Obligations of Society* (1949), 29.
[2] In 1082 he was arrested and deprived of his earldom, apparently for enticing Normans in England to join him on an Italian expedition.

uncritically the belief that Norman influence in the English Church was invariably for the good.

A more thorough and sympathetic study of the literature, personnel, and activity of the late Old English Church, the work very largely of R. W. Chambers, R. R. Darlington, and Dorothy Whitelock,[1] has proved that the reforming impulses of the second half of the tenth century had by no means died out in the generations before the Conquest. The problems which exercised the best minds in the Church were the lack of education among the rural clergy, the failure of many canons serving the great cathedral or minster churches to lead a disciplined life, and the almost incorrigible tendency of English churchmen to marry in defiance of Canon Law. Some ecclesiastical leaders, notably Archbishop Ealdred of York (died 1069), Bishop Leofric of Exeter (1046-72), and Bishop Wulfstan of Worcester (1062-95), were fully alive to these shortcomings, and tried to remedy them in their own spheres of authority. But they were hampered by a fundamental weakness of the English Church as a whole which William I and Lanfranc, with the advantage of a fresh start, were able to remove. This was the fact that in practice there was no single undisputed head of the Church in England, and no machinery by which decisions taken by the whole Church could be enforced effectively in every diocese and parish.

It says much for Lanfranc's political insight that he at once grasped the necessity of tackling this problem first. Within a year and a half of his consecration, at Winchester in April 1072, he held the first of the great councils that distinguish his primacy. Archbishop Ealdred's death had made it easier for Lanfranc to establish the unequivocal supremacy of Canterbury over York, for not only had his successor, Thomas of Bayeux (a royal clerk), been consecrated by Lanfranc, but his personality and status were quite inferior to those of the new primate. On the basis of Lanfranc's arguments, and of evidence which (almost certainly without the archbishop's knowledge) included a number of forged documents, the council of 1072 declared that the Archbishop of Canterbury should be undisputed head of the Church of England, and that the province of Canterbury should comprise all the English dioceses south of the

[1] Cf. R. W. Chambers, *Exeter Book of Old English Poetry*; R. R. Darlington, " Ecclesiastical Reform in the late Old English Period ", *E.H.R.*, li (1936), 385-428 ; D. Whitelock, " Archbishop Wulfstan ", *Trans. R. Hist. Soc.* (1942).

Trent, together with those of Wales. York's metropolitan authority was to operate from the Trent-Humber line " as far as the uttermost limits of Scotland ". This accorded with Pope Gregory the Great's plan (*c.* 600) for the organisation of the Church in Britain, but in practice the Scottish kings would not allow their bishops to acknowledge the supremacy of York, and the northern province was therefore confined to the country between the Humber and the Scottish border. Even in this restricted area the bishops of Durham, by reason of their see's rich endowments and political importance, ranked almost as the archbishops' equals, and often took a highly independent line.

Once the supremacy issue was settled, the Church under Lanfranc set about three major reforms, which may be briefly described.

(1) *Diocesan reorganisation.* A council convened by Lanfranc at London in 1075 accelerated the process, begun in 1049-50, whereby each bishop's see was to be located in the most considerable town or city of his diocese. This accorded with continental practice, but not with that of Anglo-Saxon England, which had seen nothing strange in a bishop's having his cathedral in a country village. Three bishops—Sherborne (Dorset-Wilts-Berks), Selsey (Sussex), and Lichfield (Mercia)—were allowed to refound their cathedrals at the appropriate towns of Salisbury, Chichester, and Chester respectively. At about the same time, the first Norman bishop of the huge midland diocese of Dorchester-on-Thames (a village near Oxford) set up his cathedral in the growing city of Lincoln, while in the same general period the first Norman bishops of East Anglia moved their seat from the village of Elmham first to Thetford, finally to Norwich. There were to be some further changes in the generation following Lanfranc's death—the abbey of Ely became the endowment of a new see, covering Cambridgeshire, *c.* 1109, and Henry I set up another new see at Carlisle in 1133—but broadly speaking the organisation of the Church as Lanfranc left it was to endure for the next four centuries.

(2) *Clerical celibacy.* Although at least one English bishop, Wulfstan of Worcester, was prepared to compel all the clergy in his diocese to be celibate, Lanfranc was statesman enough to realise that so revolutionary a change would have to be brought about gradually. In 1076 another Winchester council decreed that in future no one was to be ordained as deacon or priest unless his celibacy were proved, and that clergy professing to be canons—that is, most of the

priests serving the cathedral and minster churches—should be unmarried, or lose their prebends. Parish priests already married would not be forced to choose between their wives and their churches; but none was to marry henceforth, and obviously, if the decree were made effective, there would not, within two generations or so, be a single married clergyman left in England. Clerical marriage did in fact decline considerably during the next hundred years, but complete celibacy had not been achieved even by the thirteenth century.

(3) *Monastic reform.* Lanfranc was himself a Benedictine monk, and naturally took a lead in imposing on all the English monasteries an acceptably high standard in their observance of the Rule of St. Benedict, and some degree of uniformity in monastic customs generally. His approach, however, was far from doctrinaire : he said himself, " No one church can exactly imitate the practices of another ".[1]   But he co-operated with King William in the appointment of Normans as abbots over many of the English monasteries, and the cohesion of the Norman abbeys from which these men were drawn, coupled with their respect for Lanfranc personally, meant that English monasticism was given a measure of unity and discipline which it had lacked for nearly a century, while it was also brought more directly in contact with the currents of monastic life on the continent. Lanfranc's belief in the value of a reformed Benedictinism for the English Church as a whole is shown in the fact that he retained the English arrangement by which certain cathedrals were served by monks, and, indeed, in his time monks were established in the important cathedrals of Durham and Rochester, while before *c.* 1109 the Bishop of Norwich had obtained a monastic chapter, and the first Bishop of Ely had taken as the chapter of his new see the monks of Ely abbey.   By an unusual arrangement, the ancient dioceses of Somerset and Mercia each acquired two cathedral churches and a pair of chapters of which one was secular and the other monastic.   In 1090, John of Tours, Bishop of Wells, a secular foundation which had hitherto served as the see of the Somerset diocese, transferred his see to the abbey church of Bath, preferring to have a monastic chapter.   But a later bishop, about 1140, restored Wells as a second chapter, and his thirteenth-century successors came to be known as the bishops of Bath and Wells jointly.   Almost

[1] *Lanfranc's Monastic Constitutions*, ed. D. Knowles (1951), 1.

the same thing happened in Mercia. The original bishop's see was at Lichfield, a secular cathedral. In 1072 it was transferred to Chester, also a secular foundation. In 1102, however, Bishop Robert de Limesy transferred his see to the abbey of Coventry. Despite these changes, Lichfield did not lose its cathedral status, and from 1228 the bishops were regularly given the double style of Coventry and Lichfield. They were also known, unofficially it seems, as bishops of Chester, but the claim of Chester to be considered a true cathedral foundation in the middle ages is doubtful.

If Lanfranc's primacy left its mark on the internal character of the English Church, it was also momentous for its relations with the Crown and the Papacy. In his work of reform, the archbishop had had the constant and close support of the king. This co-operation meant that while Lanfranc could make a particular reform effective because the king would enforce it through his agents, the archbishop for his part acquiesced in certain features of royal policy towards the Church which later leaders of the episcopate would strenuously oppose. For example, it was in accordance with the aims of the contemporary Church reformers that, in the early 1070s, William ordered his sheriffs to see that in future no one dealt with spiritual cases—that is cases involving the transgression by lay men or women of the laws of Christianity—in the ordinary secular courts of the hundred (and, no doubt, of the shire also). The older practice had been for the bishop to sit with the sheriff who presided over the suitors of these " popular " courts. Offenders against the laws of the Church, or disputants whose quarrel involved some religious precept, were sentenced or obtained satisfaction in company with parties to civil suits, e.g. over the ownership of land, or with ordinary criminals. After William's order, the Church was able to go ahead with the setting up of its own separate system of courts to deal exclusively with ecclesiastical cases.

In two other respects, however, the king imposed burdens and limitations on the Church. First, he decided that some of the Old English monasteries and cathedral churches were so richly endowed with landed property that they ought to be subjected to the same sort of feudal service—the provision of knights for his army—as the greater baronial honours. No doubt it was true that most of the ecclesiastical dignitaries chosen to bear this burden—for example, the Abbot of Peterborough or the Bishop of Lincoln—were well able to afford it, but by bringing a number of important churches within the feudal complex, William I was laying up for the Church as a whole a store of trouble in the future. The abbots and bishops became in effect feudal barons, with obligations to the king which were not only quite irrelevant to their ecclesiastical duties, but through which, indeed, they might well be diverted from them.

Secondly, William held firmly to the view that the relations of the English Church with the Papacy were for him to determine. He was out of sympathy with the second phase of the reform movement in the western Church, which had as its aims the exaltation of the papal see so that the Popes could exercise a direct and constant supervision over the entire Church in the west, and also (at least in the intention of the extremists) the *ultimate* supremacy of ecclesiastical or spiritual authority, represented by the Pope, over all laymen, even over those rulers of nations who were acknowledged to be divinely ordained. It followed that William would not allow his churchmen to recognise anyone as Pope officially until he had made his own decision in the matter ; that correspondence between the Pope and the leaders of the English Church should be subject to royal censorship (a condition made easier by the English Channel) ; and finally that he would not consider himself in any way subject to the Papacy on the grounds, advanced by Gregory VII, the greatest of the eleventh-century reforming Popes, that the English people were specially bound to allegiance to Rome because their conversion had been carried out under the personal direction of Pope Gregory I. This restraint by the king on the aspirations of the reforming section of the clergy was tolerated because behind it lay the mutual respect of William and Lanfranc, and because the king did much to encourage what he considered to be wise and beneficial reform. With a different king or archbishop, this pragmatic compromise might very quickly break down.

CHAPTER V

THE CONQUEROR'S SONS

1. *William Rufus, 1087-1100*

THE settlement devised by William I may have seemed equitable, but it could not be permanent. None of his sons was willing to identify his interests with those of the country Duke William had conquered. They remained Normans at heart, and England they valued merely because it conferred the prestige of kingship, an independence of any feudal superior, and a tremendous increase of wealth. In consequence, neither William Rufus, who was crowned by Lanfranc, September 26th, 1087, nor his younger brother Henry, who seized the throne on Rufus's death in 1100, was prepared to allow the eldest brother, Robert " Curthose ", peaceful possession of the duchy of Normandy itself. Their ambitions were helped by the endemic rebelliousness of the Norman baronage. This was serious enough even when the duke was a strong ruler, like William the Conqueror. When he was as lenient and feeble as Duke Robert proved to be, baronial insubordination rapidly reduced the duchy to anarchy, leaving the ordinary inhabitants at the mercy of any leader of knights attracted by a career of plunder.

Moreover, the planting after the Conquest of many prominent Normans in English estates meant that rebellion on one side of the Channel almost inevitably involved those who held political power on the other. The problem could be solved in one of two ways. Either the King of France, as feudal superior of Normandy, could use force to bring its duke and his tenants firmly under his control, or else the King of England could throw over the Conqueror's settlement and take Normandy for himself. As it happened, the French monarchy did not possess for the next hundred years the resources to subjugate Normandy. Into the vacuum of power created by the weakness of Robert Curthose and of both Philip I (1060-1108) and Louis VI (1108-37) of France moved, first Rufus, and after him Henry I, with the help of disaffected Normans and troops raised from among the native English.

That these foreign kings could make use, apparently without any difficulty, of the English *fyrd* to fight their wars in Normandy is an indication that the majority of Englishmen had, by 1087, accepted the Conquest as an irreversible fact. From this time onward, the English in general supported the monarchy against the feudal baronage, since for them a foreign king, however brutal and tyrannical (and Rufus was both) was preferable to a group of foreign barons dominating some local countryside with unchecked power. The English, moreover, had a long tradition of reverence both for the institution of kingship and the person of the king, a feeling not shared by the great feudatories. They, on the contrary, tended to regard the king merely as a lord among his barons, a leader of those who were very nearly his equals.

There were two serious baronial revolts against William Rufus. The first broke out not long after his accession, in 1088, its chief instigator being Bishop Odo of Bayeux (unwisely restored to his earldom of Kent after the Conqueror's death). Within his own field of operations, the counties of Kent and Sussex, Odo had a capable ally in Earl Roger of Shrewsbury's son, Robert of Bellême, who brought knights from Normandy with the connivance of the duke. There were sympathetic revolts in East Anglia, Leicestershire, and the Welsh march. The king himself dealt with the main centre of revolt in the south east, and Rochester, the rebels' last and strongest castle, fell to him in the early summer. It was his English subjects, together with such Normans as remained loyal to the Crown, who successfully overcame the local risings, Bishop Wulfstan of Worcester, for example, stoutly heading the resistance to Robert of Bellême's father in the Severn valley.

The second revolt, in 1095, was the work of Robert of Mowbray, whom the Conqueror had made Earl of Northumberland in 1081. Earl Robert had brilliantly checked a Scottish invasion in 1093, when the King of Scotland himself had been slain. It is probable that Rufus feared the resulting enhancement of the earl's power, and that Robert, for his part, mistrusted the king. Earl Robert allied himself with some of the barons who had rebelled in 1088, and they invited a cousin of the king to take the English throne. The position was made more grave by the unconnected but contemporary outbreak of warfare in Wales, where, during the years 1094-5, two Welsh princes, Cadwgan of Powys and the now freed Gruffydd ap

Cynan of North Wales, had driven the Normans east of the River Conway, captured the new castle of Montgomery, and threatened the whole structure of defence against the Welsh erected by the Conqueror. But Rufus was equal to the situation. First he took an army north, which reduced Earl Robert's castles at Tynemouth and Bamburgh. Then he spent the autumn of 1095 penetrating into the southern fastnesses of Snowdonia. The Welsh prudently destroyed food stocks and gave no battle, but the king had for the moment scotched the danger from that quarter. Towards the rebels in England he was unmerciful. Earl Robert was imprisoned, and he never recovered his lands or power. His fellow-conspirators received harsher treatment, and Rufus was troubled with no further outbreaks of rebellion.

The attempt to wrest Normandy from his elder brother occupied Rufus from 1089 until 1096, during which time the utter incompetence of Duke Robert and the military and political superiority of William were convincingly demonstrated. Briefly, the position was that those Normans without military power wished to have the King of England in the duke's place, while the unruly barons were equally anxious not to be saddled with a ruler of Rufus's ability. That Rufus was not in fact able to conquer the duchy outright was due to the fluid nature of political allegiance and the desperate slowness of warfare which consisted not in open battles but in besieging one castle after another. By 1091, Rufus's conquests in the east of Normandy were recognised by his brother in the Treaty of Rouen, and during the brief spell of reconciliation which followed they turned upon their brother Henry and drove him out of the fiefs in western Normandy which his skill and a good use of his father's legacy had won for him.

In 1096, however, the actual rule of all Normandy came to Rufus, not by war, but through a simple financial deal. Duke Robert responded with characteristic chivalry to the Pope's appeal (1095) for western rulers to lead a crusade to capture the Holy Land from the Seljuk Turks. To raise money for this expedition, he pawned Normandy to his brother for over £6,500, which Rufus raised by levying Danegeld throughout his kingdom. For the last three years of his reign, Rufus governed Normandy as he governed England. harshly, but with a maintenance of peace.

Little can be said in defence of William Rufus personally. He

was extravagantly generous to members of the knightly order, a fact
which brought men flocking to his service from every part of the
west. But he was cruel and violent, cynical in his dealings with
other men, and (except when in fear of death) contemptuous of
religion, though if we can believe a curious story told by William of
Malmesbury, he at least took an intelligent interest in it.[1] Nevertheless, with all his faults, William Rufus had some conception,
however dim and crude, of the chief business of his office. He was
energetic, and could show political shrewdness, as, for example, at
the siege of Rochester when he proclaimed that any Englishman
who did not come to his aid would be judged *nithing*, " worthless ",
a term of opprobrium which no free Englishman could bear to incur.
There is no doubt that during the thirteen years of his reign, the
highly centralised royal government which was to dominate twelfth-
century England steadily extended its influence. Under Rufus, it
has been said,[2] we see " the widening of the king's relations beyond
those of mere overlord to tenant-in-chief, the increasing interference in local affairs through itinerant justices and use of shire
courts ".

The king could not have done this without the services of skilled
administrators. Few of the great barons were either willing or able
to undertake the day-to-day tasks of government, and so the burdens
—and the rewards—of this work came to the personal servants of
the king. Rufus's chief agent in ruling England was a household
chaplain, Rannulf, nicknamed " Flambard " from his burning
ambition. Rannulf Flambard was active throughout the reign, as a
conveyor of the king's will to sessions of the shire courts, an enquirer
into royal rights, or a royal justice deciding the issue between parties
to an important dispute. He might be called on to supervise a levy
of taxation (finance seems, in fact, to have been his strong point),
or to organise military support for the king. Both these operations
might be combined, as in 1094, when Flambard met the English
fyrd gathered at Hastings in readiness to cross to Normandy, and
dismissed it after taking from each man the ten shillings he had

[1] Malmesbury, writing a generation after Rufus's time, says that Rufus
convened a debate between spokesmen for Christianity and Judaism,
promising to join the Jewish religion if the Jews got the better of the
argument.
[2] R. W. Southern, " Rannulf Flambard and Anglo-Norman administration ", *Trans. R. Hist. Soc.* (1933), 127.

been given as subsistence money. With money thus raised the king could hire better-trained troops on the continent.

The chief method by which the Norman and, after them, the Angevin kings of England developed a government with a strength and efficiency unrivalled in western Europe was through interfering in the relations between one free subject, even though he was a great lord, and another. When a king like Rufus concluded a writ with the words, " so that I hear no further complaint about this matter ", it meant that he was putting into practice the theory that everyone had the ultimate right of access to the king to obtain redress for an injury. William II and Henry I may have limited this practice to highly-favoured subjects, but they were nonetheless setting precedents which were later used by their successor, Henry II, to establish the supremacy of royal justice and administration over all other kinds.

In addition to keeping England and Normandy in relative peace and order, William Rufus showed a business-like grasp of the problems produced by the frontiers with Wales and Scotland. It is true that his achievement in regard to Wales was not impressive, but it was not less than that of any English king of the period. His show of strength in 1095 had been only temporarily effective, but eighteen months later he again invaded Wales and ordered the construction of a group of castles to hold down the country which, in the south at least, remained at peace until well into Henry I's reign. Rufus, like his father, gave his barons on the Welsh march a wide degree of freedom to pursue their own territorial ambitions. It was principally these men, the earls of Chester and Shrewsbury, for example, in the north, and their fellow-Normans established in the south, Arnulf of Pembroke, Robert fitz Hamon in Glamorgan, and Philip of Briouze in Radnor, who pressed the Anglo-Norman settlement of Wales by using their own small resources and exploiting the differences among the native Welsh. In the lordships they had carved out for themselves, with their own castles, boroughs or market towns, and religious houses, these marcher lords formed a self-sufficient and independent community which was to leave a troublesome legacy to the English kings of the thirteenth century.

Towards Scotland, Rufus took more determined and effective action. His treaty with Duke Robert in 1091 had been accompanied by the expulsion from Normandy of Edgar the Atheling, who still possessed a nuisance value in northern English politics. Edgar went to his brother-in-law's court in Scotland, and soon afterwards King Malcolm launched his fourth incursion into English Northumbria, gaining nothing politically, but as usual carrying off much booty. Rufus promptly crossed the Channel, bringing Duke Robert with him, and together they led north a large combined force of ships and cavalry. The fleet sank, but William met the Scottish king with his land army, and through the mediation of the Atheling and Robert of Normandy made peace on the terms of Abernethy. William followed this up in the next year, when he took another army to Carlisle, hitherto ruled by a lord dependent on the King of Scots. Rufus ejected him by force, and built a castle at Carlisle, thus setting the border of his kingdom emphatically at the line of the Solway. The Anglo-Saxon chronicle says that the king then sent into the Carlisle district from the south " very many peasants with their wives and live-stock to settle there and till the soil ". The practical sense of Rufus is nowhere more clearly shown than in this combined planting of a Norman castle and a southern English peasant population in the vitally important border area of Cumberland.

The king's greatest success in regard to Scotland was still to come. In 1093 he snubbed King Malcolm by summoning him to Gloucester and then refusing to see him. Infuriated by this rebuff, the Scottish king at once raised an army and invaded Northumberland, " intending ", says one chronicler, " to reduce it to utter desolation ". But he was trapped, it seems, by a small force under the earl, Robert of Mowbray, and both he and his second eldest son, Edward, were slain. On Malcolm Canmore's death, his half-Scottish, half-English kingdom fell apart in civil war. Rufus exploited this situation successfully by supporting claimants to the Scottish throne who, since they depended on military assistance from the English king, were in effect his vassals, and could not take the independent and aggressive line adopted by Malcolm Canmore.

William Rufus had never been in a stronger position, on either side of the Channel, when, on August 2nd, 1100, while hunting near Lyndhurst, in the New Forest, he was killed by the shot of his companion, Walter Tirel, a baron of Ponthieu. It will never be known whether the arrow was shot on purpose to kill the king, or struck him accidentally. Tirel fled the country, and Rufus's brother, Henry, who had been a member of the hunting party, abandoning the king's body,[1] hurried at once to Winchester to seize the royal treasure. Within three days of Rufus's death, he had been crowned king at Westminster. Such was his haste that sooner than wait for the return of the Archbishop of Canterbury, Anselm, from the exile into which Rufus had driven him, Henry had his coronation performed by the Bishop of London.[2] Since Duke Robert of Normandy was on his way home from Palestine and had at this date reached Sicily, it is hard to resist the conclusion that Rufus was slain deliberately, and that his younger brother had at least an inkling of what was to occur and had made his plans accordingly.

2. *Henry I, 1100-35*

The older view that Henry I's reign marked a sharp contrast with and improvement upon the rule of his brother has more recently come under criticism from two directions. In the first place, it is now realised that William II's government of the country, though often arbitrary, was not different in kind from that of his successor. Secondly, the reputation of Henry I himself has diminished, until it is possible for an eminent modern authority on the twelfth century to write, " it was fear rather than love or even respect that he inspired in his subjects. He had by his exactions and by his arbitrary rule strained the obedience of his barons nearly to breaking-point." [3] Clearly, these are words which might equally well be applied to Rufus. Yet, although Henry I could at times be as ruthless as his brother, his long reign did in fact see the constructive development of methods and instruments of more efficient royal government and, on the other side, the creation of some important precedents through which the almost unlimited power of the Anglo-Norman monarchy might be brought in check.

Henry I (his largely unjustified nickname of " Beauclerk ", " fine scholar ", was given him only in the fourteenth century) had a less impulsive, more calculating character than Rufus. He was probably cleverer and better educated ; he was undoubtedly meaner and more avaricious. As the youngest of three quarrelsome brothers, he had had to fight and scheme for his rights, often entirely on his own.

---

[1] Some peasants had the decency to carry Rufus's corpse, on a farm-cart, to Winchester cathedral, where it was buried without any formality.
[2] The Archbishop of York was old and ailing.
[3] A. L. Poole, *From Domesday Book to Magna Carta* (Oxford, 1951), 130.

Like all the Normans, but in a degree more acute than most, he possessed a precocious sense of the value of money. In his early struggles also, he had learned the necessity of making concessions in order to gain an immediate advantage. In short, like many men who have risen to power instead of being born to it, he was an opportunist.

Having seized the crowning opportunity of Rufus's death, he at once set about consolidating his position as king. At his coronation he issued a solemn " charter of liberties ", a lengthy document remarkable for the fact that the king frankly narrates in it the enormities practised by his predecessor and promises to abrogate them. Copies of this coronation charter, addressed to the appropriate bishop and sheriff, were sent to every shire. The abuses which figured most prominently in it were Rufus's retention of vacant churches and his disregard of the feudal contract. These were matters, of course, which affected only a handful of the greater churchmen and barons. But it is significant that Henry added to his promises to remedy these restricted matters more general assurances to mint only good money and punish the coiners of false, to remit murder fines dating from before his coronation, and to dispense to his subjects the " law of King Edward (the Confessor) ",[1] with such amendments as the Conqueror had made with his barons' counsel. To symbolise the monarchy's change of heart, Rannulf Flambard, though he had been since 1099 Bishop of Durham, was imprisoned in the Tower of London, and Archbishop Anselm of Canterbury was recalled by a most obsequious personal letter from the king. Finally, Henry brought from her retreat in Wilton nunnery on November 11th, and married, Edith (who now took the name of Maud), daughter of King Malcolm of Scotland and Queen Margaret, the Atheling's sister. In English eyes, the family from which, through her mother, she was descended, carried the legitimate claim to the Crown.

This open bid for native English support paid a dividend in the next year, when Henry (as he must have expected) was faced by a baronial attempt to place Duke Robert, newly returned from the crusade with greatly enhanced prestige, on the throne. The revolt was largely instigated by Flambard, who had escaped from prison,

---

[1] In the charter a native English word for law, *laga*, is used instead of the Latin *lex*.

but it was soon extinguished, and within a short while the king was actually employing Flambard to extend his own influence in Normandy at the expense of Robert, who ruled the duchy no better for his crusading experience.

Far more dangerous to Henry than his brother was Robert of Bellême, who, since 1098, had acquired his father's earldom of Shrewsbury and other English estates, including the important West Sussex castle of Arundel. Henry saw rightly that he would never have peace with such a man in the kingdom, and determined to ruin him. By 1102, Robert had been provoked into fortifying his castles against the king. One by one, however, they were reduced, and before Shrewsbury itself surrendered Robert was forced to submit to perpetual exile and total confiscation of his English lands. This was the last serious revolt with which Henry I had to deal, and he was now free to concentrate on the conquest of Normandy.

That he was able to accomplish this in four years, succeeding where Rufus failed, was due in part to the greater weakness of Duke Robert, now compelled to rely on the support of such hated men as Robert of Bellême, but chiefly to Henry's good luck in being able to bring his brother to a pitched battle, at Tinchebrai, in western Normandy, on September 28th, 1106, the fortieth anniversary of William I's landing at Hastings. Henry's army consisted of men from the western parts of Normandy, where he had long been influential, of cavalry from Maine and Brittany, whose counts he had made his allies, and finally of foot-soldiers from England. Just as Hastings, by which the Normans conquered England, was the victory of cavalry over infantry, so Tinchebrai, by which the English helped their king to conquer Normandy, was to a surprising extent the victory of foot-soldiers against mounted knights. The king himself and many barons fought on foot ; but the decisive turn was given to the battle by a charge of the knights from Brittany and Maine. Robert of Bellême was apparently the first to turn in flight, whereupon Duke Robert's force, in any case much smaller than Henry's, broke in disorder, the duke being taken prisoner. Tinchebrai was far from being the half-serious, half-sporting encounter often characterising warfare among the feudal barons of north-western Europe : it was the decisive battle in a determined bid to conquer Normandy outright. In proof of this, Duke Robert was kept in captivity until he died, while his six-year-old son, William the "Clito" (prince), was only released because of his tender age.

Tinchebrai was to prove the beginning of a new era. For forty years from 1066 the members of a small but powerful feudal dynasty had first fought to maintain their hold over the entirely foreign country of England, and had then squabbled among themselves for possession of their ancestral domain of Normandy itself. From 1106 onward, the successful surviving member of this dynasty, Henry I, in complete and unchallenged control of an English kingdom in which Norman conquerors were already beginning to merge with the native inhabitants, was also Duke of Normandy. The English monarchy now stood astride the Channel, and for two or three generations could use the resources and draw on the loyalty of territories north and south of what was no longer a political, if it remained a physical, frontier. If it was a liability that the King of England was independent in his own realm yet a vassal of the King of France in respect of Normandy, nevertheless the union brought England fully into the community of western European nations, and during the long reign of Henry II the country enjoyed a prestige and assumed a responsibility within this community which it never again attained until the sixteenth century.

The effects of Tinchebrai were not at once apparent. Instead of enjoying peace in Normandy for the rest of his life, Henry I found that his very success had aroused the fear and enmity of Flanders and Anjou, fiefs which bordered Normandy, and of the French king himself. Until 1128, when William the Clito was killed, Henry was much occupied in frontier warfare, in the course of which he gained suzerainty over Brittany and Maine, while Robert of Bellême, that arch-fomenter of baronial rebellion, was finally captured and imprisoned for life. Henry's successes, however, were more than offset by the loss of his only legitimate son, William, who was drowned in November 1120, when the magnificent new *White Ship*, in which he and many notables were sailing for England, sank off Barfleur. The chroniclers do not speak highly of the young prince's character, but his death meant that all the work of the Norman kings might be dissipated at Henry's death in a war of succession. The king's remarriage in 1122 did not bring him the son he hoped for, but in 1128, the year of the Clito's death, he secured the marriage of his only legitimate daughter, Maud, widow of the Emperor Henry V of

Germany, to Geoffrey Plantegenet,[1] soon to be Count of Anjou. In this way, the strife of Anjou and Normandy might be healed. If the barons of England were reluctant to take Maud as Henry's successor—though they had sworn a solemn oath to do so in 1127—at least they might acknowledge as king her eldest son by Geoffrey of Anjou, the future Henry II. It was a real tragedy for England that the Anjou marriage could only come about at the end of Henry I's life, for when he died, at Rouen in December, 1135, his namesake, Henry " Plantagenet ", was an infant not two years old.

With regard to the government of England, two processes make the reign of Henry I notable. First there was a strengthening of centralised royal control over the affairs of the king's free subjects, whether tenants-in-chief or vassals. Secondly, there was a gradual but important change in the character of royal justice, accompanied by an improvement in its administration. These two developments were really part of a single process, but the significance of each can be seen more easily if we consider them separately.

There is no question that Henry I was well served in government by a body of able if ruthless men. A contemporary chronicler, in a famous passage, emphasised what seemed to him to be the salient feature of this administrative *cadre* when he said that they were all men whom the king had " raised from the dust ", and promoted over the heads of the hereditary nobles. To us, not needing to draw the writer's aristocratic moral, and aware that many kings before Henry had used the services of men of obscure origin, it seems more remarkable that so many of these new creatures of the monarchy were not the usual clerks who could be rewarded with Church dignities, but laymen, raised to baron's rank and requiring fiefs to support them. Such men were Geoffrey of Glympton, sheriff of Warwickshire, Gilbert, sheriff of Cambridgeshire, Huntingdonshire and Surrey, and Ralph Basset, who as an itinerant justice at Huncot (Leicestershire) in 1124 hanged forty-four thieves, " so many as never were hanged before ". These men certainly impressed the country with the length of the king's arm, but they founded powerful local dynasties whose next generation had to be dismissed wholesale from their offices (1170) by Henry II.

[1] The broom, or " genêt ", was a family emblem of the Angevins. " Plantagenêt " means literally " plant broom ", a nickname of similar formation to Drinkwater and Shakespear.

But by far the most influential of Henry I's servants was a clerk of the type of Rannulf Flambard, though more responsible and statesmanlike. This was Roger,[1] whom the king made Chancellor and then (1102) Bishop of Salisbury and Justiciar. For almost the whole reign, Bishop Roger governed as "lieutenant of the realm of England under King Henry", and during the king's long absences across the Channel the full responsibility exercised by the bishop as Justiciar gave that office a vice-regal quality as the highest in the state under the king.

It was Bishop Roger who devised the Exchequer, the most notable single means by which the Crown brought under its direct control the agents of local government. We have seen that even before 1066 many of the sheriffs rendered to the king each year the *firma*, or "farm", of their counties, representing the king's food-rents, his share in the profits of the shire and hundred courts, and other revenues. Under Bishop Roger, it became the rule that every sheriff must appear twice yearly, at Easter and Michaelmas (September 29th), before the highest officials and members of the King's Council. At the Easter session the sheriff had to pay in that part of the farm he had already collected, and state the expense to which he might already have been put in carrying out the king's orders. For these amounts, he would be given as receipts wooden "tallies", sticks split zig-zag into two. Whole numbers of pounds, shillings and pence were receipted on separate tallies, the particular currency unit being indicated by making the indentations in the zig-zag cuts of different lengths. The actual number of indentations showed the total sum represented by each tally. One part was handed to the sheriff and the other kept in the Treasury. At Michaelmas, the sheriff had to account for the full farm, and if he duly proffered the remainder of it together with his receipts from the Easter session he was declared "acquitted" for that year. The Treasurer kept a special roll, known as the "Pipe Roll", on which every sheriff's expenditure and payments into the Treasury were entered. By looking up the relevant entry on this roll, the Treasury clerks could tell whether a sheriff was acquitted from the previous year, or whether he still owed money: the Pipe Roll remorselessly recorded such debts from year to year, and a chronically defaulting sheriff

[1] Like Flambard, he was a native of the Calvados district of Normandy.

might be heavily fined or put into jail. When the king's court was in session with the sheriffs appearing one by one before it, the Justiciar and Treasurer and other great barons composing the court sat round a table covered with a big chequered cloth. The accounting was done on this cloth by means of movable counters—on the principle of the abacus—so that the sheriff, doubtless unable to read or write, could know that he was not being cheated. It was from the cloth, the *scaccarium* or " chequer-board ", that these solemn meetings of the King's Council took the name Exchequer.

The Exchequer was a noteworthy advance in written and methodical government. It was paralleled by an extension of the use of written precepts, or " writs ", which might be sent either direct to a royal officer for immediate action, or to a subject who could then show it to the appropriate official and obtain the action desired. The king inherited from his Anglo-Saxon predecessors the extremely useful brief vernacular writ authenticated by a wax seal. Henry I used such writs very freely for every sort of governmental purpose. By his day they were nearly always written in Latin, instead of English (which the Norman clerks probably understood but could not write). The vast outpouring of these writs from Henry I's chancery remains a monument both of Old English inventiveness and of the Norman capacity for fruitful adaptation.

All this was only characteristic of a more literate age, but the Norman and Angevin kings of England must be given credit for making more advances in this direction than most of their contemporaries. The extension of written government on the one hand and of the royal authority on the other went closely together. The King's Chancellor and Treasurer, who had originally been only household servants, began to need officials of their own to cope with the additional business done by the Crown ; and these groups of trained administrators gradually became " departments of state ". During the twelfth century, it has been said,[1] " the personal will and wishes of the sovereign cease to be co-extensive with the activities of his officials ". This, of course, meant the arrival of what we should call " bureaucratic " government, though still in primitive form. With some exceptions, it was generally welcomed in twelfth-century England, for through it the subject might obtain effective legal

[1] V. H. Galbraith, " The Literacy of the Medieval English Kings ", *Proc. British Academy* (1935), 222.

remedies, and the excesses of local lords or royal officers might be checked. Before we can appreciate the change in the nature of royal justice under Henry I, we must understand how justice was ordinarily administered in twelfth-century England. No one, not even the king, enjoyed anything like a monopoly of justice. On the contrary, there were several distinct types of justice, applicable in different circumstances or to different sorts of people. The king, it is true, did hold courts in which the most final and solemn judicial decisions were reached. The king's court, the *Curia Regis*, was in fact simply the king sitting in judgment with his barons and bishops. In the king's absence overseas, the Justiciar might hold a court in his name ; but what gave the royal court its supreme authority was in the last resort the belief that the king himself was the " fount of justice ", that to dispense justice was an essential function of kingship. But the king's court did not open its doors unconditionally to all the king's free subjects. Where what we should now call " civil " actions were concerned, that is, disputes between one subject and another, for example, over property, the king's court normally dealt only with cases involving the king's own tenants-in-chief. Since most of these were great barons who, in any case, would often be present with the king as he travelled about the country, it was easy for them to have their disputes heard in the *Curia Regis*, while for a poorer freeman to have done so would have been very difficult or expensive. There were three kinds of court familiar to men and women of this class *c*. 1100, popular or communal, baronial, and ecclesiastical.

The courts in which the disputes of most freemen were decided, and where minor criminal offences were tried, were those of their local hundred and of the county or shire of which the hundred was a subdivision. These courts are called " popular " because the justice dispensed in them is thought to have derived not from the king but from the immemorial custom by which the substantial men of a district—ultimately of a tribe—sat in judgment on the disputes and wrong-doings of their neighbours or kinsmen. The hundred courts met every three weeks, the shire courts once a month. Originally, the " suitors " of these courts, that is, those who attended with full power to transact their business, consisted of every free holder in the hundred or county. By 1100, however, it is probable that only the holders of certain estates whose tenure carried this duty with it regularly attended the communal courts. Though under the presidency of the bishop and sheriff, or of the hundredman, all the suitors together were the judges of the court. However they might look to certain particular individuals to propound the law in cases of difficulty. Nevertheless, the fact that the bishop or sheriff presided and could easily dominate the proceedings, gave a strongly " official " tone to the shire court. The hundreds also were brought under official supervision by the sheriff's practice, well-established by Henry I's time, of visiting each of the hundreds twice a year on tour (or *tourn*, to use the technical term) to inspect the frankpledges. Moreover, neither hundred nor shire was a court of last resort : if a person failed to obtain justice in each of them in turn, he could appeal to the *Curia Regis*.

Every lord of any standing held a court in which the disputes between his own free or unfree tenants were settled, and which had the power to try and to punish minor criminal offenders guilty of petty theft, brawling in public, pursuing a man into his own home, and other acts which, while not (by twelfth-century standards) of a very serious nature, did constitute a " breach of the peace ". The lord exacted toll on all sales of cattle on his estate, and if a buyer were afterwards suspected of having stolen cattle, he could come to the lord's court and call for the testimony of those who had been present when he had duly paid his toll. Finally, most lords had the right of executing summary justice upon men caught red-handed in the act of theft : such men were straightway hanged without chance of making a defence.

Though deriving ultimately from a royal grant, it would have been hard for any twelfth-century king to deny a baron this relatively minor but valuable jurisdiction, which was summed up in the famous alliterative phrase " sake and soke, toll and team, and infangene-theof ".[1] In fact, all the kings of this period not only allowed barons this jurisdiction but often added to it the franchise of a hundred court, delegating to the private lord the right of viewing the frank-pledges instead of the sheriff. By 1272 well over half the 628 hundreds of England were in private hands. Not every lord, of course, enjoyed this privilege, and many had estates so small that

---

[1] " Infangenetheof " was the lord's right to do justice on a thief caught red-handed on his estate. It is doubtful whether the other terms still had a precise technical meaning in the twelfth century.

the majority of the court's suitors must have been villeins and not free holders.   At this end of the scale, a lord's jurisdiction amounted to no more than a manor court, whose business would be the extremely local affairs of a small agricultural community.

Such were the typical " baronial " or " seignorial " courts of medieval England.   We must be careful to distinguish them from two much less common types of court which, because they were held by lords, are easily confused with them.   First, as we have seen,[1] the greatest barons held courts for the military tenants of their " honours ".   They were intensely feudal assemblies which in the twelfth century certainly performed a useful function, though they affected only a tiny minority of the population.   Secondly, a very few highly privileged lords enjoyed in the territories subject to them virtually all the powers normally confined to the king himself or to the shire and hundred.   These exceptional jurisdictions, " franchises "[2] or " liberties " as they were naturally called, usually had a military or political *raison d'être*.   The palatine earldoms of Chester and Durham (the latter combined with the bishopric) belonged to this class, and they guarded the borders against the Welsh and Scots.   Of the rest, the most renowned was the liberty created by Edward the Confessor in favour of the abbey of Bury St. Edmunds.   This consisted of the western half of Suffolk (eight and a half hundreds), with shire and hundred jurisdiction and even the purely " regalian " right of levying Danegeld.   The Norman kings did not diminish this great franchise, though they saddled the abbot with the burden of providing forty knights for their service.

When William I forbade the hearing of spiritual offences in the popular courts, he gave royal backing to separate courts set up by the Church.   In Henry I's time, laymen in most parts of England were probably familiar with the courts held by the bishops and by their chief subordinates the archdeacons.   The dioceses were being divided into archdeaconries, often corresponding to shires, and these in turn were divided into " rural deaneries ", similar to, though not always corresponding with, the hundreds or wapentakes.   Probably a layman who committed an offence against the law of the Church would in the first place be reported to the rural dean (chief of the local parish clergy), and by him to the archdeacon.   The same

[1] Above, pp. 50-1.
[2] Norman-French : *franchise* = liberty.

system held good for disputes involving churchmen themselves, for example, over parish boundaries and the possession of tithes. Ultimately, a case might go, on appeal, from the archdeacon to the bishop, and from the bishop to the appropriate archbishop, whether of Canterbury or York. The time was close at hand when the Church would press for the right to carry appeals for final decision to the court of the Pope himself.

This picture of multiple and sometimes competing jurisdiction was not drastically altered by Henry I.[1] He directed that the shire and hundred courts should be held at their accustomed times and places (sheriffs and lords doubtless convened them too often, for financial gain). He did nothing to discourage the judicial activity of private lords or Church dignitaries. But he seems to have added to the Crown's monopoly of serious criminal cases, and to have made what amounted to an innovation in actions over property. Most important, he set up the machinery which greatly extended the scope and effectiveness of the *Curia Regis*.

Henry I inherited from the Anglo-Saxon kings a monopoly of dealing with certain crimes, including treason, murder (whether open or secret), arson, violent robbery, and coining. If a man were suspected of any of these crimes, it was the duty of the local community to bring a collective accusation against him in the hundred and shire courts. This was in addition to the personal accusation made by the individual victim of a crime or by his kinsmen. For all these crimes a fine had to be paid to the king, in addition to the compensation payable, in some cases, to the criminal's victims. Arson, secret murder and robbery, and treason to one's lord, were reckoned too serious for compensation, and the penalty was death. William I may have mitigated this in favour of mutilation, but Henry I, enacting early in his reign a " new statute " against thieves and coiners of false money, decreed that thieves should be hanged ; and it is hard to believe that murderers would receive more lenient treatment. He also extended the practice of giving his peace personally or by writ to individuals or groups, and for any injury done to subjects thus favoured, the offender was answerable to the king alone.

In the field of " civil " actions, Henry I's reign is notable, first,

[1] On this, see N. Hurnard, " The Anglo-Norman Franchises ", *E.H.R.*, lxiv (1949).

for the definite protection which the king began to offer to those who were merely in *possession* (as distinct from undisputed *ownership*) of landed property, so that they need not be ejected from it without the due judgment of the proper court,[1] and, secondly, for the establishment of the custom, which should probably be ascribed to this period, whereby a man who claimed to *own* an estate freely and hereditarily (as distinct from merely *possessing* it) need not have his ownership challenged unless his challenger first obtained a writ from the king ordering the dispute to be heard in the proper court—the writ afterwards known as the "writ of right", because it concerned a man's proprietary *right* in a landed estate. In Henry I's time, however, these legal benefits were available only to those who were prepared to pay heavily for them, or who, like monasteries and churches, could appeal successfully to the king for his protection on other grounds.

With these changes, scarcely perceptible at first but full of importance for the future, there came also fresh methods of enforcement. At the top, the appointment of a permanent Justiciar meant that the *Curia Regis* could transact business at all times, even in the king's absence. Under the direction of the king or the Justiciar, trusted officials were from time to time sent on tour through the shires to give judgment in serious criminal cases and to enquire into infringements of royal rights. It is clear that they had authority to punish criminals and to impose heavy fines on those guilty of such infringement. In certain shires Henry I appointed local magnates to be permanent royal justices. Where judicial business was concerned, these local or county justices seem to have replaced the sheriffs as presidents of the shire courts, and they may perhaps have functioned as judges. It was through the activity of itinerant and local royal justices that the older practice whereby judgment was a matter for the collective decision and pronouncement of the free men who composed the shire court gave place to the notion that the shire court was merely the king's court in the provinces. Probably at first the local justices were more directly responsible to the king than were the sheriffs. In time, however, some of them, e.g. Geoffrey de Mandeville in King Stephen's reign,

---

[1] Thus the king ordered the sheriff of Northants to restore to the monks of St. Andrew's, Northampton, the land in Stuchbury of which they had been dispossessed, and as the men of the hundred shall judge.

became too powerful, and under Henry II local justices were replaced by itinerant justices.

It is the evident increase of royal authority in the field of jurisdiction that makes the reign of Henry I especially noteworthy. Little that we know of King Henry personally makes him a sympathetic and likeable figure. If his death was regretted, it was not because of any attractiveness or altruism in his character, for he was harsh, overbearing and extortionate. The Peterborough chronicler, who was not lavish with his praise for his country's foreign rulers, could yet say of Henry that he was " a good man, and was held in great awe. He made peace for man and beast."

CHAPTER VI

ENGLISH SOCIETY IN THE TWELFTH CENTURY

1. *The Classes of Society*

THE conventional division of medieval society was into those who worked, those who fought, and those who prayed, or in twelfth-century terms, into peasants and labourers, knights and serjeants, and priests and monks. The description may have been very broadly true, but any attempt to apply it in detail breaks down at once. Nevertheless, our review of twelfth-century society may conveniently take this analysis as its starting point, dealing first with the military order, secondly with certain groups, such as townsmen, who fall outside our threefold classification, thirdly with the peasants, and finally, in a later section, with the Church and clergy.

The generation after 1066 had planted across England a land-holding aristocracy of knights, most of them tenants of the two hundred or so barons who were the natural leaders of this small but dominant class. But within this group there was room for much variety of status, while as we have seen there were many knights who had no land at all. Among these landless knights the military temper of the Conquest generation doubtless remained strong. The knights who had been enfeoffed with small landed estates, on the other hand, tended to lose the character of professional cavalry soldiers, and became, like the thanes whom they had replaced, country gentry, developing local interests in their manors and tenants. They remained, it is true, closely attached to their lords by the accepted feudal ties ; but the feeling, which must have been strong in the eleventh century, that all the Normans formed a self-contained group united under the king in a common military enterprise, was confined thereafter to the great barons. The end of the " pioneer " days of Hastings was signalised, *c.* 1100, by an important change in the way in which the king obtained the feudal military service of his barons and knights. Normally every knight had to serve the king at his own expense for forty days [1] a year, any longer

[1] Two months in time of war.

period being at the king's expense. But it was not always easy to raise the feudal host at the time and place where it was urgently needed or, once raised, to keep it intact. It often suited William Rufus and Henry I to hire mercenary troops (a plentiful supply could almost always be had from Flanders, Brabant or Brittany), since these men were not only in better training but could be recruited for long campaigns at fixed wages. Consequently these kings, while not abating by one jot their feudal tenants' obligations of service, claimed the right to take money from them in any given year instead of service in person. This levy in lieu of service was known as "scutage" ("shield levy"), and in the second half of the twelfth century became an important item of Crown revenue.

We must not imagine, however, that because the knights were settling down into country landowners and paying scutage instead of riding off every year in the hauberk (the heavy coat of chain-mail distinguishing the knight from lesser soldiers) and armed with lance and sword and shield, they were ceasing to be a military class. Warfare was less common in England than in Normandy, but it was far from unknown. Henry I recognised that knights holding "hauberk lands" must be in a state of readiness for war and exempted them therefore from the burden of Danegeld. Over sixty years later (1166), Henry II sent a questionnaire to all his feudal tenants asking how many knights they could produce for his service. Doubtless he could base future scutages on the figures revealed by the replies, but that money was not the only consideration is shown, for example, by the proud answer of a baron of Northumberland, where men had an aptitude for arms which two Scottish invasions during the century and the memory of many others made not unjustified.

' To his most revered lord, Henry, King of the English, William son of Siward [1] sends greetings.

Your command, promulgated throughout England, has come to me (as to others) by your sheriff of Northumberland, that we should inform you of our fee and the tenure which we hold of you. Therefore I notify you by this letter that I hold of you a certain village named Gosforth, and half of another one, called Middleton, for the fee and service of one knight, which I perform faithfully to you as my ancestors did to your ancestors, and I have enfeoffed no-one with the estate but hold it in my own demesne.

[1] He was ancestor of the well-known family of Surtees.

Besides real war, there was mock war, "jousting" or tournaments, to keep barons and knights familiar with the practice of arms. With many, such sport was more keenly entered into than war itself. Moreover, if jousting was perhaps too expensive for the average knight (it was the great earls, we are told, who in 1141 were especially adept at tilting), he could certainly afford to indulge in what was probably the ruling passion of medieval Englishmen—hunting. Hunting the red deer was reserved almost exclusively for the king. It involved the establishment of special forest rules—the Forest Law —over enormous tracts of country, by no means all waste ground, and the harsh operation of the forest laws by all the Norman and Angevin kings was the greatest single source of resentment against the monarchy in the period covered by this book. Large parties of horsemen might take part in stag hunting, keeping their respective stations, or " trysts ", around the coverts, while hounds and huntsmen roused the quarry within. For those of humbler rank there were the pleasures of pursuing smaller game with highly-trained falcons, the contemporary equivalent of modern grouse or pheasant shooting. Roe deer, wolves, wild-cats, foxes and hares were also hunted in many parts of the country.

Less important in the feudal structure than the knights, but scarcely less honourable, came the men who held their lands by " serjeanty ", that is, by performing some feudal service other than that of a heavily-armed cavalry soldier. Such men might be standard-bearers, esquires who bore their lord's arms, butlers or stewards in the lord's hall, or doorwards (ushers) at its door. These offices were hereditary, their holders enjoying tenure of their lands only so long as the service was performed. An interesting example of a specialised serjeanty comes from Ely, which as we have noted was often cut off by water. After Ely was made a separate diocese, the earliest bishops evidently found that a boat was a most necessary piece of equipment, and one of them enfeoffed his helmsman, Ingram, hereditarily in a local fishery, so long as he and his heirs performed their service in the bishop's *esnecca*,[1] or galley. The typical " serjeant ", however, was a man entrusted with organising foot-soldiers and light horse attendant on the feudal host, and it is from him that our modern use of the word derives.

Between those who fought and those who laboured came numbers

[1] Literally, " snake ", from a Scandinavian word for a fast ship.

of free men who did not fit neatly into the feudal pattern. After the Conquest, the thanes as a class disappeared, save in the far north, while many of the village peasants, the villeins, were regarded as legally unfree. The only native group left over in the process was that of men who held their land freely but were subject to some lord for purposes of jurisdiction—the " sokemen ". Hence it became normal to regard every man who held his land neither freely and honourably, like a knight, nor unfreely, like a villein, as a tenant in " socage ", a free but unmilitary (and therefore socially inferior) tenure. The Crown appreciated the importance of this group more than is perhaps always realised. It must have been largely for their benefit that Henry I promised to hold fast to the law of King Edward. His grandson Henry II distinguished between knights and other freeholders in the shires in 1166, while in 1181, in regulations concerning the arms and equipment his subjects must maintain in accordance with their wealth and social position, the same king went out of his way to mention three kinds of freemen not in the knightly class—those as wealthy as the average knight, with £10 a year in land, those with two-thirds of this income, and finally, " all burgesses (townsmen) and the whole community of free men ", a remarkable phrase from the chancery of an autocratic king.

The townsmen here grouped with the general run of free men formed another class which fitted ill into the threefold analysis we have described. They were for the most part merchants, with an admixture of craftsmen. They did not specialise in prayer, were not supposed to be fit to fight, and had little time to till the fields. Yet their importance in twelfth-century England was very considerable. Trade certainly flourished in Anglo-Saxon times, but during the twelfth century and beyond it grew to such an extent that the country's economy had ceased entirely to be that of a self-contained agrarian society. In every part of England there were seasonal fairs, at which commodities such as cloth from the Mediterranean or timber, pitch and furs from Scandinavia and the Baltic were sold to Englishmen, and native products, such as Lincolnshire and Yorkshire wool, Devon tin,[1] or hides and corn, were bought for export by foreign

[1] Since prehistoric times, Cornwall has been the normal source of tin in Britain ; but during the twelfth and early thirteenth centuries, tin mining on Dartmoor in Devonshire enjoyed a boom which temporarily displaced Cornish production in importance. See G. R. Lewis, *The Stannaries* (1924), Chap. II.

merchants. Markets, often held regularly once a week, were largely the reason for the existence of many small towns, founded or encouraged by lords for the benefit of themselves and their tenants. That distance was no object to ordinary men of the age is shown, for example, by the fact, related casually by a twelfth-century author, that two men bought an ox in the Durham Saturday market for work in Lothian, at least seventy miles away. The great fairs might also be held in towns, such as Boston, one of the chief ports for Lincolnshire and the north midlands, or Winchester (St. Giles' Fair), close to the busy port of Southampton. Sometimes the venue of a fair was open ground just outside a town, as at Smithfield, north-west of London, or Stourbridge Fair outside Cambridge.

The Old English word *tūn*, of which our word town is merely the modern form, meant " village ". In the twelfth century the word used to describe a settled locality which possessed undoubtedly urban characteristics was *burh*, " borough ". Now many boroughs of the period were far from imposing and would assuredly not deserve the style of " town " in its modern sense. All that distinguished them from the rural *tūn* of early medieval England was the holding of a regular market and the fact that a population of free burgesses had taken the place of unfree villeins. Occasionally, the villeins themselves might perhaps have been promoted into burgesses through their lord's favour. But there were other boroughs, towns in the modern sense, whose importance, ecclesiastical, administrative and military, gave them a genuinely civic quality. Such cities as York, Lincoln, Exeter, and Norwich, were proud of their noble cathedrals, which even in course of construction must already have dominated the surrounding countryside, of their numerous parish churches, and of their tall narrow merchant-houses, perhaps with a shop below and a decent living chamber, or " solar ", above. If the presence of a strong royal castle under a resident sheriff or constable was a burden, nevertheless the king's government made for a city's importance, and brought trade and wealth.

It has been established by recent studies [1] that, in one important respect at least, the towns of eastern England were centres not only of marketing but also of a textile industry organised upon a capitalistic footing. In the late twelfth and early thirteenth centuries

[1] See E. M. Carus-Wilson, " The English Cloth Industry in the late XIIth and early XIIIth centuries ", *Econ. Hist. Rev.*, xiv (1944), 32-50.

urban cloth-making in England reached its medieval zenith. A thriving export trade caused cloths to be known abroad by the names of the towns of manufacture: " Stamford hauberget ", " Lincoln scarlet " (not necessarily red at this date), and " Beverley burnet ". The dyers, most of whose materials had to be imported from over-seas, evidently formed the wealthiest group among the textile crafts-men. They belonged to the merchant gilds of their towns, and in some places were employers of the men and women who carried out the initial processes of turning wool into cloth, combing, spinning, weaving and fulling.[1] Often the weavers and fullers were Flemings and lived as a distinct and unpopular community in the towns where they had settled. Well before the end of Henry I's reign they possessed their own gilds in many cities. These were craft gilds, representing the special interests of the major manufacturing section of the industry, distinct from (and often in opposition to) the more widely based gilds of merchants. In the later twelfth century, the fullers and weavers at a number of towns, e.g. Beverley, Winchester, Oxford, and perhaps London, were definitely subordinated to the merchants who exported cloth.

Outstripping all other towns in size and affluence, then as both earlier and later, the great port, cathedral city and mercantile centre of London proved to be beyond even the power of the Conqueror and his followers either wholly to overawe or normanise. A century before Henry I's time, a Flemish author thought of London as the capital of England, and " a most populous place ",[2] and c. 1180 a Londoner, William fitz Stephen, sang the praises of

> " the city of London, seat of the monarchy of England, (which) spreads its fame wider, sends its wealth and wares further, and lifts its head higher than all others ".[3]

With an exaggeration which may perhaps be forgiven a native, William tells us that merchants were glad to bring their trade in ships to London from " every nation that is under heaven ". The city was dignified by St. Paul's Cathedral, 13 monasteries, and 126 parish churches. Among London markets, William mentions specially that of the horse-dealers at Smithfield, frequented, naturally

---

[1] See below, p. 344.
[2] *Encomium Emmae Reginae*, ed. A. Campbell (Camden Soc., 1949), 23.
[3] *Norman London*, F. M. Stenton, H. E. Butler, E. Jeffries Davis, M. B. Honeybourne (1934), 26-32. This admirable essay gives a very full picture of twelfth-century London.

enough, by earls, barons, and knights, for whose benefit horse races were held to show off the animals' paces. He admired the riverside restaurant, so useful when one was entertaining visitors to the city, " for there all things desirable are ready to hand ". He has much to say of the citizens' sport : ball-games and the baiting of bears and bulls were doubtless widespread throughout the country, but less common may have been the pastimes of water-tilting on the Thames, and skating when the great marsh north of the city wall was frozen over in winter.

During the twelfth century the citizens of London made a notable advance towards self-government, securing the right to appoint their own sheriff (briefly, under Henry I, finally in 1199), and to collect their own " farm " or rents due to the king. Before the end of the century, they had set up an embryo " corporation " for the city's government, consisting of a mayor (after 1215, elected annually) and aldermen. The office of mayor was a foreign importation, but that of alderman went back to Old English times. The city was divided into wards, with an alderman in charge of each. These wards held their own courts, corresponding to the hundred courts of rural areas, while a mass folkmoot for the whole of London took the place of a shire court. The characteristic London court, however, was the intermediate " husting ",[1] in which the aldermen dealt with the city's business week by week.

No other town approached the degree of self-government attained by London, but many had their own elected officers or " reeves ", and the right to account independently of the sheriff for their annual " farms ". Moreover, a vigorous merchant community, with its own association or " gild ", its own rules, subscriptions and benevolent funds, often made up for the absence of official self-government. In some towns it is impossible to distinguish between the personnel of local government and merchant gild, for the same prominent merchants held chief office in both. It is, however, far from true that the merchant gild was always a small oligarchy—in a number of large towns, e.g. Leicester, membership was open to merchants and craftsmen alike, and in the twelfth century low entrance fees may have been the rule rather than the exception. The chief aim of the town communities, as expressed through their gilds, was to be exempt

---

[1] A Scandinavian word meaning " household court ", perhaps borrowed from intercourse with Scandinavian merchants.

in as many markets as possible from the universal payment of toll. The king, or a lord with several boroughs on his estate, might give " free trade " within his own territory to all his burgesses ; but it was naturally the latter's object to prevent outside competitors enjoying similar freedom. Hence arose the familiar medieval distinction between the " denizens " (privileged natives) and " foreigners " (merchants from another town or from some other lord's territory). Yet despite the high rate of tolls and customs which they had to meet, it was merchants from Italy, the Rhineland and the Low Countries—" foreigners " *par excellence*—who largely controlled overseas trade through the south country ports of England.

No account of twelfth-century English commerce would be complete without mention of the Jews, who formed another community of " foreign " merchants as important in their own specialisation, money-lending, as were the Italians or Flemings in the wool trade. To lend money at interest ran counter to the teaching of Canon Law, and in northern Europe, where the influence of the Church was not tempered by any secular commercial traditions, Christians could not practise usury, though they had begun to see its advantages. This need was therefore met by small groups of Jewish financiers, tolerated rather than welcomed because of the services they could render to kings, barons and even churches in want of ready money. Successful Jews became extremely wealthy, and as such doubly the object of popular envy and hatred. Legally they were counted personal serfs of the king, and so long as he protected them they were secure. But when that protection failed, they were liable to become victims of savage outbursts of mass-hysteria : at York, for example, on Henry II's death in 1189, some local barons in debt to the Jews incited a city mob to murder a large number of them and pillage their houses. Yet if it had not been for the Jews, many enterprises requiring large amounts of capital, especially the construction of some of the great cathedrals and monastic churches, could hardly have been carried through. By the end of the thirteenth century, Christians had found it possible to engage in usury without hurt to their consciences, and in 1290 Edward I actually expelled all the Jews from England, a small and unlamented community which had first attained much wealth, had then suffered prolonged persecution, and had finally, in the Crown's view, outlived its usefulness.

Knights, serjeants, unmilitary freeholders and townsfolk formed a decided minority of the population, albeit one of the utmost importance. The vast majority of English people in our period—indeed, until the eighteenth century—were village peasants and farm labourers. Today we should not think of ignoring the peasants as an element in social history, and would regard as incomplete any view of society which omitted to give an account of their life and labour. Such was far from the contemporary attitude. Politically the peasants had no voice, militarily they could avail little against mounted and armoured knights. Few of the leaders in the Church or world of learning could have come from their class, and the chances were against their rising far in the mercantile community. In the eyes of the law, nothing which the villein possessed, neither his land, nor his house, his beasts nor his implements, could strictly be deemed his own. The villein's lot was one of ceaseless toil, and appeared wholly unenviable.

Yet what little we do know of the period comes to us from records which were the work of the literate, educated minority, and the bias of this minority against the illiterate, inarticulate serf must be borne in mind. The average educated man's opinion of the agricultural population was probably that expressed by an anonymous Breton clerk of the early twelfth century, who dismissed the peasant witnesses of a legal document which he was drawing up in the phrase, " many others, the rustic imbecility of whose names forbids them being mentioned here ".[1] There are indications, however, that in reality the peasants counted for rather more than might be supposed. They formed the majority population on every manor, and the lord's demesne could not be cultivated without their co-operation. This, it is true, they could hardly refuse to give ; but there might well be variation in the quality of the work performed by peasants for their lords. Strikes, though not unknown, were uncommon ; but " ca' canny " is a traditional peasant device, and although during our period the legal status of the villeins declined, it is probably true to say that England provided no exception to the rule that in the long run a stable peasant population cannot be coerced beyond endurance.

In accordance with medieval belief, the peasant had his due place in society, even though it was a humble one. A document of the mid-twelfth century gives us an example of this concept in action. A

[1] A. de la Borderie, *Recueil d'actes inédits des ducs de Bretagne* (1888), 45.

legal decision had been arrived at concerning the Northamptonshire village of Gretton, on the " honour " of the Earl of Northampton. This decision was formally promulgated by the earl himself—one of the greatest magnates of the realm—at an assembly attended by the earl's " good and lawful men ", clergy and laymen, both of the town of Northampton and the village of Gretton, by the earl's steward, by four of his knights, and finally by the reeve of Gretton (himself probably a villein) and several of the villeins of the village. When in Magna Carta King John promised not to impose fines upon villeins so heavy that they would have to sell the necessaries of life, their seed-corn, crops and implements, he was acknowledging a fundamental principle of medieval society.

Something has already been said briefly of the manorial system by which the majority of peasants outside East Anglia, the northern Danelaw, and the far north, were bound to labour on the lord's demesne as well as on their own smaller holdings. The typical peasant service was " week work ", which meant spending perhaps three or four days a week working his lord's land, with the remainder for his own. To this basic obligation were often added heavier duties at certain busy seasons, e.g. winter ploughing, spring sowing, haymaking and harvest. These additional burdens might be described as " boon works ", implying that originally the peasant had performed them out of grace ; but as happens not uncommonly the boon of one century became the compulsory custom of the next. By our period, there is no doubt that on many manors the villein tenant was bound by an onerous cycle of labour dues throughout the year.

Nevertheless, the system was not weighted conclusively in the lord's favour. For one thing, labour service was due not from the tenant but from his or her holding, the whole or half " virgate " or " bovate ", measures of about thirty and twenty acres respectively. Now, our period was a time of rising population, and many peasant families must have included adult sons who could perform the lord's work while their father attended to the family holding. For another, it must be allowed that a system which might provide for two men to work for the lord on Monday, one on Tuesday, two again on Wednesday, and one on Thursday, during a busy part of the farming year,[1]

[1] Cited by A. L. Poole, *From Domesday Book to Magna Carta*, 42, from B. A. Lees, *Records of the Templars in England* (1935).

cannot have made for efficiency. No lord's steward with the faintest conception of proper estate management could have reached such an arrangement unless it represented the best bargain he could make with peasants whose time and labour were far from being wholly at their lord's disposal. No doubt because of this inefficiency, and perhaps because of the more widespread use of money, it became the practice for many twelfth-century lords to commute their peasants' labour service for money rents. When this happened, the individual peasant had more freedom to devote to his own land, and, if he were a good husbandman, more chance to share in the thirteenth-century phenomenon of deliberately producing a surplus from the land to be sold off the estate at a profit. It also meant an increase in the numbers of men who depended for their livelihood throughout the year on being hired as wage-labourers by the owners of land.

What did the manorial system mean for the typical peasant ? We can best answer this by looking at actual examples, and the two which follow, which both belong to the same date, *c.* 1185, show incidentally how much contrast there could be between different manors. First,

---

MAP III. AN OPEN FIELD HAMLET IN THE MIDLANDS : THURLASTON ON DUNSMORE HEATH, WARWICKSHIRE (*see opposite page*).

This diagram is based on a survey made in 1717. Although the quantity of arable had probably increased considerably since the twelfth and thirteenth centuries, the basic lay-out of the village and its cultivation had probably undergone little change.

The arable lay mainly to the south of the village. The original number of great fields cannot be determined from the 1717 survey, which shows " Rye Field " to the north, " Field next Draycote " on the west, " Foxley Field " in the south-east, and between the last two, " Middle Field ". These four fields may represent two early medieval fields.

The names of many of the furlongs are shown, and in some furlongs are shown the " strips " or " selions ", which were the basic units in the composition of individual holdings of arable. Where the selions themselves are not marked, their direction is shown by arrows. This illustrates the way in which the lie of the land influenced the direction of ploughing. Note the unploughed " roads " giving access to the furlongs, and the unploughed " sikes ", unfit for cultivation because of the nature of the ground.

The meadow lay beside the cottages and also along the River Leam. The enclosed pieces nearest to Dunsmore Heath, and that part of the heath which belonged to Thurlaston, probably formed permanent pasture.

(Based upon a survey of 1717 reproduced in the *Victoria History of the County of Warwick*, vol. vi (1951), facing p. 79, by kind permission of the General Editor of the *Victoria County History*.)

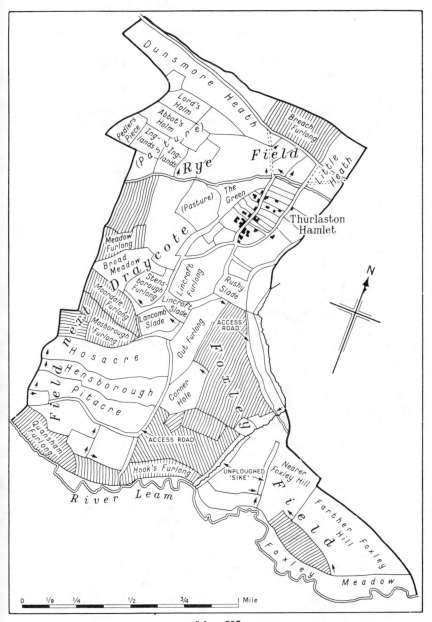

Dunsmore Heath

Lord's
Holm

Abbot's
Holm (re)

Pedler's
Piece

Ing- Ing-
lands lands
(Pa)

Rye Field

Breach
Furlong

Little Heath

(Pasture)

The Green

Thurlaston
Hamlet

Meadow
Furlong

Draycote

Broad
Meadow

Stens-
borough
Furlong

Lincroft
Furlong

Rushy
Slade

Moordale
Furlong

Mosborough
Furlong

Lincroft
Slade

Lancomb
Slade

Out Furlong

ACCESS
ROAD

N

Field next

Hosacre

Hensborough

Pitacre

Corner
Hole

Foxley

Quansham
Furlong

ACCESS ROAD

Hook's Furlong

UNPLOUGHED
'SIKE'

Nearer
Foxley Hill

Farther Foxley Hill

River Leam

Field

Foxley

Meadow

| 0 | 1/8 | 1/4 | 1/2 | 3/4 | 1 Mile |

MAP III

95

we have this description of the peasants' duties at Rivenhall in Essex : [1]

Roger Strong has 3 acres for 1*s.* a year, and must provide one man for one boon work.

William the Furrier has 3 acres for 2*s.*, must do the same boon work and provide one man for haymaking.

Adam Godwinson has 9 acres for 1*s.* 6*d.* and 2 hens at Christmas.

Geoffrey Williamson has half a virgate for 3*s.* 4*d.* He must work four days a week and provide six men for two boon works. He must give six hens at Christmas, when he will be given his food. He must go to London for carrying twice a year, each trip being counted as four days' work. He must make two loads of malt before Christmas, and he and a fellow must plough 5 acres as rent. If they harrow as well, they shall be given 5 loaves and 10 herrings, if not, 4 loaves and 8 herrings.

All the villeins of the manor shall mow for nine days and carry the entire hay-meadow, and they shall give 6*d.* and 6 loaves and a full scuttle of salt and 5*d.* ground-rent, and 2*d.* at Whitsun.

Ailward has half a virgate, and works three days a week. He must carry to London twice a year, and to Maldon on Saturdays and Sundays (not counted as a day's work) and on Mondays (counted as one day's work), whenever required.

Widow Alvid has 1 acre for 8*d.*, and must provide one man for carrying hay and another for one boon work.

Here we see great variety and, indeed, confusion, in the nature and amount of labour which the peasants had to perform and in the rents they must pay.   In contrast with this the manor of Merton, in Oxfordshire, shows an almost rigid uniformity.   The peasants held twenty virgates at a practically standard rent of 5*s.* a virgate.   From June 24th till September 29th four days' work a week had to be provided from every virgate, the men bringing their own food, while in the autumn three days' boon work must be done for each virgate, when the lord provided food for the men.   In addition, the whole group of peasants made a payment of 8*s.* at Christmas.

There were, of course, very large regions of England where this manorial system either did not find a place at all, or obtained only in a modified degree.   It was especially the case in East Anglia and the northern Danelaw that the typical peasant, whether his holding was large or small, owed little more to his lord than a money rent. In this area many peasants seem to have " by-passed " the manorial organisation of society, and to have moved direct from a system of payments in kind (which prevailed in northern England, and, as we

[1] This and the next example are taken from Lees, *op. cit.* 8-9 and 44-7, translated and slightly abridged.

shall see, in Scotland) to one of payments in coin. We should be wrong to suppose that the typical peasant of medieval lawbooks, the serf " bound to the soil ", toiling in the fields from sunrise to sunset, was the only person normally to be met with in the countryside of twelfth or thirteenth-century England. Countrymen followed a wide range of crafts and trades which, though often ancillary to agriculture, were not simply farm labouring. Many English surnames of the present day recall these occupations—Cartwright, Wheelwright, Carter, Mason, Carpenter, Miller, and many others— and their chief characteristic is variety. In one document of *c.* 1200 we even hear of the land held in a Lincolnshire village by Ralph the bell-founder. We must remember that in all likelihood carpentry no more than bell-founding was a full-time occupation for a man of that period, and that many, perhaps most, countrymen would have at least a " toft and croft ", an acre or two of land, the produce of which could eke out the living made from the pursuit of one of the specialised crafts.

2. *Religion, Church and Clergy*

The religious beliefs and observances of the English people in the twelfth and thirteenth centuries were woven so closely into the texture of their ordinary life that although it is convenient it is also unhistorical to study the Church of the period in isolation from society as a whole. It is true that a nation's Church is not the same thing as its religion, but in the minds of most men and women of the age the Church in England meant not merely its dignitaries, bishops, abbots, archdeacons, cathedral deans, and canons, or even all those in holy orders, but rather the whole body of the faithful, " the Christianity " as it was sometimes called, which made up the Church's full membership. It is in fact a paradox in this period, when many Church leaders were successfully urging that the clerical order ought to be especially privileged and sacrosanct, that the dividing line between ordinary laymen and the religious life was never more indistinct. It was open to lay men and women, just as much as to clergy, to see visions of the saints, to experience miracles, to adopt the contemplative life of a hermit and be revered as such, or to enter a monastery. Religious feeling was entirely unsophisticated. The hand of God might be apparent in every detail of daily experience, and a difference of degree rather than of kind was

97

felt between the worship accorded to one's local lord here on earth and the profounder worship by which the Lord of Creation was reverenced by all.

It was not merely that God and Christ were felt to be close at hand, overseeing every action of man—such has been the familiar belief of the Christian in all ages. What was characteristic of our period was that the near and intimate presence of the departed faithful, of long dead saints and venerated martyrs, was taken for granted. The lack of sophistication was such that both God and the saints might even be portrayed as taking part in a secular ceremony. A clerk of Canterbury, for example, named as witnesses to a gift of land in Holbeach (Lincolnshire) to Canterbury Cathedral, Our Lord Jesus Christ, the Virgin Mary, and five saints of the Church, following up these names—apparently without any sense of incongruity—by those of nine or more humble men of the district.

No doubt the clergy, by direct intercession in a ceaseless round of prayer, could help the soul of sinful man to pass through purgatory to heaven ; but many people sought as well the help and protection of a saint locally revered or chosen as patron for some personal reason. Pilgrimages to the shrines of such saints were universally popular. After the murder of Archbishop Thomas Becket in 1170, his tomb at Canterbury was the most frequented goal of English pilgrims ; but in many other places besides Canterbury the real or supposed relics of saints drew the pious from distant parts. Overseas, probably the most popular pilgrimage for English people, after Rome, was to Saint James (Santiago) at Compostella in north-west Spain. For the poorer or less adventurous, the shrines of such native saints as Alban (at St. Albans in Hertfordshire) or Edmund (at Bedricsworth in Suffolk, renamed Bury St. Edmunds) would suffice, or else churches associated with the apostles, e.g. York Minster, dedicated to St. Peter, or Hexham in Northumberland, which treasured supposed relics of St. Andrew. This apostle, however, had his British shrine *par excellence* on the east coast of Fife in Scotland, at the place known as St. Andrews since the twelfth century, and this was a resort of many pilgrims from England and elsewhere.[1]

---

[1] It seems to have been at this time that Andrew replaced Columba as the special patron saint of the Scots. No doubt this was partly because St. Andrews was accessible and much visited, while the real shrine of Columba, on the island of Iona, was almost impossible to reach, and was not even on Scottish territory.

This total acceptance of the Christian faith did not mean that the Church or society in general was complacent in its religious adherence. Quite the opposite was true. It was not only that in the medieval world many beliefs and practices from the pre-Christian, pagan, past survived in a subdued or modified form, particularly in the superstitious reverence for healing or magic wells, and in the observance of pagan feasts. The Church had on the whole successfully suppressed, tamed, or adapted much of this latent heathenism. It was rather that Christianity by its very nature implies a constant struggle towards the good life and salvation, which has to be waged afresh in every generation. It was not, therefore, disbelief or indifference which had to be combated by the Church in our period, but rather what it saw as the positive and recurring sinfulness of mankind, the backsliding from Christian standards to which all readily subscribed.

Nevertheless, the Church and Christian society generally in western Europe were acutely conscious of the existence of religious beliefs which, while far from pagan, were either non-Christian or even anti-Christian. Jewish communities in the midst of Christian ones were a constant reminder of this, while along the southern fringes of Europe, pushing, on the west, far into the Iberian peninsula, there stretched an impressive chain of Islamic powers, most of which were established in areas which had once lain at the heart of the Christian world. The fear and revulsion felt by Christians towards these highly-developed, opponent faiths found an outlet, as far as the Jews were concerned, in occasional local persecution. To counter the threat of Islamic penetration, however, called for a military effort on the part of the whole of Christendom, eastern and western alike. From 1095 onwards, there was a continual response in the west to appeals for men and money to be sent to Palestine or Spain, and in the resulting " crusades " contingents from Britain played a notable part. Here the desire to go on a pilgrimage was combined with the impulse to recover the Holy Land from its Muslim conquerors. Naturally, it was powerful barons and their knightly tenants who figured most prominently in these enterprises. We have seen that Duke Robert of Normandy was an active crusader. No king of England took part personally in a crusade until Richard I in 1190-2, but one of the chief English earls, William de Warenne of Surrey, was killed in the rearguard battle fought against the Turks in the defiles of Laodicea in 1148, and we shall see that the departure of many English nobles for Palestine in the later 1140's helped to restore peace after several years of civil war.

Military prowess, Christian piety and the appeal of a quasi-monastic life were curiously combined in the crusading orders of knights, so typical of western Europe in the twelfth century. The "poor brethren of the Hospital of St. John of Jerusalem "—the Knights Hospitallers—and the " brother knights of the Temple of Solomon "—the Templars—began as associations to protect pilgrims and rapidly became military religious orders of international scope and with vast financial resources. Recruiting membership from every nation of western Christendom, the crusading orders naturally provided many leaders in the feudal Christian states established in the Levant during the twelfth century. Both the Hospitallers and Templars possessed many estates in Britain, their manors being in effect a mixture of recruiting depôt and source of income.

The crusading impulse was by no means confined to the military classes. It was, for example, men of quite humble origin, seamen from the ports of southern England, who seized Lisbon from the Moors in 1147, establishing a friendly Anglo-Portuguese relationship which has endured to the present day. Another instance of crusading by men even more obscure—and also, a glimpse of the human side of the great crusading movement—is given by the following report of 1197, describing what had become of some men of Lincolnshire, simple peasants, who had accepted the sign of the cross in earnest of their intention to fight in the Holy Land. It shows that crusading had other perils than the weapons of the Saracen, and that first enthusiasms could easily wane in the face of domestic hardships.

" At Wyberton, John Buchart had set out for Jerusalem in the time of King William II of Sicily, who forbade him to cross the Mediterranean. On his return, he was released from his crusade by the Lord Pope, and as his neighbours testify, brought back with him the pope's letter of release, until he may be able to undertake his pilgrimage more easily. He is married with many children, very poor and of middle age.

" At Sutterton, William son of Swift, married, with children, a poor man in middle age, asserts that he has been to Palestine, but he has no witnesses to this.

" At Bicker, Elias son of Hervi, is married, with seven children, poor—almost a beggar.

" At Surfleet, Herbert son of Guy was marked with the sign of the cross five years ago. He set off, but was robbed in Lombardy. He works for his brother, and is not fit to go on this crusade.

" Ulf Poucer, marked with the sign of the cross eight years ago, on the testimony of the priest who placed the sign on him (and his neighbours say the same), denies that he ever took the cross. He has a wife and seven children, is exceedingly poor and a young man." [1]

That poor countrymen of this type from the desolate marsh villages round the Wash could attempt the arduous journey to Jerusalem apparently without organised assistance says much for the power of the crusading motive, itself only one aspect of a more general religious feeling. This feeling found its most characteristic expression within our period in the life of the monasteries. Although, as we have seen, English monasticism had already had a long history before the Norman Conquest, the twelfth century is rightly judged to have been the great age of the English monasteries. Not only did religious houses, usually founded by local magnates, proliferate in all parts of the country, but men and women from every walk of life were drawn to the religious order. The leadership and inspiration of many such men, who moved from the cloister to high ecclesiastical positions, enormously benefited the Church as a whole.

We cannot say why there should have been this flowering of monasticism in the period : we must accept it as a fact whose causes lie too deep for explanation. But by examining some of the different types of religious life, the diverse " orders " of monks, nuns, and regular canons, we may at least discover something of the aims of the men and women who in very large numbers gave up their worldly possessions to take the monastic vows of poverty, chastity, and obedience.

The dominant mode of monasticism, as we have seen, was that which observed the Rule of St. Benedict of Nursia (d. *c.* 550). Under this rule, a group of men or women lived a communal life within the walls of a single habitation, consisting of the bare essentials of a church, a common " frater " (refectory) and dormitory, with servants' quarters, infirmary, store-houses and such other buildings as were needful. The monks wore a simple black habit, and their day was chiefly occupied by a long programme of prayer and chanting, though some time was found for intellectual pursuits such as the copying of manuscripts or composition of chronicles, and some— but surprisingly little—for eating and sleeping. The earliest of

[1] Translated and abridged from Historical MSS. Commission, *Report on Various Collections*, i. 235-6.

these communities were independent, ruled by an abbot who in some respects was the equivalent of a bishop,[1] though subject to the local bishop for jurisdiction. But often an abbey of this type grew to such an extent that it was able to set up a " daughter house " or cell, ruled by a prior dependent on the abbot of the parent foundation, from which it might be many miles distant. This expansion might come about in a number of ways. A lord wishing to found a monastery might request the abbot of a house of great repute to let him have some monks for whom he would provide the necessary buildings and income (usually in the form of land). This happened, for example, at Belvoir in Leicestershire, where the Norman lord, Robert de Todeni, a few years after the Conquest, obtained monks for his new priory from Abbot Paul of St. Albans. Alternatively, the incoming Normans might actually replace native English monks by others from a Norman monastery better known to them. Gilbert, Count of Eu, and his son Richard, in turn lords of Eynesbury in Huntingdonshire, made over an old English monastery there (dedicated to the obscure St. Neot) to the great abbey of Bec. Or an abbey might of its own volition establish a group of its monks on an outlying manor : Reading abbey did this at Leominster in Herefordshire. A daughter house did not always remain in subjection to the parent. It might itself become an abbey, or the mother house might fail to exercise control over its cell, which, though still nominally a priory, would then develop along independent lines.

The twelfth century was not only a golden age for the stricter, " reformed " Benedictine orders, of which more will be said presently. It was a flourishing period for the old established Benedictine abbeys and priories. Many of the new Norman abbots and monks were men of outstanding sanctity of life or with notable powers of leadership and organisation. Under their inspiration, the numbers of professed monks grew rapidly, reaching in many abbeys totals never exceeded before or later. Famous houses like St. Albans or Canterbury cathedral priory counted over a hundred monks, and other abbeys expanded in proportion. The old Benedictine tradition of copying manuscripts and writing histories took on a new force, and in this period Winchester and Canterbury

---

[1] An abbot did not have power to ordain or confirm, but stood to his monks in much the same relation as a bishop stood to the clergy and people of his diocese.

produced manuscripts of unsurpassed beauty, while St. Albans and Durham were the home of historians on whom we rely for much of our knowledge of contemporary events. Naturally, this was a time of large-scale monastic building. New churches were begun, such as the magnificent cathedral of Durham, dating from the end of the eleventh century ; and round these churches were grouped enlarged cloisters, fraters, dormitories and other quarters, often covering many acres. Round these again were gardens, orchards and vine-yards, and beyond these the agricultural land on whose produce the whole populous community of monks, servants, craftsmen, and peasant tenants was maintained.

The greatest single weakness of the Benedictine monasteries was that everything depended upon the individual abbot. If he was a firm disciplinarian—and a man of sound business sense—all was well ; if not, lack of control made for lax observance of the rule, the disrepute of the monks, and their possible exploitation by unscrupulous outsiders. To counter this danger, the Benedictine abbots of Cluny kept their daughter houses firmly within a single " family ". The head of each new dependent Cluniac cell, always a mere prior and never an abbot, had to make a profession of obedience to the abbot of Cluny himself. But the obedience and discipline imposed by Cluny from above was too harsh and rigid for many men who were nevertheless deeply imbued with fervour for the true Benedictine life, and the elaborate round of religious offices, of chant and prayer and Mass, by which the Cluniacs' day was filled, seemed too rich and luxuriant for minds drawn to a puritan ideal of simplicity and self-denial.

It was men so motivated who, about the turn of the eleventh and twelfth centuries, brought into being the most remarkable development of monastic life to be found in our period, the " reformed " Benedictine orders, which reached their highest exemplification in the family of abbeys founded from Cîteaux, near Dijon in Burgundy.

This new movement began in various places in northern France, but its leaders possessed one common intention—to go back to what they considered the true Benedictine life of primitive austerity and even asceticism. These leaders usually began, in fact, by being simple hermits. When joined by growing bands of disciples, they were compelled to form monastic houses with a fixed constitution in order to preserve the purity of the way of life they had adopted. Monasteries of this type were founded (*c.* 1109-12) at Savigny and

Tiron (north-west France), and daughter houses from both these abbeys were soon set up in England. But by far the most famous of the reformed Benedictine orders was that founded at Cîteaux, *c.* 1098, by Robert, Abbot of Molesme, and Stephen Harding, an English monk from Dorset. It was the genius of Stephen Harding which gave his fellows the *Carta Caritatis,* the " charter of spiritual love ", perhaps the most perfect constitution for a monastic order that has ever been devised.

First, the Cluniac practice of retaining all the abbeys of the movement within one family was adopted, but with a striking improvement. Instead of Cîteaux ruling over every Cistercian [1] offshoot, each house was made an autonomous abbey, subject, however, to an annual visitation by the abbot of its immediate parent house. Once a year all the Cistercian abbots had to meet at Cîteaux in " general chapter ", to order the affairs of the whole Cistercian family. Finally, Cîteaux itself was subject to an annual visitation by the abbots of its first four daughter houses. By this simple and masterly scheme, the needs of discipline and independence were reconciled. The order was fortunate in attracting to its membership the most remarkable figure of twelfth-century monasticism, and one of the great formative personalities of the Middle Ages, Bernard, abbot of Clairvaux (one of Cîteaux's earliest daughter houses) from 1115 to 1153. Within St. Bernard's life time, and owing chiefly to his unflagging enthusiasm and force of character, the Cistercian movement grew from a primitive hermitage in the woods of Burgundy into a great international religious society.

Within their monasteries, the Cistercians, or "white monks", [2] lived a life of practical austerity. Instead of their day being occupied by almost continual chant and liturgical ceremony, communal devotion alternated with manual labour and private prayer. Learning and art were discouraged. Few manuscripts or histories come from Cistercian houses, though the letters and sermons of St. Bernard fill many volumes, and biographies were permitted of notable Cistercians and of other persons revered by the order. Their conventual buildings were extremely simple, and the severe beauty of their abbeys in England, e.g. Tintern, Herefordshire (1131), and

[1] The adjective comes from the Latin form of the name Cîteaux' *Cistercium.*

[2] So called because their habit was of undyed sheep's wool.

Rievaulx and, above all, Fountains (both in North Yorkshire, 1132), springs in part from the grandeur of their surroundings and in part from the lucky accident that the advent of Cistercianism coincided with that of Gothic architecture in its purest form. The white monks deliberately sought remote, sparsely inhabited places in which to build their monasteries, for their aim was to dwell as completely self-sufficient communities, cut off physically from the contagion of worldly life. They had no tenants, avoided feudal obligations, and even claimed exemption from the payment of tithes.[1] The land they owned was worked not by hired labourers, but by lay brothers, *conversi*, who, though humble and illiterate laymen, were as fully members of the convent as the monks themselves. The abbey's estates were divided into separate farming units known as " granges ", worked mainly by lay brothers, though in distant granges there might be a number of monks as well. Hard and lonely though the life must have been, it has been said that " the appeal made by this vocation to the illiterate, who had for many centuries been neglected by monasticism, was immediate and widespread ".[2] It was especially potent in the north of England, where the older monasticism had never recovered from the collapse of the Northumbrian kingdom and the Scandinavian invasions. In the wild dales at the edge of the moors of Yorkshire and Lancashire, the great abbeys of Rievaulx, Byland, Jervaulx, Fountains, and Furness stood as outposts of peace amid political turbulence, and busy centres for the recolonisation of an unfruitful soil. On the moors (as, farther south, on the wolds of Lincolnshire), the Cistercian monks raised vast flocks of sheep, originally to provide their own clothing, but soon growing so large that a valuable export trade throve in the wool they produced. The very success of the white monks in fulfilling their early aim of self-sufficiency proved in part their undoing, for they became wealthy, and with their wealth lost their original humility and simplicity of life.

From its arrival in 1128 until the last quarter of the twelfth century, the Cistercian order enjoyed an immense popularity in England. The total membership of the greatest Cistercian houses, taking monks and lay brothers together, far exceeded the numbers to be found even in the biggest of the older Benedictine abbeys, and

[1] They were allowed not to pay tithes from land which they had reclaimed from waste, a process in which they specialised.

[2] M. D. Knowles, *The Monastic Order in England* (Cambridge, 1949), 215.

in addition to its monasteries for men the Cistercian order had many less well-known houses for nuns also. Nevertheless, we should remember that the movement appealed to a numerically tiny minority of the population, that its members sought complete seclusion from the world, and that its influence on society was indirect, or felt through outstanding individuals like the Northumbrian Englishman Ailred, Abbot of Rievaulx (1147-67), one of the most saintly men of his age. The needs of the Church were not met by such isolated communities. It was to provide a better service of ordinary parish churches, especially those in towns, in constant use by the laity, that there was brought into existence an order of reformed canons, who were to live communally like monks, renouncing personal property, and follow a fixed rule. The rule adopted was associated with the great St. Augustine (d. 430), and from this they were called Augustinian or Austin canons. In the fifty years from *c.* 1100 groups of Austin canons were established in scores of churches, especially parish churches, up and down England, and they brought to parish ministration the stricter standards of conduct, and the more elaborate form of worship, associated with the monastic orders.

Some canons determined to go further in the direction of reform. The followers of Norbert, Archbishop of Magdeburg and famous as a preacher in eastern Germany, adopted, along with a modified version of the Augustinian rule, the constitutions and habit of the Cistercians. Under the name of " white canons " or " Premonstratensians ",[1] these extreme advocates of the reformed canonical order established several houses in England from the middle of the twelfth century, beginning with Newhouse in Lincolnshire (1143). Within fifty years, however, they had become almost exclusively monastic, and it becomes hard to distinguish their work and life from that of the white monks. Another adoption of Cistercianism may be noted in the mixed order founded by Master Gilbert of Sempringham, an English priest and teacher comparable in stature with Ailred of Rievaulx. To meet the needs of women desirous to lead the religious life in an area where there were few Benedictine nunneries, Gilbert arranged that they should have their own convent, living communally and austerely on the Cistercian pattern. To provide their spiritual ministration, he annexed to this a group of

[1] From the Latin form of Prémontré, near Laon, where Norbert founded his first community.

regular canons, and finally added a body of lay brothers, who, as at a Cistercian abbey, performed the manual labour. The " Gilbertines ", the only religious order to originate in medieval England, enjoyed a similar vogue to that of the white monks and Austin canons, being especially popular in the eastern midlands.

Thus we may see twelfth-century monasticism in England as composed of two main stems—first, the old Benedictine type, infused with fresh vigour and purpose in its reformed branches, whether of Cluny, Tiron or Cîteaux ; secondly, the Augustinian movement, the adoption of a fixed rule and a common life by canons serving parish churches. These stems were not quite distinct, for the Austin canons were influenced by Cistercianism, while on the other hand monks from all the orders we have mentioned were prepared to return to the world, as it were, and become bishops. Between 1070 and 1307, for example, six archbishops of Canterbury were monks. In a sense, therefore, English monasticism, even in Cistercian houses, took the way of compromise, the *via media* between mixing with the world and the total asceticism of the desert hermit. There was only one order outside the main stream of Benedictine monachism to find a place in England. This was the congregation of La Grande Chartreuse (in the foothills of the Alps near Grenoble), whose members lived almost as solitary and silent anchorites within the walls of their monastery. It was hardly by chance that the Carthusians [1] founded only one English house in our period, at Witham in Somerset (1178). Its third prior, Hugh of Avallon, was revered as a saint in his own lifetime, and despite the Carthusian ideal of seclusion Prior Hugh became an outstanding bishop of Lincoln.

Monasticism was not sharply divided from the life of ordinary men and women. Those who would not or could not become monks or nuns themselves frequently made benefactions to some local religious house. These donations were by no means confined to the richer landowners—poor peasants in the Danelaw, for example, made gifts of an acre of land or a few shillings rent. Most classes would have experience of monastic hospitality, for the monks gave lodging and alms to all in need, and even the king was not above staying, as an unpaying guest, in one of the wealthier abbeys. Monasteries functioned as safe deposits for money and valuables,

---

[1] Again from the Latin form. In English, " Chartreuse " became the more homely " Charterhouse ".

and they also took in elderly people wishing to end their lives in the peace of the cloister, usually in return for a small gift. Again, monks or their servants were farmers on a large scale, sellers of agricultural produce and buyers of a variety of manufactured goods and of the services of many different craftsmen. Boroughs grew up at the gates of abbeys, such as St. Albans and Bury St. Edmunds. In short, the monastery in our period might impinge on human life at every turn.

We may fittingly round off our survey of monasticism and its place in English society with an example of a lay baron's donation to a religious house—in this case, the great abbey of Reading, founded by Henry I, who was afterwards buried in its church. The letter which tells of the gift, with its naive mixture of religious piety, feudal reverence, and practical common sense, could hardly be a more characteristic product of the age.

To Hilary, by God's grace Bishop of Chichester, and to all the sons of holy church, Jocelin, brother of Queen Adelaide,[1] sends greetings. Know that I have granted to God and to Saint Mary and the church of Reading and the brethren serving God there that land in the village of Petworth [Sussex] which belonged to Robert of Diddlesfold, and the land of Theoderic and the land that belonged to Edwin Hunt, with everything belonging to those lands, in wood and open country, in meadows and pastures, and together with these, one piggery for 10 sows and one boar, and pasture free of charge for that piggery and its farrows. And in addition to this, when I was at Reading for the funeral of my lady and sister Queen Adelaide I granted to the monks those assarts in my own demesne [2] which the above-mentioned three men used to occupy and for which they rendered no service either to me or to the monks. Furthermore, I granted to the monks one virgate of arable. I have also given them permission to have 40 swine along with my own swine in my parks and fenced enclosures, from Martinmas (11 November) to St. Thomas's day (21 December). I have granted them all these things for ever, for the soul of my lord and father, Duke Godfrey, and of the soul of my lady and sister the Queen, and for the weal of my lord William, Earl of Chichester, and of his children, and for the souls of my brothers and sisters and of all my ancestors, and for my own weal.[3]

We should be wrong to think of the English Church in this age as dominated completely by the monasteries, whether of the reformed orders or of ancient foundation. Though many of the bishops had

---

[1] Henry I's second wife, daughter of Godfrey, Duke of Brabant. Her brother Jocelin settled in Sussex as tenant of the Earl of Arundel or Chichester.

[2] Note especially the encouragement given by Jocelin to the " assarting " (clearing) of his estate by letting the tenants hold rent-free.

[3] British Museum, MS. Cott. Vesp. E xxv, folio 57 (my translation).

been professed monks before their election, half the English cathedral churches were served not by monastic but by secular chapters. They included several of the largest and most important : York, St. Paul's, Lincoln, and Salisbury.[1] For much of our period, the constitution and customs of Salisbury cathedral, which in any case closely resembled those of York and Lincoln and dated like them from 1091, formed a model for a number of other cathedrals. Consequently, if we now look briefly at the salient features of Salisbury, we shall gain also a reasonably accurate picture of the manner in which the majority of English non-monastic cathedrals were organised.

The head of the cathedral church and clergy, under the bishop, was the dean. At one time strictly subordinate to the bishop, the dean in the twelfth century had come to wield more authority than his superior within the cathedral church and its precincts. Unlike the bishop, who travelled about the diocese and might actually be absent from it for long periods, the dean had his lodging close to the cathedral and spent most of his time within the precincts. He was elected by the chapter, and represented the interests and viewpoint of the permanently resident clergy who officiated at the perpetual round of services. He was in effect the parish priest of the cathedral clergy, with power to review and correct their faults. He was the president at meetings of chapter, and bore the responsibility for the general administration of his church and of the numerous community which served it.

The next senior officer was the precentor (" chanter ", in plainer English).[2] He directed the essential choral and liturgical aspects of the divine office, and supervised the choir school. In church, his coign of vantage for overseeing the choir was the extreme western stall on the north side. The dean's stall was immediately opposite, and it was normal to refer to the north and south sides of the choir respectively as *cantoris* and *decani* (" precentor's " and " dean's "). In addition to the choir-boys and choristers, the organist came under the precentor's surveillance, and the degree to which the music provided by the somewhat primitive organs of the twelfth century

[1] The remaining secular cathedrals were Exeter, Lichfield (paired with monastic Coventry), Wells (likewise paired with Bath), Hereford and Chichester.

[2] The order of seniority differed somewhat at St. Paul's and Exeter.

was employed to support the plain song was doubtless a matter for the precentor's direction.

Third place among the cathedral dignitaries was taken by the chancellor. He was responsible for the readings which formed a part of the services in church; for the official written business, correspondence and the like, of the chapter; and for keeping the chapter seal. In some ways the most important of his duties was to have charge of the school for the training of clergy which had an essential place in the cathedral foundation. To carry out the actual teaching, the chancellor normally appointed a special master of the school. Finally, there was the treasurer, the fourth major dignitary in the cathedral. Dr. Edwards has emphasised [1] that he " was in no sense a financial or business officer concerned with the income derived from the chapter lands. . . . His first duty was to keep the treasures of the church, the gold and silver vessels, the ornaments, relics, jewels, embroidered silk copes, and altar cloths, while at the same time he provided the lights, bread, wine, incense and other material necessaries for the services."

These were the four principal officers at Salisbury cathedral, and authority rested chiefly in their hands. At the same time, the archdeacons, the bishop's senior assistants in the diocese as a whole, were accorded a position of some dignity at the typical English cathedral church, and might have both stalls in choir and seats and votes in chapter. But the chapter was of course composed in the main of secular canons, perhaps twenty or thirty in number. Most cathedrals had sufficient endowments to provide " prebends " (fixed incomes, usually from parish churches and landed estate) to support as many canons as this, and a few of the richest cathedrals had considerably more. A proportion of the canons themselves filled subordinate offices under the four dignitaries, but the great majority neither resided at their cathedral nor were expected to do so. They were commonly clerks in the service of the king or the Papacy, or else teachers at the university. In consequence, the actual services at the cathedral church were in our period carried out not by the whole body of canons, as had once been the case, but by specially appointed " vicars of the choir ", junior clerics who stood in the

---

[1] Kathleen Edwards, *The English Secular Cathedrals in the Middle Ages* (1949), 220-1. Dr. Edwards's study has been the basis for this brief account of the secular cathedrals.

place of the canons and were permanently resident at the cathedral, under the watchful eye of dean and precentor. By the thirteenth century, the vicars-choral of most English cathedrals had become fully-organised corporate bodies, like the cathedral chapters, with their own rules and constitutions.

The Church which produced men like Ailred of Rievaulx and Gilbert of Sempringham among its monastic leaders did not lack statesmanship or sanctity of the highest order in its secular clergy. During our period, the western Church as a whole, through its governing minority of zealous reformers, was enlarging its influence, extending its functions of moral and spiritual guidance, of supervision and correction, into every sphere of human activity. This was not to be achieved without a hard struggle with secular authorities often out of sympathy with the more extreme aims of ecclesiastical reform. In England we have examples of this struggle at its crudest, between William Rufus and Anselm, and at its most developed, first between Henry II and Thomas Becket, later between Edward I and Robert Winchelsey.

Rufus's policy towards the Church was to exploit its wealth but otherwise ignore it. He treated Church offices like lay fiefs. If a bishop or an abbot died, he authorised no appointment of a successor until he had reaped a good profit from the revenues of the see or abbey ; and then he made the new holder of the office pay a " relief " for the privilege of taking over its plundered estates. After Lanfranc's death he appointed no one as archbishop until 1093, when desperate illness frightened him into giving the primacy to Anselm, Abbot of Bec and an old pupil of Lanfranc. But Anselm, as stubborn as he was saintly, insisted on his freedom to recognise the Pope, Urban II, regarded as canonical by the reform party in the Church, while the king favoured an " anti-pope ", Clement III. There was much other matter for dispute. The king's immorality offended Anselm, the poor showing of the archbishop's feudal contingents in war angered the king. William, as the price of recognising him as Pope, tried to persuade Urban to depose Anselm ; but he was outwitted by papal diplomacy and forced to see Anselm confirmed in his office. The final crisis came in 1097, when Anselm left the country without William's permission, in order to consult the Pope. William held the archbishopric forfeit, and its revenues remained in royal hands until the accession of Henry I.

Relations did not at once improve after 1100, despite Henry's anxiety to have the Church's support. He recalled Anselm from exile, only to find that the archbishop, returning with his prestige immensely enhanced, was determined to press demands that had never been made of the Conqueror or Rufus. The immediate question at issue turned on the appointment of bishops. Could a bishop, whose office was spiritual, lawfully accept it at the hands of the king, a mere layman, having first done homage and sworn allegiance ? Anselm took the view, advanced by the reform party, that a bishop could be invested with the symbols of his office, the ring and pastoral staff, only from the hands of other bishops, and that homage was not due to any layman in respect of a Church appointment. The king for his part could not surrender his control —and the ceremony of homage which symbolised that control—over the bishops of his realm, who possessed vast baronies and were answerable, in England at least, for the service of some hundreds of knights. Though investiture lay at the centre of the dispute, the struggle ran deeper and involved the question of whether Church or State was to have ultimate supremacy. Fortunately, Henry was of a temper very different from his brother's, and in 1107 a compromise was reached. Henry agreed not to confer ring or staff on new bishops : Anselm accepted bishops already appointed in the old manner, and conceded that a priest nominated as bishop might do homage to the king before he received full episcopal orders in the rite of consecration. Bishops were to be elected by the chapters of their sees ; but the king made sure that this took place under his eyes in a royal chapel, and though " elections " were nominally free, they were guided by the royal will. This compromise formed the basis of relations between Crown and Church for the rest of the Middle Ages.

In substance, Henry I had yielded scarcely any ground. The English Crown, even in the relatively unsure grasp of Stephen, exercised considerable authority over the Church in the appointment of bishops and the greater abbots. Consequently, the king could still reward his deserving councillors with bishoprics, and they in turn tended to take his side either against the Pope or against the reforming section of the Church which would have liked to see ecclesiastical offices separated entirely from lay interference, and churchmen holding aloof (as they seldom did in England) from secular business. The compromise, however, sometimes broke down badly. Even a pliant king like Stephen might provoke an Archbishop of Canterbury to exile. A more serious breakdown, the famous quarrel between Henry II and Becket, must form part of a later chapter.

CHAPTER VII

THE CIVIL WAR, 1135-54

THE nineteen unsettled years which come between the successful autocracies of Henry I and his grandson Henry II are usually described as " The Anarchy ", and explained by a desire on the part of the English baronage to kick over the traces of government and indulge in an orgy of plunder and private war. The truth of this interpretation seems highly doubtful. A few members of the military order may have welcomed the Crown's weakness, and it is true that some individuals of preternatural infamy, for example, Geoffrey de Mandeville, Earl of Essex, did indeed take up careers of pillage and commit atrocities of every description. But these men were a minority. The magnates of an entire nation, even in the feudal age, do not so readily abandon all traditions of good government for the sake of transient gain. The plight of the country under Stephen was due rather to perfectly genuine political difficulties for which there was no clear-cut solution, and the period is better regarded as one of civil war rather than feudal anarchy.

Despite their sworn oath to accept the Empress Maud as queen and duchess, the barons of England and Normandy disliked the idea, unprecedented in their history, of a woman ruler. The Empress had been away from England for twenty years and, what was worse, was married to the Count of Anjou, the traditional enemy of Normandy. Moreover, she was known to be personally high-handed and wilful. Even so, she might well have acceded to her father's throne had not another candidate, her cousin Stephen, younger brother of the Count of Blois and in his own right one of the greatest landowners in England, carried out a swift *coup d'état*. If Maud's claim were discounted, Stephen was almost certainly the best choice ; but Stephen moved with such speed that Maud was not seriously considered. He was in England when Henry I died, his younger brother, Henry of Blois, was Bishop of Winchester, where the royal treasure was kept, and he had the support (doubtless at a price) of the citizens of London. The English Church followed the line taken by the influential Bishop of Winchester, and on December 22nd, 1135, Stephen was duly crowned at Westminster by the Archbishop of Canterbury. Across the Channel the greater part of Normandy acknowledged him as duke, and soon the Pope also declared his support. Nor was this the limit of his advantage. A consequence of the Church's attitude was that Roger, Bishop of Salisbury, the pillar of Henry I's administration and controller of the financial resources of the realm, placed the weight of his experience and wealth—and that of his relatives, who held two bishoprics and the chancery, and shared Roger's control of the exchequer—at Stephen's disposal.

Yet in the circumstances of the time, it was unthinkable that Maud would give up her hereditary claims without a struggle, and in fact she had powerful allies. At one extremity of Stephen's dominions her husband Count Geoffrey invaded Normandy, while at the other her uncle [1] the King of Scots, David I, occupied the district of Carlisle and the county of Northumberland. The Angevin army, however, which committed atrocities even at the expense of those Normans who were friendly to the count, was driven out with much slaughter, and for the moment Maud was forced to give up her attempt to seize the duchy. Meanwhile Stephen gathered a very large force for the defence of northern England, and by an agreement with David at Durham recovered Northumberland, but at the price of surrendering the border fortress of Carlisle and its district to the Scots. It has been said that David I's policy towards Stephen was one of opportunist aggression. Opportunist he certainly was, but Carlisle had once been part of his father's kingdom and the earldom of Northumberland he claimed in right of his wife, Earl Waltheof's [2] daughter. There is in fact no reason to question the statements of contemporary writers that David was prompted by the oath of 1127 to support Henry I's daughter, which he had been the first layman to take. We should also remember that the Scottish king, like a number of English barons who took Maud's side, owed much to Henry I's generosity and patronage and had been bound to him by close ties of feudal loyalty.

[1] King David was the younger brother of Maud (Edith), Henry I's first wife. He was also the uncle of King Stephen's queen, another Maud, daughter of the Count of Boulogne by David's other sister Mary. See Genealogical Tables.   [2] See above, p. 40.

The first round had gone to King Stephen. Even after his efforts to remove the Angevin threat to Normandy failed (1137), his position seemed far stronger than that of his rivals. But at this juncture (1138) the Empress and her party launched their most strenuous attempt to dislodge him. Maud appealed to her uncle, David of Scotland, and to her half-brother, Robert, Earl of Gloucester, the most notable and powerful of Henry I's many illegitimate sons. The Scots invaded Northumberland in the winter, bringing misery to the countryside by the pillaging, burning and massacre which they wrought. The king again marched north, and while David, afraid to give open battle, vainly waited in some hidden glen to entrap and ambush him, Stephen and his army unconcernedly laid waste the eastern border district of Scotland. As summer approached, however, Stephen was tied to a laborious war of castle sieges against Robert of Gloucester, who declared openly for his sister in May. David I judged the moment ripe for as massive an onslaught upon northern England as the resources of his kingdom would allow. A vast ill-assorted host of Scots, Northumbrians,[1] " Picts " of Galloway,[2] Normans, Flemings, islesmen, and even Danes, poured southwards down the old Roman route of Dere Street, which led directly from the Scottish king's chief castle at Roxburgh into the north Yorkshire plain. Near the southern end of this road, on Cowton Moor by Northallerton, the invaders were met (August 22nd, 1138) by the *fyrd* of Yorkshire and a strong contingent of Anglo-Norman barons (including a force of knights sent by Stephen), under the dual leadership of William of Aumâle, Earl of Yorkshire, and Thurstan, Archbishop of York. The English army rallied beneath the standard of St. Peter of York to defend its homes against the ravages of an invader who spared no one in his barbarity. The Scottish attack was weakened by regional jealousies and by the inadequacy of the half-naked Galwegians when pitted against archers and armoured knights fighting as infantry. A turning point came when the Earl of Lothian was slain and his men fled, and the " battle of the Standard " ended in the utter rout of the Scots and the withdrawal of King David first to Carlisle and then to Roxburgh.

Unhappily for King Stephen, he was in no position to exploit

[1] Part of historical Northumbria, Lothian, was in Scottish territory.
[2] Some English chroniclers of the time used the word " Pict " to distinguish the native of Galloway from the Scots living north of the Forth.

the Scottish defeat. The forces of Robert of Gloucester still held Bristol and the west, and they were powerfully reinforced in 1139 by Henry I's hereditary constable, Miles of Gloucester, and Brian, son of Count Alan " the young ", one of the old king's Breton allies. Brian " fitz Count " held command of the great fortress of Walling-ford-on-Thames, midway between Oxford and Reading, a dangerous salient thrust into Stephen's territory. The friendship which Henry I had maintained since his earliest days with the barons of the march between Normandy and Brittany bore fruit at Tinchebrai and was now, years afterwards, to stand his daughter in good stead. Brian fitz Count was only one of several Breton leaders who took her part, among the others being the two sons of Alan of Dol, William, a powerful landowner in the upper Severn valley, and Walter, who took service as hereditary steward of King David of Scotland and was enfeoffed by him in a great estate. In the face of southern opposition, the best that Stephen could do (May, 1139) was to buy David off with the cession of Northumberland and Car-lisle and they remained in Scottish hands for eighteen years.

Shortly after this, Stephen—instigated it is said by the baronial family of Beaumont—turned upon his most valuable supporters, Bishop Roger of Salisbury and his family, accused them of treason, treated them with the utmost ignominy and even violence, seized their castles, and confiscated their enormous stocks of money and valuables. The old bishop never recovered from the indignity of his imprisonment and died before the year was out. He was far from being a model churchman by the standards of his time—apart from his colossal wealth, he was married and had secured a bishopric for his son ; but the Church could not easily forgive Stephen for this outrage. Even the king's brother broke with him and led the episcopate over to Maud's side. The profit Stephen made from looting the bishop's castles was soon spent, and it was far outweighed by the permanent loss of the men who could best operate the Ex-chequer. This institution did evidently continue to function, but its working was badly dislocated.

The fall of Bishop Roger marks a definite climacteric in Stephen's reign. Almost from the first, he had been driven to admit that his possession of the crown depended on the goodwill of the different sections of the nation to whom in his second charter of liberties (April, 1136) he had made concessions. To the Church he had promised abolition of simony (the sale and purchase of ecclesiastical offices), the restitution of all its property as it had been held in 1087, and the confirmation of all subsequent accretions. Free election of bishops and abbots was not explicitly permitted,[1] but the clergy were to have custody of sees and abbeys while they were vacant, a concession which, if it had been observed, would have been extremely valuable. Afforestation—that is, the creation of hunting preserves —carried out by Henry I was to be cancelled ; but the king reserved the still substantial forests of the two Williams. Otherwise his charter was general in its terms and not so far-reaching as that which Henry I had published in 1100. If Henry had been able to ignore his promises, there seemed no reason why Stephen should not follow suit. But his contemporaries knew him for a different man from his uncle. He was, as the Anglo-Saxon chronicle said, " mild and soft and good, and did no justice ", and his barons took advantage accordingly. The more he tried to win their loyalty by concessions of one kind or another the less he could trust any of them. For example, in 1135 only six English magnates and the King of Scots held the rank of earl in England. In the next few years Stephen gave this honour to no fewer than nine of his adherents. Yet hardly one was loyal to him, except Earl Simon de Senlis of Northampton, and he only because the Angevin party thought his earldom belonged to the King of Scots. It may be true that this wholesale cheapening cost the Crown little in material terms, but it was recognised at the time as a sign of weakness. The most unscrupulous of the barons, Geoffrey de Mandeville, alternately bargained with Stephen and Maud (who also gave earldoms away freely) for concession after concession, until his double-dyed treachery to both parties had won him the earldom, county justiciarship and hereditary shrievalty of Essex, the hereditary keepership of the Tower of London, the offices of hereditary justiciar and sheriff of London and Hertfordshire, and a royal stewardship. If he was an extreme case, others, e.g. Aubrey de Vere, the Chamberlain, behaved with like opportunism. Ironically enough, the only man Stephen could really trust was his chief mercenary captain, William of Ypres.

[1] Henry, Archdeacon of Huntingdon and an historian of this period, asserts that Stephen did promise free elections and the abolition of Danegeld ; but the king's charter does not contain these promises. (See Stubbs, *Select Charters* (9th edn.), 143-4.)

The nadir of Stephen's power came in 1141. Early in February, while he was besieging Lincoln castle, held by the men of the rebellious Earl of Chester, he allowed himself to be captured by a relief party under the earl himself and Robert of Gloucester, and was carried off a prisoner to Bristol. Two months later, Bishop Henry of Winchester proclaimed Maud queen in his cathedral. In June, she and her supporters, including King David, moved to London for her coronation. It now became clear that Stephen was not the only one who knew how to throw away his advantages. Maud refused to listen to her councillors, and instead of making a judicious concession to the citizens of London demanded from them an immediate levy of taxation. The infuriated Londoners took to arms and drove the Empress, still uncrowned, from her lodgings at Westminster. By now Bishop Henry had changed sides again, and wishing to punish him for this *volte face*, Maud and her entourage decided to lay siege to his castle of Wolvesey, south of Winchester. The bishop escaped, and the Empress's small force found itself in turn beset by a larger army sent by Stephen's queen and William of Ypres. A food shortage forced the Angevins into retreat, and in the panic flight which this became Earl Robert of Gloucester was captured, while King David and his niece only escaped with difficulty. Maud found refuge in the west country, and her cause never recovered from this débâcle. Without her brother she was powerless. To his lasting honour he refused the most tempting offers to change sides, and before the close of the year he and the king were exchanged.

Matters now stood as they had in 1140, but both parties were in fact exhausted. Stephen was again recognised as king throughout the midlands and east, but although his military energy was as conspicuous as ever, he had spent all his treasure, and could not raise the forces required to drive Maud and Earl Robert out of Gloucester and Bristol. His greatest success was the reduction of the important castles of Oxford (1142) and Faringdon (1145), thus isolating Wallingford and confining the main Angevin forces west of the Thames valley. More than this he could not do, and even in the parts of which he was nominally ruler he could not prevent the worst kinds of lawlessness. Geoffrey de Mandeville, when threatened with hanging or the loss of his lands and offices, merely established himself in the fenland abbey of Ramsey, which he coolly converted into a fortified centre for the systematic and brutal pillage of the surrounding countryside. Fortunately he was killed in 1144; but there were others who followed his example on a smaller scale. The Earl of Yorkshire made himself a castle out of Bridlington priory, the Earl of Richmond plundered the minster church of Ripon. Many lords of castles ruled their districts like petty kings. In default of strong central government, the great men of the realm were forced to make elaborate agreements among themselves, so that in pursuing their own policies they would not inflict unnecessary injury on one another's castles, men and resources. Such was the well-known treaty between the earls of Chester and Leicester (1148-53), which has been called " an approach towards the restoration of order by the only means effective in a land where the royal power had fallen into temporary abeyance ".[1] An agreement of the same kind was made between the earls of Gloucester and Hereford. Only north of the Tees where the land had fallen wholly under the rule of King David was an effective peace maintained. It was at least some relief to the war-stricken country that in 1147 two earls and a good many barons and knights responded to the call of the Second Crusade.

In this year too the mainstay of the Angevin cause, Robert of Gloucester, died, and in 1148 Maud left the country to rejoin her husband, who since 1144 had held the duchy of Normandy, and was ruling it in the name of their son Henry, now a youth of fifteen and a force to be reckoned with. The young prince had indeed tried to win his spurs against Stephen in 1147. His expedition was a ludicrous failure which ended in Stephen magnanimously paying the expenses of his return to Normandy. But England had not seen the last of him. He came again in 1149, and at the Scottish court at Carlisle in the summer tried to revive an Angevin party to consist of himself, the King of Scots, and the powerful but fickle Earl of Chester. On this occasion, King David made the young prince a knight, obtaining in return an oath that should the English crown pass to Henry, the Scots would be left in possession of the northern counties. The defection of the Earl of Chester brought to nothing the scheme of 1149, and Henry of Anjou had to wait until 1153 before he could make another attempt. By then, however, his prospects had become immeasurably brighter.

[1] Stenton, *English Feudalism*, 254. A full translation of the treaty is given, *ibid.* 249-52.

In the first place, his father's death in September, 1151, made him Count of Anjou as well as Duke of Normandy. Secondly, in March, 1152, a brilliant marriage turned him into one of the greatest secular rulers in western Europe. His wife, some years older than himself, was Eleanor, in her own right Duchess of Aquitaine, nominally a fief of the French Crown but in practice an extremely independent principality covering most of south-western France. The match, moreover, reversed the balance of power south of the Channel, for Eleanor had previously been married to the French king, Louis VII. It was therefore no longer as a stripling, a penniless adventurer, that Henry of Anjou crossed to England in January, 1153. His force, it is true, was small, but it made up for the lack of numbers by efficiency and purposefulness. Malmesbury castle in Wiltshire was captured at once, and soon afterwards Henry was able to relieve the town and garrison of Wallingford, which with wonderful loyalty had held fast to the Angevin cause throughout the civil war.

As the young duke's star waxed, so that of the old king waned rapidly. His gallant and determined queen had died in 1152. He had for the second time forfeited the support of at least a section— the important reforming section—of the Church through his prolonged endeavours to give the archbishopric of York to his nephew. The leaders of the Cistercian order, Bernard of Clairvaux abroad as well as the influential Yorkshire abbots at home, played a notable part in rousing ecclesiastical opinion against Stephen and his candidate, and in favour of the Abbot of Fountains, Henry Murdac. At the crucial time the Pope himself was an old disciple of Bernard. By his authority, Murdac was consecrated archbishop, but Stephen showed remarkable firmness in denying him possession of the see, and refusing admittance into England to the Pope's own legate. The Archbishop of Canterbury from 1139 to 1162, a monk of Bec named Theobald, also belonged to the reforming party. He was patron of a small but highly influential group of younger churchmen, including the theologian, philosopher and historian, John of Salisbury, who had been a clerk at the papal *Curia*, Roger of Pont l'Evêque, afterwards Archbishop of York, his rival Thomas Becket, and Master Vacarius, an eminent Lombard teacher of the Roman civil law, whose lectures King Stephen for a time suppressed as subversive of Anglo-Norman feudal custom. Acting on papal instructions, Archbishop Theobald refused Stephen's request to crown his elder son Eustace as his successor (1152); and when Eustace died, in August, 1153, the king himself began to lose interest in his own cause.

At last, in November, 1153, a treaty was agreed on at Winchester which brought the civil war to an end. Stephen was to remain king until his death, but with Henry's co-operation in government. His younger son's vast estates were to be confirmed to him. All the barons and major feudatories of England, whichever side they supported, were to do homage to both Stephen and Henry. Much of the year 1154 Henry in fact spent on the continent, and Stephen was left for the first time in peaceable possession of his kingdom. He died on October 25th. A man of much more attractive personality than any of his Norman predecessors and most of his Angevin successors, a generous and straightforward pattern of knightly character, Stephen of Blois was totally lacking in either the gifts of leadership or the ruthlessness which were essential to a king of twelfth-century England. Although the contemporary chronicles probably overstate the extent of the misery engendered by the civil war, although there seems to have been no ruinous cessation of economic activity, although more monasteries were founded between 1135 and 1154 than in any other two decades of English history, nevertheless the nation had been gravely weakened by lack of good government. Much would be pardoned in his successor if only he would restore the justice and firmness of which Stephen had proved himself incapable.

CHAPTER VIII

THE EMERGENCE OF SCOTLAND, 1058-1124

When we speak of the emergence of Scotland in the eleventh century, we should understand this expression in two different senses. First, for the historian, this is the period in which Scotland emerges into the light of record. Although the main outlines of Scottish history may be constructed for five centuries before this time, the materials are lacking for anything like a continuous political narrative until the important reign of Malcolm III " Canmore " [1] (1058-93), while evidence for the structure of Scottish society does not become adequate until the twelfth century. Secondly, it was in this period that the kingdom of Scotland began to emerge decisively into the main stream of western European history. During the century and a half (*c.* 900-1050) which followed the most devastating phase of Scandinavian invasion, Scotland had shared with Ireland, with whose general culture she had much in common, a period of isolation from the formative currents of European history. As in England, there had been no growth of the continental type of military feudalism, but in Scotland the monarchy did not possess either the prestige or the widely based power and unifying influence of its English counterpart. There is no reason to think that the strength of Christian belief had seriously declined in eleventh-century Scotland, and at least one king of the time, Macbeth, went on pilgrimage to Rome, where, with the true provincial's anxiety not to appear mean or penurious, he is said to have " scattered his money like seed to the poor ". Nevertheless, the Scottish Church was hardly an organised institution, and its clergy were undoubtedly more secularised than those of England. On the eve of David I's reign (1124), by contrast with this relative obscurity and isolation, the Scottish king was in correspondence with the Papacy, his monarchy was modelled to some extent on the Anglo-Norman pattern, and a place had been found in his kingdom for the first elements of Norman feudalism and for convents of religious belonging to the orders

---

[1] This by-name means " big head ".

familiar in the west. As a token of the country's sense of unity with western Christendom, a Scottish contingent had gone forth to the crusade of 1095, arousing in their march the curiosity of a French historian, amused at their bare legs, rough cloaks, and purses slung over their shoulders.[1]

Nearly everywhere mountainous, and covered in many parts by thick tracts of natural pine forest, the country now known as Scotland supported at the close of the eleventh century perhaps a third of a million people. Theirs was not a rich land. A heavy rainfall drained quickly enough from the steep hillsides in countless streams and rivers, but was slow to reach the sea. Instead, the water saturated the often peaty soil of the lower lying districts, and either turned to unworkable morass the only ground level enough for the plough, or filled the declivities with lochs, of which there were many more in the period covered by this book than exist today. Indeed, if one takes the modern map of Scotland and considers the enormous number of names on it which contain an element denoting marsh or bog, the wonder is that any room was found at all for permanent habitation. Doubtless the adaptation of the Scots to their damp and inhospitable environment was responsible for their already well-established reputation for hardiness. Broad firths cut deep into the land, and with the hill ranges separated it into well-marked regions, though as obstacles to communication these features may easily be exaggerated.

The geographical divisions of the country were in some degree reflected at the start of our period by cultural and political divisions more sharply pronounced than those we have noted in England. North of a line drawn roughly from Grangemouth to Glasgow, the unity of the Gaelic language and the effective fusion of the once opponent Pictish and Scottish peoples were expressed in a single, homogeneous kingdom, the kingdom of *Scotia*,[2] or Scotland proper. There were sub-regions in Scotia, but they were made from within and were not the result of holding together parts which were really

[1] A. A. M. Duncan, *Scot. Hist. Rev.* xxix (1950), 211-12.
[2] Its natives knew it as *Alba*, a name which seems once to have applied to the whole of Britain.

MAP IV. THE DIVISIONS OF SCOTLAND, 1058-1153 (*see opposite page*). The stippling indicates land over 1,200 feet.

MAP IV

125

centrifugal. These sub-regions went back far into Scoto-Pictish history ; in our period they were ruled by mormaers [1] who, like the English earls, were in origin royal officers, but had become powerful territorial nobles. Traditionally, but hardly in fact, the mormaers and their regions were seven in number. The seat of the Scottish kingdom was located at Scone in the centre of the sub-region of Gowrie, near the lowest point at which the River Tay could be bridged or forded. Adjacent to Gowrie lay Fife, and it was chiefly from these two districts that the house of Malcolm Canmore derived its power. North of the "mounth",[2] the great mountain lump stretching east and west across Scotland, was the important sub-region of Moray, with whose rulers King Malcolm fought a bitter dynastic struggle. Scottish history, however, cannot be explained in terms of Scotia only. There were at least three other elements, Scandinavian, British, and English, which were integral to her development, and something must be said also of Galloway, a separatist south-western enclave of the Gaelic tongue.

We have seen that pre-Conquest England was really an Anglo-Scandinavian state, in which the results of Danish colonisation remained in evidence well into the Middle Ages. For Scotland, the period of aggressive Scandinavian pressure lasted four and a half centuries, from *c.* 800 to 1266. Here the invaders were Norwegians rather than Danes. In 1050 they were strongly entrenched in all the islands off Scotland's northern and western coasts, and controlled the mainland south as far as Dingwall,[3] as well as much of the western seaboard. Although the Vikings had never been able to conquer the richer lowlands between the Moray Firth and Yorkshire, Scandinavian influences were strong in northern Northumbria, perhaps by penetration from the Danish and Norse kingdoms of York (867-954), while to an extent greater than is usually realised some Scandinavian settlement or infiltration had taken place in Scotland north of Forth. So much is shown by the use in the twelfth century of Scandinavian personal names among the native Scottish aristocracy. Scottish rulers had been forced to come to terms with their Norse neighbours, and in a sense Scotland belonged to the Scandinavian world. The families of Orkney Vikings intermarried with those of

[1] Literally, " sea officer".
[2] From a Pictish word akin to Welsh *mynydd*, " mountain ".
[3] Scandinavian " thing vollr ", " place of assembly ".

the mormaers of Scotland. An early eleventh-century Scottish king had given a daughter in marriage to one Earl of Orkney, and Malcolm Canmore himself married the daughter of another as his first wife.

The British element in Scotland was the remnant of the old kingdom of Cumbria or Strathclyde, reaching from Dumbarton to the English Lake District. The natives of this region were not wholly British : there had been Gaelic and Northumbrian penetration, and what is now Cumberland was in fact a thoroughgoing mixture of Briton, Northumbrian, Scandinavian, and Gael. Nevertheless, the region had had a king of British race as recently as 1018, and its own episcopal see of Glasgow only fell into abeyance in Malcolm Canmore's own time. Cumbria, in fact, though under Scottish suzerainty, was ruled as a distinct political entity, and the arrangement by which an earlier king, Malcolm II, had made it an appanage for his successor, Duncan I, was repeated on several occasions before 1124. The overlordship of Cumbria gave the Scottish Crown a strong claim to modern Cumberland and Westmorland, " as far as the Rere Cross on Stainmore ",[1] the traditional boundary mark of the Cumbrian kingdom.

West of Cumbria the smooth hills of Clydesdale give place to a genuinely highland zone of wild mountains and inaccessible lochs. In the valleys of this rough peninsula of Galloway, which were more easily reached from Ireland and the Hebrides than from the Scottish mainland, dwelt the " foreign Gael ",[2] cut off from their kinsmen in the north. At the start of our period, the history of Galloway is obscurity itself ; but when we do begin to have information we see that Galloway emerges as a strongly separatist region, posing a challenge to the Scottish monarchy in its efforts to unify the mixture of communities nominally under its rule.

East of Cumbria, beyond the watershed which divides Clyde from Tweed, and separated from Scotia by the Forth and its tributary the Avon, lay the northern part of the old Anglian kingdom of Northumbria, most of which was known by the regional name of Lothian. Lothian provided the English element in the composition of Scotland, and though it has been left to the last in our survey, it was in fact more important than either the Scandinavian or the British for the future development of the medieval kingdom.

[1] See Map IV.
[2] In Gaelic, " gall ghaidhil ", whence the name " Galloway ".

Lothian had been settled by English folk as early as the seventh century. Three hundred years later it had proved beyond the power of the West Saxon monarchy to hold the district directly, and *c.* 975 it had been surrendered, probably conditionally, to the King of Scots. Its definite annexation to the northern kingdom came *c.* 1016 with the great battle won at Carham by King Malcolm II of Scotland and King Owen of Strathclyde against an earl of Northumbria. It is clear from the evidence of personal and place names that, preponderantly Anglian as it was, Lothian had received by *c.* 1100 an appreciable Gaelic settlement, especially strong in the west of the area and along the southern coast of the Firth of Forth. The firth was no impassable barrier. Northumbrians made pilgrimages to St. Andrews, and the cult of St. Cuthbert, the especial patron of Northumbria, was observed in Fife. In view of Scandinavian influences in Scotia and Gaelic penetration south of the Forth, it would be wrong to regard Lothian, as it often is regarded, as a completely Germanic intrusion into purely Celtic territory. Nevertheless, the River Tweed in the eleventh and twelfth centuries divided into two a district essentially homogeneous. The border was long felt to be artificial, and a protracted struggle was fought out between the English and Scottish rulers for control of the country between the English Tyne and the Tweed.

Malcolm Canmore, whose reign of thirty-five years (exceptionally long for a Scottish sovereign before the twelfth century) was to see the beginnings of a real unity brought to these diverse and hostile regions, was in many ways well-fitted for the task. His grandfather had been lord of Dunkeld in the heart of Scotia ; his father had ruled Cumbria under Malcolm II. Malcolm Canmore himself had spent his youth in exile at the court of Edward the Confessor, learning English and winning the friendship of Siward, the warrior Earl of Northumberland (d. 1055). During Malcolm's exile the rival royal family of Moray, in the person of Macbeth, held the Scottish throne, and as is well known from Act IV of Shakespeare's play of *Macbeth*, it was Earl Siward's help that enabled Malcolm to defeat his rival (1054), though fact as opposed to drama places the final overthrow and slaying of Macbeth three years later, in north-east Scotland, while Malcolm could not take the throne until Macbeth's step-son and successor was killed in the same region in 1058.

The political centre of gravity shifted in Malcolm III's reign to southern Scotia and Lothian. On five separate occasions Malcolm invaded English Northumbria, and it is hard to judge whether his motive was chiefly to annex the land, to plunder it, to distract the Scots from internal strife, or to forestall any serious invasion of Scotland from the south. Whatever his reasons, his aggressive policy cannot be called an unqualified success. It is true that, save for one occasion, the Moray men seem to have kept quiet in his time, and doubtless the Scots carried off much booty from England. But against this must be set the undying hostility of the very region which King Malcolm wanted either to annex or at least to keep friendly. Earl Siward had been his patron, Earl Tostig was his " sworn brother " ; yet he laid waste their land with fire and sword. The foolishness of his policy becomes clearer after the Norman Conquest. As we have seen, the Northumbrians had no love for the Normans, and had the Scots King given them security and military aid the history of Britain might have taken a radically different turn. As it was, his support for the Atheling was tempered by the devastation of English land, and a notable opportunity was lost.

The Atheling's reception by Malcolm (1067) did, however, have one result of paramount importance for Scottish history. As the price, no doubt, of Malcolm's support, Prince Edgar gave him in marriage (*c.* 1070) his sister Margaret. Just as Malcolm's first marriage to the Norwegian Ingibjorg had denoted a Scandinavian alliance (probably directed against Moray), so his marriage to Margaret stood for an alliance with the legitimist royal house of England, and, had Scots strategy comprised ought save repeated pillage, might have been a means of rallying the men of English as well as Scottish Northumbria against the Norman usurpers. During the 1070s a number of Englishmen did in fact take refuge in Scotland. Their number was not large, but they were all men of high rank and considerable wealth. As we have seen, by going into Lothian they were merely exchanging one part of Northumbria for another, while even if they penetrated north of Forth they would not have found themselves in completely alien territory. The greatest man among the refugees was Cospatric, the deposed Earl of Northumbria.[1] He was given a large estate in eastern Lothian which formed the nucleus of the later earldom of Lothian, Dunbar, or March. What became of the others is not known, but some at least probably settled in

[1] See above, p. 42.

Scotland for good. Certainly English influences had begun to weigh equally with Celtic by 1093, and it is difficult to believe that this was due to Queen Margaret alone.

For all that, Margaret was clearly one of the outstanding personalities of her time. Austere in her private life, though not without a vanity which in a lesser person might have been mere ostentation, devoutly religious, forceful in her relations with those about her, charitable as a saint, the impression she left upon contemporaries was lasting and profound. She was very conscious of belonging to the ancient West Saxon dynasty, but she had been born and brought up in Hungary, on the other edge of Christian Europe, among a people who had only been converted to Christianity in her father's lifetime, and who were still experiencing relapses into heathenism. We may perhaps ascribe the sense of mission which Margaret undoubtedly possessed to this double fact, that she was a returned exile and had personally witnessed the triumphs and setbacks of the evangelising policy of St. Stephen. Her influence in her adopted country was pervasive. She brought a new refinement to the royal household, and furnished the king's palace (probably at Dunfermline) with silk hangings and objects of gold and silver. Merchants were invited to come from foreign parts with wares hitherto unknown in Scotland, and " the people rejoiced in the prosperity of commerce ". She encouraged the St. Andrews pilgrim traffic by providing lodgings at each end of what is still called, after her, the " Queensferry ", as well as boats to carry pilgrims free of charge.

But it is especially for her influence upon the Scottish Church that St. Margaret is remembered. Her career makes uonsense of any supposition that in her time women were debarred by custom from theology or ecclesiastical politics. She discussed problems of scripture with the learned men of the country ; she corresponded with Archbishop Lanfranc of Canterbury and Master Theobald of Étampes, a teacher of Caen. She convened councils of the Church to reform matters of doctrine and observance. At one of them the Scots clergy were compelled to admit defeat when the queen had debated with them for three days, and they duly brought their practices into conformity with her wishes. Not that she found the Church in Scotland entirely without merit : she revered certain of the native clergy who practised an ascetic life either in solitude or grouped in communities of anchorites which represented the Egyptian or " desert hermit " type of monachism rather than the Benedictine. But under her influence there began a gradual transformation of the Scottish Church which was to be carried on, as we shall see, by her sons, especially David I. From a close resemblance to the Church in Ireland, a Church lacking in organisation, dominated by an hereditary clerical caste, and exposed to strong lay influence, the Church of the Scots was brought into line with that of western Europe generally, in accordance with the reforming ideas which we have already seen at work in England. At Dunfermline, as a symbol of the new order, Queen Margaret founded the first Benedictine monastery in Scotland, for which Lanfranc, who naturally approved her labours on behalf of religion, sent her monks from his own cathedral priory at Canterbury.

Last but not least of the benefits conferred by Queen Margaret on her husband and his kingdom, she bore Malcolm six sons who all survived to adult life. The importance of this was considerable. According to ancient custom, the Scottish throne passed not to the direct heir of the dead king but to some near relative of the collateral line, the " tanist ", usually chosen before his predecessor's death. The elective principle contained in this system of tanistry, and still more the impossibility of founding a single strong royal dynasty, permanently weakened the Scottish monarchy. Malcolm III appreciated this and was determined to break the custom. He himself had won the throne from the collateral family of Moray, but he wished his own eldest son to succeed him on it. By his first wife he already had one son, Duncan, but obviously in the conditions of the eleventh century the success of a " Canmore dynasty " depended on a plentiful supply of direct heirs. A secondary but not uninteresting point is that not one of Malcolm's and Margaret's sons were given Scottish names : the four eldest, undoubtedly at their mother's instance and perhaps with some notion of making a political appeal to the English, were named in order after their four immediate lineal ancestors on the English side ; the other two being called Alexander and David.

Malcolm III fell in 1093 on his fifth invasion of England. His second son Edward was slain with him, and Queen Margaret died of grief a few days later. At once the succession was disputed. An anti-foreign reaction seized the Scots, as it had seized the English in the 1050s. King Malcolm's English followers were expelled, and his brother, Donald Bán ("the fair"), as a collateral claimant after the old fashion, was made king instead of Duncan, who since 1072 had remained half hostage, half protégé, at the courts of the Conqueror and Rufus. With Anglo-Norman help Duncan drove out his uncle and ruled for a space as King Duncan II, but in 1094 he was killed by the mormaer of Mearns, and Donald Bán was restored. For three years Donald ruled a kingdom from which Anglo-Norman influences were seemingly eliminated, but in 1097 William Rufus provided Edgar the Atheling with a large army and sent him off to conquer Scotland. The Atheling's expedition was successful and his nephew Edgar, the fourth [1] of Malcolm's and Margaret's sons, was set on the Scottish throne.

The silence of the chronicles about the ten years of Edgar's reign (1097-1107) and the fact that he died peacefully at Edinburgh show that his government was effective. The single event of importance was a treaty with the King of Norway, Magnus Bareleg, in 1098. King Magnus with a great fleet had completely subdued the scattered Norse settlements of Shetland, Orkney and the "Sudreyiar" [2] ("southern isles"), as the Norse called the Hebrides and Man. His agreement with Edgar provided that the Scots should recognise Norwegian rule over all the northern and western isles and the long peninsula of Kintyre. The treaty merely acknowledged an established fact, but the rulers of Scotland did not remain satisfied indefinitely with a situation which exposed them to constant attack from Hebridean pirates and deprived them of much of Argyll, the cradle of their race, including Iona itself, the shrine of St. Columba and the immemorial burying ground of their ancestors. If Edgar was in general a competent king, the legacy of Malcolm Canmore's misguided policy nevertheless meant for him and his successors too great a dependence on the kings of England. If they could win and hold their throne only with help from the south, it was clear that the Scottish monarchy would soon be placed in much closer subjection to the English than was signified by Abernethy. Even Alexander I, who succeeded the childless Edgar and ruled strongly for seventeen years (1107-24), was appreciably dependent on his brother-in-law Henry I. He had to take for his bride Sibylla, one

---

[1] Edward was dead and Edmund and Ethelred had entered religion.
[2] Hence "Sodor" in the name of the episcopal see of Sodor and Man.

of Henry's illegitimate daughters, and his participation in Henry's Welsh campaign of 1114 probably (though not necessarily) bespeaks a position as the King of England's vassal.

The brief reign of Duncan II, who had been knighted by William Rufus in 1087, and the much longer reign of Alexander I, who had also spent many years at the English court, heralded a new era for the Scottish kingdom. Malcolm III had been a strong king, but there is no evidence that he saw much of value for Scotland in the continental type of heavy cavalry warfare or in the system of castles and knights' fiefs with which this warfare was associated. At his death Scotland remained a loose confederacy of semi-independent regions, and even within Scotia a mormaer might rule more like a sub-king than a royal official. It is probable that there already existed in Malcolm's time those lesser officers who appear in the next century as thanes, with charge of certain royal estates. The origin of the thane is one of the unsolved problems of Scottish history. In view of their English name and nature, thanes are unlikely to have been introduced into Scotland under Norman influence, i.e. after 1093. The probability seems to be that the thane, long familiar of course in Northumbria, was regarded by the Scottish kings as a useful official to have in Scotia, and that the adoption was made easy by the presence north of the Forth of a Celtic officer, the *toisech* (literally " first " or " chief "), not dissimilar to the thane in function. However this may be, at the close of the eleventh century Scotland was not feudalised, and in particular the king's ability to mobilise the full military resources of his kingdom depended on the goodwill of the mormaers, whose duty and privilege it was to raise the host. A reliable chronicler tells us significantly that the terms on which the Scots would accept Duncan II as king in 1094 were that he should introduce no Normans or English nor allow them to perform knight service for him. Under Alexander I the Scots could no longer dictate such terms, and he probably retained a small force of cavalry of the new type. We are told that he himself possessed up-to-date Turkish armour and a beautiful Arab steed, and it may have been with a band of knights that he chased some rebel islesmen from Gowrie to Ross. But it was not until his brother's time that the thoroughgoing feudalism of post-Conquest England was imported into the Scottish kingdom.

CHAPTER IX

DAVID I, 1124-53

ALEXANDER I left no children, and in 1124 the only surviving legitimate descendant of Malcolm Canmore was his youngest son, David, then a man of about forty. Ailred of Rievaulx, who afterwards knew David well, says that his distaste for power was so great that the bishops could barely persuade him to go through the ancient ceremony of enthronement. Since David had already been ten years Earl of Huntingdon and lord of Cumbria, his reluctance may have been due rather to a feeling that the ceremony at Scone was alien and (compared with the English coronation) unchristian. If so, it was a symbolic beginning to his reign. For the Scotland of his time was ready to enter fully into the main stream of European development, and in so doing to sacrifice something of her own heritage of custom and culture. The tide of new ideas and institutions had turned to the flood and could not be stemmed at every point or for a much longer time. The substitution for Celtic tribal custom of the feudal custom of Neustria, including especially the harsh but politically valuable rule of primogeniture; the first glimpses of the tremendous edifice of Roman law which the schools of northern Italy were unfolding; an exalted notion of kingship and advances towards centralised royal administration; the use of towns and coined money, with a resultant enlargement of trade; the integration of a local Church within a European ecclesiastical framework, and the gradual transformation of Rome from a pilgrims' shrine into the seat of government for the whole Church of the west —these were some of the experiences and experiments in which twelfth-century Scotland was ready to share. It was her great good fortune to find in David I a man exceptionally sensitive and receptive to these changes in the contemporary world and a king who could hold the balance between the foreign institutions which he introduced and the deep-rooted traditions and customs of his native country.

Between 1093 and 1107 most of David's time was spent at the courts of Rufus and Henry I. Henry took a liking to him, gave him the usual education of a young Anglo-Norman of high birth, and made him a knight. Some time after 1107, his brother, King Alexander, allowed him as an appanage the rich provinces of south Lothian and Cumbria. Somewhat later, in 1114, Henry I gave him in marriage a lady who was perhaps the richest heiress in England, Maud, only daughter of Earl Waltheof by his wife Judith, who was the Conqueror's niece and inheritor of Waltheof's vast estates in the eastern midlands. Maud was the widow of a Norman, Simon de Senlis, by whom she had three sons ; nevertheless, King Henry granted to David with his bride the rank and title of earl and the estates of her earldom of Northampton-Huntingdon.[1] The favour in which he was regarded by King Henry may be further judged from the fact that his earldom was to be specially exempted from Danegeld, bridge and castle work, murder fines, scutage, and a great many other burdens.

During the next ten years David began to show in his earl-dom and his Scottish lands something of the activity which was to make his reign of outstanding importance. He evidently acted as a justice for Henry I, and he became the patron of religious houses in several parts of England. His marriage brought him a household and retinue composed of prominent feudal tenants of his wife's " honour " of Huntingdon, among whom we should note especially the families of Moreville, Soules, Corbet, Lindsay, Somerville, and Brus (a family powerful in their own right as lords of Cleveland). In Scotland the chief centre of David's power seems to have been the lower valleys of Tweed and Teviot. It was here that he built the castles of Roxburgh and Berwick, both of immense importance to the Scots throughout our period. Round each of them grew up a thriving burgh, thanks probably to David's importation of mer-chants and craftsmen from England and Flanders. He decided to revive the defunct episcopal see of Glasgow, appointing, after initial setbacks, his own chaplain John as bishop, ensuring him an en-dowment of land around Glasgow and in Teviotdale, and assigning money from Northamptonshire for the rebuilding of his cathedral. From Tiron, north of Chartres, where a famous reformed Bene-dictine abbey had been founded in the woods of Perche, David

---

[1] There is evidence that the earldom included authority over the shires of Bedford and Cambridge as well, and its lands were spread over eleven counties.

(1113) brought monks to Selkirk, on the edge of the Forest of Selkirk or Ettrick, the great forest of southern Scotland. This spot may have proved too wild even for the Tironians, for in 1128 they migrated to Kelso beside Roxburgh, where their abbey soon became the richest, as it remained one of the most famous, in the whole Scottish kingdom. Earl David was already a mature and experienced ruler when he succeeded to the throne of Scotland in 1124. His reign had profound consequences for both Church and State. It will be easier to understand its achievement if we arrange our account chiefly under these two headings.

The Church

Until the twelfth century, the character of the Church in Scotland varied from one region to the next. Lothian and Teviotdale, ecclesiastically as well as socially, resembled the rest of Northumbria. Lothian had been placed by the Scottish kings under the authority of the Bishop of Scotland who had his see at St. Andrews. Teviotdale came under the see of Durham until David transferred it to Glasgow, *c.* 1114. In both areas there seem to have been churches of parochial type, served by priests who were clearly men of standing locally and who probably inherited their benefices and expected to pass them on to their sons. There was plenty of room for lords to found new parish churches, but on the whole, as in England, a close correspondence persisted between the parish church and the village settlement. Farther west, in Cumbria and Galloway, Church organisation reflected a Celtic society of scattered hamlets, not a Germanic one of compact villages. Instead of a few parish churches there were numerous chapels and shrines often dedicated to Celtic saints of the old British and Irish church. We do not know how these upland chapels were served, but there may well have been a number of more imposing ecclesiastical foundations of the type of Kirkcudbright ("St. Cuthbert's kirk"), which is known to have been served by a body of clergy and was perhaps not altogether dissimilar to an English "old minster". When, during the twelfth century, new landowners were established in this region, they tended to regard themselves as the undoubted proprietors of the churches on their estates. At some churches, e.g. Dumfries, there were priests who apparently had something like proprietary rights ; yet it was possible for the lord of Renfrew to endow the monastery he had founded at Paisley with " all the churches in Strathgryfe " (Renfrewshire), without mentioning the consent of the clergy. We hear also in this region of hermits, dwelling in what were probably recognised hermitages. It is unlikely that the Cumbrian and Gallovidian clergy were subject to any sort of supervision, and until *c.* 1110-20 only a memory remained of the bishoprics of Glasgow and Whithorn. Moreover, this lack of close episcopal control throughout southern Scotland was not offset by a flourishing monasticism : there was not a single monastery south of the Clyde-Forth line before 1113.

In Scotia the Church was similarly unorganised. It is probable that the majority of the clergy, as in Ireland, belonged to hereditary clerical castes attached to the ruling families or tribes of the various sub-regions. The merging of ecclesiastical with secular institutions was certainly more thorough than in pre-Conquest England. It affected monastic life, for (as an early chronicler puts it) " many abbeys were created there in ancient times which many laymen still hold by hereditary right ". No doubt this was due to the strength of the hereditary—or, to be precise, the family—principle in Celtic society. A monastery was founded and endowed with land. Some of its monks would be celibate, but not all ; and the families of the married ones would in time gain control of the church's property. Eventually most of the monastic lands and the title of abbot would pass to complete laymen who made no pretence of performing spiritual offices, though force of tradition would compel the lay abbot to leave room in his " abbey " for a community of genuine clergy. There were a number of ancient, well-endowed, and half-secularised religious centres of this kind in Scotia *c.* 1100, including Dunkeld, Brechin, and Abernethy. An abbey would normally have some lands subject to it, known as the " appin " from a Gaelic term denoting the jurisdiction of an abbot.[1] Where the abbey had passed into lay hands, this territory would of course form a lay lordship. Even at St Andrews church incomes were going to laymen. It is true that in the ninth and tenth centuries a reform movement had brought to certain Scottish churches groups of " culdees ", monks of the desert-hermit type who lived according to a fixed rule. It

[1] The district of Appin in modern Argyllshire is the best known of these areas. It was subject to the Abbot of Lismore.

was the culdees, e.g. those at Loch Leven, who found favour with Queen Margaret. But by the twelfth century the culdees also had undergone a decline in the strictness of their life.

Outside the monastic churches which dominated the ecclesiastical landscape of Scotia, there were obviously many lesser churches, chapels, shrines and cemeteries of an undefined character. There were "mother churches" of large districts, and these along with smaller chapels may have served the laity as the parish churches did in England. But there was no systematic division of the country into distinct parishes. Clergy were supported by allotments of land, as also were a few solitary hermits, for whom three acres seems to have been the standard allowance. Neither monastic nor other churches were aloof from secular business. Some had custody of sacred relics which may have been used in the courts for oaths and judgments, and we learn that *c.* 1180 the Abbot of Glendochart—doubtless because he was custodian of a very famous relic, the Staff of St. Fillan [1]—had the duty of fetching from south Argyll those vouched to warranty [2] by men accused of stealing cattle.

The status of the pre-twelfth-century bishops in Scotia is nearly as obscure as the origins of the Scottish thane. Provision was undoubtedly made for bishops in the Celtic church, for there as elsewhere clergy in episcopal orders were needed to perform the rites of ordination to the priesthood, confirmation of the laity, and consecration of sites to religious use. But the Scottish Church does not seem to have been under episcopal governance and there was no division of the country, as in England, into well-defined territorial dioceses. There was a bishop—significantly known simply as the " Bishop of Scotia " [3] or " of the Scots "—who had his see at St Andrews and held a position not unlike that of a bishop of the Old English Church. But there is no evidence that there existed besides St. Andrews any fixed number of bishops' sees. On the contrary, we hear of at least one wandering Scottish bishop, John (*c.* 1065), who was made a suffragan of the Archbishop of Bremen and savagely done to death by heathen Slavs.

In short, the Scottish Church was diverse, unorganised and in some important respects markedly different from the Church of most

---

[1] Now in the National Museum of Antiquities in Edinburgh.

[2] I.e. called to give proof that the cattle or goods in question had been lawfully bought.   [3] In Gaelic, *escob Alban.*

of western Europe. It was the aim of Alexander I and David I to give it uniformity and to bring it more into line with the Church in England and France. This they did by encouraging non-Celtic monasticism and establishing a system of territorial dioceses. Between 1115 and 1120 Alexander brought Austin canons from Yorkshire to serve the church at Scone, important for its associations with the symbolic seat of Scottish kingship. Shortly before his death, he appointed one of these canons, Robert, Bishop of St. Andrews. Bishop Robert, who ruled till 1159, administered the territory assigned to his see as a diocese on the English pattern, with the help of archdeacons and rural deans hitherto unknown in Scotland. At St. Andrews he built a small cathedral [1] and installed Austin canons as its chapter. King Alexander had made a start, but his brother carried the work on so vigorously that tradition has held " Saint David " solely responsible for an ecclesiastical revolution. As usual, tradition contains truth but also exaggeration.

In fact, David I was the founder, either on his own or working closely with his bishops and his only son Prince Henry, of at least a dozen monasteries, in addition to raising his mother's priory of Dunfermline (which had now become the royal burial place) into an abbey and building for it (c. 1128) a great new church, in its day the largest ever built north of the Forth. The king showed a catholic choice in his patronage of religious orders. Benedictines, " reformed Benedictines " whether of Cluny, Tiron or Cîteaux, Austin canons from England and France, all found a place in his kingdom, from Moray in the north to Jedburgh and Kelso, within a few miles of the English border, while his Constable brought a convent of white canons to Dryburgh on the Tweed. In fact, most of the major abbeys of medieval Scotland were of David's foundation. Their importance in our period, as bringers of a new spiritual life and of fresh economic and industrial activity, is not easily overstated. And in the twelfth century, the close bond uniting the Tironians of Kelso and Cistercians of Melrose, Newbattle, Holm Cultram,[2] and Kinloss to their ultimate mother-houses in France meant a continuous link between remote Scotland and the continent.

[1] Partly surviving as St. Rule's Tower.
[2] This daughter-house of Melrose was actually in Cumberland, but until David's death was more a Scottish than an English abbey.

The changes wrought in David's time in the secular Church were perhaps still more important. The whole country was brought within a system of nine territorial dioceses, or ten if Whithorn (Galloway), established independently of the Scottish king, is included. We have already noted the formation of the two largest, St. Andrews and Glasgow (Cumbria). Certain others, e.g. Caithness, Ross and Moray, coincided with political divisions. Elsewhere the arrangement was far less symmetrical, because respect had to be paid to the property rights of the ancient monastic centres, such as Dunkeld, which were turned into sees for bishops of the new type. David I's bishops, however, unlike his monks and canons, were not all foreign newcomers : two native bishops at least were his close counsellors. Nor was the Scottish episcopate obscure and backward, and in John of Glasgow, who had argued the case of the Scots Church at the papal court, had been the honoured guest of Gurmond, Latin Patriarch of Jerusalem, and had lived for a time as a monk at Tiron, it possessed a leader of European outlook. Under the direction of these bishops, cathedral churches began to be built with organised chapters of clergy to serve them, and a start was made, at least at St. Andrews and Glasgow, with proper diocesan administration. Much progress was made in dividing the various dioceses into parishes, and to help the clergy in this work the king, by an edict later known as the " Assize of King David ", commanded tithes to be paid to parish churches, an order which seems to have been obeyed, at least to some extent. In this period, too, clerks from Scotland went to the schools of England and the continent and returned with a training in theology and the canon law. The Scottish Church entered into closer relations with the Papacy, and the Pope's legates held councils at Roxburgh (1125) and Carlisle (1138). But despite the great reputation which David I enjoyed at the papal *Curia*, he was unable to accomplish the one thing necessary for the *ecclesia Scoticana* to become a normal member of the western Church : he could not obtain papal sanction for St. Andrews to be made a metropolitan archbishopric like York or Canterbury. The Scots clergy were subject to bishops who lacked a constitutional head and spokesman, a weakness which found no remedy until the fifteenth century when it was too late to have effect.

David I, 1124-53

The Government of the Country

The objectives of both Scottish and English monarchies in the earlier twelfth century were the same : (1) the establishment of undisputed hereditary succession, and (2) the building up of a centralised government supported and obeyed in every corner of the realm.   Judged by these aims, the work of David I was brilliantly successful and quite as momentous for Scottish history as his reform of the Church.

(1) We have noted that Malcolm Canmore wished to replace tanistry by hereditary succession.   The alternate slaughter of rival claimants after his death was followed by the peaceful accession of three of his sons in turn, and as the first two were childless, the rule of succession was not seriously put to the test until 1130.   That is not to say there were no other claimants.   The family to which Macbeth belonged was represented by Angus, mormaer—one source actually styles him " king "—of Moray.   Then Alexander I had apparently left an illegitimate son, Malcolm Macheth.   In 1130, taking advantage of David's absence in England, Angus and Malcolm took an army southward to seize the kingdom.   The rebels were opposed near Stracathro in Angus, after crossing the North Esk, by a force under the King's Constable Edward, and in a battle of whose details we know nothing suffered a disastrous defeat.   Angus and many of his following were killed, and though Malcolm Macheth escaped to cause more trouble, he was captured in 1134 and imprisoned at Roxburgh for twenty-three years.   King David wisely annexed Moray to the Crown, and there were no earls of Moray until 1312.   The only other pretender of note was a strange individual named Wimund, who would be comical if he had not so violently· disturbed King David's peace.   Rapid promotion from scribe to monk and from monk to Bishop of Sodor and Man evidently turned his head : he proclaimed descent from the line of Moray, raided Scotland, and was eventually captured, blinded and mutilated.[1] In order to ensure the succession of his son Henry, King David, from *c.* 1139, associated him in the work of government, giving him the style of " king-designate ".   All his contemporaries speak well

[1] He ended his days at Byland Abbey, where, according to the historian William, from nearby Newburgh, something of the old man's fiery past still smouldered within him.

of Prince Henry, who besides his Scottish position was Earl of Northumberland from 1139 until his death and Earl of Huntingdon from *c.* 1135 for an uncertain period. To the intense grief of his father and the whole nation, Prince Henry died in June, 1152, while still in his thirties. He left three sons, but the eldest, Malcolm, was only eleven years old. The old king commanded one of the greatest of the native magnates, Earl Duncan of Fife, to take Malcolm with him through Scotia at the head of an army and show him to the people as the heir to the throne. There could be no more eloquent tribute to the respect inspired by King David and to the strength of his monarchy than the fact that Malcolm " the Maiden ", a boy of twelve and hereditary successor after a new-fangled fashion, was accepted as king throughout most of the realm. After 1153, the hereditary principle of succession was never challenged.

(2) David I's power to make changes in the government and social structure of Scotland largely depended (as his friend Robert Brus once reminded him) on the support of his Anglo-Norman vassals. The strength and above all the sanctity of his character, which even the wild Scots respected, had to be supplemented by the reaction of military fiefs on the Norman model, to be held by men of proven loyalty who were experts in cavalry warfare. He found most of these men, naturally enough, in his English honour of Huntingdon, and equally understandably the parts of Scotland where he enfeoffed them with estates and castleries were Cumbria and Lothian, where he himself was lord of immense tracts of land. To Hugh de Moreville he granted his constableship and the districts of Cunningham and Lauderdale ; to Robert Brus, Robert Avenel, and Rannulf de Soules respectively the adjoining border valleys of " Strath Annan " (Annandale), Eskdale, and Liddesdale. David was rescued from the rout of Winchester (1141) by his godson David Oliphant (Olifard) of Northamptonshire, who was rewarded with land in Berwickshire, and was given by the next king an estate near Glasgow which became the famous lordship and castle of Bothwell. The king attracted to his service many who had no ties with Huntingdon. After Moray fell to the Crown, for example, a Fleming named Freskin, tenant of Strathbrock in West Lothian, was enfeoffed in Duffus near Elgin and founded a great feudal dynasty. Best known of the " outsiders " was the Breton Walter fitz Alan, already mentioned, who became hereditary steward and was granted Renfrew

and other lands. The sixth " Stewart " in succession to Walter was to found his own royal dynasty.

We must not exaggerate the " Norman " settlement in Scotland under David I, or its value to the Crown.[1] In 1153 Anglo-Normans formed a minority among landowners, none of them held earl's rank and in Scotia (except for Moray) they were scarcely to be found at all. They cannot have mustered all the knight-service which the king required, and which he could not get from the mormaers or (because of his respect for the Church) from the lands of bishoprics and abbeys. His household, it is true, was Anglo-Norman. Its chief officers were the Chancellor, Chamberlain (equivalent to the English Treasurer), Steward, Constable, and Marischal. Alexander I had introduced the office of Chancellor. Invariably, of course, a cleric, he held the same high place at the Scottish as at the English court. He kept the king's seal, modelled on that of England, and his staff of clerks produced the writs which in ever-increasing numbers under David I made known the king's will to his " French ", English, Scots, and Gallovidian subjects.

Native magnates, however, were not excluded from court. David made no effort to reduce the power of the mormaers, or earls as they were coming to be called, but he evidently took the first steps towards feudalising them : he granted the earldom of Fife to its native heir, Duncan, as a fief. Moreover, he extended into parts of Scotia the new system of local control which he had first set up in Lothian, the system of castles and sheriffs. David adopted the office of sheriff from Norman England, but in Scotland it underwent certain changes. The early Scottish sheriffs appointed by David I were mostly based on royal castles, and if they were not always the keepers of these castles they nevertheless administered the king's interests from the castle, supported by its garrison. Most of them belonged to the incoming Anglo-Norman class, though in Scotia—a notable indication that David carried out no drastic suppression of the old order —some " new sheriffs " might be but " old thanes " writ large, native Celts who even with the new title did not administer areas as large as the sheriffdoms of the later medieval period. It is probable that from the first the sheriff did not merely collect the king's food-rents and other revenues from his district, but was also associated in

[1] For a view somewhat different from that offered here, see R. L. G. Ritchie, *The Normans in Scotland* (1954).

the dispensing of justice alongside the native *brithem* [1] ("judge") whose duty it was to pronounce the law. Gradually the sheriff court became the standard court for the free man in Scotland. In the field of justice, as in religion, David I took his duties seriously. His kingdom was too primitive and divided for there to have been anything like a standard code of law or custom, but he issued edicts on judicial matters which applied to the whole country, and his new sheriffs could ensure their enforcement. The king also dispensed justice in person. "It was his custom", Ailred of Rievaulx says, "to sit at the entrance to the royal hall and carefully hear the cases of poor men and old women who on certain days were called to him individually, in whatever district he came to, and to satisfy each, often after much deliberation." He remained accessible, and we know, again from Ailred, that he possessed the gift, characteristic of those on whom authority rests naturally, of making each petition of the moment his own exclusive concern.

The country's economic progress was closely associated with the developments in the Church and in royal government. Monasteries and castles created new needs, and a money economy was required in place of the barter of cattle and foodstuffs. The earliest known Scottish coinage, silver pennies copied from those of England, was minted under David I and his son Prince Henry, at Roxburgh, Berwick, Edinburgh, Carlisle, and in Northumberland. Trade was fostered by the development of burghs, which grew up in the shelter of royal castles. Probably Berwick was the biggest town in David I's kingdom, but Roxburgh, Edinburgh, Rutherglen, Stirling and Perth, likewise developed by the king, and St. Andrews, made into a burgh by its bishop, were all well-established as towns by 1153. As in England, religious houses created burghs, and Dunfermline and Canongate beside Edinburgh came into being in this period, the latter belonging to the canons of Holyrood. Many of the craftsmen and merchants who peopled the early towns were Flemings, driven from their own country by repeated waves of unemployment, and welcomed by a far-sighted king. By 1153 the racial composition of Scotland had become more mixed than ever. In the south the Anglo-Norman feudatories mingled and intermarried with the indigenous aristocracy of Old English or Cumbrian

---

[1] Pronounced roughly like "brieve", in which form the word was in use in the Outer Isles until the seventeenth century.

stock, in the north with the Gaelic-speaking inhabitants of Scotia who might themselves have some Scandinavian or English ancestors. Over this heterogeneous complexity of race and language the strong monarchy built up by Alexander I and David I imposed a very considerable measure of unity.

King David died at Carlisle in May, 1153, when he must have been about seventy years old. His body was taken over the hills to the crossing of the Forth at Queensferry, and was buried beside those of his family in the abbey church of Dunfermline. Altogether, his reign made a fitting entrance for Scotland into the medieval European world. The devotion for religion which he inherited from his mother made him famous throughout the west. He led a strict private life, keeping a simple, and, by the standards of the age, perhaps a somewhat puritan court. But there was clearly something more than piety in his character : he possessed the power of winning the loyalty and obedience of many different sorts of men. In the latter part of his reign he regained control over the far north of the Scottish mainland, lost in the eleventh century. Galloway was more closely subject to the Scots crown under him than previously and for long years to come. He anticipated gaining direct control over the western highlands, a task which proved beyond his powers. But for the last ten years of his reign, he came nearer than any of his predecessors or successors to building up a Scoto-Northumbrian state, which he governed chiefly from Carlisle. His son's early death, and the accession of Henry II of England, put an end to this state, but its importance in the twelfth century, when there were more large landholders of English stock north of the border than in England itself, should not be forgotten. As for Scotland, its people in later ages looked back to the reign of David I, not without reason, as a time of justice and the observance of good customs.

CHAPTER X

ENGLAND UNDER HENRY II, 1154-89

IN 1154, not for the last time in its history, the English nation rallied to the leadership of a young man who had come from oversea to claim his right. The force of Henry of Anjou's personality was recognised from the first. " All the people loved him, for he administered justice fairly and made peace. . . . No man dared to do other than good, for he was held in great awe ", wrote the Peterborough chronicler not long after Henry's accession. He was then twenty-one years of age, not at all a personable figure, stockily built, of middling height, with a freckled face and a head of reddish fair hair on a neck which seemed to be set somewhat low on the shoulders. His bright blue-grey eyes became fierce and bloodshot when he was angry : his bad temper, a Norman trait, could at times be almost ungovernable. His strong physique bore him through a life of constant and often violent activity. In 1174, when directing the surrender of some rebels in Norfolk, Henry was given a severe kick on the thigh by the horse of a former Master of the English Templars, Osto of St. Omer. A weaker man might have been laid up by such an injury, but within a few days Henry was chasing the King of France out of Normandy. Three years later, the same injury brought on an illness that confined him to Winchester for some weeks ; but again, as soon as he was able, he made the crossing to Normandy, and within a month or two was campaigning in Aquitaine. The management of his vast empire, with its two chief capitals, London and Rouen, separated by 200 miles of road and 100 miles of sea,[1] imposed a heavy strain on the king and his court, to say nothing of the burden on the treasury. Much depended on ability to cross the sea speedily. The king's fast galley was kept at Southampton, clearly in constant readiness, and to the standard cost of its passage

---

[1] Measuring via Southampton or Portsmouth and Barfleur, by far the commonest route taken by Henry II.

to France, £7 10s., must be added that of the warships and transports that carried the king's councillors, mercenary troops, treasure and munitions. Nor was all this without risk, for though there was nothing in Henry II's time to compare with the disaster of the *White Ship*, a number of his servants, some of them in important posts, were lost through the sinking of their ships in Channel storms.

Henry II's seemingly limitless energy was quite equal to these severe demands ; indeed, he set new standards of royal devotion to business, being constantly in the saddle riding from one corner of his dominions to another. He often turned aside, it is true, to hunt or hawk, but almost never to rest or be idle. The energy of his body was matched by that of his mind. Highly educated for a layman of the twelfth century, he was not only fond of books and of intellectual disputation himself but was also a generous patron of writers and scholars. His court was a focus for the intercourse of the keenest minds of the day, which were regularly being applied to the practical tasks of government. Among them, for example, were an Exchequer official, Richard fitz Nigel, who was prompted to write a systematic account of the working of the Exchequer, and a judge, Rannulf Glanvill, who has left us a methodical treatise on the law he administered. A solid Yorkshireman, Roger Howden, who served the king in several capacities and wrote what amounts to an " official history " of the reign, had as fellow-courtiers two lively Welshmen, Walter Map, accounted an extremely witty raconteur and satirist, and Gerald of Barry (" Giraldus Cambrensis "), who wrote voluminously on many topics and who is revealed by his writings as a keenly interested, if prejudiced and credulous, observer of the human and the natural scene. These men were fully conscious of belonging to the most brilliant court of western Europe, and paid ready tribute, which was not always mere flattery, to the king they served. Richard fitz Nigel, for example, praises the clemency which Henry II undoubtedly showed to his enemies, while in a famous passage Glanvill wrote of the king thus :

No-one doubts how spiritedly, strenuously and ardently our king has used his military skill to ward off the hatred of his enemies in time of war, since his praise has already gone forth to every land and his great deeds are bruited to the ends of the earth. Nor is there any uncertainty of how justly, wisely and mercifully the same king, himself the lover and maker of peace, has in peace-time treated his subjects, since his majesty's care has been to hold so even a balance that not one of his judges, however impudent of face or bold in his presumption, has dared to depart in any way from the highest paths of truth and justice.[1]

These royal servants were in fact fascinated by the business of government, and responded gladly to the lead which Henry Plantagenet gave them.

In the generation after the civil war there was much work to be done by an energetic king and a capable council. We have already seen the Crown under Henry I making the first approaches towards establishing the supremacy of its courts and of the justice dispensed in them. The country was now ready for an extension of this process. The lasting fame of Henry II as the prime founder of the English Common Law rests on this fact, that under his direction and inspiration the variations of local custom and privilege and the fierce tangle of competing jurisdictions which characterised English justice in the early twelfth century began to give way, slowly but for all time, to a single type of justice, royal justice, standard over the whole kingdom and available to all the king's free subjects through the precepts or writs which could be obtained at any time from the royal chancery. It was to England's immeasurable benefit that Henry Plantagenet, schooled to be a king in every particular, was above all else a lawyer, one of the outstanding lawyers, indeed, in English history. For all his faults and shortcomings, and they were many, he remained, as a great historian has written, " the man the age required ".

The king's peace must be established before legal reforms could be worth anything. The castles built in the civil war without licence from the crown—the " adulterine castles " as they were called—must be demolished, and barons who showed a recalcitrant spirit must be brought to heel. This was soon accomplished. Some years later (1166) the allegiance of the entire feudal class was secured by a searching enquiry into the amount of knight-service due to the Crown from its tenants-in-chief.[2] The amount of knight-service owed to the Crown in 1135 was taken as the standard : some tenants-in-chief had enfeoffed more knights than this figure, others fewer.

---

[1] There is irony here, for Glanvill was once dismissed from sheriff's office presumably for misconduct, and once nearly had an innocent man hanged because of a private grudge, but the King stopped the execution.

[2] For an example of a reply to this enquiry, see above, p. 85.

The penalty for having enfeoffed an excess was that the lord might have to pay scutage on the larger number, though Henry II did not enforce this ruling in every case. At the same time, all men of knight's rank were made to take individual oaths of allegiance to the king direct—the oath " de dominio solo ", i.e. in recognition of the king's lordship alone, irrespective of whether those taking the oath held any land of the king.

The king's choice of responsible servants was extremely important. He appointed as joint Justiciars two adherents of Stephen, the dependable Richard de Lucy, and Earl Robert of Leicester. He restored to the Treasurer's office Nigel, Bishop of Ely, nephew of the great Bishop Roger of Salisbury ; this remarkable " Exchequer dynasty " was continued by Nigel's son Richard and their kinsman William of Ely, successively treasurers for the last part of the twelfth and early years of the thirteenth century. A clerk of much promise from Archbishop Theobald's household, Thomas Becket, of a London merchant family, was made chancellor, and soon became the young king's boon companion. In 1162, more than a year after Theobald's death, Henry made Becket his new primate.

It was an essential part of the king's policy that he should have as head of the English Church a man who saw eye to eye with him on the question of what should be the proper boundaries between the sphere of Church influence and the jurisdiction of the Crown. Henry's zeal to reform the working of justice was guided by the same principle we have seen applied to knight-service : the restoration of things as they were in his grandfather's day, without any precedents being admitted from the reign of the " usurper " Stephen. Chief among these false precedents was the encroachment of the Church upon royal prerogative. The clergy had in fact gained more than the baronage from the civil war. Not only had elections become too free, in the king's view, but appeals were going from English Church courts to the court of the Pope without the intervention of the Crown. Moreover, the privileges successfully claimed by the clergy in respect of judicial proceedings appeared to be exempting them from the ordinary operation of the law.

We may find it hard today to understand why the criminal activity of men in holy orders should have consumed the attention of King and Council and led to a quarrel which ended with the murder of an Archbishop of Canterbury. We should remember first that in twelfth-century England a very large proportion of men were counted as clergy, the greater part of them not fully ordained priests but merely in one of the minor orders, which might involve no more than tonsuring the hair in the prescribed clerical manner. There were many among the " clergy " in this wider sense who possessed no religious vocation whatever and who conducted their lives certainly no better than laymen and sometimes quite disreputably. Secondly, we must not underestimate the importance to King Henry of the principle involved. He considered it wrong that there should be such a glaring disparity between the treatment suffered by a layman who had committed a crime—hanging, mutilation, or loss of property—and that accorded to a convicted clergyman, which might amount to nothing more than unfrocking. In the eyes of the Church, on the other hand, degradation, even from minor orders, was regarded as a severe spiritual punishment, and moreover the procedure used in the Church courts was more advanced and rational than the crude proofs of hot iron, water and compurgation by which laymen were acquitted or condemned. If ecclesiastical penalties seemed too lenient, at least they were awarded after a fairer and more foolproof trial.

It seems clear that Henry sincerely believed that his old friend and chancellor Becket would use his great influence as primate to persuade the bishops and clergy to accept some curtailment of clerical immunity. But the archbishop's behaviour since his consecration had been strangely ominous. He had broken William the Conqueror's rule that a royal minister should not be excommunicated without consulting the king, and had spoken against Henry with needless vehemence on matters unrelated to the Church. From the moment he became archbishop, Thomas Becket seems to have conceived himself, in a dramatic fashion, as the fearless and single-minded defender of the Church in England against secular forces that were bent upon injuring it. At all costs the clerical order must be preserved inviolate.

A number of complaints which reached the king's ears in the 1160's brought matters to a head. A rural dean had blackmailed a burgess of Scarborough. Philip de Broy, a canon of St. Paul's Church in Bedford and a member of a substantial family of gentry in the county, having previously been tried and punished in a Church court for the homicide of a knight, had publicly insulted a royal justice, who on the king's orders had summoned him before the royal court on the same charge. Henry pressed the subject of criminal clergymen at a Westminster Council in October, 1163. He first asked the bishops to agree that clerks convicted of crimes in Church courts and then degraded should be handed over to royal officers to be punished as laymen. Becket, to the king's fury, persuaded his colleagues to refuse the request. The king then asked if they would agree to abide by the ancient customs of the realm. Becket again refused, but the other bishops assented " saving their order ", a proviso which made the assent almost worthless. The breach dividing king and archbishop was now complete, and the next stage would clearly be an open battle of will, influence and political skill between the two men. Henry was much helped by the neutral position of Pope Alexander III, who vainly urged Becket to compromise. After some further resistance, the archbishop reversed his stand of October and agreed to observe the ancient customs. It has been suggested that this apparently unaccountable submission was prompted by Becket's anxiety for popularity. This had evidently been a trait of his earlier career, and might have made him " unable to bear the bitterness of the reproaches of the king and his friends ".[1] However this may be, the king was not satisfied. Having got the Church to agree to follow the customs of his grandfather's time, he was determined that he and his trusted councillors should declare in detail exactly what these customs were. At a Council called at the hunting lodge of Clarendon, near Salisbury, in January, 1164, the king promulgated a record of sixteen customs concerned with the relations between Church and State. Some of these " Constitutions of Clarendon ", as they are called, dealt with minor matters, but several were highly important, and three in particular call for our attention.

First, legal disputes over the right to present incumbents to Church livings—the right known as the " advowson ", and treated as a type of real property, to be inherited, bought or sold—were to be the exclusive concern of the king's courts. Secondly, when decisions in Church courts were made the subject of an appeal by one or other party, the *ultimate* court of appeal was to be the king's court, unless the king permitted the appeal to go " further ", i.e. to

[1] M. D. Knowles, *Archbishop Thomas Becket : a Character Study* (British Academy, Raleigh Lecture for 1949), p. 12 of the separate reprint.

the Papacy. Thirdly, and most controversially of all, clergy accused of criminal offences were to have their cases examined by a royal justice before going for trial in an ecclesiastical court. Even there, the trial was to take place before an observer sent by the royal justice, and if the accused were convicted the Church was no longer to give him protection. As an ordinary layman, the degraded cleric could then be dealt with like other laymen. Whether or not this procedure had been the rule under Henry I, it agreed substantially with the practice recommended by Canon Law. Nevertheless, Becket opposed it strenuously and bitterly, holding it unjust that a man should be punished twice for the same offence. Then, by another inexplicable *volte face*, he suddenly gave way and accepted the Constitutions.

In the autumn of 1164, however, feeling on both sides had hardened. The Pope had declared all but six of the Constitutions invalid, while Becket recanted his acceptance of them. Henry vindictively demanded that the archbishop should give an account of his income and expenditure of public money while Chancellor, and at a Council at Northampton contrived a charge against him of contempt of court. Truculent barons went through the motions of a hanging in front of Becket, who fled by night to the Channel and took refuge in the French abbey of Pontigny. The next six years formed a stalemate highly characteristic of major disputes in the Middle Ages. On the whole, the Pope supported Becket, and was only occasionally moved by Henry's threats to transfer his recognition to the imperialist anti-pope, Paschal III. In 1166, Becket, though still in exile, was made papal legate in England (save for York diocese), and received the Pope's authority to excommunicate the king's servants who had taken possession in their master's name of the property of the see of Canterbury. In England, however, Becket commanded less support. His vacillation in 1163 and 1164 had lost him the confidence of many English bishops, while some had never been on his side. The Archbishop of York, Roger of Pont l'Evêque, added to a feeling of personal rivalry the traditional hostility of his see for Canterbury. The most notable of the English bishops, Gilbert Foliot of London, though believing as sincerely as Becket in the preservation of the Church from lay domination, was convinced that the primate's tactics were misguided and dangerous.[1]

[1] He was once provoked to exclaim that Becket " always was a fool and always will be ".

His own view of the proper relations of Church and State seems to have been based on the moderate teaching of a German ecclesiastical reforming writer, Gerhoh of Reichersberg.[1] Foliot remained a consistent critic of Becket throughout his years of exile, and his influence on the opinions of churchmen in England and on the continent was considerable.

It is in the closing stages of his life that Thomas Becket's character becomes most difficult to fathom. Some historians have concluded that he was bent upon martyrdom almost for its own sake. Professor Knowles, taking a more sympathetic view of Becket's motives, believes nevertheless that "during those last months of 1169 . . . he had become convinced that only by his death would a solution be found ".[2] It seems to be true that Becket's personality made difficult any gradual adjustment in his relations with those about him. While not fanatical in temperament, he was a man of extremes, and while he commanded the deep respect of the faithful clerks of his household, he was actually loved by very few. To such a man, especially after six years' harsh exile, sharing the austere life of the Cistercians of Pontigny, the idea of offering his life in the cause to which he had dedicated himself might seem attractively logical. It is doubtful if any estimate of Becket's character will ever be thought to do justice both to him and to his opponents. Not only were contradictions implicit in it, but controversy remains implicit in the cause for which he stood, the freedom of an authoritarian Church from secular authority. Ever since his own time, Becket has been referred to either with the adoration proper to a martyr and saint or in terms of bitter hostility. It is in large part the very nature of the contemporary material on his life which makes it unlikely that any "received opinion" with regard to Becket will ever gain currency.

In the summer of 1170, while the issue of the Constitutions of Clarendon was still unresolved, Henry II felt in a strong enough position to proceed with a scheme on which his heart had been set for some years—the coronation of his eldest surviving son Henry as king in his father's lifetime. Although this was a French and Imperial method of ensuring the succession foreign to English

---

[1] M. D. Knowles, *The Episcopal Colleagues of Archbishop Thomas Becket* (1951), 83-4, 153-4.
[2] *Archbishop Thomas Becket*, 20.

custom, the lay and ecclesiastical magnates of the realm accepted the proposal. It was clear, however, that despite the precedents set by the Conqueror and Henry I the ceremony itself could be performed only by the Archbishop of Canterbury. Yet, on June 14th, 1170, in spite of failure to obtain papal permission, the king had his son crowned at Westminster by the Archbishop of York assisted by six other bishops. The act moved Becket to a fury of indignation and stirred the Pope to threaten an interdict, or suspension of religious services, throughout Henry II's kingdom.

It was presumably in the hope that Becket would modify his opposition on this issue that the king offered, shortly afterwards, to meet the archbishop and be reconciled. It is much less easy to account for Becket's agreement to the meeting, for it seems clear from his subsequent actions that he had forgotten and forgiven nothing. The conference took place on July 22nd near Fréteval, in the French county of Blois but close to the border with Angevin territory. The two men came together in a purely formal reconciliation. King Henry withheld the symbolic " kiss of peace ", though he declared that in so doing he meant no harm to Becket. After two rather more friendly meetings, the archbishop returned to England on December 1st. But he was preceded by letters which he had obtained from the Pope, in which sentences were pronounced against certain of the English bishops who had presumed to assist at the unlawful coronation of the young king. In consequence, Becket was given a cold or hostile reception by those in authority. In Southwark, however, which he visited in a vain attempt to interview the younger Henry, he was given an enthusiastic welcome, and at Canterbury clergy and people flocked to greet him, celebrating his homecoming with the ringing of church bells, the music of organs and the singing of hymns and songs of praise.

The archbishop's actions during these last few weeks seem to have been almost deliberately provocative, yet even he may not have realised how quickly his provocation would be answered. His last act of defiance was on Christmas Day, when he pronounced the excommunication of his enemies from the pulpit of his cathedral. Already, four knights from the royal household had made up their minds to murder him. Stealing unnoticed from the court in Normandy, they took ship at once for Kent. They reached Canterbury on December 29th. About three o'clock in the afternoon, when it was already growing dark, they roused the archbishop from his house in the precinct. His clerks persuaded him to seek the sanctuary of his own cathedral. The four knights found him in the north transept, near the entrance to the choir, and after some confused altercation, they hacked him to death with their swords.

The guilt of this enormous crime settled at once upon the entire English nation and in a sense upon the whole Christian world. It could not be lifted easily or in a short time, and in the popular imagination it may be said to have persisted for some hundreds of years. Its expiation involved everyone in Henry II's dominions, from the king himself, who had to found three monasteries, maintain a force of knights in Palestine, and (1174) submit to a public whipping near the scene of the murder, to his ordinary subjects south of the Channel, who were forced to endure for some time an interdict imposed by the Pope. Popular horror reflected itself almost immediately in a veneration for the martyred archbishop which spread with extraordinary rapidity to every country of the Christian west. Naturally, the news that Becket had worn an ascetic's hair-shirt and also the stories of miracles wrought at his tomb or in his name had greatest force in England itself, and among the common people the cult of Becket as a saint actually anticipated the Pope's official act of canonisation (March, 1173).[1] The murder of course affected the king's policy towards the clergy. The clause of the Constitutions of Clarendon most obnoxious to the Papacy—the prohibition of appeals to Rome—was unreservedly withdrawn. Yet in spite of the profound shock and revulsion which the act caused, King Henry's defence of the " ancient customs " for the most part held good. Advowsons remained the preserve of lay courts, as did all suits concerning land held by a secular tenure as distinct from tenure in charity or " free alms ". It is true that in 1176 the king promised that clergy should not be summoned before a lay court except for an offence against his forest laws. But in practice this concession was not the unqualified " benefit of clergy " for which Becket had striven, for in order to have his trial and punishment solely at the hands of ecclesiastics the accused had first to prove to the satisfaction of royal sheriffs or judges that he really was a clergyman. Otherwise, the Constitutions of Clarendon became part of the law of the land. In particular the king kept a tight grip on

[1] E. W. Kemp, *Trans. R. Hist. Soc.* (1945), 19-20.

elections to bishoprics and abbacies, so that, for example, the monks of the great abbey of Bury St. Edmunds, whose abbot died in 1181, were uncertain until the last moment whether the king would allow them a " free election ".

We cannot say how much more Henry II would have accomplished if the Becket controversy had not beset him with so many problems for so long. But as it was, the sum of his achievement in the fields of what we should call civil and criminal law was impressive. We may look first at his reforms of criminal law, which, if indeed they are rightly called reforms, were in the main conservative. It is in the nature of the matter that we cannot judge the success of Henry II's measures here. Statistics of twelfth-century crime are lacking, and criminal activity fluctuates notoriously. It can only be said that Henry II maintained his initial reputation for keeping the peace, and that his successors built upon his methods.

For the first ten years of his reign, Henry II may have been content to see royal justice administered chiefly by local justices of the type who held office under Henry I and Stephen, acting in conjunction with the sheriffs. But in 1166 a number of judges were specially appointed to tour the country, and this practice of sending out " itinerant justices " or " justices in eyre " [1] quickly became normal and regular. In this respect, Henry II's itinerant justices mark an important advance on the occasional tours of royal agents acting as judges under Henry I. The judges of 1166 were given elaborate instructions, known collectively as the " Assize of Clarendon ", many of which were directed towards a tightening up of criminal justice. As the judges travelled from shire to shire the successive sheriffs were to bring before them all those accused or publicly suspected of being murderers, robbers, thieves, or their harbourers. The sheriffs were to have these men " presented " to them by juries of twelve law-worthy men from each hundred and four from each village, who were to declare on oath the names of all such accused or suspected criminals. No baronial or other private franchise could claim exemption from this procedure. Foreseeing that the judges' eyre would cause a countrywide flight of criminals trying to escape being brought to justice, the king ordered each sheriff to help his fellows by arresting men who had fled from other counties, and by compiling a list, for circulation among

[1] From the Old French form of Latin *iter*, a journey.

156

the justices and other sheriffs, of outlaws and fugitives from his own county. In anticipation of much business for the justices, the sheriffs were to construct jails to hold those whom they arrested. The " jury of presentment " already had a long history in English law when its duties were described in the Assize of Clarendon ; it seems probable that such a method of bringing criminals to trial had supplemented the individual accusation of the victim or his kinsman since Anglo-Saxon times. But from 1166 its working became for the first time closely linked to the central government.[1]

The Assize of Clarendon was followed up ten years later, when the rebellion of 1173-4 had produced a fresh wave of lawlessness, by the Assize of Northampton. Northampton shows advances of method compared with Clarendon ; it was also harsher. The itinerant justices were sent out in groups each of which toured one of the six circuits into which the country was divided. The king and his judges were clearly dissatisfied with the antiquated customary methods of proof, the ordeals of being plunged, trussed, into a pit filled with water which had first been blessed by a priest [2] (normal for men), or of carrying the red-hot iron (customary with women). By the Assize of Clarendon men convicted at the ordeal were punished by loss of a foot and by exile ; Northampton directed that they were to lose their right hands as well. Moreover, this later assize added forgery and arson to the list of grave crimes. When we consider that both assizes decreed that men of known bad fame should be exiled even though they passed the test of the ordeal, we see how much judicial power was in effect given to the presenting jury, which in this respect became almost a trying jury of the modern type. But the true criminal jury of today arose rather later than the time of Henry II (*c.* 1200), when the justices either gave the accused the option of paying to have a jury instead of the ordeal, or else allowed his counter-accusation that he had been charged out of " hatred and spite " to be adjudged by a jury, whose verdict would be final if it favoured the accused. This example, from 1199, shows

---

[1] N. Hurnard, " The Jury of Presentment and the Assize of Clarendon ", *E.H.R.* lvi (1941), 374-410, demonstrates the antiquity of sworn present-ments, and believes that such presentments were used at the visits of itinerant justices as early as Henry I's time (*ibid.* 379).

[2] It was believed that water thus blessed would receive only an innocent person, who therefore sank ; if guilty he floated. By the twelfth century men were already sceptical of this test.

a defendant asking for such a jury ; it shows too, incidentally, the difficulty of being a subject of both the King of England and the King of Scotland, and how an individual accusation might be kept alive for a quarter of a century. Robert, laird of Hoddom in Dumfries-shire, claimed Gamblesby and Glassonby in Cumberland against Richard, Troite's son, his claim being countered as follows :

Richard, Troite's son, accuses Robert of Hoddom of wickedly deserting his lord King Henry and being false in his faith to him and destroying his land and besieging his city and castle and allying himself, as a wicked traitor, to King Henry's mortal enemy the King of Scotland. He alleges that he accused him of this in King Henry's presence outside the village of Geddington (Northants), and as he did not then dare or wish to defend himself in the king's court King Henry drove him thence in flight. If Robert should wish to deny this, Richard offers to prove it by his own body or that of one of his free men (i.e. offers trial by battle).

Robert comes and offers to defend himself of the felony, word for word, or, since he is a man of over sixty, through one of his sons. Richard, asked before which judges he made the accusation in King Henry's time, says it was before King Henry in person and not before any judge or anyone else before whom the charge might be shown or named. Robert comes and says that at the time when Richard alleges he was with the King of Scotland at the siege of Carlisle castle (i.e. in 1173 or 1174) his father Odard was in possession of the land which he claims against Richard and was in King Henry's service at the time, in the castle, and that he died in possession, and that he, Robert, held no land at that time. And Robert places himself upon a jury of law-worthy men of the county that the accusation has been made from spite in order to disinherit him. . . . Then it is judged that since Richard has kept quiet about his accusation for such a long time the accusation is quashed and he is liable to a fine and Robert is acquitted.[1]

In 1215, the Fourth Lateran Council of the Church forbade priests to assist at the ordeal, a rule which brought to an end an already discredited device. But in other respects, Clarendon and Northampton formed the basis of criminal procedure for generations. In 1195, the ancient duty of local people to raise the hue and cry was again emphasised, and in every shire knights were appointed to receive oaths from every male over fifteen to keep the peace. These knights were soon known as " guardians of the peace " ; their successors in the fourteenth century were promoted to be " justices of the peace ". Criminal justice in our period was often rough and ready and sometimes savage. We should remember that men in that age were quick to use fists and knives, that there was no police force, and that the odds were against a really determined criminal being caught at all.

[1] *Rotuli Curiae Regis*, ed. Sir Francis Palgrave (1835), ii. 30-1 (translated).

Henry II's reforms were most beneficial and enduring in regard to disputes about property (especially land) between subject and subject, an aspect of what we should now call civil law. A subtle but vital distinction was drawn between what was termed " seisin ", that is, merely being in possession of a piece of property, and *ius*, or complete proprietary right over property held freely and heritably. As we have seen, the concept of outright ownership was foreign to feudalism. Nevertheless, even under feudalism it could well happen that one man might have a better title to a holding of land than another who was actually in possession. Apart from disputes over inheritance, it was not uncommon, especially in the civil war, for one man to seize another's land by violence. The genius of Henry II's policy lay in the fact that it stopped self-help to right such wrongs and made their remedy the exclusive business of the royal courts. It may seem unjust that the king protected the man who claimed possession often at the expense of the man with a better title ; but the decision of the king and his advisers to protect possession first, and allow the question of proprietary right to be determined afterwards, was probably the greatest single advance towards the rule of law ever made in English history. To understand the methods used, we shall be best advised to follow the order preferred by King Henry, taking possession first and proprietary right second.

The first and simplest case was that of a free man, X, who complained that he had recently been dispossessed of his land by another, Y, unjustly and without the judgment of a court. Under Rufus or Henry I, X might, if he had been very wealthy or influential, have persuaded the king to help him. But from 1166 (probably as part of the reforms outlined in the Assize of Clarendon), all that X or any other free man had to do was to obtain the appropriate writ from the royal chancery. This writ ordered the sheriff of the county concerned to empanel a jury of twelve men of the neighbourhood, to whom was put the question, " Has X recently been dispossessed, unjustly and without judgment, by Y ? " If the answer were affirmative, the sheriff restored the land to X without further argument. The jury was called an " assize ", by another use of this rather overworked term, and the whole remedy was known as the assize of recent dispossession, or in twelfth-century language, the Assize of " Novel Disseisin ".

The second case concerned inheritance. X claims that he ought to inherit the land of his father (or other lawful ancestor), Z, but Y has taken possession instead. Again, X obtains a writ from chancery, which authorises the sheriff to summon a jury of twelve neighbours who know the land. The following questions are put to them : " Did Z die in lawful and hereditary possession of the land ? Is X his lawful heir ? " If both questions are answered affirmatively, the sheriff at once gives possession of the land to X, and Y is ejected. This assize, dating from between 1166 and 1176, was known as the Assize of " Mort d'Ancestor " (death of one's predecessor). For both assizes to work effectively, it was necessary that the events alleged should be recent and therefore fresh in the minds of the jury of neighbours on whose verdict so much weight was placed. But it should be emphasised that in neither case did the assize settle the question of who had the ultimate, proprietary right in the land.

The third of these remedies dealt with advowson, claimed, as we have seen, for the royal courts by the Constitutions of Clarendon. A church living falls vacant, and X and Y dispute the right to present the next incumbent. As before, the machinery of royal writ, sheriff, and jury is set in motion. The jury are asked " Who presented the last incumbent? " They answer according to their memory, and the person whom they name, or his heir if he is no longer alive, is adjudged the rightful person to make the next presentation. This assize was called " Darrein Presentment " (last presentation).

These Petty Assizes, as they were collectively known,[1] were swift, simple, relatively cheap and soon immensely popular. But they dealt with only half the problem of property disputes, the matter of possession. It was probably in 1179 that Henry II and his legal advisers introduced a parallel method of settling the question of proprietary right. To mark the fact that this concerned the more important of the two aspects of property disputes, this new remedy was called the " Grand Assize ". Hitherto, cases concerning right in land had been settled by judicial combat (or compromise) in the courts of the barons of whom the contestants claimed to be tenants. The king's court heard only disputes between the king's own tenants-in-chief, or between men who claimed to hold of different lords. But from 1179 an alternative procedure was open to any free man, whereby he could, as Glanvill says, " decline the doubtful

---

[1] A modern alternative term is " possessory assizes ".

issue of combat " and have a jury instead. The Grand Assize was complicated, slow and solemn, but it was final, and much more rational than trial by battle. X claimed the right over land held by Y. He obtained from chancery a " writ of right ", ordering the appropriate lord to do justice between him and Y. Y, instead of agreeing in the old way to give battle in the feudal court, obtained in turn a " writ of peace ", whereupon X, if he wished to proceed with his claim, had to get another writ, which ordered the sheriff to appoint four knights who were to empanel a jury of twelve other knights. These twelve knights then decided which of the two litigants had the better right.

Henry II's reforms in the field of property actions were completed by an important procedure known as the final concord. Where two rival claimants to a piece of land were prepared to reach agreement and have its conditions certified once for all by the king's judges, a document (itself called the " final concord " or " fine ") was drawn up which set forth the terms of the settlement. Two copies were written on one piece of parchment, and were then separated by making a zig-zag cut. One copy was given to each disputant. Should their dispute be resumed thereafter, the copies would be produced in court. If their indented edges fitted together exactly, their authenticity was held to be proved and the judges ordered a strict adherence to the terms of the settlement. If one of the parties tried to forge a version more favourable to himself, it would be almost impossible for him to reproduce on another parchment the exact indentations of the genuine copy. But for added security, the cut in the original was made through the middle of large letters written between the two copies of the agreement, thus " A B C D . . . " or *Cirographum* (literally, " signature ") or some other word.[1] In 1195, an improvement of this simple duplicate fine was introduced. The new fine was in triplicate, and the third or bottom copy, the " foot of the fine ", was kept by the king. Any dispute could thus be settled at once by reference to the copy in the royal archives. It is clear that some pride was taken in the new device, for the very first fine to be made in this way was endorsed as follows :

---

[1] We use the word " indenture " for such a duplicate or tripartite document because originally they were all cut through in an indented or zig-zag line. In our period they were also known as " chirographs ".

This is the first chirograph to have been made in the court of the lord king in the form of three chirographs [? according to what was ordained by the Archbishop of Canterbury and the other barons of the lord king for this purpose]. In order that in this form it could be a record, it was handed over to the treasurer to be placed in the treasury.[1]

And in the " treasury " Feet of Fines have remained ever since, many thousands of them steadily accumulating from the reign of Richard I to the year 1833 : an astonishing testimony to the continuity of English legal administration ! The final concord was expensive, but it gave an absolutely secure title to landed property. From about 1200 until the eighteenth century it was perhaps the most popular of all methods of making a conveyance of land, since the royal judges allowed it to be used to settle a purely fictitious " dispute ", the real purpose of which was simply to transfer ownership from one person to another.

The Petty and Grand Assizes were a royal monopoly, since they involved the compulsory (and unpopular) appointment of knights and freemen of wide local neighbourhoods, and not merely estates or franchises, to serve on juries. As the remedies they provided became more and more welcome, the royal courts took on a great increase of business, much of it at the expense of the baronial courts. It meant also an increase in the number of royal servants who were required to serve as judges, and a new permanence in the sessions of the king's courts. By the end of Henry II's reign the eyres of itinerant justices had become a regular part of royal administration, and there had already come into existence at Westminster an almost permanent session of the king's court, held, no matter whether the king were present or not, by his " justices of the bench ", the forerunners of the court of Common Pleas. The king's peace was furthered, and, since the assizes were not obtainable *gratis*, a great deal of money was paid into his treasury. But we should be wrong to suppose that the whole edifice of law and its administration, inherited by the Norman kings from Anglo-Saxon England, extended by them, and wonderfully developed by Henry II, arose merely from the king's need to accumulate money. The twelfth-century kings of England were conscious, in however rudimentary a fashion, that it was their business to provide good government. In their efforts to supply this need, much of what they created was enduring.

[1] *Feet of Fines, Henry II and Richard I* (Pipe Roll Soc., 1894), 21.

CHAPTER XI

HENRY II's EMPIRE

OF his thirty-five years as king, Henry Plantagenet spent some twenty south of the English Channel. We have seen his Norman predecessors showing a similar apparent neglect of their kingdom, but in Henry's case the reasons were essentially different. Born and buried in France, more of a Norman than an Englishman and as much an Angevin as either, there are nevertheless grounds for believing that Henry II had a greater love for England and a better opinion of its inhabitants than any king since the Conquest. The fact was that Henry found it an easier matter to govern England than to hold together the vast continental dominions of which inheritance and marriage had made him nominally master. To understand why this was so we must look briefly at the component territories of what, even in Henry's own time, was recognised as his " empire ".

Through his mother Henry II was Duke of Normandy, inheriting to the full the status and rights enjoyed by William the Conqueror. Thanks largely to Henry I, twelfth-century Normandy was a highly centralised feudal principality, over which the duke maintained a control firmer than that exercised by any other secular ruler in western Europe. It is almost certain that the experience of the dukes as kings of England furthered their development of Norman government. For example, there grew up during the century a Norman exchequer, which held its sessions at Caen, where the treasure was kept, and closely resembled in staff and function the exchequer of England. Again, Normandy was governed in the duke's absence by a seneschal whose position was very similar to that of the English justiciar. He kept the duke's peace, and supervised the management of his demesnes, which under Henry II were being extended through a systematic recovery of lands alienated by his predecessors. Ranking almost equally with the seneschal, however, was an hereditary officer of more feudal type, the Constable, recalling the fact that Normandy was still more like the private fief of a great baron than an

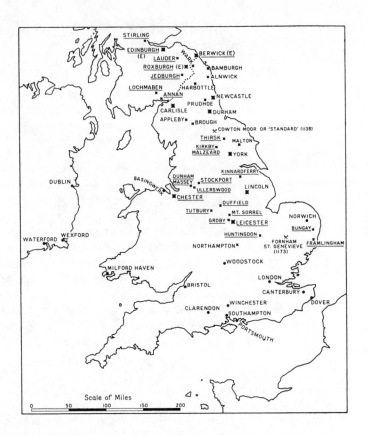

MAP V. THE CHANNEL STATE, 1154–1216 (*see above and opposite page*).
North of the Channel, castles of importance in the rebellion of 1173–4
are shown thus :

First-class castles . . . . . . ■

Less important castles . . . . . . ▰

Held by rebels or enemies of Henry II . . CHESTER

Scottish castles garrisoned by Henry II after 1174 EDINBURGH (E)

embryo state. The Constable had charge of the knight-service of
Normandy, and in Normandy, more than anywhere else in Henry II's
lands, knight-service was part of the very fabric of society. Local

South of the Channel, the boundary of Henry II's dominions at their widest extent is shown thus : //////////////.

administration was in part controlled by *vicomtes* (" vice-counts ", viscounts), who despite their name were originally agents of the duke, but had become largely hereditary and independent. To offset their failure to take proper care of the duke's affairs, Henry II began to promote more direct agents of his own, *baillis* (lit., " subordinate officers "), who were given the duty of watching over ducal rights and interests in certain fixed areas or bailiwicks.

Immediately south of western Normandy stretched the three " Loire provinces " of Maine, Anjou, and Touraine. Maine bordered Normandy and had long been coveted by the Norman dukes ; but in 1110 it passed by marriage to their old enemy the Count of Anjou. The union of the families of Anjou and Normandy in the person of Henry II softened this ancient hostility, greatly to the benefit of Maine, which now ceased to be subject to regular devastation from north and south. As tenth Count of Anjou— though only fourth count of his line by direct male descent—Henry Plantagenet may be said to have found the heart of his empire in the Loire provinces, and he certainly spent much time in the great castles of this rich country, at Le Mans, Angers, or Chinon, where the count's treasure was stored. His building works and hospital foundations in this ancestral region were famous, yet his control over its great lords was more personal, less buttressed by political institutions, than in England and Normandy. The constitution of Anjou was primitive by Norman standards, and its government much less centralised. The king-count was represented by a seneschal who lacked the powers of his Norman counterpart, and to remedy this Henry II sometimes appointed a genuine viceroy.

On the west, the Plantagenet strongholds of Normandy and Anjou were bordered by the duchy or county of Brittany, " little Britain ", a remote peninsula which had been intensively settled from early times by people of British stock from north of the Channel. Celtic in culture and memories, separatist by inclination, the Bretons had little in common with their neighbours to the east. In 1154 the duchy did not form part of the Angevin dominions, but there was already a long history of Norman interference in Breton affairs and of attempts by the Norman dukes to impose a permanent overlord-ship upon the rulers of Brittany. For the first half of the twelfth century, as we have seen, relations between the two duchies were sensibly improved by the friendship offered by Henry I to many Breton nobles. But the Bretons wished for no closer relationship, and were alarmed by the union of the two powerful, but hitherto mercifully hostile, principalities which menaced their eastern frontier. It may be politically significant that in 1160 a double marriage alliance seems to have been planned between Brittany and Scotland, half fulfilled in the wedding of Duke Conan IV to a sister of King Malcolm IV.[1] Even when Brittany was drawn, as we shall see shortly, into the sphere of Angevin dominance, the social structure of the country, a land of scattered hamlets whose service to a lord was expressed in primitive food-renders of corn, pigs and malt, remained sharply distinct from the other territories of King Henry.

The most important distinction within these territories, however, if not the sharpest, was marked by the border dividing the Loire provinces from the vast, sprawling and disunited conglomeration which made up the duchy of Aquitaine. Here, in a region of great natural wealth, the more rigid military feudalism of Neustria did not prevail, and political power was shared, equally but turbulently, by a bellicose aristocracy, quarrelsome urban communities, and powerful and independent ecclesiastical lords such as the Archbishop of Bordeaux or the Bishop of Limoges. By his suzerainty over Aquitaine, Henry II cut in two the lands dependent on the French crown, for in the east of the duchy, beyond the mountainous Dauphiné of Auvergne, the county of Velay marched with the Dauphiné of Viennois, which was subject to no suzerain. But this appears more impressive on the modern map than it was in the reality of the twelfth century.

Angevin rule over these easy-going but tumultuous southern barons was not the same as that exercised in Anjou, Normandy or England. Henry II did not attempt to exploit to anything like their full extent either the financial or the military resources of this area, though they were doubtless substantial. The most he could do was to try to secure some control over the key border districts of Aquitaine, the counties of Poitou, Angoulême and La Marche (the last two straddling the route from Paris to Bordeaux), and Toulouse, whose count was claimed by King Henry as his vassal. Henry bought La Marche outright in 1177 for nearly £4,000, but with the Poitevin nobles he had little success. Guy of Lusignan, perhaps

---

[1] Apparently King Malcolm himself was to marry Duke Conan's sister, Constance. She told the King of France that she would sooner marry a Frenchman of lower rank than be Queen of Scotland, while Malcolm, for his part, evidently wished to remain celibate. Princess Constance's letter to King Louis is printed in the *Recueil des Historiens des Gaules et de la France*, xvi (1878), 23.

the most prominent among them, actually killed (1168) the English Earl of Salisbury whom Henry had appointed as viceroy, and appears hardly to have suffered for this deed. One factor of Aquitanian politics favoured the English king : if the baronage were chronically insubordinate, they were also as chronically at feud with the rich merchant towns, especially La Rochelle and Bordeaux, which plied a thriving trade with England. By showing favour to the towns Henry II was able to provide some counterpoise to the rebelliousness of the Poitevin and Gascon nobility. Not surprisingly, his Aquitanian queen Eleanor, beautiful, passionate and strong-willed, a patron of the troubadours, was more skilful than her husband in the management of southern affairs, and her decision to side with their second son Richard (made Duke of Aquitaine in 1172) against the king was a serious blow to Henry's command of the far south.

All these diverse dominions were not only in themselves liable to dismemberment : they were the object of a fairly constant campaign of attrition by the French monarchy. For the Capetian [1] kings of France this was less a matter of aggression than of sheer self-preservation. There was a real danger in the earlier twelfth century that the French monarchy might be engulfed by the great feudatories who were nominally its vassals. We have already seen the extreme independence of Normandy, Brittany and Aquitaine. Flanders, Toulouse, and Barcelona were scarcely in any closer subjection. Even in the Ile de France itself, the district of Paris and the very heart of the French royal demesne, the king was hedged about by the fiefs of Blois and Champagne, which in our period were possessed by a single powerful family. Respect for the ancient crown of France and persistent emphasis upon their feudal rights constituted the French kings' chief hope of survival. They must reassert their control over the outlying provinces or perish.

An independent Normandy was the most imminent danger to the French kingdom. Not only did Normandy control the entire lower part of the River Seine, a major trade route into Paris, but her border fortresses rose only forty miles from the French capital. The crucial area for defence or attack was the Vexin, the district which covered the right bank of the Seine midway between Paris and the sea. Though the River Epte was the recognised boundary between the " Norman " and the " French " Vexin, the whole district was

[1] From their ancestor Hugh " Capet " (987-96).

perpetually in dispute and, with each successive attempt by French and Normans to secure it, was fast becoming an intensively fortified zone that bristled with castles of the most modern description. In 1154, King Louis VII of France was in possession of the whole Vexin, but four years later he unwisely assigned it as dowry for his infant daughter Margaret as soon as she should be old enough to marry, as was arranged, Prince Henry, the English king's eldest son. Still more unwisely, Margaret was placed in her prospective father-in-law's custody, and in 1160, when she was not yet three and the prince barely six, King Henry had them married, thus recovering the Vexin much sooner than the too simple Louis had bargained for. Such a marriage of infants was not usually tolerated by the Church, but quite extraneous causes produced papal approval for the match. The German Emperor, Frederick Barbarossa, ambitious to revive a western Roman Empire and bent upon the conquest of Italy, was determined to establish a line of popes amenable to his policy. In 1159, on Pope Adrian IV's death, Frederick flagrantly intruded his own candidate against the majority vote of the cardinals for the anti-Imperial Alexander III. Alexander had to flee to France, and his approval of Henry II's piece of sharp practice was given in return for the king's recognition that he was the rightful Pope. The recovery of the Vexin was thus a minute but not trivial consequence of great events.

The year before he won back the Vexin, Henry II made a great effort to subdue the Count of Toulouse, his most powerul south-eastern neighbour. A large army was led south, but King Louis, with only a few troops and showing surprising promptitude, entered Toulouse in person. The English king, who feared the bad example to his own vassals if he attacked his feudal superior directly, was forced to retire baffled. Fourteen years later, however, in 1173, the Count of Toulouse voluntarily gave his homage to King Henry in return for arbitration in a dispute with Barcelona.

Breton fears of Angevin domination began to be realised in 1158, when a succession dispute of ten years' standing had split the duchy into rival factions. Henry II, ostensibly acting in the Count of Anjou's capacity of " Seneschal of France ", took possession of Lower Brittany, the district round the mouth of the Loire, and then arranged a marriage between Duke Conan's only child Constance and his own third son Geoffrey. The westerly, more completely Celtic parts of

Brittany exchanged Conan for a leader of tougher fibre. Summer campaigns in 1166 and 1167 made little impression, but in 1168 the king pushed far into the west and forced the Breton nobles (1169) to recognise Geoffrey as heir to the dukedom or county, which he held from 1171 to 1186.

This steady success of Henry's efforts to hold his continental empire together, for which credit should be given both to his state-craft and his demonic energy, was paralleled in his relations with Scotland and Ireland, but was strikingly absent in regard to Wales. One result of the civil war in England was a major reversal of the Anglo-Norman penetration of Wales which began under the Con-queror. Two outstanding Welsh princes, in the north Owain, son of Gruffydd ap Cynan, known from his territory as Owain Gwynedd, in the south Rhys ap Gruffydd, grandson of Rhys ap Tewdwr, had succeeded between them in re-establishing an unchallenged native power almost throughout Wales. To Henry II, the independence of Gwynedd and Deheubarth, whose rulers had done homage to his grandfather, was an affront to the dignity of the Crown, quite apart from its potential military danger. The first English expedition occupied July and August of 1157. The king was lucky to escape from an ambush near Basingwerk (Flintshire), but he forced Owain Gwynedd to do him homage, and he restored the English frontier to the Clwyd at Rhuddlan, whose castle he strengthened. In 1165, however, a second and larger expedition, intended to put down a serious revolt, proved an ignominious failure. Owain emerged as powerful as ever, while in the south Rhys ap Gruffydd pinned down the Anglo-Norman settlers to tiny coastal pockets. Henry, indeed, came to terms with Rhys, acknowledged his power in Deheubarth, and was rewarded by a loyalty on Rhys's part which lasted until the king's death.

The setbacks encountered by the Anglo-Normans in South Wales go far to explain the conquest of Ireland (1171-2), which may be called the culminating point of Henry's successful imperialism. Whether because her efforts to fight off Scandinavian invaders had left her exhausted, or whether from deeper, more unfathomable causes, Ireland in the eleventh and twelfth centuries had tended not towards the unified monarchical government developed in England and developing in Scotland, but away from it, in the direction of chronic anarchy and tribal war. The Norman and Angevin kings spoke of conquest but were too busy to undertake it. The reforming section of the Church, however, especially the Papacy itself, was keenly interested in Ireland. In 1152, a papal legate convened at Kells a representative council of the Irish Church which saw established a system of archdioceses and dioceses and sanctioned much-needed reforms in the faith and conduct of the Irish clergy. It was, in fact, for ecclesiastical reasons that the Pope in 1155 gave his approval to a projected conquest of Ireland by Henry II. The project was shelved, and in the upshot it was an accident of Irish domestic strife which precipitated the " Norman " invasion.

In 1166, Dermot MacMurrough, King of Leinster, whose seaports were in regular contact with those of western England, was driven out of Ireland by the " High King ", Rory O'Connor of Connacht, acting in support of a sub-king of Brefni whose wife Dermot had previously abducted. Dermot was welcomed at Bristol and asked help from Henry II, who issued a general licence for any of his subjects to go to Dermot's aid if they wished. Dermot quickly found subjects who did so wish among the restless and frustrated Anglo-Norman and Flemish settlers of South Wales, perhaps the last stronghold of the pure Norman type of military adventurer so common in the previous century. Robert fitz Stephen and Maurice fitz Gerald (both sons of Nesta, the beautiful but promiscuous daughter of Rhys ap Tewdwr), and greater still their lord Richard of Clare (" Strongbow "), Earl of Pembroke, crossed in turn to Leinster (1169-70), overran much of the country, and captured Dublin against the disunited opposition of the Irish and the half-Scandinavian, half-Gaelic " Ostmen " whose ancestors had founded the trading towns of the Irish coast. Strongbow established himself as prospective King of Leinster by marrying Dermot's daughter Eva. Dermot, having thus sown the dragon's teeth, died in 1171, but not before Henry II, disturbed at this winning of kingdoms by his own tenants-in-chief, had forbidden further reinforcements and ordered the conquerors home. Strongbow obediently surrendered his newly-won lands to the king, who in the autumn of 1171 made the passage to Waterford himself with an impressive army of knights and mercenaries.

Henry took possession of the coastal towns, of which Dublin was already the most considerable, and granted the rest of Leinster to Strongbow for knight-service. During his six months' sojourn in

Ireland the kings and chiefs of the southern half of the country submitted to his overlordship, as did, perhaps more sincerely, the leaders of the Irish Church. In 1177, Henry granted the lordship of Ireland to John, his almost landless youngest son, then but ten years old. John was sent to Ireland eight years later for his first taste of government. The episode was a signal failure. Its tone was set at the beginning by the famous incident in which some of John's youthful companions, sniggering at the long beards of the Irish chiefs who had come to give their homage, gave them a disrespectful tug, " none too becomingly ", to quote the understatement of an eye-witness. John had to be recalled, but there were able deputies to rule and administer for him. Although for the rest of our period only a part of Ireland, Leinster, Meath and eastern Munster and Ulster, was actually governed by the English Crown, through its Justiciar and the feudal settlers, the authority of Henry II and his sons was remarkably effective. Many institutions of the Anglo-Norman state were set up in Ireland, and on the whole the conquered districts enjoyed well over a century of good government.

If it was difficult for Henry II to keep his empire together in his own lifetime, he found it still harder to know how best to dispose of it after his death. Many sons were usually reckoned a blessing to a medieval king, but Henry Plantagenet was cursed in his offspring. His eldest son and namesake, gay, likeable, feckless and easily influenced, was intended for the English kingdom and the rule of Normandy and Anjou. He was, after the French manner, crowned king in his father's lifetime, first, as we have seen, in 1170 and for a second time, because of the Becket affair, in 1172. But even then he was only seventeen, and his father had no mind to entrust him with any real political power, still less to see his younger son, Richard, whom he had had enthroned as Duke of Aquitaine in the same year, actually trying to govern that unruly province. The boys chafed at their tutelage, and though they were powerless the king reckoned without their mother, infuriated by Henry's persistent infidelity, and King Louis of France, longing for an opportunity to retake the Vexin, if not to annex the whole of Normandy. In the spring of 1173 the queen and the young princes, supported by the King of France and the Count of Flanders, plotted a grand revolt. Casting about for a third force to enter the conspiracy, Louis remembered the King of Scots, William the Lion, who felt sorely aggrieved that Henry II had failed to honour his promise of 1149 [1] regarding the northern counties. Far from leaving the Scots in possession, Henry had compelled Malcolm IV in 1157 to surrender Carlisle and Northumberland, of which William had up to then been earl. A Scottish knight-hospitaller was sent to Henry to raise the matter again. He returned with the answer that the English king did not fear his enemies and would grant no increase of land to the King of Scots, whom, he said, he took to be a sensible man, not a child. William was in fact thirty, in the prime of life, ardent to prove his knightly prowess. Against the better judgment of his native counsellors, the earls of Fife and Lothian, he let himself be persuaded into war by the young Norman and Flemish hotheads at his court, and also by the younger Henry's promise of Northumberland.

The revolt of 1173 was the most serious challenge which the English Crown had faced since the civil war.[2] Three of the greatest earls, Chester, Leicester, and Norfolk, and a powerful minority of barons came out in support of the young king, and if their risings had been co-ordinated with the attacks from France, Flanders, and Scotland, Henry II's position would have been critical. The movement was not, however, a " feudal " revolt, with the baronage on one side and the king and the non-feudal classes on the other. A long schedule of Henry's supporters drawn up at the time includes, along with all the English bishops, nine earls and many barons of middle rank. It is true that the towns and the peasantry fought the rebels with zest. The Londoners rejected the young Henry's advances, the burgesses of Dunwich in Suffolk told the Earl of Leicester " they did not feel a pennyworth of fear for him ", and it was peasants of north-east Nottinghamshire who captured the Yorkshire rebel Robert Mowbray. But the king's cause would hardly have triumphed in England had it not been for the energetic measures taken by the loyal Justiciar, Richard de Lucy, his colleague Rannulf Glanvill, and the Constable, Humphrey de Bohun, not to speak of the resolute loyalty of the barons of Northumbria.

The first phase of the revolt consisted of attacks on Normandy, in the north-east by the Count of Flanders, at Verneuil by King

---

[1] See above, p. 120.
[2] For the topography of the revolt, see Map V, p. 164.

Louis. Both came to nought, while in August a rising in Brittany led by the Earl of Chester collapsed with the surrender of the chief rebels at Dol. When his peace-terms were then rejected, King Henry moved to Anjou and subdued the revolt there. Meanwhile the Earl of Leicester and a band of Flemish weavers landed in Suffolk, and, failing to take Dunwich, were marching towards the earl's town of Leicester, when they were set upon at Fornham St. Genevieve (near Bury St. Edmunds) by the knights of Humphrey de Bohun and the local country people. The earl and his wife were taken prisoner, the Flemings were massacred. The King of Scotland then entered the stage, gathering so great a host of " naked men " as had not been seen in England since 1138. He also had many knights and some Flemish siege engineers who failed, however, to reduce the vitally important castles of Carlisle and Wark,[1] though Appleby and Brough were captured. It is probably significant that while the Norman baronage of the north remained loyal to King Henry, at least two prominent Northumbrians of English race went over to the Scottish king.

The Justiciar and Constable arranged a truce for the winter, but early in 1174 the pattern of rebellion was repeated. Another force of Flemings landed in Suffolk and led by the Earl of Norfolk seized Norwich, while the Scots again invaded Northumberland. The threat was so grave that in July Henry himself crossed to England and after public penance at Canterbury for Becket's murder moved to Westminster to direct operations. He had just retired to bed on the evening of his arrival when a messenger who had ridden for three days without sleep brought the news that William the Lion and many of his barons had been captured at Alnwick. Early in July the Scots king, having failed in the previous months to take the strongest castles in the north, had dismissed his main army to plunder the countryside, and with a small company of knights was waiting at Alnwick, preparing to besiege the castle when the army returned. There on July 13th the barons of Yorkshire, under Rannulf Glanvill, surprised him at dinner,[2] and after a brief fight took him prisoner.

---

[1] The layman's readiness to laugh at the expert showed itself at the siege of Wark, when a knight among the besiegers was nearly killed by one of the siege engines of his own side. " Much must he have hated the engineer who engineered that one for him " was the comment of a lively chronicler of the rebellion, who may have seen the incident himself.

[2] Other accounts say the Scots were jousting.

The rebellion now collapsed : the Earl of Norfolk surrendered, and a feeble attempt by the French to take Rouen was easily repulsed. The King of Scots and many prominent Scottish subjects, lay and ecclesiastical, were brought to Normandy, where by the Treaty of Falaise (more precisely Valognes, December 8th, 1174) William the Lion did homage to Henry II for his kingdom, and his barons for their lands, while the Scottish clergy swore, less unequivocally, to render such obedience to the primate of York as ought to be rendered.[1]

The suppression of the rebellion and the subjugation of Scotland were great triumphs for the king, yet the last decade of his reign was a time of mounting disaster. As the royal princes grew up they became more reckless and insubordinate, while their father showed an unhappy bias in his strong dislike of Richard and quite misplaced love for John. The younger Henry, having failed to oust Richard from Aquitaine, died of dysentery in 1183, while his brother Geoffrey of Brittany died equally young in 1186. Their father thought it reasonable that Richard should succeed to England while John should be compensated with Aquitaine. But Richard had no intention of surrendering his duchy. He had ruled it with vigour, and in curbing its rebellious barons had shown the first proofs of the military skill which was to make him famous. A change of king in France made it easier for Richard to resist his father. Louis VII died in 1180, and the son who succeeded him, a boy of fifteen at his accession, was soon to show himself the shrewdest, most calculating, and yet withal the most successful and admired king of his time in western Europe.

Philip II—" Philip Augustus " as his biographer called him in tribute to a greatness which no one has since denied—took a cool and methodical advantage of the squalid family quarrels which marred the last few years of Henry II's life. He entered into military alliances with Henry's rebellious sons, and received their direct homage for lands which, strictly speaking, they held only of their father. When, on the other hand, they did the French Crown an injury, Philip took pains to call the father to account, holding him responsible for the transgressions of his children. When the

[1] Under the treaty English garrisons were placed in the Scottish castles of Edinburgh, Roxburgh, and Berwick. Edinburgh was restored to Scottish control in 1186 when King William married the bride provided for him by Henry II, Ermengarde of Beaumont.

younger Henry died without a son, the Vexin once more became a bone of contention. As the dowry of the Princess Margaret it should have reverted to the French crown, but Henry II refused to give it up, proposing instead a similar marriage settlement between Richard and Margaret's sister Alice, which, however, he failed to implement. The Vexin was to be the key area in what became a grim struggle between Richard and Philip Augustus. But before this broke out, a temporary alliance between the two, formed in the autumn of 1188, had brought Henry II's life and reign to a humiliating close. By a rapid campaign in the following summer the allies deprived King Henry of the Loire provinces, and forced him to submit to the stringent terms of surrender dictated by King Philip. Though still only fifty-six, King Henry had been for some time in the throes of a serious fever ; the knowledge that his favourite son John had gone over to his enemies took away his will to live, and shortly after his submission he died (July 6th, 1189), consoled in some degree by the love and loyalty of his illegitimate son Geoffrey, then Chancellor and soon to become, as his father intended, Archbishop of York.

CHAPTER XII

THE LOSS OF NORMANDY

THE turn of the twelfth and thirteenth centuries in England presents two curious paradoxes. First, a period of over twenty years of strong, and in the main remarkably efficient, government ends in a powerful and ordered protest against the activities of the Crown and in the production of the most famous document of English constitutional history. Secondly, the " Channel State ", built up by Henry Plantagenet on the foundation laid by Henry I, collapses abruptly and unexpectedly. The political merging of the English kingdom within a continental feudal empire, which had appeared to be successful under Henry II, was not only terminated by the military defeat of his youngest son John ; it was thwarted by the growth of an English isolationism among the French-speaking aristocracy of England whose origins and cultural affinities lay south of the Channel. The events which led to the break-up of the Angevin empire and to Magna Carta were in fact closely connected ; but it will be as well for us to examine the two processes separately, taking first the military and dynastic struggle between the Angevins and the Capetians, and reserving for the next chapter a study of England in the years before the Great Charter.

If the collapse of the Channel State was important for England, for France it was fundamental. The student of English history should never forget that what he calls the loss of Normandy by the English kings was also the deliberate winning of Normandy by the monarchy of France. It was the intentional victory of an extraordinarily able ruler, Philip Augustus, who seldom allowed himself or his resources to be deflected from the single-minded pursuit of a definite policy, the reduction of Angevin power in Gaul. Nevertheless, when ·Richard of Aquitaine succeeded his father as King of England in 1189, the integrity of the Angevin empire hardly seemed to be in doubt. It is true that through Richard's own treachery Philip Augustus had gained a footing on Angevin soil, but he must have realised that Richard would never tolerate this encroachment once he had become an independent ruler. Moreover, Richard was not only his superior in military ability, but could also match him in diplomacy. Only one factor of overriding importance told in the French king's favour : the crusade.

Two years before Henry II's death, the Kurdish soldier Saladin, who had made himself ruler (1174) of both Syria and Egypt, succeeded in recapturing Jerusalem for the Islamic world. The effect of this disaster on the Christian states of western Europe was instantaneous. Within two years the Emperor of Germany himself set off for the Holy Land at the head of an army, while King Henry of England and King Philip of France were both compelled, perhaps somewhat reluctantly, to take the vows of a crusader. But where his father had hung back, Richard I by contrast was all eagerness to bend his energies wholeheartedly upon the crusade. He was prepared to consider every device for raising troops and money, and regarded his kingdom merely as a source of supply. " If I could find a suitable buyer I would sell London itself ", he is said to have told his courtiers. He certainly sold offices such as justiciarships and shrievalties, sometimes for large sums, and one of his first acts was to release the King of Scotland from the vassalage to which the Treaty of Falaise had subjected him in return for the payment of 10,000 marks.[1] Most significantly of all from the standpoint of his continental empire, Richard was ready to pay in money and land for the company of Philip Augustus on the expedition to Palestine, not merely for the sake of his military co-operation but quite as much to ensure that he could not try to filch some Angevin territory while Richard's back was turned. By an arrangement at Gisors in the Vexin (July, 1189), Richard for the moment yielded Auvergne and part of the adjacent district of Berri and promised to pay a huge indemnity, really a bribe, of 24,000 marks. It was settled that the two kings should leave together for the east in April, 1190.

Richard spent the autumn in England and the winter in Normandy and Anjou making ready for the great enterprise. He had a fleet of unprecedented size assembled from many English and continental ports, chiefly consisting of merchant vessels, and with him in the army went a considerable number of the barons and knights of England. But his arrangements for the government of

---

[1] A mark, much used in reckoning payments and accounts though not represented by any coin, was worth 13s. 4d., or two-thirds of a pound.

the realm during his absence were confused and imprudent. The biggest problem was presented by his irresponsible and ambitious brother John, now twenty-two years old. Richard was as yet unmarried, and in his view the heir presumptive to the English throne was not John but Arthur of Brittany, the three-year-old son of their brother Geoffrey. It was widely believed that the king would never return from the crusade alive, and John was determined that he and not Arthur should succeed his brother. It would probably have been better for Richard to have taken John with him, but perhaps it was thought that for both adult members of the royal family to risk their lives thus would have endangered the kingdom. It was, however, scarcely less perilous for Richard personally to leave John at home as he did, in possession of the senior Norman county of Mortain, newly-married to an heiress of the great earldom of Gloucester, and holding, independently of the royal administration, the English shires of Nottingham, Derby, Devon, Cornwall, Somerset and Dorset, together with five important castles and four rich " honours ". Having given his brother this generous slice of landed wealth and political and military power,[1] Richard then excluded him from the government and even tried, unsuccessfully, to keep him out of England altogether. The administration was placed in the hands of a committee of justiciars. While the king dismissed the old chief justiciar, Rannulf Glanvill (who went on crusade and died in Palestine), he failed to make clear who was to have pre-eminence in his stead. At first the Bishop of Durham, Hugh du Puiset, and the Earl of Essex, William de Mandeville, shared the leading position, but three months after the earl's death Hugh was replaced by the king's Chancellor, William of Longchamps, Bishop of Ely (March, 1190). The change was more than an administrative convenience: it involved the clash of incompatible personalities. Hugh du Puiset had ruled the see of Durham since the end of Stephen's reign: he was a great-grandson of William the Conqueror, an elderly, cultured nobleman who could look back on a lifetime's enjoyment of wealth and political influence. William of Longchamps, on the other hand, belonged by birth to the petty official class of Normandy. He had worked his way up in Richard's service to the high positions of chancellor and bishop, but he remained essentially Richard's creature. The leading men in England resented his bumptiousness, feared his

[1] We should note that John retained his lordship of Ireland.

ambition, and made fun of his squat and ugly appearance. The clergy in particular professed to be shocked at his habit of touring the country with a vast retinue which he billeted on abbeys that could ill afford the burden. It was thought a proof of his arrogance that he issued acts of government under his own personal seal instead of using the duplicate royal seal (the " exchequer seal ") which the king had left behind for the authorisation of royal precepts. Yet Longchamps retained the king's confidence, and there is no question that he was both a loyal and a capable servant of the Crown.

Even before he was made chief justiciar Longchamps had decided to show his colleagues who was master of England. He ousted Hugh du Puiset from the Exchequer and deprived him of the shrievalty of Northumberland. The king tried to compensate Bishop Hugh by appointing him justiciar north of the Humber, but far from allowing him to exercise this office Longchamps actually brought him to London under arrest, made him surrender his castles and some hostages for good behaviour, and then confined him as a prisoner in his own palace at Howden. Through the king's influence Longchamps obtained the office of papal legate in England. Since the Archbishop of Canterbury went on crusade and died before the end of the year, while the newly-elected Archbishop of York, the king's half-brother Geoffrey, was not yet consecrated and was banned from England by the king's wish, Longchamps's position was supreme in both Church and State, resembling that of Thomas Wolsey under Henry VIII. He overawed his fellow-justiciars, of whom the most important were William the Marshal,[1] occasionally styled earl (in right of his wife who was Strongbow's daughter and heir), and Geoffrey fitz Peter, a protégé of Rannulf Glanvill and a professional judge and administrator.

He was, nevertheless, in a difficult position. The mere fact that he was Richard's loyal servant made him an enemy of Count John, and as it seemed more than likely that John would soon try to step into his brother's shoes, Longchamps naturally felt he must strengthen his defences militarily and diplomatically. He asked the King of Scotland to be ready to support the claims of Arthur of Brittany, whose grandmother Margaret, still living, was King William's sister.

[1] He was a younger son of the hereditary Master Marshal, succeeding to the office himself in 1194 on the death of an elder brother. Confirmed in the earldom of Pembroke in 1199, he is usually known simply as William the Marshal.

He fortified Windsor, Dover, and the Tower of London. But he could not prevent John from seizing the two important north-midland castles of Nottingham and Tickhill, or eject one of John's supporters, Gerard de Camville, from the equally important castle of Lincoln. An open struggle was imminent in the summer of 1191 when an impartial agent of the king, Walter of Coutances, Archbishop of Rouen, arrived from the Mediterranean with authority to super-sede Longchamps as chief justiciar if he felt it necessary. Arch-bishop Walter was not a dominant personality, but he made a good committee chairman. He temporarily patched up the quarrel be-tween Longchamps and Count John, and it seems likely that he and the other justiciars would have succeeded in maintaining John's exclusion from government had not Longchamps overreached him-self by a foolish outrage.

Archbishop Geoffrey of York, having at last been consecrated in August, 1191, landed at Dover in defiance of the express orders of Longchamps, who seems on this point to have been carrying out the king's wishes. But there was little excuse for the rough manner in which Longchamps's agents dragged the archbishop out of sanc-tuary and threw him into jail. Count John seized his opportunity. Placing himself at the head of a " popular " movement of protest against the high-handedness of the chief justiciar, he drew over to his side the moderate men in the government, including William the Marshal and Geoffrey fitz Peter. Longchamps now took fright and ordered Archbishop Geoffrey to be released, but it was too late. At a Council held at St. Paul's on October 8th, without, of course, the king's authority but with the full participation of the Archbishop of Rouen and the other justiciars, Longchamps was deposed and exiled and the Archbishop of Rouen appointed in his place. The way was now open for John to put himself in an impregnable position. He took over the castles of Windsor and Wallingford, and in 1192, when the King of France had returned abruptly from the crusade to annex part of the county of Flanders, he began treasonable negotiations with him regarding the future of Richard's continental empire. The one thing John still lacked was news of his brother's death; but when news did come, early in 1193, it told a different and entirely unexpected tale. The king was still alive, but he had fallen into the hands of his enemy, the Duke of Austria, and was being held captive by him and his overlord the Emperor in the heart of Germany.

Richard had journeyed overland to Marseilles in July, 1190, and had sailed thence to Messina in Sicily ahead of his fleet, which had to make the long passage by way of Gibraltar. Messina was Richard's rendezvous with Philip Augustus (September), but instead of proceeding at once to Palestine, the two kings wintered in Sicily. Richard waited to be joined by his mother Queen Eleanor, who was making a leisurely traverse of Italy bringing with her the king's prospective bride, Berengaria, daughter of King Sancho of Navarre. It was during his stay at Messina that Richard entered into the alliance which made the German emperor his enemy. It will help us to understand this complex situation if we consider two marriages arranged by Henry II for his daughters Maud and Joan. In 1168, in token of Anglo-German alliance, Maud had been married to Henry " the Lion ", head of the powerful German family of Welf, duke of Saxony and Bavaria, and at that time on friendly terms with the Emperor Frederick Barbarossa. Long before Richard's accession, however, the Welfs had become bitterly hostile to the Hohenstaufen family which Barbarossa represented, and when Barbarossa himself was accidentally drowned in Asia Minor on his way to the Holy Land (June, 1190), his son, who succeeded as the Emperor Henry VI, already regarded the King of England as an enemy. Again, in 1177, Henry II had given his daughter Joan in marriage to King William II of Sicily, a Norman kingdom of the far south with which Norman England had many connections. The Hohenstaufen emperors were anxious to gain control of both Italy and Sicily, and Henry VI married a Sicilian princess who, on King William's death in 1189, ought to have inherited his throne. The Sicilian nobles, however, chose as king one of their own number, Tancred of Lecce. One of Richard's first tasks on arriving at Messina was to compel King Tancred to allow his sister Joan her proper dower, i.e. her portion as King William's widow. As part of his settlement with Tancred, Richard declared that Arthur of Brittany should be heir presumptive to the English throne, and should marry one of Tancred's daughters. The result of this treaty was to confirm Count John in his treachery and give mortal offence to the German emperor and his followers, since it involved the recognition of Tancred who in their eyes was a usurper. When Richard finally sailed for the east in April, 1191, he had made sure of rebellion behind him and hostility ahead, for the German crusaders who had pushed on to

Palestine after Barbarossa's death were naturally supporters of the Hohenstaufen. This inauspicious start was lightened only by the brilliant navigation which brought the fleet through the eastern Mediterranean, and by Richard's marriage to Berengaria of Navarre on the island of Cyprus, which he had turned aside to conquer.

The long voyage had shown something of Richard's outstanding powers of leadership. As soon as he arrived in Palestine (June, 1191), the excellence of his generalship became equally apparent. The town of Acre, a key sea-port of the Levant coast, was recaptured in July, and on September 7th a lightning victory at Arsuf put Richard in possession of Jaffa, some miles to the south. The crusaders, however, were hopelessly disunited. Apart from the quarrels among the three main western contingents there was a fundamental cleavage of outlook and method between the westerners as a whole and the resident Christians, descendants of the earlier crusaders who had founded the Frankish kingdoms of the Levant. Philip Augustus abandoned the crusade altogether after a few months and returned to France. The Germans and such of the French as were left were so deeply embroiled in the question of who was rightful King of Jerusalem that they seem almost to have forgotten that Jerusalem itself had still to be recaptured. Richard, hampered as much by friend as by foe, did make some effort in this direction, but he can hardly be blamed for deciding that negotiations with Saladin would probably be more fruitful than a military campaign. At one point he even suggested that his sister Joan (who had accompanied him to the Holy Land) should marry Saladin's brother Safadin, with whom Richard was on excellent terms. Queen Joan became extremely angry when she heard of this proposal, but Richard blandly reported to the Muslim leader that " the difficulty might be got over if Safadin would become a Christian ".[1] Finally, in September, 1192, after a year's ineffectual skirmishing, Richard and Saladin concluded a three-year truce which gave the Christians peaceful possession of a thin belt of coastal territory and the right of access to Jerusalem for pilgrims to the Holy Places. It was not the glorious achievement on which Richard had originally set his heart, but every circumstance of dynastic quarrel, disunity of command, climate and disease had combined against him. The news that Count John and Philip Augustus were conspiring to seize his kingdom

[1] L. Landon, *Itinerary of Richard I* (1935), 57.

and empire prompted him to leave for home in the following month. Because of French hostility, he sailed by way of the Adriatic, where a storm drove him ashore east of Venice. After reaching Vienna *incognito* [1] he was discovered by men of the Duke of Austria and taken prisoner (December, 1192).

Richard remained in captivity for over a year while the Emperor Henry VI (as his captor's overlord) drew what profit he could from this precious windfall. He needed money, and England was a rich country. He needed an ally against Philip of France and Tancred of Sicily. If Richard refused to abandon Tancred and to authorise the ransom fixed, the Emperor could threaten to hand him over to King Philip, his mortal enemy. The terms finally agreed on were hard. The ransom was to be 150,000 marks (two-thirds to the Emperor, the rest to the Duke of Austria [2]), the hostages to be handed over to ensure its payment included Richard's young Welf nephews, Otto and William, sons of Henry the Lion, and Richard himself was to surrender his kingdom to the Emperor and receive it back as a fief. Throughout this trying period the king was served well and loyally. A treacherous attack on Normandy launched by Philip Augustus as soon as he heard of Richard's capture was beaten off by the Earl of Leicester. At home, the justiciars and Queen Eleanor made everyone take a special oath of allegiance to the king, placed the country in a state of defence, and then (greatest triumph of all) raised an unprecedentedly large tax with which to pay off the ransom, an aid of £1 on every knight's fee and a levy from the whole population of no less than 25 per cent. of the value of income and chattels. In the next chapter, we shall see something of the career of the man who as chief negotiator of the ransom now came to prominence in the government, Hubert Walter, whom Richard, while still in Germany, rewarded with the archbishopric of Canterbury.

King Richard returned to England in March, 1194, and began to prepare almost at once for the warfare with Philip Augustus which was to last for the remainder of his reign. At Winchester on April 17th he underwent a second coronation, " to wash away the shame of his captivity " and cancel the surrender of the kingdom. Less

---

[1] It has been suggested that Richard was trying to reach Hungary, whose king was friendly ; but the movements and motives of Richard in this period are in fact mysterious.

[2] Not all the ransom money was paid, and Duke Leopold had received only 4,000 marks before he died.

than a month later, he was in Normandy, never to return to England. The next five years was a period of fierce border skirmishes and castle sieges, punctuated by impermanent truces (Tillières, 1194-5; Louviers, January-June, 1196). The points at which Philip Augustus harried Angevin territory with most vigour were the Vexin and the district of Berri, possession of whose castles would open the way to Normandy and Aquitaine respectively. The French had the advantage of interior lines, but Richard was more than a match for his opponent in the field. Two events stand out from the confused welter of siege and counter-siege plot and counter-plot. In 1196 the leading men of western Brittany, fearing Anjou more than France, met Richard's demand for the custody of his nephew and heir Arthur by handing him over to King Philip. This act extinguished any serious claim Arthur might have had to the English throne, and, since Richard and Berengaria had no children, greatly improved the prospects of John, whose past treachery Richard, with characteristic generosity, had agreed to forget. The other event was the building of Château Gaillard, the " saucy castle ". At the confluence of the little river Gambon with the Seine, well within the Norman Vexin, the Archbishop of Rouen possessed the estate of Andely, which included a perfect site for fortification, an isolated rock overlooking the river. During the fighting for Normandy, the kings of France and England had both trespassed on Andely, and Archbishop Walter, loyal as he was to Richard, stoutly resisted this encroachment on his property. Nevertheless, in the autumn of 1196 Richard began to construct on the rock the largest and strongest castle yet known in the west, whose nickname was doubtless due to its being built in brazen defiance of the King of France and the Church of Normandy. A year later the archbishop was bought off by a grant of the valuable port of Dieppe and other property.

Castle building in the twelfth century was so much in advance of siegecraft that Château Gaillard would be impregnable in ordinary circumstances. With it and the other Vexin castles as his base, Richard was easily able to repulse French attacks in 1197 and 1198. At the same time he threatened Philip Augustus with encirclement by means of skilful diplomacy. He offered subsidies to the emperor's vassal rulers who controlled the principalities on the north-eastern borders of France, Holland, Brabant, Hainault, and Limburg. Better still, the counts of Flanders and Boulogne, who were strictly

King Philip's vassals, switched their allegiance to Richard in 1197. One of his Welf nephews became Count-Palatine of the Rhine, and Richard's own relations with the Emperor grew more cordial. On the southern border of Aquitaine, Navarre and Toulouse were bound to him by marriage alliances. And then in 1199 Richard was killed, as William Rufus had been killed a hundred years before, violently and unexpectedly, at the very height of his fame and power. A ploughman at Châluz in the Limousin had unearthed an ancient treasure of gold. His lord took possession of it and, when the king heard of the find and pressed his right to " treasure trove ",[1] refused to give it up. Richard impetuously besieged the castle of his disobedient vassal—as, on his way to the crusade, he had stormed a town in Provence whose inhabitants had jeered at the crusaders, or had conquered Cyprus because of the unfriendly attitude of its ruler Isaac Comnenus. Under the walls of Châluz an unlucky shot from a cross-bow gave him a wound which turned gangrenous, and on April 6th he died.

The balance of strength between France and the Angevin empire shifted at once in Philip's favour. Despite Richard's declared preference for John, there were two claimants to the throne of England and the continental fiefs. If John were preferred to Arthur in both Normandy and England (largely owing to the prompt support of Hubert Walter, William the Marshal, and, it is said, of William of Briouze, an Anglo-Norman baron who was in the confidence of the late king and with him when he died), he was preferred as the lesser of two evils, not as the welcome successor of Richard the Lion Heart. For all that, John acted at first wisely and promptly. From Brittany (where, oddly enough, he was staying with Arthur) he rode to Chinon to seize the Angevin treasure, and then on to Rouen to be installed as Duke of Normandy—all within three weeks. A month later he was in England and on May 27th was crowned at Westminster by Archbishop Hubert Walter. Meanwhile, his mother, Queen Eleanor, anxious as ever lest her duchy of Aquitaine fall into French hands, had herself taken the homage of its lords on John's behalf. But the barons of the Loire provinces between Normandy and Aquitaine, and of course the Bretons also, declared for Arthur, and in this region John was left only with the two castles of Chinon

---

[1] Literally, "found treasure". In England it belonged to the king, but the rule regarding treasure trove in Aquitaine may have been uncertain.

and Loches, which were guarded by the Seneschal of Anjou, a Kentish baron named Robert of Thornham. By the time John was back in Normandy, Philip Augustus had received Arthur's homage for all the Angevin lands south of the channel, and declared Normandy forfeit because John had taken possession of the duchy without obtaining Philip's permission first. This was, of course, a wholly new though strictly legal argument; so was the demand that John should pay a relief of 20,000 marks. John's weakness compelled him to yield to these aggressive innovations, and at Le Goulet (May, 1200) he not only agreed to pay the relief but surrendered the whole Norman Vexin, except Château Gaillard, and the neighbouring county of Evreux as well.

The scene now shifts to Aquitaine. Here, too, Philip Augustus had been patiently whittling away the solid block of Angevin territories. The key castles of Berri had been handed over to him under the treaty of Le Goulet, and a few months later John himself took a step which gave the French king a perfect occasion for interference in Poitou, the district between Berri and the sea. The two leading baronial families of northern Aquitaine, the counts of Angoulême and the lords of Lusignan, both claimed the county of La Marche, in spite of its sale to Henry II in 1177. To forestall a dangerous marriage alliance between these unruly feudatories whose mutual enmity was to his own advantage, King John himself took to wife [1] Isabel, the child heiress of the Count of Angoulême (August, 1200), much to the fury of the Lusignans to whose chief she was already betrothed. After further provocation, they appealed to Philip Augustus, who ordered John to appear in his court to answer the complaint and, when John naturally refused, sentenced him to lose all the lands which he held of the French Crown (April 30th, 1202), proposing to transfer most of them to Arthur of Brittany.

The war which followed this second sentence was begun by John with a stroke of great boldness and resolution. While at Le Mans in July, 1202, he learned that Arthur and his chief supporters, including the Lusignans, were besieging the old Queen Eleanor (she was nearly eighty) in the castle of Mirebeau in Poitou, eighty miles to the southward. The king and his small band of mercenaries covered

---

[1] His marriage to Isabel of Gloucester, by which there were no children, was dissolved in 1199 on grounds of consanguinity; John and Isabel were both great-grandchildren of Henry I.

this distance inside two days, a truly astonishing feat, well worthy of his father and brother whose capacity for swift movement had filled their enemies with dismay or terror. Arthur and his knights had already gained a lodgment in the castle bailey and were besieging Eleanor in the keep. It proved possible for John's men to carry one gate into the bailey by storm, and, taken utterly by surprise as they were, the besiegers could make only an ineffective resistance. Arthur himself and over 200 barons and knights of Poitou, Brittany and the Loire provinces were captured and despatched to some of the king's strongest castles, Chinon, Rouen, Corfe in Dorset, and Bristol. At one blow, John had put out of action a rival whose nuisance value for Philip of France was very considerable. He had taken alive a number of well-connected noblemen who could be ransomed for a substantial sum. Yet it was precisely at this moment of initial triumph that everything began to go wrong for the King of England. To be on the crest of victory seemed to bring out the worst in John's variable character quite as emphatically as it was later to be brought out when he was in the trough of defeat.

John's relief of Mirebeau had owed much to the counsel and co-operation of the Angevin William des Roches, who had taken Arthur's side in 1199 but had joined John a year later and been appointed Seneschal of Anjou. William was no mere royal agent but a baron powerful in his own right. Yet the advice which he gave the king to treat his prisoners decently, and his well-founded claim that nothing should be done with Arthur without his being consulted, were blatantly ignored. The less valuable prisoners were coldly starved to death, while the dangerous Lusignans were released for ransom without sufficient safeguards. The young Prince Arthur, fifteen years old, seems to have been immured at Falaise and Rouen for nine months and then murdered in secret, it is thought by the king's own hand. In English history, Arthur is almost as dim and legendary a figure as his famous namesake. But for the people of Brittany Arthur was very real and, as his name shows, a symbol of their fiercely resurgent nationalism. Their belief, which spread rapidly after Arthur's capture, that he had been foully done to death filled them with an implacable fury. If the Bretons' certainty of John's guilt were motivated largely by political feeling, the ugly disappearance of Arthur raised enough of a question in other men's minds to cause fairly general disaffection. William des Roches changed sides again and the other barons of the Loire provinces were confirmed in their opposition to John. Philip Augustus was able to take swift advantage of the disloyalty which, not unjustifiably as it seems, dogged John at this time. Two great castles of Normandy, Alençon on the southern border and Vaudreuil on the Seine, were surrendered to the French "before a stone had been cast", the latter, ominously enough, by joint-castellans who were men of more consequence north of the Channel than in Normandy.[1] William du Hommet, the hereditary Constable of Normandy, went over to the French king. The Normans suspected that John had no serious intention of defending the duchy. He spent his time either flitting purposelessly from castle to castle or staying idly at Rouen where he " minded nothing but feasting, luxury, and lying in bed till dinner-time ". He was up early enough, however, on November 14th, 1203, when he slipped away from Bonneville before the court knew he was awake. He made for Barfleur by a devious route, and took ship for Portsmouth early in December. Normandy had seen the last of him. Some of his castles remained loyal, e.g. the massive fortress of Arques in the east and Verneuil in the south. Château Gaillard itself had to bear the brunt of Philip Augustus's onslaught and held out gallantly under Roger de Lacy until March, 1204. But after John's flight the French conquest of Normandy was only a matter of time. Most of the Norman towns gave in without a struggle, and King Philip entered Rouen at midsummer.

Back in England, John began to scheme for the recovery of his French lands with far more concentration than he had ever shown in Normandy. He still held part of Poitou which could make a base for operations. In 1205 a large fleet and army were assembled at Portsmouth ready to sail for La Rochelle ; but opposition to the plan by the English baronage, supported by the king's most influential counsellors, Hubert Walter and William the Marshal, compelled its abandonment. A year later, however, John was able to take a force to Poitou. A brief campaign confirmed his authority over much of Aquitaine, but he was unable to reconquer the Loire provinces, much less strike northward into Normandy. For the next few years, serious troubles at home prevented any exploitation

---

[1] Robert fitz Walter was a great landowner in Hertfordshire and Essex, and his colleague Saer de Quinci besides having estates in Northants, was an important baron of the King of Scotland.

of this small victory, but renewal of the war was never far from John's mind. In 1212 he began, with notable success, to rebuild the system of encircling, offensive alliances which Richard I had employed after 1193. Boulogne, Flanders, Brabant, and Hainault were each brought in by the offer of subsidies. Since 1209 the king's nephew Otto of Saxony had been recognised as Emperor by at least a part of Germany and he was ready to help his uncle by harassing the French from the east. To complete the encirclement, John tried to include the southern powers of Toulouse and Aragon. Unhappily the widespread hold upon the people of this region of an anti-Christian religious movement, the so-called " Albigensian heresy ",[1] had given the French an excuse for a military invasion or " crusade ", and in the autumn of 1213 the Tolosan and Aragonese forces were annihilated at the battle of Muret. It was a year later before John could bring all his diplomatic labours and military preparations to fruition. The campaign of 1214 would, if it had been successful, have altered fundamentally the history of France and England. It consisted of an attack on two fronts, first by the King of England thrusting northward from Poitou, secondly by the Netherlandish princes and the Emperor Otto IV striking south-westward from Hainault. But the attacks were not co-ordinated. In Poitou John at first repeated his success of 1206, and even won over the Lusignan clan. But early in July King Philip's son, Louis, already reputed an able commander, came up with John while he was laying siege to La Roche-aux-Moines, near Angers. The Poitevins deserted and John had to retreat to La Rochelle. The French, having thus taken the measure of one opponent, concentrated all their forces on repelling the Germans and Flemings. The decisive battle was fought (July 27th) at Bouvines, between Lille and Tournai. The two armies were spread out across a hot dusty plain, where the French, preponderant in heavy cavalry, were at a great advantage over the foot soldiers of Flanders. At the end of the day the coalition forces were completely shattered, and scores of prisoners were being led in triumph towards Paris. The King of England stayed on in Poitou until October ; but the Channel State of the Norman and Angevin dynasty, which had first been brought into existence at Tinchebrai in 1106 by another pitched battle, was destroyed for ever.

[1] I.e. the heresy of the *Albigeois*, or inhabitants of Albi, near Toulouse, one of the centres of the movement.

CHAPTER XIII

THE YEARS BEFORE THE CHARTER, 1189–1215

LESS than a generation elapsed between the death of Henry II and the sealing of Magna Carta, and in that brief period the government of England saw the fulfilment of a revolution. The steps by which Henry II restored the authority of royal government, whether wholly innovations like the permanent court at Westminster or the Grand Assize, or new and fruitful developments of older devices, like the Petty Assizes, the strengthening of criminal jurisdiction, and the regular use of itinerant justices, became during the reigns of Richard I and John an accepted, indeed, an indispensable, part of the national life. The king and his agents steadily widened the field of governmental activity, both at the centre and in the local areas. At the beginning of the twelfth century, royal government had amounted to little more than the king and his immediate entourage, continually on the move from one royal castle or manor to another, together with the few trusted servants whom the king might on occasion send into distant parts of the realm to carry out particular commissions. Government, for the ordinary inhabitant of England, meant not this ambulatory royal court or its agents, which came his way only seldom, but rather the rule of his local lord, a lay baron or a prelate of the Church. The meetings of hundred and shire courts might be disturbed now and then by the imposition of a heavy murder fine or a command from the king to do justice to a plaintiff who had gained his ear ; but normally they took their course without royal interference. The sheriff was certainly an important and active figure ; but from the standpoint of the countryside, he was more often than not a powerful private baron with whose administration the king seldom meddled unless he failed to account for the farm of his shire at the Exchequer. Local loyalties were stronger than national, local differences of law and custom almost sacrosanct.

The work of the first Angevin kings and the small group of remarkably able ministers who served them wrought a gradual but decisive change in this picture. In justice, in finance, and in the provision of adequate forces for war and defence, they turned the king's government in this period into the ordinary immediate government of the majority of men and women. To their achievements in these three fields must be added their invention of elaborate new devices by which the business of government was made easier and through which it became possible to increase its scope immensely.

Richard I, because of crusade, captivity and war with France, spent but six months all told in his own kingdom. The royal officers whose duty it was to dispense the king's justice learned to carry on their work without the king. The reforms of Henry II would have been sterile if there had not been a supply of trained men prepared to devote almost their whole time to administering and developing the law. A new phenomenon emerges in this period, the professional judge and legal administrator, trained in the court of Henry II or in the households of his powerful ministers, especially Glanvill. Such were Hubert Walter (Justiciar, 1193-8), who happened to enter the Church and ended by being Archbishop of Canterbury, and Geoffrey fitz Peter (Justiciar, 1198-1213), who happened to remain a layman and ended by being Earl of Essex. They were both Glanvill's pupils, as was their master King John. Hubert, clearly marked out for promotion at an early date, had been made Bishop of Salisbury and had gone on crusade with Richard. He was among the first to seek out the king in his imprisonment, he had been the chief collector and custodian of his ransom, and he became the indispensable right-hand man of both Richard and John. Geoffrey fitz Peter perhaps specialised more in judicial work, but even he led an army against the Welsh in 1198 with brilliant success. The influence of these men, and of those whom they trained, on English legal history is incalculable. " Geoffrey fitz Peter and his colleagues were moulding the Common Law of England, as described by Glanvill, into the form known to us in Bracton.[1] Geoffrey had a favourite clerk, Martin de Pattishall (i.e. of Pattishall, Northants), who was to be the justice most admired by Bracton. These three generations of jurists constructed the Common Law of England." [2] They devised improvements in the final concords and in the writs already

---

[1] Henry of Bracton (Bratton Fleming, Devonshire), royal justice *c.* 1245-68, was author of the greatest medieval work on English law, *The Treatise of the Laws and Customs of England.*

[2] Sidney Painter, *The Reign of King John* (1949), 82.

discussed by which litigants could obtain remedies in the king's court. They invented many more types of writ to meet needs which royal justice had not hitherto satisfied, of which we may mention the important and useful writ called *unde nihil habet* (" whence she has nothing "), by means of which a widow deprived of her rightful dower by her husband's relatives or others could force them to give satisfaction in the king's court.

The judges did their work indiscriminately in the Bench at Westminster (which came later to be called the court of " Common Bench " or " Common Pleas "), in the eyres which took them into every part of England, or, especially in John's reign, in the king's company as he travelled about the realm, holding the court " before the king " (*coram rege*), later known as the court of King's Bench. It must be emphasised that all these occasions were sessions of the *Curia Regis*, for the king's justice was equal and undivided. There was no distinction of personnel, and no sharp distinction of function, between eyre, Bench and *coram rege*, though naturally the justices holding the first two courts often deferred difficult or important cases for final judgment by the king and the great barons, ministerial and feudal, who constituted, *par excellence*, the *Curia Regis*.

Nevertheless, the germs of differentiation were there. We have already seen that the Exchequer, itself merely an aspect of the *Curia Regis* concentrating upon financial affairs, was located at Westminster from early times, and met there in full session twice a year, at Easter and Michaelmas. The Justiciar was presiding officer alike in the Exchequer and the Bench and many of the judges were also barons of the Exchequer. It was natural that Westminster, close to London, with its great hall built by Rufus, its lodgings for royal servants and storage space for records, should be regarded as a genuine administrative centre or even capital. It was equally natural that the institutions which operated there almost continuously should develop their own routine which marked them off from the *Curia Regis* as a whole. In time it was felt that the Bench should be confined to cases between subject and subject, and in 1215 Magna Carta required that such cases, " common pleas ", should not follow the king's court but should be dealt with in a definite place, which came in practice to mean Westminster. This branching out of permanent offshoots of the *Curia Regis* in no way diminished the right and duty of the king and his immediate court to settle any cases affecting the Crown directly or to provide remedies for aggrieved subjects. The judges travelling with the king continued to hold the pleas *coram rege* in the place where the king was, though increasingly rarely in his physical presence.[1] Their court of King's Bench tended to deal with important criminal cases. Many cases of great moment were still reserved for the king and his council personally, and King John in particular took a lively if erratic interest in the working of his courts, sometimes to the annoyance of his clerks,[2] though his participation in judicial matters was probably more stimulating to his judges than Richard I's comparative indifference.

The judicial eyre underwent a like process of differentiation. In the twelfth century, the itinerant justices were maids-of-all-work for the Crown, who might in the course of one tour deal with criminal and civil cases, enquire into royal rights, receive money owed to the king, suppress disturbances or conduct negotiations with the Welsh or the Scots. The judges on the great eyre organised by Hubert Walter in 1194 had to carry out over twenty-five separate instructions. These general eyres continued with increasing unpopularity right through our period. But after 1215 special judges in eyre were appointed to hold the popular Petty Assizes, while other eyres might concentrate on criminal business, " delivering " (i.e. emptying) the jails in which sheriffs had lodged accused persons against the judges' coming. We have fairly full records of several early eyres, e.g. that sent into Cornwall in 1201, when the judges delivering Launceston jail tried four murder cases, a small number when it is remembered that Cornwall had had no eyre for seven years. Either Cornishmen were exceptionally law-abiding, or (as seems all too probable) were exceptionally reluctant to present local bad characters for trial.

The king's justices wherever they functioned continued to work in close co-operation with the sheriffs. Many of the new writs which originated litigation were addressed to the sheriff for action, and the empanelling of juries was his responsibility. But though busier than ever, the sheriff moved to a less dominant position. In 1170 King Henry II, returning from France to find loud complaints

[1] D. M. Stenton, *Pleas before the King and his Justices, 1198-1202* (Selden Society, 1953), i. 100.

[2] Lady Stenton, *op. cit.* 90, cites an instance in 1199 when a clerk commenting on a land case concerning Shepperton wrote, " be it known that this inquest was made by command of the Lord King and not by a judgment of the court or by the custom of the realm ".

against royal officials, had dramatically asserted his authority over the sheriffs by suspending nearly all of them from office and holding a searching enquiry into their conduct, as the result of which twenty-three (out of thirty-five) were dismissed. The sheriffs as an official class never recovered their old predominance. The greater use of itinerant justices and juries diminished their judicial activity, and in 1194 sheriffs were forbidden to act as justices in their own shires. The " guardians of the peace ", already noted, shared the sheriffs' peace-keeping duties. Under Henry II and Richard I other persons (after 1194, three knights and one clerk in each county) were appointed to keep a record of pleas of the Crown and these " coroners ", as they have since been known, developed a preliminary jurisdiction of their own over certain well-defined Crown pleas, unexplained death, wreck and treasure-trove.

Altogether, English justice made great strides forward in the period from 1189 to 1215, in intellectual content, in speediness and availability, in procedure and in administration. It need occasion no surprise that at least thirteen chapters of Magna Carta relate to judicial matters.

The men who were clever and industrious enough to produce a revolution in English justice were extremely fertile in experimenting with new taxation.[1] The words of the Treasurer, Richard fitz Nigel, in his *Dialogue of the Exchequer*, " in the collection of taxes the most up-to-date practice is seldom milder than that of former times ",[2] sound a note of grimly ironical understatement when applied to the fiscal policy of Richard I and John. Not that the Crown normally practised extortion for its own sake. The cost of government was rising sharply. The country was unquestionably rich and prosperous, while the Crown, operating largely on fixed and customary income, was slow to share this prosperity. There were primarily two ways in which the Crown could secure a revenue proportionate to the work it had to do : (1) It could try to tap more of the country's increased wealth at source by augmenting its customary revenues. (2) It could skim the cream of the new prosperity from the surface, by means of extraordinary taxation.

---

[1] The paragraphs which follow owe much to Painter, *The Reign of King John*, chap. iv.

[2] *Dialogue of the Exchequer*, ed. C. Johnson (1950), 50. My translation differs slightly from Mr. Johnson's.

(1) The ancient and regular sources of Crown revenue consisted of the farms of the counties and boroughs, feudal incidents (e.g. reliefs, income from fiefs held in wardship, the sale of marriages of heiresses and widows), profits of justice and various special profits, e.g. from minting coins (almost a royal monopoly), from the tin mines of Devon and Cornwall, the lead mines of Derbyshire and the silver mines of Cumberland, and from forest revenues. The county farms had last been fixed in the middle of the twelfth century and were so much below what the counties could be made to yield that men were willing to pay enormous premiums to have the office of sheriff. Under Richard I and John, therefore, a sheriff was sometimes asked to pay an " increment " over and above his farm. This seems to have been no more than equitable, but in Magna Carta John was made to promise that increments should be discontinued. An alternative method of raising more from the county was not to set it at farm to a sheriff but to assign it to a custodian who instead of rendering an agreed lump sum accounted in detail for each individual item of revenue. John tried out this device from 1204 to 1207. It was not well liked among the class of local administrators ; it was too new-fangled and made too great a demand on their skill in estate management and accounting. John had more success with cities and boroughs. The reason why the earliest charters of so many English towns were issued by Richard I and John is that both these kings readily sold liberties and privileges to townsmen at a high price.

Feudal incidents were of course tolerated by a feudal class whose members depended on them as much as the king. But it is generally agreed that both Richard I and John, especially the latter, exploited their rights in this respect beyond all precedent. In this period, £100 was reckoned a " reasonable " relief for an heir to any but the richest barony to have to pay ; yet in 1214, a year before Magna Carta emphasised, in its second chapter, the promise to ask no more than this figure, a Shropshire baron of middle rank was charged the fantastic relief of 10,000 marks (over £6,600). John also sold the marriages of heiresses and widows in his custody for exorbitant sums.

(2) General taxation, drawing revenue from all classes, was unknown in our period, and is, indeed, a comparatively modern phenomenon. The nearest approach to it was the Danegeld, a tax on arable land levied not infrequently down to 1162. Its value for

Richard I and John was small since many landholders were exempt and the assessment was hopelessly out of date. It was therefore levied only three times by these kings, despite efforts to make a fresh assessment. It was found more profitable to exploit two other old occasional sources of revenue, scutage and tallage, and to experiment with sources which were almost wholly new, customs duties and taxes on income and movable property.

Every lord was accustomed to mulct, at least occasionally, the men of his own demesne. This imposition, the tallage, was normally laid on villeins; it became associated with villeinage and among free men was extremely unpopular. King John was well aware that in law most of the wealthiest towns in England and the entire community of Jewish money-lenders formed part of the royal demesne, and he tallaged both merchants and Jews with a will. From the former he is reckoned to have raised over £25,000, while he mulcted the Jews so fiercely in 1210 that many fled the country. The Crown guarded jealously its monopolistic control of Jewish usury, and in 1194 a special exchequer was set up to deal with future lending and the vast sums of money already owed. Under Richard I this exchequer was in part supervised by prominent Jews, but John appointed only non-Jewish supervisors and his behaviour towards the Jewish community was harsher than his brother's.

Scutage affected directly only the knightly class. Theoretically it could be demanded as often as knight-service, that is, once a year, but in practice levies of scutage during the twelfth century had been much less frequent. Henry II and Richard I had taken eleven scutages in forty-five years. John took eleven scutages in sixteen years. The rates normal before 1199 had been £1 or one mark on the knight's fee. Only two of John's scutages were as low as this, and in 1210 and 1214 he levied £2 per fee. Scutage, in short, became in his time almost an annual exaction from military freeholders and came to be identified with those vague " aids " which a feudal lord sometimes demanded from his tenants with their consent on occasions other than the three sanctioned by custom.[1] The merging of these two different types of levy explains why in Magna Carta the king had to promise to levy " no scutage or aid " other than on the customary occasions except by the common counsel of his realm.

[1] Above, pp. 44-5.

The most novel experiments were those made in the field of customs duties and property taxes. From 1202 until 1207 a duty of a fifteenth was imposed on all goods exported and imported. This was vastly more productive than the wine duties and " prise of wine " [1] levied hitherto. Although it was not originally intended as a permanent form of taxation but merely as a threat or punishment for Philip Augustus's Flemish vassals, the precedent of these customs duties (which brought John some £15,000) could not be ignored in a century which saw the volume of English wool exports to the Netherlands swelling yearly. Under Edward I, the custom of wool and hides became a major item of Crown revenue. The fall of Jerusalem in 1187 provided the thin end of another wedge. In 1188 the Church instigated lay rulers to raise the so-called " Saladin Tithe ", a levy of a tenth of income and chattels (movable property, both live and inanimate) for the recovery of the Holy Land. Richard I's ransom seemed to call for an even more drastic tax of the same type, this time 25 per cent. John levied two such taxes, the best-known being the " thirteenth " (actually 1s. in the mark) of 1207, which, despite widespread evasion, yielded over £57,000. This tax was so dangerously novel that the king acknowledged that it had only been authorised by the common advice and consent of his Council.

Such were the principal methods by which King John raised money and, in so doing, stirred up an opposition to the Crown which provided the barons of Magna Carta with much of their motive and support. In addition, as we shall see, he drew off colossal wealth from the Church, and was also able to save the Crown expense in two ways, one old-established, the other fortuitous. First, by keeping bishoprics and abbeys vacant he could either take their revenues himself or use them to provide the rewards which were expected by loyal servants and useful supporters. Thus in 1200 he gave custody of the rich abbey of Peterborough to the Bishop of St. Andrews, brother of his friend the Earl of Leicester, who promptly carried off all its stocks of food and fodder. A second type of saving became possible after the loss of Normandy in 1204, for the king could grant his adherents the English lands of those

[1] This was the king's right to buy a tenth of imported wine below market price, one tun of inferior wine stowed before the mast and one of the best from abaft the mast.

Norman lords who had gone over to Philip Augustus. In this way the Lincolnshire towns of Grantham and Stamford formerly held by the Constable of Normandy, William du Hommet, passed to the English Earl Warenne.

The period we are considering was one of almost continual war. New techniques of castle building and siegecraft, some brought from the east, made warfare more expensive and enhanced its professional element. Longer campaigns, mostly fought south of the Channel, increased the use of mercenaries and made the English knight a luxury, no longer a mere unit in the line of battle but a commander of light horse or infantry. Moreover, English barons and knights were sometimes unwilling to serve in France, and on many baronial honours the knights' fees had been so minutely divided, by the process known as " subinfeudation ", that many sub-tenants owed fractions of a knight's service and preferred to pay scutage rather than serve in person. In 1205 the sheriffs were ordered to have every tenth knight in their bailiwicks ready for service " as long as the need shall last ", the arms and equipment of each being provided by nine other knights. We are not told how this " quota system " was to be operated in detail ; it cannot have been easy. The Crown continued to stress the military obligations of all free men in addition to the knights and serjeants. Henry II's Assize of Arms (1181) laid down a scale of armour and weapons to be maintained by every class of free man in accordance with his income. In 1205 when attack by the French seemed imminent, John organised a militia of free men for the defence of the realm under chief constables for each shire and constables for each hundred and borough. For the most part, however, John depended on mercenary troops under foreign captains, of whom the colourful rascal Fawkes de Bréauté is the best known. When compelled to wage war in England, in 1215-16, John owed much to his control of most of the first-class castles. His practice of not only putting foreign captains in command of castles but even appointing them to English shrievalties called forth intense resentment among the native baronage. The loss of Normandy turned the Channel into a battle zone for the first time for 150 years. The royal navy became a matter of some concern. Many warships were built and seamen pressed into service under the supervision of a special keeper of the King's ships.

With the fleet thus created the English and their Flemish allies were enabled to destroy the ships of Philip Augustus at Damme in 1213, a victory without which the campaign of the following year would hardly have been possible.

We see the influence of the government—of the king, of Hubert Walter and Geoffrey fitz Peter—in matters less important than justice, finance or defence but of great interest to the ordinary subject. When Archbishop Hubert was still Justiciar, for example, in 1196 and 1197, decrees were published standardising measures of quantity throughout England and ordering the removal of fish-weirs which blocked the River Thames, navigable for commerce (in the thirteenth century at least) as far up as Lechlade. Again, it was the baker of Geoffrey fitz Peter, presumably when his master was Justiciar, who set the standard of weight and fineness for the Assize of Bread and Ale, designed to make the weight of the quartern loaf and the price of a gallon of ale correspond reasonably to the current price of cereals. In 1199, when Hubert Walter had moved to the chancellorship, the king and he issued an ordinance under which the exorbitant fees taken by the Chancery for royal charters and letters of protection were to be reduced and fixed at reasonable levels.

The orderly mind of Hubert Walter has usually been credited with the truly astonishing advances made during this period in the arrangement and recording of acts of government. The *Curia Regis*, in its capacity of law court, began to record its cases in 1194. In the Chancery the distinction, already grasped in practice, between the solemn charter which granted land or rights in perpetuity, the open letter (" letters patent ") conveying the king's will to several addressees simultaneously, and the closed letter (" letters close ") sent to a single individual and dealing with ephemeral business, was confirmed. Copies of all three types of document were henceforth kept on separate rolls, which " in their hey-day, in the thirteenth century, supply the material for a day-to-day administrative record unique in medieval history ".[1] Other rolls commenced at this time recorded the debts owed to the king and the moneys paid out by him, an account of casual income and expenditure standing in relation to the Great Roll of the Pipe somewhat as a petty cash book

[1] V. H. Galbraith, *Studies in the Public Records*, 76.

does to a ledger. It became the rule (a most useful one for historians) to date royal letters by the day of the month and the regnal year. The volume of business transacted in the king's name compelled the Chancellor, who kept the king's seal, to become the head of a large department, and made it impossible for the king to use his seal whenever he wanted, at short notice or for extremely private matters. To meet this difficulty, a new seal, the " small " or " private " seal (later called the privy seal), was brought into use. Its keeper was free from departmental duties and could be in constant attendance upon the king. In one way and another, the production and recording of official acts had reached an unprecedented pitch of efficiency. By the end of John's reign, the king and his servants were in a position to know in vastly more detail than any of their predecessors the things which had been done or authorised in the government's name.

John came very near to being one of the most successful kings of English history. His expeditions to Scotland (1209), Ireland (1210) and Wales (1211) gave him a mastery throughout the British Isles possessed by no English king before or since. In his own view, doubtless, his greatest failure was the loss of Normandy, which he felt keenly to be a lasting dishonour, though we can now see that it was to England's advantage. Conversely, the quarrels with Church and baronage which we take to be signs of weakness John probably attributed to treachery and misfortune. In fact, he was his own worst enemy. Several recent historians of eminence, attracted by John's acute intelligence and undoubted administrative capacity, have so successfully rescued him from the evil reputation which he used to enjoy in our history books that there is a danger of redressing the balance too far in John's favour. Certainly he had some pleasing attributes, a sense of humour, education, a fondness for reading. His library was trans-shipped from Normandy on the eve of its fall, and for a sojourn at Windsor in 1202 he commanded one of his servants to lay in wine and a " history of England in French ". As Professor Painter says,[1] " the picture of John sitting in Windsor castle preparing for the council with two tuns of wine and a book on English history is thoroughly entrancing ". But cleverness by itself does not make for statesmanship. The two fatal flaws in his

---

[1] *The Reign of King John*, 56. It should be added that Mr. Painter is not one of the historians who seem to judge King John too favourably.

character, his intense suspicion and occasional savage cruelty, cannot fairly be dissociated from his conduct as king, for it was precisely in their appraisal of John's character that the barons of Magna Carta found a motive for pushing their opposition to the limit. We have seen that after 1189 there were many grounds for protest not only against particular strokes of tyranny but also, more deeply, against the manifold expansion of royal government and its bureaucratic interference in the affairs of daily life. Yet at the same time the Crown could offer many advantages to its free subjects, especially in the field of justice ; the king's peace was much preferred to baronial lawlessness ; and loyalty and reverence towards the monarchy remained instinctive and strong. It is, in fact, doubtful if the opposition would ever have spread beyond a few disaffected magnates if John had not almost simultaneously alienated the Church and a great part of the baronage.

The quarrel with the Church arose over the election of an Archbishop of Canterbury to replace Hubert Walter, who died on July 13th, 1205. Secular interests had taken first place in Hubert Walter's life. He had been an invaluable but over-mighty servant of the Crown. The king wished to replace him by John Grey, Bishop of Norwich, whose career had been of the same kind but who was entirely the king's creature. It was traditionally the king's right to exercise a weighty influence upon the nomination of all new bishops, especially of an Archbishop of Canterbury. But he might not always exercise this right, and the actual election was the prerogative of the monks who formed the chapter of Canterbury cathedral priory, though the bishops of the province also claimed to participate. The monks probably knew that John Grey was the king's choice, but it so happened that they had just weathered a long-drawn-out dispute with the last two archbishops which had made them extremely sensitive about their electoral rights. They realised that while English custom gave the right of appointment to the king, the Canon Law of the Church claimed " free election " for cathedral chapters. With papal backing, they might defy both the king and the bishops. They therefore secretly elected the sub-prior and sent him to Rome, first to represent their interests, and secondly, but only if the Pope seemed to favour the rival parties, to declare his own election. In fact the sub-prior announced his election at once, but the Pope, Innocent III, waited to hear the arguments from the other side. In the meantime King John, pointing out to the chapter quite rightly that they could not lawfully choose an archbishop without royal licence, bade them elect Grey, which they duly did on December 10th. By this time, however, the Pope was not satisfied that the rights of the Church were being respected. It must be realised that in Innocent III John had to deal with a man of exceptional genius, one of the greatest of all holders of the papal office, possessed of a highly-developed legal sense, an iron determination and an unshakable belief in the supremacy of spiritual over secular authority. Pope Innocent deferred a decision until late in 1206. The monks, to whom he had finally adjudged the exclusive right of free election to belong, could not decide between the sub-prior and Grey, and at Innocent's suggestion elected an English cardinal named Stephen Langton, for many years a teacher of distinction in Paris University but not well-known in his native country. In 1207 the Pope consecrated Langton and gave him the *pallium*, the vestment which symbolised his metropolitan authority as archbishop.

John could not accept an election which contravened a fundamental right of the English Crown. He refused Langton entry into England, drove all but the oldest monks at Canterbury into exile, and confiscated the estates of archbishopric and priory alike. It was the first act of a quarrel which continued with increasing bitterness for six years. Both sides were convinced of the rightness of their cause, and judged by the irreconcilable standpoints which they adopted there was indeed right on both sides. Innocent put the Church's view clearly enough in a letter of August, 1207.[1]

> God forbid that the English people, who are truly Christian and zealous for the orthodox faith, should in this wicked project follow their earthly king in opposition to the Heavenly King, preferring the corporeal to the spiritual, for there are not only clergy but also laity who are men of such wisdom and devotion that they have both the knowledge and the will to distinguish between the things which should be rendered to Caesar and those which should be rendered to God.

King John replied with equal firmness that his essential rights as King of England must be respected ; but while he argued fairly with the Papacy he treated the English clergy with an old-fashioned

[1] C. R. Cheney and W. H. Semple, *Select Letters of Innocent III concerning England* (1953), 92.

violence and rapacity which William Rufus himself could scarcely have equalled. The Papacy invoked the usual penalties of interdict and excommunication. John's answer to the former was to confiscate the property of all clergy who refused to perform the prohibited services of religion (only baptism of infants and extreme unction for the dying were allowed). He was then (1209) excommunicated, whereupon he commenced a systematic pillaging of Church property. It is estimated that during these years John took some £100,000 from ecclesiastical sources. Excommunication hit him hard, for no one who set any store by religious sanctions dared stay in his company, and the only bishops prepared (apparently) to risk damnation out of loyalty to him were Grey of Norwich and Peter des Roches, the Poitevin Bishop of Winchester with whom John was on close terms, and whom, on Geoffrey fitz Peter's death in 1213, he appointed Justiciar.

At last in the autumn of 1212 the king gave way. There was treason among the English baronage and danger from Philip Augustus. Before negotiations were completed, indeed, the Pope had either deposed John or threatened to do so, and the French king may have received papal encouragement to invade Britain. By May, 1213, John had decided on abject surrender. Langton was to be admitted, Church property restored and the kingdom of England itself granted to the Pope to be received back as a fief. By this shrewd stroke King John transformed the Pope into a staunch ally. Not only was Philip of France deprived of a moral motive for invasion, but the English barons, already feeling their way towards a formulation of their grievances, were now opposing a dutiful son of the Church, the Pope's own vassal.

Baronial opposition to King John had shown itself from the very beginning of his reign, but the movement which led to Magna Carta had its origins in the time of the interdict. In 1210 William of Briouze, hitherto the most intimate of all the king's close friends and supporters, fell into deep disgrace. It is thought that he knew the truth about Arthur's death and his wife had been indiscreet with this dangerous knowledge. Whatever the explanation, William fled from South Wales, where his family had long been powerful, to Ireland, where he himself had been granted land through John's favour. The king pursued him thither with an army which enabled him, incidentally, to bring Ireland into complete submission to the Crown. William got away to France, but his unlucky wife, with one of their sons, tried to escape to Scotland and fell into the hands of the Gallovidian lord of Carrick who, by John's authority, was enjoying a share in the contemporary plantation of Ulster. He promptly betrayed them to the English king, who had them starved to death at Windsor. William of Briouze had influential relatives and friends, but anger and dismay at John's arbitrary cruelty was felt by a much wider circle of the baronage. Two years later Robert fitz Walter and Eustace de Vesci (a prominent lord in Northumberland and brother-in-law of the King of Scots) also fled to the French court. In the autumn of 1213 a group of north-country barons, men whose estates lay chiefly north of the River Welland, refused to give service south of the Channel and later withheld their contributions to the scutage of 1214. It seems likely that their grievances were set down in writing and have been preserved in the unhappily-named " Unknown Charter of Liberties ",[1] which dealt chiefly with the king's abuse of feudal incidents and forest rights and sought to limit overseas service to Normandy and Brittany, " and that decently ". But the king, strengthened for the moment by his surrender to the Church, was giving nothing away to the baronage. It was the catastrophe of Bouvines which made the Great Charter inevitable. One contemporary account says that the first open resistance came from " knights ", who were then joined by men of higher rank. Early in 1215 the dissident barons, now including a considerable number from East Anglia and one or two others, chose Robert fitz Walter as their leader. They gave him the pompous and (since the king was now reconciled with the Papacy and had even taken crusader's vows) the inappropriate title of " marshal of the army of the Lord and of Holy Church ". They had an extremely important ally in Stephen Langton, and it was perhaps at his suggestion that the Coronation Charter of Henry I was adopted as the basis of negotiations with the king. The barons assembled at the favourite midland tournament grounds of Stamford and Brackley and then moved on London, where they were admitted to the city (May 17th) by a minority of the citizens.

Even with London lost the king had a preponderance of military power, but he was still ready to negotiate. He suggested arbitration,

[1] Conveniently found in W. S. McKechnie, *Magna Carta* (1905), 569-70.

but since he proposed the Pope as chairman of the arbitrators the barons not unnaturally declined. The Pope, who seems to have believed that John's submission to the Church was sincere, was impressed by his decision to become a crusader. The barons, and doubtless Langton with them, knowing John at first hand, realised that it was merely a quite unscrupulous move on the king's part to gain clerical and public sympathy. John did, however, concede the demand, given first place in the " Unknown Charter ", that a man should not be seized without trial, but should have the law of the land and the judgment of his equals. This alone did not satisfy the opposition. Since John remained unwilling to go to war, Langton was able to bring the two sides to a meeting, " in the meadow which is called Runnymede, between Windsor and Staines " (June 15th, 1215). In earnest of the king's intention to accept the baronial demands the Great Seal was fixed to a schedule of some forty-eight reforms, the " Articles of the Barons ", a unique memorandum which still survives and " is perhaps the most momentous single document in our history ".[1]

The Great Charter of liberties, into which in the course of the next four days the preliminary articles were more methodically and comprehensively rearranged, was in a sense a commentary upon the whole range of government during the past two or three reigns. With few exceptions Magna Carta retained and even extended the legal reforms of Henry II and his sons, the Petty Assizes, the criminal jury, the new machinery of justice. But in a few immortal chapters it was made clear that these reforms were to operate for the benefit of the whole community of free men, not for the sake of the Crown, and that the king in carrying out his lawful and necessary duties of dispensing justice and keeping the peace was not to oppress the men and women of any class, be they gentlemen, merchants or only humble villeins. " A free man shall not be fined for a petty offence except according to the scale of the offence. For a greater offence he shall be fined according to its magnitude, saving his social status ; likewise a merchant, saving his trade, and a villein, saving his tillage." [2] " No free man shall be taken, imprisoned, dispossessed,

[1] Galbraith, *Studies in the Public Records*, p. 124. It is preserved and normally displayed at the British Museum.
[2] My translation of the technical terms here follows J. Tait, *E.H.R.*, xxvii. 720-8, and A. F. Pollard, *op. cit.* xxviii. 117-18.

outlawed or exiled or in any way ruined, nor will we pursue him or send after him, except by the lawful judgment of his equals or by the law of the land." " To none will we sell, deny or defer right or justice."

Naturally enough the greater part of Magna Carta is taken up by matters which touched the feudal aristocracy closely or exclusively. Feudal incidents are not to be an excessive burden, the rights of wardship and marriage must not be abused. Heiresses and widows of English barons, e.g. must not be forced to marry beneath them, to take foreign mercenary captains as husbands. Scutages and aids must be levied with the common counsel of the realm. The king must not claim feudal incidents in respect of those who held land of him by some non-military tenure simply because they happened to be tenants of another lord by knight-service. Barons whose ancestors had founded religious houses were to have custody of them while the office of abbot or prior was vacant. The writ of right must not be used to deprive a lord of the jurisdiction over a case with which his court was competent to deal. Foreign mer-cenaries were to be banished, and (a hit at Peter des Roches) only men who knew the law of the realm were to be made justiciars or sheriffs. Many of the concessions keenly desired by the baronage also benefited the wider community. This was true not only of the chapters dealing with legal matters, but even more in respect of those which restricted the king's forest privileges and ordered a special enquiry by twelve knights in each shire into the " evil customs of forests and warrens ". Miscellaneous chapters include certain liberties for London and other towns, freedom for merchants to enter and leave the country except in wartime, and a re-enactment of Hubert Walter's decrees on standard measures and fish-weirs in the Thames.

Magna Carta, coloured as it inevitably was by the narrow outlook of the feudatories who compelled the king to seal it, remains for all its limitations a fundamental statement of constitutional right. " In age after age a confirmation of it will be demanded and granted as a remedy for those oppressions from which the realm is suffering, and this when some of its clauses, at least in their original meaning, have become hopelessly antiquated. For in brief it means this, that the king is and shall be below the law." [1]

[1] F. W. Maitland, in *The History of English Law,* by Sir F. Pollock and F. W. Maitland (2nd edn., 1911), i. 173.

The events which filled the sixteen months between the Charter and the death of King John were dictated by the utter disbelief of the opposition that the king had any sincere intention of mending his ways, and by the king's own desire, manifested at the latest by the end of July, to have the Charter annulled by the Pope. It had been provided that if John failed to implement it a special committee of twenty-five barons should have power to coerce him by force of arms. John did in fact do much in June and July to give effect to some important clauses, but wholehearted implementation was impossible because trust was lacking on both sides. The opposition knew they were a minority and that if they dispersed peaceably to their homes there was nothing but the king's good faith to preserve them from destruction. In 1215 it was too late to expect them to believe in John's good faith. John, on the other hand, complained with reason that while he tried to carry out the terms of Magna Carta the barons remained in arms against him, retained control of London, and were in correspondence with his enemy the King of France.

The Pope's letter condemning the Charter root and branch reached England late in September. It merely confirmed the king in the course of action he had begun already, for he had recovered his nerve and was raising mercenaries against his opponents. Before this, Stephen Langton, one of the few steadying influences during the Magna Carta crisis, had been suspended from office by delegates of the Pope for failing to excommunicate the rebellious barons. The delegates, who included Peter des Roches, were biased in John's favour. In Langton's opinion, they had not tried as they ought to explain to Innocent that Magna Carta was more than an impious restraint imposed by rebels upon the anointed of the Lord. We can be certain that much of what is permanent in the great charter was owed to the archbishop's patient persuasion of the barons during the months preceding Runnymede. Now the programme had failed, the Pope had misunderstood his motives, and in England there was no place for his moderate viewpoint. He travelled to Rome to lay his case before the Pope in person and to attend the great General Council of the Church which opened in this year. For the next few months John carried all before him. He captured all the strongholds of importance held by the rebels outside the city of London,[1] swept

---

[1] The Tower of London was still in royalist hands.

northward to devastate Lothian in order to punish the young King Alexander II of Scotland for supporting his opponents, and made ready to attack the main body of rebels in London itself. But in May, 1216, their promise to give the Crown to the French king's son Louis at last brought this able young prince to Kent with a force of experienced knights. Dover held out for the king under Hubert de Burgh, a Norfolk man who had served John loyally as Seneschal of Poitou and who had been Justiciar since the issue of Magna Carta. Elsewhere in south-eastern England the king soon lost any general control of the countryside. Only in the western counties, where at Corfe in Dorset he possessed a fortress strong enough to defy the fiercest onslaught, was John completely secure. But in the east many isolated castles were still held by his supporters, and in September he crossed the country to East Anglia and Lincolnshire to comfort his friends and plunder the lands of his enemies. He fell ill with dysentery, aggravated, it is said, by a surfeit of peaches and new cider, and by the news that all his household belongings, his wardrobe, jewels and holy relics, had been lost in the treacherous tide and quicksands of the Nene estuary. He died at Newark on October 18th. His son Henry, eight years old, had been left at Corfe in the safe keeping of William the Marshal and other loyal adherents of the Crown, who had supported the king faithfully throughout his quarrel with the barons.

PART IV : WALES AND SCOTLAND

CHAPTER XIV

WALES UNDER THE TWO LLYWELYNS, 1194-1277

THE peoples of Celtic speech who have inhabited the British Isles are usually divided according to their language into two broad groups, Goidelic or Gaelic and Brythonic or Brittonic.[1] The Goidelic form of Celtic became dominant in Ireland, the Hebrides, Man, and, as we have seen already, in Galloway and the rest of Scotland north of the Clyde-Forth line. Brythonic dialects prevailed in Strathclyde or Cumbria, in Cornwall, in Brittany, and above all in Wales, the wooded mountainous western projection of Britain which had become by our period the heart and centre of the Brythonic division of Celtic culture. The people for whom Brythonic was a mother-tongue were not the only inhabitants of Wales and perhaps did not even form a majority of the population. In North Wales there was an ad mixture of Goidelic stock, while throughout the country in the twelftht and thirteenth centuries the lower strata of society probably represented a number of older, pre-Celtic strains. Nevertheless, the Brythonic-speaking element was politically and socially pre-dominant. The princes and tribal chiefs and the clergy of Wales, who were fully conscious of their inheritance, remote as it was, from Romano-Celtic Britain, were almost entirely Brythonic, and it was this branch of the Celtic family of languages which became the sole vernacular tongue of early medieval Wales.

The Welsh inhabited a thickly-forested land of rugged hills, rising in places in precipitous mountain-bastions, and of torrential rivers, all teeming with salmon and trout and at least one, the Teifi, still harbouring in the twelfth century colonies of beavers. There was little ground suitable for agriculture, except the isle of Anglesey, the " granary of the north ", and parts of modern Pembrokeshire and Glamorgan. In Wales the 600 foot contour seldom runs far

---

[1] Brythonic is more usual, but Brittonic is preferred by a recent authoritative writer on the subject, K. Jackson, *Language and History in Early Britain* (1953), 3.

from the coast or the English border, and above this line the land that could be utilised was mainly given over to the pasturing of cattle and sheep. Instead of dwelling in well-defined, compact, " nucleated " villages, each surrounded by its great open arable fields, such as composed the pattern of midland and southern England, the people of Wales occupied scattered pastoral townships, or even quite isolated family homesteads. Save in the small areas already mentioned, the Welsh were not an agricultural but a pastoral people. Their food was not bread but meat and milk, butter and cheese, from their huge flocks and herds, their drink mead or metheglin, the fermented honey of their bees. Like other pastoral folk, they were almost entirely self-supporting, with no need to import foodstuffs or clothing materials and little use for foreign manufactured articles. Money was not in much demand and no Welsh ruler ever had coin minted for him. The Welsh did not take easily to town life, and urban development in Wales came very late in comparison with that of England. It was, indeed, when it came, an English introduction, at first undertaken by the foreign marcher lords and later accelerated under royal direction, especially in Edward I's time.

It followed also from the pastoral character of the Welsh people that they were semi-nomadic, moving from the lower ground to the heights in the summer and back to the valley shelter in the winter. They possessed the mobility which this implies. Their personal belongings were few and easily transported, their dwellings were of simple timber or wattle construction, which, if they were easy to destroy, were as easy to rebuild. A frugal life in the mountains had inured the Welsh to hardship and privation. " In mid-winter ", an observer of Welsh soldiers wrote in 1297, " they were in the habit of running about with bare legs, wearing a red tunic. They could not be warm. The money which they received from the [English] king was spent on milk and butter." [1] Hunting and inter-tribal warfare ranked highly among their congenial pastimes, and in both pursuits the qualities of endurance and reckless daring were most admired. This hard obverse of the Welsh character had its softer, mellower reverse in the practice of an unstinted hospitality [2] and in

[1] John Edwards, *Scot. Hist. Rev.*, v (1908), 15.
[2] If the lady of the house failed in hospitality she might be the victim of such a witticism as that uttered (according to Gerald of Barry) by a guest of a certain greedy woman : " I have only one fault to find with our hostess : she puts too little butter in the salt ". (*Opera*, Rolls Ser., vi. 191.)

a passionate love of poetry and of music, both vocal and instrumental. At the close of the twelfth century, Gerald of Barry, who shared Welsh with Norman descent, declared the outstanding powers of the Welsh in the playing of the harp, flute and " crowd ",[1] and of their gifts for part-singing (shared in Britain, it seems, only by the Yorkshire folk). Every Welsh ruler of note had his own bard to compose poems in his honour, and despite its conventionally heroic and stilted character the language of many of these poems may still be moving. The Lord Rhys, the prince of Deheubarth respected by Henry II, convened in 1176 the earliest-recorded *eisteddfod*, and in this great gathering for the performance of instrumental music and the recitation of poetry the prize for the former went to Rhys's own men of the south, for the latter to the men of Gwynedd.

The social organisation of Wales in the thirteenth century was still tribal. Clan feeling was paramount. The Welsh considered themselves one great family, the *Cymry* (literally, " men of this country ", " fellow-countrymen "), from which only slaves and obvious aliens were excluded. Within the *Cymry*, the free-born were all of one rank under the princes, and belonged to innumerable small kindred-groups, whose calculable limits were reckoned to be the relationship of fifth cousins. These groups owned the land of the kindred, were collectively responsible for their members in law, maintained blood-feuds on their behalf, and supervised such important social matters as the entry of new members and the marriage of their young men and women. Male descent alone was socially significant. When a girl married out of her kindred-group, her children would automatically belong to that of her husband. But though Welsh society was tribal, the township or *tref* in which a kindred lived would be grouped with others territorially, for administrative and judicial purposes, into a district known as a cantred (Welsh, *cantref* = " 100 *trefs* ") or a commote (Welsh, *cymwd* = " neighbourhood "). In size the typical Welsh cantred came half-way between the hundred and the shire of England. Originally, the whole of Wales was divided into cantreds, but in our period the more recent commote, usually rather smaller than the cantred [2] but

---

[1] An early Celtic forerunner of the fiddle.
[2] There were notable exceptions ; e.g. the commote of Gower, in modern Glamorganshire, was larger than the cantred of Emlyn (modern Pembrokeshire).

having exactly the same functions, had tended to displace the older division in Powys and the eastern half of South Wales.

The cantred and commote, through their freemen in the scattered free townships and their villeins huddled together in their own more compact hamlets, contributed renders of food to the local ruler, which were brought in to some recognised centre of his power. Here stood his *neuadd* or long timber hall, and here dwelt along with himself and his immediate family the *teulu*, or band of warlike retainers, indispensable to the dignity of a Welsh prince. Only the ruler's young sons might be absent, for the Welsh aristocracy practised the custom of fosterage by which sons were sent away from home to be brought up in the households of kinsmen ; because of this, adult brothers might scarcely know one another, and fighting between brothers was a common occurrence. At the *neuadd* the princes dispensed justice and received their revenues, which, in addition to the food-renders, included certain customary perquisites and payments, e.g. the salvage of wrecked ships and fines due in respect of serious crimes.

In our period the Welsh princes had begun to emerge from the limited position of tribal chiefs, and though they did not style themselves *rhi*, " king ", they were taking on more and more of the character of territorial rulers. The large-scale division of Wales into three major principalities recognised this fact. The tribes of Gwynedd acknowledged the rule of the lords whose ancient traditional seat of power was Aberffraw in Anglesey. In this family, Owain Gwynedd was succeeded by his sons David and Rhodri ; but they were soon supplanted by their nephew, Llywelyn ab Iorwerth. The men of Powys or mid-Wales were subject to one ruling family from the eleventh century until the death in 1286 of their last prince, Gruffydd ap Gwenwynwyn. The southern Welsh house of which the Lord Rhys was head lost its power and unifying influence after his death, yet his descendants, as we shall see in a later chapter, retained more than a memory of the great days when the men of Deheubarth had led resistance to the foreign invader.

In between the three major divisions, however, were large tracts ruled by minor princelings, or areas which had so little cohesion that they might be known colourlessly as " the four cantreds " (roughly modern Denbighshire and Flint) or " between Wye and Severn " (Radnorshire). All along the eastern and southern fringes of purely

Welsh territory were ranged the lordships of the " marcher barons ".
The palatine earldom of Chester was held at the turn of the twelfth
and thirteenth centuries by Earl Ranulf of "Blundeville" (Oswestry),
the descendant of Hugh of Avranches. He seems to have adopted
a relatively aloof position in the politics of his time, preserving
something like neutrality in the struggle between King John and the
barons and holding to the friendship of Llywelyn of Gwynedd when
most of his fellow-marchers regarded the native Welsh as unreliable
at best and mortal enemies at worst. South of Cheshire the old
earldom of Shrewsbury had come to an end with the overthrow of
Robert of Bellême, and the dominant families of the valleys of
Shropshire were now the Fitz-Alans of Oswestry and Clun, the
Corbets of Caus, and, soon to be most powerful of all, the Mortimers
of Wigmore and Chirk.

South of the River Teme, the political landscape had also changed
since the early twelfth century. The earldom of Hereford had been
revived (1141), and had passed in 1200 to the king's hereditary
Constable, Henry de Bohun, whose son, grandson, and great-
grandson, all named Humphrey, were successively earls of both
Hereford and Essex, and among the very greatest baronial leaders of
thirteenth-century England. West of Hereford stretched the hilly
and strongly Welsh districts of Radnor, Builth, Elfael, Brecknock,
and Over Gwent (upper Monmouthshire), which had long been

Map VI. The Divisions of Wales in the Thirteenth Century
(*see opposite page*).

(Based on the map of Wales in Sir J. E. Lloyd, *History of Wales* (1911,
3rd ed., 1939), end of vol. ii by permission of Longmans, Green and Co. Ltd.)

For the dioceses, see Map VIII, and for the Welsh shires after the Statute
of Wales (1284), see Map IX.

The names of the more important Anglo-Norman marcher
families are shown thus : .   .   .   . *(BOHUN)*

Religious house shown thus :   .   .   .   .   .   +

Episcopal sees shown thus :   .   .   .   .   .   ☨

The stippling indicates land over 1,200 feet.

YNYS
MON
(ANGLESEY)
Beaumaris
Aberffraw
Aberconway
MENAI STRAITS
Aber
Bangor
Carnarvon
RHOS
Rhuddlan
St.
Asaph
Denbigh
TEGEINGL
(ENGLEFIELD)
Basingwerk
Flint
Chester
Hawarden
Conway
RHUFONIOG
DYFFRYN
CLWYD
Ruthin
(GREY)
YALE
G
W
Y
N
E
D
D
Criccieth
Dolwyddelan
BROMFIELD
Chirk
(MORTIMER)
Harlech
ARDUDWY
Cymmer
Oswestry
(FITZALAN)
Bere
MEIRIONYDD
Dee
Severn
Maes
Moydog
(1295)
Shrewsbury
Caus (CORBET)
Montgomery
Aberystwyth
ARWYSTLI
CEREDIGION
(CARDIGAN)
Teme
Cym Hir
MAELIENYDD
Wigmore
(MORTIMER)
Strata
Florida
'BETWEEN
WYE AND
SEVERN'
Radnor
(BRIOUZE)
St.
Dogmael's
Cardigan
Teifi
Irfon
Bridge
(1282)
Builth
ELFAEL
Hereford
(BOHUN)
EMLYN
YSTRAD
Llandeilo (1282)
Dynevor
Drwslwyn
Llandovery
BRYCHEINIOG
EWIAS
LACY
Wye
D y f e d
St. David's
Haverford
DEHEUBARTH
Whitland
Tywi
TYWI
Carreg
Cennen
Carmarthen
(BRECKNOCK)
(BOHUN)
Abergavenny
Usk
Monnow
Monmouth
Wye
GWENT
Kidwelly
(CHAWORTH)
GOWER
(BRIOUZE)
GLAMORGAN
Neath
(CLARE)
Margam
Llandaff
Caerphilly
Cardiff
Striguil
(Chepstow)
(BIGOD)
Scale of Miles
0   10   20   30   40   50
Severn

MAP VI

215

ruled by the influential Anglo-Norman family of Briouze. But powerful as were the Bohuns of Hereford and the Briouzes of Brecknock, the dominant place among the marchers of South Wales was taken by the family whose head was Earl of Gloucester and Lord of Glamorgan. Henry I's illegitimate son Robert was the first to hold this position. His son left three daughters, and, by the fiat of Henry II, the marriage of the youngest, Hawise or Isabel, to Count John of Mortain, afterwards King John, brought this great lordship back for a time into the royal family. But after John divorced Isabel in 1199, Gloucester and Glamorgan passed eventually to the son of her sister Amicia, whose husband Richard of Clare, Earl of Hertford, was a first cousin, once removed, of Richard " Strongbow ", Earl of Pembroke. Like the Bohuns, and with even greater power, the Clares, Gilbert I, Richard (1230-62) and Gilbert II (1262-95), doubled the rôles of English earl and Welsh marcher lord. While the Hertford branch of the family rose to pre-eminence in South Wales, the Pembroke branch came to an end on Strongbow's death in 1176, and the earldom, together with the lordship of Striguil (a key strongpoint at the mouth of the Wye), passed to William the Marshal, the most respected baronial leader of John's reign. The Marshal was not destined to found a dynasty. Between 1219 and 1245, five childless sons succeeded him in turn and died, whereupon their vast inheritance was divided among sisters. Striguil and the marshalcy went with the eldest to the Earl of Norfolk ; the earldom of Pembroke itself passed to the Poitevin half-brother of Henry III, William of Valence, apparently without the title of earl.[1] Between Pembroke and Glamorgan came the lesser but not unimportant lordships of Kidwelly, held by the Chaworths, and Gower, given by King John to William de Briouze. Most of these lords of the Welsh march ruled with a stubborn sense of independence an area where the King of England's writ did not run. They fought the Welsh, and when opportunity offered pushed their conquests deeper into Wales ; yet they claimed the customary rights of the native Welsh princes whom they had displaced, e.g. private war and the right to a third share of the booty taken by their men. English to the Welsh, Welsh to the English, the marchers constituted a serious problem both for the King of England and for any Welsh ruler who aspired to the political hegemony of Wales.

[1] See below, pp. 266–7.

When the Lord Rhys died in 1197, his lands were divided according to Welsh custom among his sons, none of whom had the gifts of leadership needed to maintain the dominance of South Wales. Some three years, however, before Rhys's death these gifts began to be shown by a member of the ruling family of Gwynedd, Llywelyn ab Iorwerth. The turn of the century was a period of renewed conflict between the Welsh and the marchers, and Llywelyn was to prove equal not only to the initial difficulty of making himself sole ruler of the north, but also, in the end, to that wider problem of how to unite the Welsh of all districts against a resumption of marcher aggression. At first, however, he could do little more than establish his power over Gwynedd, the Four Cantreds, and certain border areas to the south. The unprecedented fact of Count John, heir to the throne and then king, being a marcher baron himself by virtue of his wife's lordship, was a major check to Welsh aspirations in the south. John understood Welsh political problems better than any English king had done before him. At first he showed favour to Llywelyn, then he played off against him the ruler of Powys, Gwenwynwyn. Between 1201 and 1210, however, Llywelyn's relations with John were close and friendly. In 1204 he was given the king's illegitimate daughter Joan in marriage, and in 1208 his rival Gwenwynwyn was deprived of his power by the king.

Two years later, by a *volte-face* as sudden as that by which he turned on William of Briouze (and perhaps because Llywelyn and Briouze had become allies), John declared the Welsh ruler a traitor and ordered the Earl of Chester to invade Gwynedd. The king followed this up the next year (1211) with two invasions of North Wales which he conducted personally. The Welsh were brought to complete submission. Llywelyn gave up the Four Cantreds, which he had previously annexed, and handed over hostages for good behaviour. He had to watch helplessly while John, who as early as 1199 had made Cardigan an advanced strongpoint of English penetration, now built an entirely new castle at Llanbadarn or Aberystwyth, thirty-five miles farther north. This was placed under the command of the mercenary, Fawkes de Bréauté, and whether because of the castle's novelty or its constable's buccaneering methods, the reaction of the Welsh to the new work was instantaneous and hostile. In 1212 a league of Welsh princes was formed with Llywelyn at its head, and Aberystwyth was stormed and captured.

John vented his fury pitilessly by hanging twenty-eight boys among his Welsh hostages ; but the baronial opposition which was gathering momentum prevented him from taking military measures against the Welsh. Llywelyn threw all his weight on the side of the opposition barons, and as a result three chapters of Magna Carta promised the Welsh substantial benefits—the restoration of the remaining hostages and the lawful judgment of equals in cases concerning the alleged wrongful seizure of Welsh land by the English, even when the complaint dated from Henry II's time. Llywelyn then took the chance offered by the civil war of 1215-16 to enlarge his own power. He overran Powys and South Wales, and by capturing the castles of Cardigan and Carmarthen isolated the Anglo-Norman and Flemish settlers of Pembroke from their fellow-marchers in Glamorgan. By a stroke of true statesmanship, Llywelyn forebore to annex these conquests to his own domains, and instead, by an agreement made at Aberdovey (1216), partitioned them among the native rulers of mid-Wales and the south. At the same time, the lesser princes acknowledged his supremacy and became his vassals.

Llywelyn was now a force to be reckoned with. In twenty years he had extended the territory and enlarged the political influence of Gwynedd so successfully that men of all parts of Wales looked to the north for what may, without anachronism, be called national leadership. He possessed the gifts, rare among Welsh rulers, of caution and foresight. His rule stood for something more than the rallying point of a frothy and emotional nationalism : he was seen by the government in England to be a stable element in the normally kaleidoscopic shiftings of power and allegiance which made up Welsh politics. His new position was recognised by the peace of Worcester (1218). By its terms, the Welsh prince was given the custody of the important castles of Cardigan, Carmarthen, and Montgomery, and of the lands of Powys, whose nominal lord was Gruffydd, the child heir of Gwenwynwyn (d. 1216). The effect was to consolidate Llywelyn's conquests and leave him supreme in Wales.

From 1218 until Llywelyn's death in 1240 relations between England and Wales were relatively peaceful. The three occasions of warfare, in 1223, 1228, and 1231, stand out as exceptional and on each occasion the underlying dispute was not with the English king but with lords who held lands in the southern march and in Ireland, men who felt personally threatened by the new power in Gwynedd.

In 1223 the quarrel was with the young William the Marshal, Earl of Pembroke, the first of the old marshal's sons to succeed to his vast estates. Llywelyn was forced to surrender Cardigan and Carmarthen. A few years later, custody of Montgomery was transferred to the Justiciar, Hubert de Burgh, whose aggressive policy in this area and also in South Wales (where he was effective lord of Glamorgan in the minority of the Earl of Gloucester) led in 1228 and 1231 to serious resistance by Llywelyn and the Welsh. Hubert had been acting for personal aggrandisement rather than as a royal official, but the king felt that he must intervene in support of his Justiciar. The campaigns proved a costly failure, and when eventually Llywelyn was brought in to a firm peace (at Middle, Shropshire, July, 1234), he was allowed to keep Cardigan and Builth, which he had captured, and for the last six years of his rule wielded very nearly as much power as he had done in 1218.

Direct relations between Henry III and Llywelyn were normally friendly if never intimate. The Welshman was given English manors, his wife, the king's half-sister, enjoyed some influence at court, his son David was formally recognised as heir to Gwynedd in 1220 and again in 1229. Henry was content to receive Llywelyn's homage in token of suzerainty, and does not seem to have interfered in purely Welsh affairs. In this domestic sphere, Llywelyn enhanced his authority to a point not previously reached by any Welsh ruler. He did not, it is true, call himself " prince of Wales ". At first he was " prince of North Wales " ; but the style he later adopted, " prince of Aberffraw and lord of Snowdon ", was for Welshmen pregnant with ancient and traditional pre-eminence.[1] He made himself the feudal superior of the lesser princes of northern Wales, and his leading position was recognised in every part of the country. For his own dynasty he was determined to break the custom of partition among male heirs and replace it by primogeniture, or at least single succession. It is clear that he was aiming at a stable territorial principality, and he went so far as to claim the same liberties and independence as were held by the kings of Scotland, which, if nowhere defined, at least included the right to harbour fugitives from English territory.

Save in his relations with the lesser princes, Wales was not feudalised under Llywelyn. The surest evidence that English

[1] Lloyd, *History of Wales*, ii. 682.

influences were not predominant lies in the fact that it was under the patronage of Llywelyn ab Iorwerth that the fullest collections of laws were compiled. These were purely Welsh in character and were expanded versions of the ancient code of laws first promulgated by King Hywel Dda (" the good ") who reigned from 920 to 950. Yet some English influences were certainly at work, notably in the prince's household and in the Welsh Church. A Seneschal, Ednyfed *Fychan* (" the young "), incidentally the direct ancestor of the royal Tudors, held a place in government from 1215 to 1246 similar to the Justiciar's in England. The Church in Wales, as in other Celtic lands, had been based on the family and tribe. The characteristic centre of the old Church was the monastic *clas*. Governed by an abbot, and including numbers of clergy living together in a community but not observing a strict rule like that of St. Benedict, the *clas* formed in effect an ecclesiastical tribe. The *clas* dominated the Church as a whole, since instead of there being a division of the country into parishes whose churches were directly subordinate to a diocesan bishop, the typical local church or chapel in Wales was closely attached to a *clas*. It is true that there were episcopal sees of ancient origin. Bangor and St. Asaph [1] divided North Wales between them more or less equally, three-quarters of South Wales came under St. David's, and the remainder fell to Llandaff. But originally the episcopal sees and the bishops themselves had been monastic in character, and it was only gradually, during the twelfth and thirteenth centuries, that a system of territorial dioceses was created. After a fruitless but prolonged endeavour on behalf of St. David's to be recognised as a metropolitan see, led first by Bishop Bernard (1115-48), then by Gerald of Barry himself, when Archdeacon of the same diocese, the Welsh Church was finally accounted part of the province of Canterbury. During the reign of Llywelyn ab Iorwerth, however, there was as little interference in the Welsh Church by the English primate as there was in Welsh domestic affairs by the English king. Save in the small diocese of Llandaff, whose territory was held by foreign marcher lords, the bishops appointed were for the most part Welshmen. An obvious channel of foreign influence in the Church lay in the religious orders ; yet even here, the Cistercian abbeys founded in Mid- and North Wales,

[1] St. Asaph seems to have been defunct between the ninth century and A.D. 1143.

e.g. Strata Florida (Cardiganshire), Cwm Hir (Radnorshire), Cymmer (Merioneth) and Conway, were almost from their inception strongly Welsh in character. The austere and puritan quality of Cistercianism appealed to the Welsh of that age much as the message of the Baptists and Methodists appealed to their descendants in the nineteenth century.

Llywelyn ab Iorwerth died on April 11th, 1240. He is commonly known to history as " Llywelyn the Great ". The epithet is used primarily because he, more than any other Welsh ruler, changed the older concept of " the Cymry ", vague and tribal, into a more feudal concept of a single lordship or principality for the whole of Wales, except, of course, for those areas already anglicised by marcher occupation. Had it been possible to do this in the mid-twelfth century it is arguable that a third feudal kingdom, a kingdom of the Welsh, might have emerged alongside those of England and Scotland. Yet there were serious difficulties in the way of such development. Welsh nationality and Welsh nationalism were alike matters of emotional feeling, of language and poetry and music, and of a particular habit of life. They were not founded in political experience and had never been expressed in concrete political acts, such as acknowledging a single effective lordship over all Wales or paying taxes to a single ruler and doing him military service. In short, Welsh tradition was nationalistic, but Welsh history was not national. And if history offered one obstacle to unity, geography offered another and a greater. No native Welsh ruler ever solved the problem posed by the physical barrier between north and south and the consequent remoteness which made it possible for Edward I to raise men from Gwent and Glamorgan to fight against men of Gwynedd, and for Henry " of Monmouth " a century later to make some appeal against the northerner Owen Glendower. If the greatness of Llywelyn was in this respect the greatness of a " might-have-been ", he nevertheless earns the description on account of his political sagacity, a rare quality among the Welsh of his day, and one not inherited by his more brilliant and ambitious grandson Llywelyn ap Gruffydd. The earlier Llywelyn knew that a few minor concessions, a little swallowing of his pride, were a small price to pay for the independence which in his lifetime Wales substantially enjoyed.

Llywelyn was duly succeeded by David, his only legitimate son, but at once the position of supremacy built up by his father was successfully challenged by the English Crown. When David died, after a rule of only six years, he had lost control of everything outside the borders of Gwynedd. Cardigan had gone to the Earl of Pembroke, the custody of Powys and influence over its prince had been resumed by the Crown, while all the lesser Welsh princes had now to do homage and swear fealty to the King of England direct. Worse threatened, for since David had no sons it seemed that Gwynedd itself would disintegrate. The claimants to rule in the north were the three sons of Gruffydd, an illegitimate son of Llywelyn the Great who is chiefly famous for having been killed on St. David's Day, 1244, while trying to escape from the White Tower of London by climbing out of a high window. Of his three sons, Llywelyn and Owen were at first the most considerable, and from 1247 to 1255 Gwynedd was divided between them. A struggle for sole power followed, in which Llywelyn ousted both Owen and the third brother, David, now of an age to claim his share of lands and lordship. The new Prince of North Wales at once began to restore the ascendancy of Gwynedd over Powys and the south. His success was so rapid that by 1257 he was exercising a control over an area even wider than that subject to his grandfather at the height of his power.

Llywelyn's rise had not been ignored by Henry III, but, as had been true of the years from 1212 to 1216 for King John, a mounting baronial opposition at home made the fifties unpropitious for military counter-measures. An English force had, indeed, met a disastrous defeat near Carmarthen in June, 1257, and the king's own expedition to Snowdonia in August gained him nothing. In the following year the launching of the baronial reform movement precluded further action. It was Llywelyn's opportunity. In 1258, probably in March, he convened an impressive assembly of all the lesser Welsh princes except Gruffydd of Powys, and received their direct homage and fealty to himself. At the same time (March 18th) he sealed a bond of alliance with a powerful body of Scottish magnates who were trying to remove the young King of Scots from Henry III's influence, and in this document Llywelyn styled himself for the first time " prince of Wales ". For the next nineteen years, Llywelyn ap Gruffydd ruled a territory as extensive as his grandfather's, but with enhanced prestige and authority and, evidently, with a more grandiose conception of his own dignity. The first half of this period was one of disturbance and civil war in England, but although it ended with the defeat of Simon de Montfort, with whom Llywelyn had made a close alliance, the Welsh ruler's power was not seriously diminished. If anything, the Treaty of Montgomery (1267) which brought him into Henry III's peace actually added to his authority, for by it his claim to be hereditary Prince of Wales was formally recognised by the English king. He was acknowledged to be the feudal suzerain of all the Welsh princes (with the exception of Maredudd ap Rhys, prince of the Tywi valley, the truncated remnant of the old kingdom of Deheubarth), while his territorial conquests of the Four Cantreds and Builth were confirmed to him. For his part, Llywelyn did homage to King Henry and agreed to pay an indemnity of 25,000 marks, mostly in annual instalments of 3,000 marks.

Yet it was just at this point of success that Llywelyn's lack of political sense began to undermine the structure of Welsh independence rebuilt by his own enterprise and daring. In trying to solve the succession problem, he failed to placate his restless younger brother David. His dealings with the men of South Wales took much the same course as those of his grandfather, but he failed to secure the same loyalty. Finally and most seriously, although Llywelyn must have known, on Henry III's death in 1272, that the new king would be altogether more stubborn and formidable, he failed to foresee the consequences. As a fresh and threatening wind began to blow, he could not or would not trim his sails.

CHAPTER XV

SCOTLAND: THE FEUDAL KINGDOM, 1153-1286

1. *Social and Economic Life*

IN David I's reign the tide of foreign influence in Scotland had been flowing strongly. The second half of the twelfth century was the time of high water. New settlers and new ideas mixed with the old to produce the distinctive society of medieval Scotland. As we should expect, foreign influence was prominent most of all in the Church, in the aristocracy, and in the development of town life. Yet all these rested upon an archaic bedrock of husbandry. The country's economic capacity lay in the rearing of stock and, to a lesser degree, in the growing of crops.

Scotland and northern England were alike in being neither mainly agricultural nor mainly pastoral, but a mixture of both. The pastoral aspect was certainly well-marked. The herd, the drover, and the shepherd are among the immemorial figures of the Scottish scene. In every part of the land there was a yearly migration of families and their animals from the lower-lying villages to the upland summer pastures or shielings; in the Island of Lewis the practice has not yet quite died out. Pastoral activity is revealed in several ways. For example, cheese, made presumably from the milk of both sheep and cows, was a staple article of diet and much used in the payment of food-rents. Other renders might be made in hides and fleeces, while live cows formed the currency for larger payments. If a man of Clydesdale failed to pay his tithe to the Church he forfeited twelve cows to the king. If from ill-will a man struck his neighbour he must pay him one cow and the king four. The lord of Galloway tried to placate Henry II of England in 1174 by offering, in addition to 2,000 marks of silver, a yearly render of 500 cows and 500 pigs.

In Scotland as in England, our period is marked by an enormous development of wool-production and the wool trade. Here the Cistercian and other abbeys, which possessed the capital and the organising ability, took a leading share. Thousands of sheep belonging to the monks of Kelso and Melrose and the canons of Dryburgh and Holyrood grazed the hillsides of Teviotdale, Tweeddale and Lothian. The Newbattle monks joyfully recorded the " marvellous concession " by a Norman lord of pasture for 1,000 sheep at Romanno in Peeblesshire. Melrose had a grange in the wilds of upper Eskdale (Dumfriesshire), no doubt a sheep station. It was on the hill route to Galloway, where cattle were bred, and we hear of it as a convenient stopping place for a lay-brother whose job it was to buy cattle for his abbey. The new large-scale farming practised by the Cistercians and the other religious orders was not always achieved without social disturbance. Melrose carried on a prolonged legal dispute with the men of Stow (Peeblesshire) over important pasture rights ; early in the thirteenth century, the monks of Holm Cultram (Cumberland) were accused of depopulating the Kirkcudbrightshire village of Kirkgunzeon and turning it into a grange. But the wool which the abbeys and their secular imitators produced in abundance and shipped to Flanders from Berwick and Inveresk (Musselburgh) undoubtedly brought new wealth to the country as a whole.

The brown heath and shaggy wood of Scotland harboured other beasts besides sheep and swine. Though we hear little of it, wolf hunting must have been a constant necessity. All that an anonymous English map-maker of about 1300 could find to say when he drew the part representing Sutherland was, " Here wolves abound " ; but they were doubtless common enough far to the southward of Sutherland. In a country of primitive agriculture hunting was more than a sport : it formed an economically important source of livelihood. The red deer were not stalked with skill, one by one, but were rounded up by fleet-footed young men, driven into some narrow defile or " elrick " [1] chosen for the purpose, and there slaughtered wholesale. As in England, the king jealously guarded his monopoly of hunting over vast areas, e.g. " *The* Forest " of Ettrick, and Stormont, the wooded terrain east of Dunkeld. But it is clear that the killing of game animals was carried out on a scale more appropriate to food production than occasional sport. This was still truer of fishing. Fish formed an extremely valuable part of the food supply, and fisheries figure in the endowment of almost

[1] Middle Gaelic, *elerc*, " ambush ".

every religious house (whose inmates, of course, required fish for fast-days) as well as being owned by private individuals. We hear little of such purely fresh water fish as carp, or of eels and lampreys, all found often at the English table. The catches sought by the Scots were of herring (which came much further inshore than nowadays), salmon, and stranded porpoises and whales, greatly prized for their oil and fat. Salmon were caught in traps, " cruives "[1] of branches and wickerwork or " yairs " of stones and stakes— usually funnel-shaped or bottle-shaped enclosures placed in river estuaries between high and low water mark. The tide brought the fish into the trap, which was then closed, so that when it receded they were left inside. There was evidently coastal fishing too, for we hear of the fishermen " who are wont to fish round the Isle of May " (in the Firth of Forth). Spey, Tay, and Tweed were probably as renowned for their fishing " beats " then as they are today, the only difference being that nets were used instead of rod and line.

Nevertheless, even if pasture, hunting and fishing occupied so large a place in the country's economic life, the people were also agriculturalists. The ploughman and his oxen were as familiar as the shepherd. Wherever the land was sufficiently level, at least in south-eastern Scotland, an open field system similar to that of England seems to have been the rule, and went hand in hand with the compact " nucleated " villages still to be found in Lothian and Berwickshire. The arable was distributed over the fields in strips, known in Scotland as " rigs ". Around 1162 we find the king offering half a carucate of arable at Selkirk " lying all in one piece " to the agriculturally progressive monks of Kelso in exchange for an equal area " which was of little use because it lay scattered about the (open) field ". Open fields cannot have been unknown north of the Forth, for in the thirteenth century we hear of a man obtaining " every fifth rig " in a village near Crail, and of " the arable land of the village of Markinch " (both Fife). But the commonest arrangement of the ploughed ground in this region was in fixed and compact units assessed (probably rather arbitrarily) as a whole, half, third or quarter carucate. The word *carucata* was used in official documents to denote the major unit of arable, with which, as in England, a definite amount of common pasture would be linked. In popular

[1] Gaelic, *craobh*, " tree ".

usage this unit south of the Forth was the ploughgate or ploughland, familiar in eastern and northern England. North of the Forth, in the territory of the old Pictish kingdom, it was the davach or dauch,[1] while in the middle west it was termed an " arachor ". In theory it consisted of the arable which one plough-team could cultivate in a year, together with proportionate pasture ; but the actual acreage varied according to the nature of the soil and the size of the team. The fact that many carucates or davachs north of the Forth had (and here and there still have) names permanently attached to them shows that they were compact and not dispersed over open fields. In any one place, the lord might have one compact davach and the peasants another.

The cereals grown in Scotland were chiefly barley and oats, with rye as the winter-sown crop. The rarity of wheat (because of climate and soil) had long been proverbial before Dr. Johnson wrote his famous dictionary definition of oats, as " a grain which in England is commonly given to horses, but in Scotland supports the people ". From barley came the malt needed for the brewing of ale. Oatmeal and its products, together with milk, cheese and fish, and probably in smaller measure, butter and meat, made up the food supply of the ordinary people. It must not be thought that these things were always to be had in plenty. One writer, about 1200, tells us casually of a serious famine which brought a crowd of folk to Melrose abbey in hope of sustenance.

Further evidence of the importance of agriculture is given by the amply recorded fact that mills were numerous, widespread and busy. Possession of a mill was highly valuable, and a lord would strive to ensure that his tenants never took their corn to be ground at any mill but his own. Unfree tenants were " thirled " to their lord's mill, that is, legally obliged to use it and pay mill-duty or " multure ". The building of a new mill could be carried out only after careful agreement with the owners of existing mills using the same river. Thus, around 1180, the Bishop of St. Andrews gave the Earl of Fife permission to build a mill at Dairsie on the River Eden for half a mark a year and on condition that if the bishop's own mill should break down temporarily, his corn could be ground at the earl's mill free of charge, " immediately after the corn already in the hopper ". At the same time the earl gave permission for the canons of the

---

[1] Middle Gaelic, *dabach*, a vat or large measure.

bishop's cathedral church to construct a mill and mill-pond on his land at Nydie, a mile or two downstream, apparently asking nothing in return.

We know very little about the peasants of early medieval Scotland. What little we do know points to an agrarian pattern very like that of northern England. There are no signs of a south-country manorial system under which most villages contained a substantial area of demesne belonging directly to the lord of the manor and worked in conjunction with the land held by the villeins. Instead, the northern peasantry usually lived in relatively scattered townships or hamlets, and fulfilled their obligations to the lord not by onerous week work on his demesne but by regular renders of food, commonly malt, cheese, grain and meal. In addition, they performed certain seasonal labour services and perhaps carriage service also. The food renders were paid by free and unfree alike. They took two forms, (i) " can " (later " kain "), a substantial yearly tribute in recognition of lordship, (ii) " coneveth " or " conveth ", which was the obligation of giving one's lord hospitality, and could be performed either to the lord personally whenever he came to stay with his tenants or in the form of a rent in a year when the lord paid no visit. The abbot and canons of Scone, who were great landlords, were entitled to the following coneveth every year from each davach of their estates : 1 cow, 2 pigs, 4 sacks of flour, 10 thraves [1] of oats, 10 hens, 200 eggs, 10 bundles of candles, 4 pennyworth of soap and 20 measures of cheese.

The typical unfree Scottish peasant was not called a villein but a " neyf " (Latin, *nativus*, one born and bred in a particular locality). The neyf might have some security of tenure, but he could be and often was transferred, with his land, from one lord to another. Much would depend on the attitude and influence of the lord, as the following case shows. Around 1180, the king had granted part of Arbuthnott in Mearns as a fief to one of his barons. For the next twenty years this baron's successors and their lessees apparently strove to bring the whole of Arbuthnott under cultivation as a single estate, turning pasture into arable and evicting small-holders in the process. But part of the village belonged to the powerful bishop and church of St. Andrews : it was the *kirketun*, the " church's village ", and, as one of the " improving lairds " related when the matter was

[1] A thrave is a number of sheaves, usually 24 or 26.

referred to a court in 1206, the inhabitants of the Kirkton of
Arbuthnott proved obstructive :

> Isaac of Benvie said that when he took the lease of Arbuthnott the
> Kirkton was well built up, with eight tenants and others under them who
> had houses and animals at pasture. The service owed him from every
> house was 10 cheeses and three men to work once in the autumn at the
> harvest. These bishop's men might use the mill on Fridays free of charge,
> and when he annoyed them by wishing them to be bound by the same
> customs as those observed by his own men, they showed him the place on
> their own land where they had formerly had a mill and said they had the
> power to re-erect a mill there. Isaac thereupon came to an agreement
> with them, realising that it was useless to quarrel with them since the
> bishop protected them as his own. But when one called Gillanders the
> One-footed was more rebellious towards him than the rest, thinking that
> if this man were got out of the way he might deal with the others at his will,
> he offered Bishop Hugh a horse worth 5 marks to remove him. *But on
> hearing that Gillanders was a neyf, the bishop replied that he would on no
> account do so.*[1]

When Bishop Hugh and the insubordinate Gillanders died, later
lords evicted the tenants one after another ; but eventually the
church of St. Andrews recovered its property and (it may be hoped)
its tenants.

This process of changing over from pasture to agriculture may
have received some impetus from a statute of 1214 which ordered
every countryman rich enough to own four cows to take land from
his lord and begin to plough and sow for his living. As for security
of tenure, it was probably less common for a neyf to be evicted than
for him to flee to another lord's lands. The surviving royal commands to restore fugitive serfs to their lawful lords have often been
taken to mean that unfree tenants suffered harsh oppression in our
period. The references are in fact too numerous and general to
admit of this interpretation. The conclusion we ought rather to
draw is that a fairly acute shortage of labour prevailed. Much
development was afoot, but for some generations at least the population failed to keep pace with it.

It is not easy to determine the degree of serfdom borne by the
various groups within the peasant class. Occasionally the term
bondus is used in early documents to denote a Scots peasant, and
some later translators have taken this word to mean " bondsman ",
with all its implications of personal unfreedom. In fact, it is the

---

[1] *Miscellany of the Spalding Club*, v. 210-11, translated and abridged
(my italics).

latinised form of a Scandinavian or Anglo-Saxon word meaning simply " small farmer ". We are not surprised to learn that the lesser men of Caithness were called *bondi*, for this was a Norse district ; but the word was also used in Fife aᵤd Stirlingshire, and we cannot be sure that the men so called were completely servile. Probably in Scotland, as in England, some depression of the majority of the peasantry took place during the twelfth and thirteenth centuries, the Scots neyf going the same way as the English villein.

It is clear, however, that there existed a substantial class of lesser free men who held only small amounts of land and could hardly have had the same social status as the incoming knights and serjeants. Men of this type possessed land individually, and place-name evidence tells us that a man's holding might be divided among his sons or pass to his daughter.[1] The real difficulty is to decide what, if any, social distinction should be drawn between such men who, though they appear to have been free, can in many cases have held little more than a peasant's holding, and the not unimportant class of native freeholders who were able to adapt themselves to some extent to the incoming military feudalism of Norman type. These freeholders were obviously too numerous to be eliminated or reduced

[1] Thus, Couttie near Coupar-Angus was Cupirmaccultin, " Coupar of the sons of Ultan " ; Shettleston in Glasgow was [Bal]inien Schedin, the " *tūn* or village of Schedin's daughter ".

MAP VII. THE FEUDAL KINGDOM OF SCOTLAND IN THE THIRTEENTH CENTURY (*see opposite page*).

Principal royal burghs are shown.

Names of notable families shown in the areas of their influence,

thus :   .   .   .   .   **MELVILLE**

The families so indicated did not necessarily enjoy this influence for the whole of the century.

Diocesan boundaries are given in simplified form.   Episcopal sees shown

thus :   .   .   .   .   ⚲

Some of the principal religious houses shown thus :   .   .   +

MAP VII

to peasant level as a class, and as the rigid structure of twelfth-century feudalism gave way to the more flexible relationships of the thirteenth century, it seems likely that the dividing line between their descendants and the descendants of the knights and serjeants became blurred and finally disappeared. One group of pre-feudal freeholders succeeded in retaining its identity throughout our period. The thanes, whose service consisted in managing the estates of the king or some other great lord, may be found in records relating to the whole of Scotland from Inverness-shire to Stirling, from the early twelfth century to the reign of Robert I and beyond. The thane was subordinate to the sheriff, and his closest English equivalent by this date might seem to have been the bailiff of a royal manor or hundred ; but since the thane's office was normally hereditary, he ranked higher in the social scale than the royal bailiff, and a few thanes held estates so large that they ranked with knights or lesser barons.

In the upper strata of Scottish society, we find that a closer equation is possible between Scotland and England. From the later years of David I's reign, and with increasing intensity under Malcolm IV and William I, tenure by knight-service became the normal mode by which the larger estates were held. But whereas in England the king had commonly granted out enormous estates in return for which their lords provided the service of some scores of knights, the Scottish king more often enfeoffed men for a single knight's service. Despite their relatively small service, such men, holding in chief of the Crown, ranked as the king's barons. In this fact lies the explanation of the important contrast between English and Scottish stratification, the former dividing barons (= great lords) from knights (= country gentry), the latter dividing nobles (= great lords) from barons (= country gentry). The typical Scots baron was poorer than his English namesake, but he was a military tenant-in-chief of the Crown and he also stood closer to the common people of the land. Nevertheless, in our period there can as yet have been little difference between the feudal classes of the two kingdoms : in many instances the knightly and baronial families of Scotland had been founded by younger sons of similar families south of the border.

In the topmost ranks of this class there were a few lords whose position was anomalous. In legal theory they were barons, but the estates they held were so large that they were in fact the equal of the earls, who still ranked first among the nobility of Scotland. Such were Brus, lord of Annandale, the Steward, lord of Renfrew, and the heads of the families of Comyn, Moray, and Oliphant. The oddness of their position is a tribute to the tenacity of the native earls, who even under the fullest impact of foreign feudalism never allowed their precedence to be entirely displaced. In this matter there was give and take, instead of the clean break with older practice which we have noted in England. The earldoms were to some extent feudalised. They were held of the king in chief, obeyed feudal rules of succession, and some owed fixed and probably military service. An earl did not think it beneath him to receive a single knight's fee from the king, while on the other hand an earldom could be a prize for an ambitious feudatory. Before 1286, four of the Celtic earldoms passed by marriage into the possession of families of " Anglo-Norman " origin, the first being Buchan, acquired by William Comyn in 1214. Moreover, the earls were not the only native lords with whom the newcomers had to share power. The lay " abbots " of Abernethy, e.g. became without any break of descent the baronial lords of Abernethy, and the hereditary lay " priest " of the ancient sanctuary of Applecross, Farquhar Mactaggart,[1] was knighted and made Earl of Ross by King Alexander II.

Between 1153 and 1286 there took place an expansion of town life in Scotland which, if smaller in scale, compares for rapidity and relative importance with contemporary English development. Almost all the well-known burghs of Scotland had become established by the end of our period, including the six which would rank today as the best known in the kingdom, Edinburgh, Glasgow (developed by its bishops from *c.* 1174), Aberdeen (really two towns, " old " and episcopal and " new " and royal),[2] Dundee, Stirling, and Perth. The four chief towns were still Berwick, Roxburgh, Edinburgh, and Stirling ; they observed common customs, based on or closely cognate with those of Newcastle-on-Tyne, and known as the " Laws of the Four Burghs ". The reign of William I (1165-1214) has a place in Scottish burghal history comparable with those of Richard I

---

[1] *Maccintsacairt,* " son of the priest ".
[2] It should be added that New Aberdeen, dating from William I's reign or earlier, ranked as a burgh in our period, while Old Aberdeen did not achieve this status until the fifteenth century.

and John in England. Many burghs trace their origin or early privileges to a grant of William the Lion, from Aberdeen and the towns of Moray north of the Mounth, to whose burghers he gave the right to have their free " hanse " [1] (gild), to the burgh of the " New Castle upon Are " (Ayr), founded in Kyle *c.* 1203-6, whose townsmen were given the same liberties as those enjoyed by every other Scots burgh. The immediate government of a burgh was in the charge of one or more *prepositi,* provosts, who, though they acted primarily as the servants and agents of the king or other lord of the burgh, may sometimes have been elected by their fellow burghers. Some degree of self-government was achieved by Scottish burghs in the thirteenth century, when a burgh might have a body of aldermen, its own burgh court, and a common seal which symbolised its power to transact business corporately. In the early charters of privileges (e.g. those given to Perth, Stirling, and Aberdeen), care was taken to provide that the fullers and weavers should be excluded from the merchant gild. This shows that the industry of cloth-making was well-established in the Scottish burghs during the reign of William the Lion. It is probable that the merchants who financed the manufacture of cloth and then marketed it and the craftsmen who wove and " walked " it,[2] were supplied by the immigration of men and women of foreign origin, Flemish and English especially. Like the Welshman, the Celtic Scot did not then take readily to town life. The burgh communities, though important, remained until the close of the twelfth century small alien outposts of commerce, sharply marked off from their rural hinterland.

The development of towns may provide part of the answer to one of the most interesting and puzzling problems of our period. By the time of Robert I (1306-29), a northern version of the English tongue had effectively replaced Gaelic almost everywhere in southern and eastern Scotland, save for Galloway in the south-west, Buchan in the north-east, and the highland parts of those modern counties which have a coastline on the North Sea. Even before the death of William the Lion (1214) a few country places north of Forth and Tay had been given English names. But they are of very rare

---

[1] The German word may have been used because of the strongly Flemish composition of the burghers in Aberdeen, Elgin, Inverness, etc.

[2] The north-country term for fulling cloth was and is " walking ", a word of Old English origin.

occurrence as early as this, and there is little doubt that well into the thirteenth century Gaelic remained the speech of the lowland countryside of Scotland north of the Forth, while in the highlands its supremacy was not challenged until the eighteenth century. To this general rule the towns formed an. exception. The recorded names of townsfolk in our period are in the main English, Flemish, and French. The burgh communities must have had a considerable share in spreading Northumbrian English beyond the Forth and Tay. We have no vernacular literature surviving from thirteenth-century Scotland, but when such a literature does emerge in the fourteenth century, e.g. in the grand epic poem of *The Bruce* by the Aberdonian John Barbour, it is far too vigorous and confident not to have had a pretty long ancestry.

Towns existed primarily for trade, not industry, which, apart from cloth-making, formed in Scotland an uncommon though not quite insignificant variation from agriculture in certain country districts. Gold and iron were mined, probably in very small quantities. The making of salt was an extremely necessary activity, for the nearest rock salt was in Cheshire and would be expensive to import. The salt was obtained by evaporating brine in salt-pans dug along the coast, often beside tidal estuaries. Salt-making evidently flourished widely, though no doubt production was designed chiefly to meet local demand. A famous episode in Scottish history tells incidentally of the importance of the industry. When King Alexander III crossed the Forth on the night of his sudden death in 1286, he was met at Inverkeithing and offered lodging by the master of the royal saltworks. The making of salt, which required great quantities of fuel, may have stimulated the growth of an industry which was to become much more famous in Britain, and in which the men of Lothian were pioneers. Already by the close of the twelfth century, coal was being won at Carriden and Preston on the southern shores of the Firth of Forth, in part " between the ebb and flow of the sea ". Coal was not mined but quarried, for the seams came to the surface. The fact that a particularly black and horrible dungeon in Berwick castle was nicknamed " Cole " in the twelfth century may show that its use was not unfamiliar ; but the domestic fuel of ordinary folk, then and for long after, was wood and peat. The country was almost certainly more thickly wooded then than it is today, even after two centuries of fairly steady planting. It was probably only in the twelfth century that the growing population of Scotland embarked intensively on that prodigal exploitation of its rich inheritance of standing timber which by the seventeenth century had almost entirely bereft the lowlands of their trees. Peat, however, was in general use, except perhaps in densely forested regions like Strathtay, Strathspey, and Badenoch.

2. The Church

The lines along which the Church in Scotland was to develop during the 150 years after David I's death had already been laid down in the first half of the twelfth century. First, we see the establishment of a diocesan system with a fixed number of bishops' sees, with cathedral churches served by organised chapters of clergy, with a steady increase in the number of parishes and a general diocesan administration in the charge of archdeacons and rural deans. Secondly, we observe how the ties by which the Church of the Scots was bound to the western Church as a whole—and especially to its nerve-centre, the papal court—were at once multiplied and drawn still closer, so that in the thirteenth century the Papacy was able to supervise ecclesiastical affairs in Scotland in astonishing detail. Thirdly, we can discern little diminution until the close of the twelfth century in the leading part played by the various religious orders in the life of the Church.

All this was foreshadowed in the history of the Church under Alexander I and David I, yet in 1153 much remained for the future. By the second half of the twelfth century the two largest dioceses, St. Andrews and Glasgow, had an organisation closely similar to that of their English counterparts. Each bishop had his cathedral church, which, if not yet completed, was at least building. About 1170, Bishop Richard of St. Andrews gave lands towards the construction of the new cathedral, which had been started some ten years earlier. He decreed that the burgesses of St. Andrews must not demand " stallage " (a kind of purchase-tax) from the masons, stone-cutters, and quarrymen engaged on the new work ; they were to be neither exploited nor enticed away to other tasks. The contemporary Bishop of Glasgow, Jocelin, formed a society to collect funds for building which was patronised by the king—a twelfth-century equivalent of the "Friends of Glasgow Cathedral" or some similar modern association. Like most other great churches of the day, Glasgow cathedral suffered severely from fire, and was almost wholly rebuilt between 1181 and 1194. It was served by a chapter of secular canons under a dean. The bishop had only one archdeacon until 1238, when the diocese was divided into two archdeaconries. The position at St. Andrews was somewhat different. It resembled Carlisle (with which it had an early connection) in having a chapter of Augustinian canons-regular under a prior, so that it was in effect a monastic cathedral, and the bishops from an early date created a household and staff quite independent of the necessarily cloistered and confined members of the chapter. In this large straggling diocese there were two archdeacons, one each for north and south of the Forth respectively. To preside over their courts both bishops had appointed officials by *c.* 1200, doubtless clerks trained in the Canon Law at the schools of Paris or Oxford. South of the Clyde-Forth line before 1153, north of it from *c.* 1180, rural deans had been appointed among the parish clergy.

These two dioceses comprised the wealthiest part of Scotland, but we should remember that there were nine others in which the setting up of a diocesan organisation had barely gone beyond the appointment of bishops. It was only gradually that endowments could be obtained to enable the lesser bishops to found their cathedral churches, establish chapters, and provide for archdeacons and officials. Often some famous English cathedral was taken as the model for a new foundation. The Customs of Salisbury, e.g. which had been adopted at Glasgow between 1147 and 1164, were also chosen for Dunkeld, *c.* 1236, while those of Lincoln were copied at Elgin when the Bishop of Moray finally established his see there in 1224. In contrast with English practice, a few Scottish cathedral chapters included the heads of the richer religious houses of their dioceses, a device probably intended to strengthen the chapter where there was insufficient income to provide prebends for more than a handful of secular canons. In one or two dioceses the parish clergy were never organised within rural deaneries.

Owing largely to its close association with the Crown, the Scottish Church during the twelfth century developed a keen sense of its own corporate unity. Although St. Andrews was not made a metropolitan see, the extremely influential Pope Alexander III

(1159-81) recognised the *Ecclesia Scoticana* as a distinct entity both by appointing a Scots bishop legate for the dioceses which were subject to the King of Scotland, and by absolving the Scots clergy from the non-committal oath of obedience to the English Church they had sworn in 1174. In 1165, moreover, he authorised the consecration of a new Bishop of St. Andrews by the other bishops of Scotland. Previously, bishops of St. Andrews recognised by the Papacy had been consecrated either by the Archbishop of York or by a specially appointed papal legate. Finally, on March 13th, 1192, Pope Celestine III issued the famous bull *Cum universi*, in which he declared that the Scottish Church ought to be subject immediately to the apostolic see " whose special daughter she is ". Henceforth, no one but the Pope or his personal legate was to utter a sentence of interdict or excommunication against the Scottish kingdom, and no disputes brought before Church tribunals were to be heard outside Scotland unless an appeal was taken to the papal court itself. The issue of this bull has been called " an epoch-making event in Scottish history ", " marking the end of York's authority in Scotland ". What it did in fact was to make clear and authoritative a constitutional independence of York which the Scottish clergy had effectively enjoyed for over fifty years, and to couple with this a statement of their direct dependence on the Papacy. Where Scotland was concerned, *Cum universi* acknowledged an accomplished fact ; where the Papacy was concerned, it was no more than the expression of standard papal policy.

The *Ecclesia Scoticana* was defined in 1192 as the nine dioceses of St. Andrews, Glasgow, Dunkeld, Aberdeen, Moray, Brechin, Dunblane, Ross and Caithness. Galloway, though subject to the Scottish Crown, was thus omitted : its bishop succeeded in preserving the historic attachment of his see of Whithorn to York, which dated back to the Northumbrian bishopric of Whithorn in the eighth century.[1] Around 1200 a new diocese was created for Argyll, so that for the rest of our period there were ten dioceses in the Church of Scotland, but the land ruled by the Scottish kings included Galloway as an eleventh and (after the annexation of the Isles in 1266) Sodor and Man as a twelfth diocese.

---

[1] This in turn had been a deliberate revival of the missionary church founded by the Strathclyde Briton Ninian, the first evangeliser of the Picts, probably in the fifth century.

The favour shown by the twelfth-century Papacy towards the Scottish Church was not maintained so emphatically by Innocent III and his successors. It is true that in 1225 the Scots clergy received an important concession when Pope Honorius III decreed that they could and should convene an annual council of their Church. But this was to be held under direct papal authority, and instead of confirming the unofficial primacy enjoyed by the Bishop of St. Andrews and making him *ex officio* convener and president of the council, the papal privilege stipulated for the inconvenient device by which any one of the Scottish bishops might be chosen as " conservator " and preside over the assembly of the Church.

In addition to legislating directly and addressing a steady stream of judicial and administrative letters to the clergy of Scotland, the Popes sent legates to convene special councils of the Church at which important disputes were settled and " canons "—i.e. ecclesiastical laws—were promulgated. Such visits took place in 1177, 1180, 1201, 1221 and 1239. The Council held at Perth in 1201 by the Cardinal John of Salerno was probably the most fruitful example of legatine activity. At this meeting, many rules and decrees approved at the Third Lateran Council of 1179 as part of the law of the whole Church of the west were formally published, and thereafter the Scots bishops and their officials proceeded to put them into effect in their various dioceses. The Scottish prelates did not always wait for a legatine visit in order to keep informed of oecumenical legislation and policy. William Malvoisin, Bishop of St. Andrews from 1202 to 1238, attended the great Fourth Lateran Council in 1215 along with Bishop Walter of Glasgow and Bishop Brice of Moray, and Malvoisin's official acts show him applying conciliar legislation in his own diocese. His successor, David Bernham, likewise attended the Council held at Lyons in 1245 by Pope Innocent IV, and he issued canons for his clergy and spent much time touring his bishopric to consecrate parish and other churches which, though long in use, had not hitherto been formally consecrated.[1]

Bishop Malvoisin was the most eminent bishop of the Scots in our period. His zeal for law and justice, his alert attention to infringements of the rights and dignity of his office and his see, any the respect which was accorded him by clergy and laity alike, mad

[1] This was in obedience to a canon promulgated at the Council held at Edinburgh in 1239 by the legate, Cardinal Otto.

all be seen in his own and other recorded acts of the time. He furthered the building of the " new " cathedral of St. Andrews, and was the first bishop to be buried within it. Belonging to a generation of churchmen who believed that the monastic orders should not be active in secular affairs, Malvoisin clearly did not favour the established abbeys and priories. On the other hand, he was a patron of hospitals, and of the mendicant friars, Dominicans and Franciscans, who first entered Scotland towards the end of his episcopate, in 1230 and 1231 respectively. Though a Norman himself, he had many clerks of Scottish origin in his household, and his episcopate marks a definite turning point in the history of the Scottish Church : from *c.* 1107 down to his time, foreign influence had been overwhelmingly dominant ; after 1238, the *Ecclesia Scoticana*, thoroughly integrated as it was within the body of the western Church, became more Scottish in personnel and outlook. David Bernham was the first native Scot to be Bishop of St. Andrews for nearly a century and a half, and after his time it was unusual for a clergyman of foreign origin to hold this pre-eminent see.

In any survey of Scottish society in the thirteenth century, there is little danger of exaggerating the importance of the Church. On the merely material plane, the cathedral foundations and, still more, the greater abbeys and priories were among the largest landowners in the realm. It is true that David I's prodigality in this respect was not matched by his descendants, but several notable religious houses were founded in the century which followed his death, e.g. Coupar-Angus (1160-4) by Malcolm IV, and Balmerino (1229) by Alexander II (both Cistercian), Paisley (1163) by Walter the Steward (Cluniac), and Arbroath (1178) by William I, and Lindores (*c.* 1194) by David, Earl of Huntingdon (both for Tironian monks from Kelso). Of these, the great abbey of Arbroath, dedicated to St. Thomas the Martyr—Thomas Becket—in reconciliation, since he was believed to have helped Henry II to overcome King William in 1174, was the most magnificent. It had property in many parts of the north and east, as well as custody of the banner sacred to St. Columba beneath which the Scots were wont to go into battle. In political affairs also the Church held a leading position. The bishops of St. Andrews and Glasgow in particular ranked among the king's most influential counsellors, and in the thirteenth century they were usually men who had spent many years in royal service before their elevation to episcopal office. We shall not comprehend the depth or obstinacy of Scottish resistance to Edward I after 1296 unless we remember that the Scots clergy inherited by long tradition a jealous desire to preserve the liberty of their Church from all external interference save that of the Papacy.

Finally, it was inevitably through the Church that Scotland was enabled to participate in the intellectual movements of the day. The learning and scholarship of continental Europe were once more brought to the Scots, who in turn contributed something of their own to the common fund of human thought and knowledge. Adam of Dryburgh (?1140-?1212), first a Premonstratensian canon in his native Berwickshire, later a Carthusian monk at Witham, was renowned before the close of the twelfth century both as a preacher and for the sanctity of his life. Michael Scot, who probably came from Scotland, had as his patron the Emperor Frederick II. He translated works by Aristotle, and commentaries upon them by the Cordovan Arab philosopher Averroes, and wrote widely on topics of natural science. Peter Ramsay, Bishop of Aberdeen (1247-56), had previously succeeded the great Robert Grosseteste as master of the Franciscan school at Oxford. At least four Scottish doctors, or as we should call them, professors, taught at Paris University within our period, and of these the Franciscan John Duns of Maxton in Roxburghshire (1266-1308), "Duns Scotus" as he is commonly known, became a philosopher of European distinction and lasting fame. Yet it must be admitted that no school within Scotland itself grew in this period to university status. The young Scots clerk who hungered after learning and the delights of research and disputation must travel either to Oxford [1] or else farther afield, to Paris and the universities of Italy.

3. *The Kingdom Defined*

To the rule that in our period kings must be as violent, callous and unfilial in their private lives as they were ruthless in affairs of state, the royal family of Scotland offered a benign exception. The mutual love of David I and his son Earl Henry was proverbial, and

[1] Here in 1282 a Scotswoman, Dervorguilla, lady of Galloway and widow of John Balliol, founded a college (later Balliol College) originally endowed by her husband with scholarships of 8*d*. a week.

it is only the unsupported and in part demonstrably inaccurate statement of a chronicler writing two and a half centuries later which tells of any bad blood between Malcolm the Maiden (1153-65) and his brother William the Lion (1165-1214). The third grandson of King David, his namesake David, Earl of Huntingdon from 1185 to 1219, remained on the best of terms with his elder brother during his long reign, and what we know of his career in no way contradicts the eulogy of a versifying clerk who knew him personally, that

> he was a very gentle knight,
> No holy church or abbey was ever robbed by him
> Nor did any under his command injure a priest.
> He was most wise, filled with good grace ;
> He protected holy church, and wished that none should harm
> A priest or a canon who knew Latin,
> Or give annoyance to a nun from an abbey.[1]

The two kings of the thirteenth century, Alexander II (1214-49) and Alexander III (1249-86), respectively son and grandson of William the Lion, did not inherit in marked degree the religious devotion characteristic of many of St. Margaret's nearer descendants, but they were forthright and honourable men.

We shall best appreciate the course of political events between 1153 and 1286 if we grasp the fact that all four rulers of the period were faced by two major problems, the preservation of their own kingdom intact and their relations with the English monarchy, and that each problem was complicated by a subsidiary issue. In the first place, King David's bequest of a united Scottish kingdom could hardly be maintained, still less enjoyed in peace, unless its boundaries towards the Norse-dominated north and west were defined much more precisely. The failure of the Norwegian rulers to exercise firm government in the Orkneys and the Hebrides led directly to the campaigns of William I and Alexander II against Ross, Caithness and Argyll, for the leading men of these remote regions, whenever they wished to rebel against the monarchy, found in the islands either an inaccessible refuge or a ready source of support. Secondly, the care which the Scots kings took not to be committed to any definite subjection to the Angevins was persistently thwarted by their own territorial ambitions south of the Solway-Tweed border and by their privileged possession, from 1157 to 1174, and again

[1] Jordan Fantosme, *Chronique de la guerre entre les Anglois et les Ecossois*, ed. Michel (Surtees Soc., 1840), lines 1102 ff. and 1141 ff.

from 1185 to 1237 or later,[1] of the earldom of Huntingdon. These ambitions and actual possessions were for the Scots kings what Normandy and Aquitaine were for the English—subordinate tenures held by a ruler who within his own domains claimed to be sovereign.

For the first few years of Malcolm IV's brief reign, while the king was still a boy, the government was in the hands of a small group of influential magnates, his mother, Ada de Warenne, Countess of Northumberland, his steward, Walter son of Alan, Bishop Herbert of Glasgow and one or two others. During this crucial minority Henry of Anjou gained the throne of England, and the initiative in Anglo-Scottish relations shifted for ever from north to south. In 1157 King Henry set the border firmly at the Solway-Tweed line, and in compensation for the lost northern counties enfeoffed King Malcolm with the honour of Huntingdon held by his father and grandfather. The Scots king regarded this midland earldom as no more than his right, and undoubtedly wished for Cumberland and Northumberland as well. But his overriding desire for the moment was to receive at his cousin's hands the belt of knighthood, the socially indispensable honour which David I had bestowed upon King Henry himself in 1149. Malcolm was kept waiting for the distinction until the summer of 1159, when it was given him while on his way to Toulouse in Henry II's abortive expedition of that year. As Earl of Huntingdon, Malcolm was Henry's vassal, obliged to ride with his contingent to the host ; but the two [2] young grandsons of King David were doubtless prompted less by feudal obligation than by the call of adventure and a keenness to win their spurs in something more serious than a tournament. The English king, however, was bent on making the relationship between himself and the King of Scots the strictly feudal one of liege lord to liege vassal. The Scots were anxious to avoid anything so precise. Malcolm IV's first homage to Henry II, in 1157, was probably ambiguous ; but the second, exacted at Woodstock in 1163, was almost certainly seen by the English to be more strictly binding. It took place, significantly,

[1] The *Complete Peerage* (ed. Gibbs, vi. 647) states that on the death of Earl John of Scotland in 1237 his honours became extinct ; yet seisin of the earldom of Huntingdon was then granted to King Alexander II (*Bracton's Notebook*, ed. Maitland, Case No. 1221). During the later part of William I's reign, from 1185 to 1214, the earldom was held by his brother David ; John of Scotland was his son.

[2] William of Scotland accompanied his brother on the Toulouse expedition.

on an occasion when homages were being rendered by the princes of Wales, and it involved the surrender as a hostage not, it is true, of Malcolm's heir William, but nevertheless of the youngest royal brother, David, " as security for King Malcolm's castles which the King of England wished to have ". Both monarchies were moving towards a closer definition of their relationship, the English wishing to emphasise Scottish dependence, the Scots on their side willing to acknowledge feudal subjection only in respect of lands that formed part of the realm of England. These might on a wide interpretation include Lothian, but not " Scotia " or Scotland proper.

Against Henry of England Malcolm the Maiden fought a rather unsuccessful rearguard action, but in his government of the Scots he was a worthy heir of David I. Deeply imbued with the spirit of chivalry and valuing his Warenne inheritance higher than his ancient Scottish lineage, he relied even more than his grandfather on the support of military tenants of foreign origin—chiefly Normans and Flemings—to whom he granted knights' fees in Clydesdale, Moray and elsewhere. Yet despite his predilection for French men and customs, Malcolm IV was accepted as rightful king throughout the greater part of Scotland. The sons of Malcolm Macheth, it is true, made a bid for power in alliance with the Hebridean chief Somerled. One of them was captured in 1156, and though Somerled himself was not induced to make peace until 1160, the king evidently discounted the seriousness of the Macheth claim long before this, for in 1157 he released Malcolm Macheth from Roxburgh castle and gave him the rank of earl. The gravest revolt against King Malcolm which was undoubtedly internal (for the Isles were not within the kingdom of Scotland) was prompted by the Toulouse expedition of 1159, which to some of the native magnates seemed an admission of Henry II's feudal overlordship. On the king's return in 1160, Earl Ferteth of Strathearn and five other earls plotted to capture him at Perth : doubtless not an attempt on his life, but the more " constitutional " device—all too common in later Scottish history—of kidnapping the sovereign and then governing in his name. Even this plot, which was foiled at once, was connected with a rising in Galloway, which at this date was scarcely an integral part of the kingdom. It was in this wild region that King Malcolm, in three expeditions in 1160, finally defeated the rebellious earls ; and thereafter we hear of no more domestic insurrection.

Malcolm the Maiden, as his almost contemporary sobriquet implies, remained unmarried,[1] probably from deliberate choice. A projected marriage with the Count of Brittany's daughter came to nothing, and when he died, December 9th, 1165, after some years of painful physical affliction, the heir to the throne was his brother William, a rash and robust young man, sharing Malcolm's enthusiasm for the ways of chivalry, but of an altogether more worldly stamp. Some account has already been given of his ill-judged interventions in English affairs, which turned a rearguard action into ignominious defeat and resulted in the subjection of the Scottish crown from 1174 to 1189 and an unnecessary submission to King John in 1209. But William's tireless assertion of royal authority within the confines of his own kingdom, which must now receive a brief notice, will to a large extent restore the balance in any final estimate of his reign. On the military side, the challenge to William the Lion came from two remote and separatist regions, Galloway and the far north, neither as yet fully assimilated to the kingdom ruled by the Canmore dynasty. The challenge may also be divided chronologically into two phases, the first lasting from 1174 to 1187, the second, much less continuously, from 1197 to 1212.

The leaders of opposition in the south-west were Uhtred and Gilbert, the sons of Fergus, lord of Galloway (d. 1161), and cousins of Henry II through their mother, a natural daughter of Henry I. Partly because of this relationship, partly because the region had always held aloof from Scotland, the English king often treated Galloway as a separate province, and occasionally played off its princes against the Scottish king. A quarrel over precedence arose between the brothers, and deepened to a bitter feud when, in 1174, Gilbert had Uhtred savagely murdered. William of Scotland took the part of Uhtred's son Roland, while Henry of England, though not condoning the crime, eventually supported Gilbert's son Duncan when his father died in 1185. At the news of his uncle's death Roland, evidently trained as a knight and schooled in Norman ways, overran Galloway with horse and foot and built castles to hold down the people. King Henry saw in this private enterprise a breach of

[1] The belief that he begot an illegitimate son, accepted by most historians from Lord Hailes (1776) to the present, is probably founded on error. For a full review of the evidence, see A. C. Lawrie, *Scot. Hist. Rev.*, xii (1915), 437-9, and R. L. G. Ritchie, *The Normans in Scotland* (1954), 413-17.

his own peace, led an army to Carlisle, and commanded William the Lion to bring Roland to submission. But William had doubtless connived at Roland's action, and by his agency a settlement was reached confirming southern Galloway (modern Wigtownshire and Kirkcudbrightshire) to Roland and compensating Duncan with the lordship of Carrick, the southern part of modern Ayrshire. In 1196 Roland became Constable of Scotland, while Duncan, son of the ruffian Gilbert, lived to become a respectable first Earl of Carrick under Alexander II.

The malcontents who were able for a century or more to rouse the north-west highlands to rebellion were chiefly the descendants of William, son of King Duncan II. Although no hereditary claim which William might have had to the Scottish throne ever seems to have been considered, David I had treated him as a protégé, friend and ally. In addition to a lawful son of his own name who died young, William had another son, perhaps illegitimate, whose upbringing in some purely Gaelic-speaking district may safely be inferred from his regular style of Donald MacWilliam. The established reigning family accorded him no recognition. He seems to have begun to make trouble in 1179, for in that year the king went to Ross and built castles to guard the Black Isle passage from Inverness to Sutherland. Two years later Donald broke into serious revolt. In 1186 one of his sons was sacrilegiously besieged and burned to death in Coupar-Angus abbey by the Earl of Atholl, but not until the following year was King William able to undertake a campaign of suppression, using Inverness as his base. None of the Scottish kings between Alexander I and Robert Brus showed any outstanding military aptitude, and it was not the king but a band of young men (including the household of Roland of Galloway) sent out by the earls to scout and forage who, in July, 1187, surprised MacWilliam " on a moor near Moray called Mam Garvia ".[1] Donald himself and many of his followers were slain, and peace restored to king and kingdom.

The MacWilliams were a prolific clan, and another of Donald's

---

[1] The locality of Mam Garvia (" rough moor "), a name which has now disappeared, has not been established. Among the possibilities are Garve in Ross-shire and Meall Garbha, at the foot of the Pass of Corrieyairack (Inverness-shire), over which General Wade found it worth while in 1731 to build a road to facilitate and control the crossing from Badenoch into Glenmore.

sons, Guthred, who had been skulking in Ireland, again brought out the men of the north-west in 1211. The north had enjoyed relative peace for twenty years, save for an incursion by a son of the Earl of Orkney in 1197, successfully countered by a royal invasion of Caithness. But in 1211 the king was old and tired, and his thirteen-year-old son Alexander scarcely of an age to lead his father's barons to war. On an appeal to King John, Saer de Quinci, Earl of Winchester and an old friend and vassal of the Scottish king, was sent north with a force of mercenaries. Guthred was captured and hanged. The MacWilliams produced another leader, Guthred's brother Donald Bán ("the fair"), who invaded Moray in 1215 but was killed by Farquhar of Ross. Still the race was not extirpated, for we hear of more MacWilliams in 1228-30. On this occasion, the custody of Moray was given to the Justiciar, William Comyn, Earl of Buchan. The lowland of Moray was already well administered by sheriffs and thanes, but the highest part of the province, known as Badenoch, hitherto ruled neither by earl nor sheriff, seems now to have been made an hereditary lordship for the Comyns, passing from Earl William to his younger son Walter (Earl of Menteith in his wife's right) and on his death to his senior male kinsman, John Comyn "the Red". Badenoch was not a rich district, but commanding as it did one of the principal passes from both north and west highlands into the basin of the Tay, it had much strategic importance.

In the perspective of seven centuries, we can see that the solid achievement of the Scottish Crown under the two Alexanders was the incorporation of the islands and the west highland seaboard. It was a triumph not because this territory was fertile and populous (it was neither), but because failure to control it had proved for the Canmore dynasty a source of chronic weakness. Every strong king of Scotland has grasped the vital importance of mastering the highlands. Agricola and Edward I failed to conquer Scotland because they were unable to hold down this difficult terrain from which continual raids could be launched against the governed areas. Cromwell succeeded in his conquest precisely because he was able to do what the earlier invaders had found beyond their resources.

Scottish history has never lacked drama, but few of its major episodes fall more naturally into dramatic form than the reconquest of the western isles. The tales of Homer and Herodotus are recalled in the violent and colourful feuds among the islesmen and their chiefs, for whom, equally with the land, the tide-swept sounds and fjords of the Hebrides were dominion and natural element. Their rivalries form a series of minor plots played against the background of greater events, the inexorable clash of ambition between two Scottish kings on the one hand, bent on the annexation of the west, and, on the other, Hakon IV (1217-63), one of the most powerful kings of medieval Norway, whose purpose was to bring under his direct governance all the outlying oceanic Norse settlements, Iceland, Greenland and the Scottish archipelagos.

Before the isles could be won for Scotland, Argyll must be subjugated. As early as 1222, Alexander II sailed along this difficult coast and received the homage of the chief men of the district. But, strangely enough, it was not the king who followed up this success with a plan to conquer the Hebrides, but one of his most independent barons, Alan (son of Roland) of Galloway. He married the Earl of Ulster's daughter, built a fleet, and laid waste the Isle of Man. Before his aggression could prove dangerous to the Crown, he died (1234), leaving only daughters. Rather than see their land partitioned among the English husbands of these three ladies, the Gallovidians rose in revolt, but were heavily defeated by a royal army in 1235. It was in the following decade that Alexander II made the annexation of the outer isles an object of his own policy. Envoys were despatched to King Hakon urging the injustice of the treaty of 1098 [1] and, when this argument failed, offering to buy the islands for silver. Hakon's answer was to give full backing to the most successful Hebridean chief of the moment, Harold, Olaf's son, coupled with his daughter's hand in marriage. But in the autumn of 1248, as Harold was bringing home his bride, a great gale off Shetland sank their ship with all her company. This was the Scots' opportunity. Collecting an army and a fleet, King Alexander set off westward to see what force could accomplish. There, perhaps on the eve of triumph, a fever seized him. He was brought to the isle of Kerrera, off Oban, and died on July 8th, 1249.

For the next twelve years, the Hebridean enterprise was postponed. The new king was only eight at his accession, and a momentous change came over English policy towards Scotland. During Henry III's earlier years Anglo-Scottish relations had been comparatively free from aggressiveness on either side. Alexander II

[1] Above, p. 132.

248

had married Henry's sister Joan in 1221, and in 1237 solemnly renounced the Scottish claim to the northern counties. But his English queen bore him no children, and after her death in 1238 he married a French lady, Marie de Coucy, who not only gave birth to the future Alexander III but replaced English by French influence at the Scottish court. Now the case was altered. King Henry was a grown man, in full control of government, with a young daughter, Margaret, whom he gave in marriage to the boy King of Scots in 1251. An understandable fatherly concern for the children went hand in hand with direct interference in Scottish affairs. The magnates of Scotland were split into two factions, and whether Henry's change of attitude was the cause of it or not the alignment was of necessity between those who received his support and stood for English influence and those—usually known as the " patriotic " or " national " party—who opposed him and tried to remove the young king from his tutelage.

The grouping of the factions was guided as much by family feuds as by private interest or considerations of state. The patriot leaders belonged to the immensely powerful family of Comyn, and their senior member, John Comyn the Red, held large estates in England. The Steward, on the other hand, with no land south of the border and everything to gain from an independent Scotland, supported Alan of Lundie, the hereditary royal " Doorward " [1] and self-appointed head of the " English " party. But it is significant that the foremost prelates of the Church, Gamelin, Bishop-elect of St. Andrews, and William Bondington, Bishop of Glasgow, were among the national party. What for the average Scotsman was merely the struggle of Doorward *versus* Comyn might threaten the Church with a revival of English interference.

The Doorward's party gained the upper hand in 1255 by a coup in which they captured the king in Edinburgh castle and haled him away to Roxburgh. Here in September the King of England was royally entertained, and supervised the issue of a statement, in Alexander's name, that the Comyns and other objectionable lords were to be removed from the king's council. At Christmas, however, Bishop Bondington was able to consecrate Gamelin in the see of

---

[1] This office was not of the first rank, but Alan was ambitious, had married a natural daughter of the king and had pretensions to the earldom of Mar.

St. Andrews in spite of strong opposition from the English party. Gamelin boldly took ship for France, laid his case before the papal court, and was unconditionally confirmed in office. The Pope, moreover, excommunicated Gamelin's opponents, and when the sentence was published in Scotland the national party, under the leadership of Walter Comyn, Earl of Menteith, promptly carried out a counter coup, seizing the king at Kinross and hurrying him off to the safety of Stirling castle (1257). The Doorward fled Scotland, and in the next year the English political crisis gave the national party almost a free hand. In the treaty which they made with Llywelyn of Wales (March 18th, 1258), in which it was agreed that neither party should make a separate peace with King Henry, the Scots barons acknowledged that they might be compelled to make such a peace at the behest of their lord the king. Nevertheless, they would do nothing against the treaty except by their king's strictest compulsion and command ; rather would they induce him to become a party to the treaty himself. Compared with the limitations which the English barons were shortly to place on Henry III's freedom of action, this was a very cautious piece of constitutionalism. Yet in proposing to give concerted counsel to their king on a matter of high policy, the Scottish barons were reaching forward from the concept of a primitive feudal *Curia* towards that of Parliament as it would be understood in the fourteenth century.

With King Henry placed under constraint and with the death of the Earl of Menteith before the end of 1258, the tension in Anglo-Scottish relations was relaxed. Not surprisingly, the young King of Scots, now approaching manhood, determined to take up his father's scheme of annexing the Hebrides. An embassy to King Hakon (1261) proved in vain, and shortly afterwards, probably with Alexander's connivance, the Earl of Ross plundered the Isle of Skye. In answer to this provocation, an army and fleet of unprecedented size were summoned to Bergen in May, 1263, and two months later set sail across the North Sea. Our sources are too meagre or ambiguous to tell us whether Hakon's intention was to invade Scotland in earnest or merely to frighten the Scots into abandoning their designs on Norwegian territory. Certainly his fleet, in appearance and conduct, gave proof that the old Viking spirit was still vigorous. The king himself was brought from Norway in a flagship which had twenty-seven oar-banks and a great gilded dragon figurehead. When, towards the end of September, the fleet anchored off the Cumbraes in the Firth of Clyde, a detached flotilla of forty ships sailed to the head of Loch Long, made the mile and a half portage into Loch Lomond, and systematically plundered its shores and islands.

But, in the event, there was no pitched battle. During the night of September 30th a violent tempest sprang up. The Norse ships dragged their anchors and several were blown aground on the mainland near Largs, where their crews were promptly harassed by Scots archers. As soon as the storm had abated slightly (October 1st), King Hakon led his men ashore to give support, though the king himself withdrew at the approach of a strong contingent of Scottish knights. A sharp fight followed, which turned to a confused mêlée as the Norwegians were pressed back on to the beach. It was late in the day when a brief rally gave the invaders breathing space to reach their boats and rejoin the fleet. With food supplies running short and demoralised by the losses they had suffered from the weather and their enemies, the Norwegians weighed anchor and sailed slowly back to Kirkwall in Orkney, where their aged king died on December 16th. Three years later, by the Treaty of Perth, Hakon's successor Magnus IV surrendered to King Alexander his rights over Man and the western isles for 4,000 marks and a future tribute of 100 marks annually. For Scotland, the Age of the Vikings was ended at last.

The twenty year peace which preceded the death of Alexander III has given rise to a legend of the Golden Age of medieval Scotland, a halcyon time before the long winter of war. To the Scottish chroniclers who set down the history of their country at the turn of the fourteenth and fifteenth centuries, the miseries of the long war were as close as its splendours, and not all their accounts of the pre-war period can be taken at their face value. Their general tone was set by Andrew of Wyntoun when, after a long passage extolling the virtues of Alexander " the Peaceable ", he quoted a lament perhaps composed at the close of the thirteenth century.

> When [1] Alexander our king was dead
> That Scotland led in lauche and le,
> Away was sons of ale and bread,
> Of wine and wax, of gamyn and glee.
> Our gold was changéd into lead :
> Christ, born into virginity,
> Succour Scotland and ramede
> That stood is in perplexity.

[1] The commoner words have been given in modern English spelling:

Nevertheless, though the legend may be coloured it contains much truth. The third quarter of the thirteenth century was a time of general prosperity, and there is every reason to believe that Scotland shared in it. Yet there were signs of impending danger. Faction had rent the nobility in 1255 and might do so again under political stress. The king's children—two sons and a daughter, Margaret, married to King Eric II of Norway in 1281—all died before their father, the last in giving birth to another Margaret, " the Maid of Norway ". As with Alexander II, a French queen (Yolande de Dreux) followed an English when, in 1285, the king was left without a son. But instead of heirs, the marriage inadvertently brought disaster. It was his desire to rejoin his new wife that induced Alexander on a night of storm (March 18th-19th, 1286) to ride from Edinburgh to his manor of Kinghorn on the coast of Fife. On the last stage of the journey his guides lost him in the dark, and when daylight came he was found on the shore with his neck broken.

The monarchy, which had survived two minorities and considerably extended its dominion, was obviously strong and stable. Its government was also fairly centralised. If there was no official capital, there is evidence that Edinburgh filled that role in effect as early as Malcolm IV's reign, and its pre-eminence was unquestioned in 1286. Based upon this and other royal castles, the king's control over local affairs, far from negligible under Malcolm IV, increased substantially during our period. The resources of the Crown, and its typical activity, may be briefly described.

Revenue derived from four main sources, (1) the ancient food renders (can and coneveth), payable at the royal manors, and largely commuted for money in the thirteenth century ; (2) profits of justice arising from cases heard by the king or his justiciars and sheriffs ; (3) profits of commerce, in the form either of customs duties or of the rents paid by the royal burghs ; and (4) taxation, assessed on the land units (carucate, davach, etc.), of which " common aid " was occasional and levied from the feudal class, but " common army " or " Scottish service " was more regular and of universal application north of Forth. " Scottish service " might mean actual attendance in the host when the king required it, but it is clear that normally it was rendered in cash or in kind. The king's dependence on pay-

---

lauche = law ; *le* = peace ; *sons* = plenty ; *gamyn* = sport ; *ramede* = bring remedy.

ments in kind is shown by the Exchequer Rolls and by incidental evidence, e.g. the fact that when two English bishops fled from King John to Scotland (1209), William I made them an allowance not of money but of cereals.

In regard to military service, the position was not unlike that in England. The king himself was attended by heavy-armed knights and more lightly equipped serjeants. For the most part these men held their estates on condition of performing this service, which might, of course, take the form of garrisoning the king's castles instead of campaigning in the field. In time of peace the king on occasion levied an aid from his military tenants, normally payable in cash. There is evidence that over much of Scotland outside the remote north and west knight-service had become by 1214 the normal tenure by which large landed estates were held. Even in Argyll, Alexander II and his son each enfeoffed native lords for knight-service or at least castle ward. The " feudal host " could never have been a numerous body, but if the King of Scots was to keep countenance in the intensely chivalric society of western Europe, some force of properly trained knights was indispensable. Besides this, common infantry service was incumbent on the whole population, apparently on free and neyf alike. For calling out this relatively untrained host, the earls were responsible in their respective provinces. Its military value in our period is hard to determine, but even in the early stage of the war with Edward I, the common soldier of Scotland armed with spear or Lochaber axe could give a good account of himself.

The Scots king, like the English, was the fount of justice. The royal obligation to do justice where lesser lords or officials had failed seems in our period to have been taken seriously. The *Curia Regis* itself was normally concerned with the pleas of the Crown's tenants-in-chief. Barons and ecclesiastical lords possessed their own rights of jurisdiction, and the free man would as a rule litigate in their feudal courts or else before the king's sheriff, who, with respect to all but the most important suits, had taken over the justice formerly administered by the royal *judex* (*brithem*) with the assistance of the free men of his district. Cases between clergy and laity were frequently settled, after appeal to Rome, by persons specially delegated as judges by the Pope—as a rule, a panel of three judges to each case. At times men's faith in this international machinery of justice and their disregard for its cost and its delays appear quite astonishing. Papal letters were not to be had for nothing, and the journey from Scotland to Rome and back might well occupy two or three months. Yet in 1225, e.g. a bishop and an unimportant baron thought it worth while to have papal judges-delegate appointed to settle their dispute about fifty acres of land in the wild country at the southern end of Loch Ness.

There are indications that Malcolm IV and William I attempted to introduce royal justices who functioned locally, comparable to the county justiciars of Henry I. This localisation of the chief royal agents of justice, flexible perhaps at first, had crystallised in the thirteenth century into a threefold division of Scotland with a justiciar for each region. Under William I there were justiciars of Lothian and *Scotia*, the country north of Forth. Rather later, a separate justiciar was appointed for Galloway. At the highest level, it became the practice for the king to hold specially solemn sessions of the *Curia Regis*, usually known as *Colloquia*, at which the most weighty legal cases were determined, and where, no doubt, the business of the realm came under discussion. On the side of criminal justice too there was steady development in our period, much of it modelled on or parallel with that of England. Malcolm the Maiden was especially praised for " bringing the inflexible penalty of the law to bear upon thieves, robbers and traitors ". His brother, *c.* 1175, adapted Henry II's Assize of Clarendon for Scottish use.

A word may be said finally about the royal household, upon which all royal government centred. Specialisation within it had not developed so far as in England, but it can be clearly discerned from the time of William the Lion. The day-to-day work of government was no longer carried out solely through the three or four feudal offices which served David I. The position of Steward, Constable and Marischal remained important, but became largely honorific. The Chancellor and Chamberlain, on the contrary, were heads of two busy departments, the former at least having a sizeable staff of clerks before 1214, under a special Clerk of the Seal. During the chancellorship of Hugh of Roxburgh (1189-99) the practice was introduced of dating royal charters and writs by the day of the month in addition to the place of issue. Naturally enough, this limited dating proved unsatisfactory, and from 1222 onwards the number of the regnal year was regularly added. The chapel of Edinburgh castle served both Chancellor and Chamberlain as a central repository for official records. While the Chamberlain continued to be responsible generally for all royal revenue, there are recorded from *c.* 1175 onward two specialist household officials, the clerks of the " provender " and the " livery ", whose duty it was to control the receipt and consumption within the household itself, as it travelled about the country, of the corn and meat and all the other varied necessaries required by the king and his servants.

CHAPTER XVI

CRITICISM, REFORM AND REBELLION, 1216-66

THE guiding theme of English history in the reign of Henry III (1216-72) is the difficulty which both Crown and baronage experienced in trying to adjust themselves to the revolution in government described in earlier chapters. As a result of this revolution, the king had gained power and the barons had lost it ; but in the process both monarchy and baronage had learned to take a more advanced view of their obligations towards a wider society. The old, simple feudal allegiance between lord and man which had sufficed for the twelfth century was gradually giving place to the notion of a political " community of the realm " in which the king was sovereign directly and equally over all and the barons had become his principal subjects and counsellors and in some sense spokesmen for the community instead of merely his tenants-in-chief. If to this change are added the factors of a better-educated baronage, a more complex machine of government, a king bent upon an inept and extravagant foreign policy, and, finally, a run of bad harvests there will be present all the elements of a major political upheaval. It is a testimony to the conservatism of English life that the upheaval was delayed until 1258 ; it is a measure of the brilliant inventiveness of the age that when it did come it came as a reform movement which proved one of the most astonishing and constructive episodes of our history.

Because of the boyhood of the king and the occupation of half the country by foreign invaders, this central theme was held as it were in abeyance in 1216. In this chapter we shall see how three subsidiary processes, (i) the recovery of royal power at home, (ii) the defence of English lands in France, and (iii) the king's relations with the Papacy, all gradually forced the main issue upon the attention of the politically conscious community of the realm.

1. *The Recovery of Royal Authority*

King John's death did not bring peace or mean the withdrawal of Prince Louis from the country. The regents, William the Marshal, Bishop Peter des Roches of Winchester, and the Pope's legate, Cardinal Guala Biacheri, together with the Justiciar Hubert de Burgh, must first beat the invaders in the field before they could begin to rule effectively in the young king's name. It was, however, a wise preliminary to their campaign to issue Magna Carta for the second time. Its formal publication by men who had been on King John's side in the crisis of 1215 emphasised that the new reign would not undo the worthwhile results of the barons' struggle, even though the opposition leaders themselves adhered stubbornly to the foreigner whom they had brought to their assistance. From the regents' point of view, the military position was grave. Louis controlled substantially the whole of eastern England south of the Trent, save for two key strong points at its extremities. In the south, Dover Castle was held by Hubert de Burgh, in the north, Lincoln Castle was defended by the widow of its late Constable, Gerard de Camville, a gallant elderly lady named Nicola de la Haye,[1] whom King John, just before his death, had appointed joint sheriff of Lincolnshire.

Dover was inaccessible, and Lincoln was threatened by a strong force of French under the command of the Count of Perche, together with the main army of the opposition barons under Robert fitz Walter and Saer de Quinci. The Marshal and Peter des Roches therefore decided to risk their smaller force in the relief of Lincoln Castle. They found the besiegers unwisely concentrated within the town walls, in a position which enabled them to surround the castle on every side except the west, where its outworks abutted on the western wall of the city. Peter des Roches (who had once been a canon of Lincoln Minster) is said to have discovered a weak point here, an old gate, disused and blocked up, leading into the town close to the north-west corner of the castle. Through this the royalists burst, taking by surprise the cavalry and men-at-arms massed in the congested streets between castle and minster. After a hard fight, the French knights were driven down the steep hill towards the

[1] Her name was a pleasant pun on " Nicole ", the inverted form for " Lincoln " habitually used in this period by those who spoke French.

south gate. Many on their side were taken prisoner, and the " Fair of Lincoln ", as it was called, ended as a victory for the regents all the more complete because they had suffered hardly any casualties (May 20th, 1217).

Only reinforcements from across the Channel could keep Louis in England now, and the French had no mastery of the Narrow Seas. The " Cinque Ports " [1] of Kent and Sussex were fiercely anti-Norman, and offered a base to Philip de Aubeney, an able lieutenant of King John, and governor of the Channel Islands, the only part of the Norman duchy which Philip Augustus had failed to conquer. De Aubeney, the Marshal and de Burgh, who had rejoined the royalists from Dover, together organised a fleet which on August 24th intercepted, off the South Foreland, the French troopships bringing Louis' reinforcements. Fetching to windward of the enemy, the English scattered powdered lime which blinded or choked the soldiers crowded above deck. The biggest French vessel, commanded by the piratical adventurer Eustace, a renegade monk, and weighed down to her gunwales by a gigantic siege-engine, was boarded and her company overpowered. The other French warships made off home, leaving all the smaller craft carrying supplies to fall into English hands. It was the finish of Louis' cause in England, and of the last seriously attempted foreign invasion until 1588. By the treaty of Kingston (September 12th), Louis renounced his claim to the throne, while the barons of the charter were to be restored to the king's peace with all their estates as they had held them before the outbreak of war two years earlier. At the same time, Magna Carta was again re-issued, in a revised form which omitted several of the more restrictive provisions in the original version, e.g. that the charter could be enforced by a special baronial committee and that scutage could not be levied without consulting the Great Council. But the Charter of 1217, which henceforth remained the " standard version ", substantially embodied the great statement of right of 1215, while the few forest chapters of the original were now expanded into a long separate " Forest Charter ", which in seventeen clauses

---

[1] Comprising in our period the following towns, of which the first five formed the original association which had been organised for defence purposes by Edward the Confessor : Hastings, Romney, Hythe, Dover, Sandwich, Winchelsea and Rye. The Cinque Ports formed a privileged urban league which other south-eastern towns were glad to join, and which at times waged bitter warfare with rival ports, e.g. in East Anglia.

defined and materially limited the king's privileges over the vast areas classified as royal forest.

The regents were men of ripe experience, and the kingdom might have enjoyed a decade or more of stable government had it not been for the death in 1219 of William the Marshal, the most influential among them, and for the withdrawal of the papal legation : Guala left in 1218, and was replaced by Pandulf, who retired three years later to hold in absence the see of Norwich. Rule by a committee of elder statesmen gave place to a struggle for power between Peter des Roches and the Justiciar, with Archbishop Langton playing the role of moderator. It was a struggle which de Burgh seemed bound to win, both by reason of his official position and because the bishop's chief interests were French, indeed, European, rather than English. In 1227 he went oversea to join the Emperor on crusade. By this time the country had been pacified. As in the late 1140's the process was helped by the departure of many barons on crusade. Not the least of the regents' difficulties had been the need to appease several of John's most loyal supporters (among them Fawkes de Bréauté), who had grievances to be remedied, and in the meantime refused to surrender the castles which their late master had committed to their charge. Bedford Castle, held against the regents by Fawkes's brother, who had the audacity to kidnap a royal justice, provided a test case. It fell in the summer of 1224, after a week's siege. Thereafter the Justiciar in the king's name resumed control over all the counties and royal castles, and on Langton's death in 1228 enjoyed a monopoly of power.

As King Henry grew to manhood, he began to resent his dependence on Hubert de Burgh. He declared himself of " full age " in 1227, and when Peter des Roches came back to England in 1231 he seems to have listened readily as the bishop told him of the unfettered power wielded in Sicily by the young Emperor, Frederick II. Because in our period high office meant great wealth and the founding of feudal dynasty, the king's sudden dismissal of Hubert de Burgh in 1232 was inevitably accompanied by an attempt to ruin his position as a great baron. It was true that Hubert had been over-ambitious, and apparently his manner was overbearing. He had aroused baronial jealousy by advancing his territorial power on the Welsh marches and by persuading the young king to make him Earl of Kent and to give him in marriage one of the King of Scotland's

259

sisters. Yet the barons had no more love for Peter des Roches, and were alarmed at the immense power given, after Hubert's fall, to the bishop's son or nephew, Peter des Rivaux, who in July, 1232, was placed in charge of the Exchequer and Chamber, and appointed sheriff simultaneously in twenty-one shires. Under pressure from the magnates, Hubert de Burgh was given a trial as Magna Carta demanded, and though he lost all his offices and was for a time imprisoned, he was not deprived of his own estates. There was in fact a reaction in his favour. A plot to set him free grew into a baronial movement of protest, led by Richard the Marshal, Earl of Pembroke. This in turn flared up into a minor war on the Welsh marches, and though peace was restored through the agency of the Archbishop of Canterbury, the saintly Edmund Rich of Abingdon, Earl Richard had withdrawn unreconciled to his vast lordship in Leinster. Here, in April, 1234, motives of private feud, made to look like an excess of zeal for the king's service, prompted Hubert de Burgh's nephew Richard and the Justiciar of Ireland, Maurice Fitzgerald, to a treacherous attack in which the earl was mortally wounded. At home feelings of sympathy for the victim were so powerful that the young king was forced to dismiss Peter des Rivaux and the lesser clerks who had helped him to reform the working of the Exchequer, while the Bishop of Winchester, once more overseas, fell into deep disgrace.

Between 1234 and 1258 the king ruled on his own, without being dominated by the personality of any single counsellor. This momentous quarter-century is sometimes called the period of Henry III's " personal rule ", as though there were in this something unusual or reprehensible. In fact normal monarchical government in medieval England *was* simply the personal rule of the king. It was Henry's long minority which had provided an exception. Moreover, the king's government was still household government, or to use modern terms, the king was himself minister in all his departments, the officials in charge being merely his servants, responsible solely to him at all times. This did not mean that the king was an irresponsible despot ; only that the checks on his power, apart from the Coronation Oath, were the negative checks of baronial or ecclesiastical opposition when the king overstepped the recognised limits of the law, and not the positive checks of parliamentary and cabinet government. Henry III, though he could often say and do foolish things, was neither unintelligent nor inept at the business of being king. His weakness lay in lack of judgment and power of leadership, and in showing something of his father's mistrustfulness.

As we should expect, progress in administration proceeded apace once the king gained full control. Peter des Rivaux might be temporarily under a cloud, but the reforms, which for a time he directed, had in fact begun before he engrossed all the plums of the higher civil service and continued after his dismissal. The most important reforms were fiscal. The " farms " rendered by each county were obviously too low. We have seen that King John tried to force the sheriffs either to account in detail for every item of Crown revenue instead of paying a lump sum farm, or else to proffer an increment over and above the farm. Magna Carta had forbidden such practices. Henry III's exchequer officials resumed them in 1224, and a fresh valuation of the revenues which could reasonably be expected from each county enabled the treasurer to impose new and larger farms, to which the sheriff could hardly demur since they were based on accurate information. Gradually the sheriff ceased to be a farmer of his county, and became what John had tried to make him, a salaried custodian. There was a closer correspondence between the amount of money which the sheriff undertook to render from his county and the total due to the Crown from its many varied sources of revenue. Estate management and accounting had made great strides, and an illiterate sheriff could now find trained clerks to help him cast his accounts and estimate his revenues for the year ahead. The Exchequer also set its own house in order. For example, instead of giving the sheriff a separate tally or receipt for every item of revenue as he accounted for it, the Treasurer's clerks began, from *c.* 1216, to acquit the sheriff with a small number of " dividend tallies ". These represented large amounts which were based on estimates of the farm and additional payments which might be due, and it became the sheriff's responsibility to divide their totals into the many minute individual sums for which he then proceeded to give receipts to the Crown's local debtors in the county. Any excess paid by the sheriff could be credited to him in the following year's account, and meanwhile the saving of time and trouble was enormous.

One of the largest single sources of profit was formed by the

feudal incidents, notably escheated estates (" escheats "),[1] marriage
and wardship.   From the time of Peter des Rivaux's treasurership
onward, it became the practice to administer escheats as a separate
entity.   Two escheators were appointed, for north and south of
Trent respectively.   Henceforward they and their sub-escheators
were responsible, on the death of every known or alleged tenant-in-
chief of the Crown, however insignificant, for empanelling local
juries to enumerate and value all the lands held by the deceased in
their own counties.   This activity went on constantly, and gave rise
to the wonderful series of public records, running from Henry III to
Charles I, known as the " Inquisitions post mortem ", which contain
details about the estates of almost every secular landholder of substance.

In other respects, the middle years of Henry III's reign saw
administrative changes which, in the king's view, made for more
efficient government.   In the first place, after Hubert de Burgh's
fall there seemed no need for a Justiciar of the old viceregal type,
whose chief function had been to govern in the king's absence
overseas.   A successor was in fact appointed, but his position was
really that of a chief justice.   Between 1241 and 1258 the office was
not filled at all.   The still older offices of Treasurer and Chancellor
likewise fell into abeyance.   Mediocrity may be said not unfairly
to characterise the treasurers of the period.   Bishop Nevill of
Chichester was Chancellor from 1226 until 1238, when the king took
the great seal from him and entrusted it to a succession of obscure
household officials.   More and more use was made of the small or
" private " seal (the later " privy seal ") to authenticate the king's
acts.   Less solemnity and publicity attended the application of this
seal, which could be conveniently kept by some trusted household
clerk and brought into use immediately on the king's oral instructions.

The barons as a group disliked these changes.   Acts of government were being decided and authorised in secret, by the king and a
handful of intimate counsellors, often not of baronial rank and
occasionally of foreign origin.   The view of the great magnates was
that they were the king's advisers by birth, his "natural counsellors ".   To dispense with the traditional offices through which
government used to be carried on in the full glare of publicity was
to infringe the accepted custom of the realm.   That was bad enough.
But Henry appeared to be excluding the barons as a class from

[1] Above, p. 44.

membership of his royal council. That was much worse. What the barons failed to realise was that Henry's more subservient treasurers, wardrobe-keepers and seal-keepers stood to him exactly as Treasurer and Chancellor had stood to William the Conqueror or Henry II. These officers had grown less amenable to the king's personal will, and buttressed by their large and growing departments had tended to take a too independent line. It was in fact the king, not the baronage, who was holding closer to ancient custom. But Henry III for his part did not see that the scope of royal government had been immeasurably increased since the previous century. Henry II's barons would hardly have grumbled at exclusion from the *Curia Regis*, because as a purely feudal court it was bound to include them, and what it did outside that capacity was—at least until the end of his reign—barely appreciable. But in the thirteenth century the King's *Curia*, now more commonly called the *Concilium*, or Council, was rapidly becoming an omnicompetent organ of government for the whole realm and for all the sorts and conditions of men that composed it. In short, England was changing from a primitive feudal state to a political society, and it was necessary to work out afresh the relationship between the ruler and his subjects.

2. *Aquitaine*

The minority of Henry III left the initiative south of the Channel to Philip Augustus and, after his death in 1223, to his son, who ruled for three years as Louis VIII. They were not slow to seize this chance of driving the Angevin out of Gaul. Yet. although the triumph at Bouvines had given momentum to the French advance, the demands of the crusade, constantly urged by the Pope, and the process of annexing Toulouse (where the campaign to crush the Albigensian heresy had given the French kings a foothold), both acted as powerful brakes or deflections. The English regents showed little skill or sense of urgency in their handling of the Poitevin problem. The Lusignans were still the chief trouble-makers, and when Hugh of Lusignan, head of the family and Count of La Marche, showed signs of defection no rival family was successfully encouraged to act as counterpoise. Hugh was first betrothed to Henry III's sister Joan. The queen-mother, Isabel of Angoulême, forestalled this match by marrying Hugh herself ; but though the princess was restored to the regents, Isabel's move had been made in furtherance of personal ambition and not to bind Poitou more closely to the English crown. When Louis VIII, in the year following his father's death, led his army south of the Loire, he met with almost no opposition. The Lusignans had been won over in advance, and the richest single prize of the county, the pro-English trading centre of La Rochelle, was obliged to surrender in August, 1224, in the absence of any support from England. This at last stirred the regents to action. A force was despatched to Bordeaux under the king's uncle, Earl William of Salisbury, while the king's young brother, Richard, who was nominally at the head of the expedition, was given along with the English title of Earl of Cornwall the Aquitanian one of Count of Poitou. No battle was fought, but the French threat to Gascony—Aquitaine south of the Gironde—was lifted, and, perhaps still more important, fresh heart was put into the loyal wine-merchants of Bordeaux.

Thereafter, though little credit can be given to Henry III or his advisers, matters went rather better for the English overseas. From 1226 until 1234, the government of France was in the hands of Blanche of Castile, Louis VIII's widow. Her statesmanship was of the highest order, but for some years it was fully tested by domestic problems arising from the minority of her son, Louis IX, and she could hardly be expected to pursue her husband's aggressive policy with the same confidence. Meanwhile the recovery of Henry II's empire remained the unquestioned aim of the English Crown. In 1230 one of the succession disputes so frequent in Breton history gave Henry III the opportunity of a military expedition. The French could not stop him landing at St. Mâlo with an army, and leading it slowly down the Biscay coast to Bordeaux, holding his court at Nantes the while. The young king may have found the adventure exhilarating, but from a military standpoint it was value-less. His next expedition took place twelve years later, in 1242. In the previous year, Louis IX had made his brother Alphonse Count of Poitou. The restless Hugh of Lusignan saw in this move a threat to his own independence and sent an appeal for help to England. This time the king acted on his own initiative, without the guiding hand of a Hubert de Burgh and without the collective judgment of his barons. There was no enthusiasm at home and much misgiving when a searching enquiry was held into the feudal service owed to the Crown and a general scutage levied from all those unwilling to go to Poitou with the king. The enterprise thus badly begun ended in total failure. King Henry was driven from southern Poitou into Bordeaux. His humiliation can be imagined when his ally, the Count of Toulouse, was checked by a French force led by Hugh of Lusignan, the very man whose fit of pique had prompted English intervention in the first place, together with Peter Mauclerc, lord of Dreux, whose claim to the county of Brittany had inspired the fiasco of 1230.

The harm done to his reputation by military failure was aggravated by Henry III in the narrow but highly-charged field of personal relationships. In 1236 he married a daughter of the Count of Provence, Eleanor, whose elder sister Margaret was already the queen of Louis IX of France.[1] It was only natural that Provençals and Savoyards—for Queen Eleanor's mother was Countess of Savoy—should seek their fortune in the rich kingdom of England. One of the queen's uncles, Boniface of Savoy, became Archbishop of Canterbury ; another, Peter, by a good marriage became an English baron. In view of the distrust already developing between the king and the greater magnates, he was perhaps too ready with his favours towards the queen's relatives and friends. Then, in 1238, without consulting his Great Council, he unwisely allowed his sister—another Eleanor—to be married to a young French nobleman named Simon de Montfort, under whose spell he had momentarily fallen. Simon was a younger son and namesake of the victor of Muret (1213) ; through his grandmother he inherited a claim to half the English earldom of Leicester, an estate which, together with the title itself, had been duly granted him in 1231. His marriage to the king's sister nevertheless aroused acute resentment among the native lords. In time the queen's uncles and the Earl of Leicester became accepted as members of English society and of the King's Council. Hardly had this happened when all the old hatred of foreigners in high places flared up again. On the death of Hugh of Lusignan (1247), Henry III offered a home in England to the count's four reckless sons, his own half-brothers, Geoffrey, Guy, Aymer and William called " of Valence ". Only the last struck any roots : he

[1] Two other sisters, Beatrice and Sanchia, married respectively the King of Castile and Henry III's brother Richard, Earl of Cornwall, who in 1257 was elected " King of the Romans ", i.e. King of Germany. The four beautiful princesses of Provence who all became queens might be characters from a fairy story.

married an heiress of the Marshals, earls of Pembroke, and his son Aymer of Valence eventually inherited that earldom. Down to 1258, however, the Lusignans caused nothing but trouble.

During the fifties of the thirteenth century, we can see a marked shift in political relationships and in the balance of power in England. Since 1234 the barons had attempted once or twice to impose their counsel upon the king, notably in 1238 and 1244. The failure of these attempts served rather to harden than to mollify the opposition to Henry's " irresponsible " rule. Yet this opposition would not have insisted on reform in 1258, nor would it thereafter have taken the course of revolution, if it had not, between 1252 and 1257, found a leader and a final provocation to rebellion.

In 1248, Simon de Montfort was given a seven-year commission to administer Gascony as King Henry's lieutenant. The appointment could not have been more fitting—nor more disastrous. Simon was methodical, clear-thinking, just, yet arrogant, and, above all, a Frenchman. The Gascons not only disliked the French on principle; they were unruly and proud of their unruliness. They were not heretics to be crushed, as their neighbours in Albi and Toulouse had been crushed by Simon's own father a generation earlier. Complaints about the new lieutenant's high-handed ways poured in to King Henry. Instead of backing to the hilt the man he had appointed he summoned him (May, 1252) to defend himself before Gascon accusers in Westminster Hall. Though Simon was vindicated, the Gascons, led by the turbulent Gaston, Viscount of Béarn, were by now up in arms. The situation was saved only by Simon's angry resignation and the appointment of the king's eldest son, Edward, thirteen years old, to be nominal lord of Gascony. Two years later Edward was knighted and formally invested with the lordship, together with those of Ireland, Chester, Bristol and the Channel Isles. The king visited Bordeaux in person, and the Gascons quietly reverted to the lawlessness so congenial to them. Henry, for his part, had made a lifelong enemy.

3. *King and Papacy*

The preoccupation of western rulers with extremely local issues disguises the very genuine desire shared by them, with the greater part of their subjects, clergy and laity alike, to recover the Holy Land from its Mohammedan conquerors. In this great enterprise, upon whose accomplishment the resources of Europe were tragically diverted for 200 years, the Papacy continued to take a lead, uneasily shared as it might be with the Hohenstaufen empire. If the thirteenth-century Popes are rightly criticised for defiling their spiritual office in the extremely secular politics of Germany and Italy, it should be remembered in their defence that their ultimate aim was to unite the lay princes of the west in a gigantic military effort in which all national, racial and dynastic differences would be submerged in a common cause. If at this distance of time the cause itself seems shrunken in stature, and even trivial and irrelevant, we should marvel not at the futility of the crusading movement but rather at the nobility of an ideal which, within the relatively narrow horizons of the age, was accepted fervently by a society barely emerged from barbarism.

Before his death in 1250, the chief obstacle to a united crusade under papal direction had been the Emperor Frederick II, the son of King Richard's enemy Henry VI. In 1252 the Pope, Innocent IV, determined to be rid of the malign Hohenstaufen influence. He offered the kingdom of Sicily, the main seat of imperial power, to Henry III of England, although it was in fact occupied by Frederick's bastard son Manfred. King Henry, who had taken the vows of a crusader in 1250, was captivated by the idea of combining a " crusade " against the Pope's enemy with a much-needed enhancement of his prestige. He accepted the offer on behalf of his younger son Edmund (1254). Admittedly, by the terms of John's surrender to the Papacy, the king was the Pope's vassal; but the conditions attached to the Sicilian offer which Henry accepted went far beyond a vassal's duties to his lord and were wildly impracticable. Briefly, a tax on the English clergy authorised by the Papacy to pay for the crusade was to be increased and used to conquer Sicily. Meanwhile, the king was to pledge himself and his kingdom to repay the money —some 135,000 marks—already spent by the Papacy in fighting Manfred. A time-limit was set on Henry's performance of his part of the contract. When, in 1258, Pope Alexander IV threatened him with the agreed penalties for default, personal excommunication and an interdict on his kingdom, the utter bankruptcy of his aspirations was forced even on Henry himself. He had raised no troops, and only a fraction of the money promised.

4. *Reform and Rebellion*

The harvest in 1255 had been an abundant one, so good in fact that a quarter of wheat sold for 2*s*.,[1] oats for half that price. Three bad years followed. In 1256 the hay crop was lost, and the corn rotted in the fields or sprouted through the flattened straw. Reaping went on until Martinmas (November 11th). After this there was rainy weather until February 1257, including a mid-winter flood which inundated the countryside like a sea and in the course of which one river alone in the north of England swept away seven bridges of timber and large stones. In consequence there was serious famine in 1257 : flour could not be made into eatable bread, and the malt was unfit for brewing ale. Again the harvest failed. A long spell of mild weather through the winter of 1257-8 was broken in February by the onset of a prolonged and bitter frost, which halted ploughing and caused severe losses among sheep and lambs. All this time the king wove his dreams of a conquest of Sicily. Unprecedented sums were raised from the clergy, yet they were not enough to serve in place of a general aid which, owing to mounting baronial opposition, could not be obtained from the community of the realm as a whole.

His quarrel with Simon de Montfort, his failure to gain the confidence of the majority of greater magnates, and finally his ill-judged acceptance of a commitment in Sicily far beyond his powers, all served to fix a dangerous gulf between King Henry and his subjects. Sir Maurice Powicke has written that the king " was rarely, if ever, so remote from his people as he was in these years ".[2] He had divested himself of allies, alienated baronage and Church, and placed his trust in a few household officials. Such was John Mansel, a clerk who, despite holy orders, had made his name fighting in Gascony. Able, diligent, and very well provided for, from 1242 to 1265 the king employed him more often than any other councillor on business of the highest importance. A colleague of almost equal eminence was the king's confessor, a Dominican friar named John of Darlington, whom Henry brought into his inner circle in 1256. However loyal and skilful they might be, these were not the men to shield their master from the storm of angry protest which broke

[1] The average price of wheat, 1261-1400, was about 5*s*. 10*d*. a quarter.
[2] *King Henry III and the Lord Edward* (1947), i. 373.

against him in the cold spring of 1258, when he asked for help to carry through the " business of Sicily ".

The Great Council which met after Easter, the " Hoketide Parliament " as it is usually called,[1] inaugurated a deliberate and thoroughgoing reform of the state of the realm, and to this end placed the king under the compulsion of following baronial advice in all his governmental actions. A plan of reform was to be drawn up and published in a Parliament which was to meet at Oxford on June 11th. The leading spirits among the baronage who had taken this momentous decision to switch from mere protest to positive reform were few in number but immensely influential both in their own class and in the country at large. They included Roger Bigod, Earl of Norfolk and Marshal,[2] and his brother Hugh ; Simon de Montfort ; the queen's uncle, Peter of Savoy ; and two men who besides their other estates were prominent marcher lords, Earl Richard of Gloucester and John fitz Geoffrey of Ewyas Lacy (son of the great Justiciar, Geoffrey fitz Peter). It is worth remarking that while xenophobia was undoubtedly one strong emotion behind the opposition to Henry III, two of these leaders, de Montfort and Peter of Savoy, owed their whole position in England to that very same royal love of foreigners which apparently excited baronial jealousy and popular hostility. As one chronicler of the time naïvely puts it : " Simon de Montfort was no traitor but a shield and defender of the kingdom of the English ; *an enemy and expeller of foreigners although he himself was one by race.*" [3]

The Sicilian adventure was tacitly abandoned. The king was promised supply (especially needed against the Welsh) on condition that he took an oath to abide by the provisions of the reform programme. This programme was put in charge of a committee of twenty-four. On this, in theory, king and baronage were equally represented, but since four of the king's nominees were his Lusignan half-brothers, who were expelled from England in June, and another the Abbot of Westminster, who died in July, its composition was in fact weighted decisively in the barons' favour. Under its general supervision, the " reform of the realm " took two main lines of

[1] It met after Hoke Day, the second Tuesday after Easter Week. In 1258, Hoke Day fell on April 9.
[2] See above, p. 216.
[3] *Chronicle of Melrose* (ed. 1936), 127-8 (abridged in translation).

action, collectively known from their publication at the June Parliament as the Provisions of Oxford.

First, certain drastic measures were taken to allay the resentment felt throughout the country by lesser folk at the abuse of power by sheriffs, bailiffs and other agents of local government. Discontent, doubtless much aggravated by the wretched harvests and consequent famine, was already finding expression in acts of lawlessness. A panel of four knights chosen in the shire court was set up in each county. Their duty was to hear and record " all complaints brought by anyone whomsoever concerning transgressions and injuries inflicted on anyone by sheriffs, bailiffs and others ". They were to take pledges from both sides to ensure their appearance before the king's chief Justiciar as soon as he was able to visit the county. In the meantime, each shire was to have as sheriff a substantial man chosen from among its own resident gentry, appointed for one year at a time, and paid a decent salary " so that he take no payment (i.e. from the people of the shire), neither he nor his bailiffs ".

Secondly, there was a thoroughgoing reform of the central administration. The old " traditional " officers were restored and their position more clearly defined. Hugh Bigod was made chief Justiciar, and together with six parties of justices embarked conscientiously upon the laborious task of touring the shires, hearing and determining on the spot, without the mediation of writs from Chancery and legal delays, the cases which arose from the scores of complaints enrolled by the panels of knights. Philip Lovel was appointed Treasurer, with a senior exchequer staff likewise appointed by the Twenty-four. All royal revenues were in future to be paid into the Exchequer, and not diverted as in the past to the King's Chamber or its sub-department, the Wardrobe. Henry of Wingham, already keeping the great seal, was confirmed as Chancellor after taking an oath not to seal any but purely routine documents except by order of the Council. All three offices were to be held for one year at a time, and their occupants were to account for their work at the end of each term of office.

There remained the problem of the king himself, and the actual direction of government. Deposition or mere suspension were out of the question : the barons were not opposing the monarchy but " evil counsel ". Consequently they hoped, perhaps somewhat naïvely, that all would be well if only a responsible—i.e. a baronial

—Council were appointed and if the king were constrained to follow its advice. Fifteen men were chosen and sworn to be permanently of the Council. They included John Mansel, the Earl of Warwick and the Archbishop of Canterbury, all sympathetic to Henry personally ; but as a whole their membership was strongly baronial, and the real leadership lay with the Earls of Leicester and Gloucester. It was to this Council that the chief Justiciar, Treasurer and Chancellor were to be responsible.

Finally, the day-to-day activity of King and Council, the feeling among the baronage that they ought to be consulted on matters of importance, and the course of reform in the local areas, were all given a common focal point in parliaments which were to be held three times a year, at Michaelmas (September 29th), Candlemas (February 2nd) and the beginning of June. In this the reformers were proposing nothing new. Since 1216 it had been customary for especially large and solemn meetings of the king's court, " great councils ", in contrast with the king's small inner council, to meet with fair regularity, often on the dates here proposed. It was admittedly an innovation to have twelve barons elected specifically to attend Parliament along with King and Council. This " standing legislative committee of the baronage ", as it has been termed, can hardly have been meant to exclude the rest of the barons from Parliament. The significance of the provision lies rather in the fact that the reformers were not remoulding the constitution but instead were making explicit and formal something that was already established custom, in order that the government of England should conform to their view of what was right. Where Magna Carta had listed certain things which the king must not do, and had clearly implied that he was below the law, the Provisions of Oxford attempted to solve the new problem of how king and baronage could still co-operate in government even though it had grown infinitely more complex in machinery and universal in application.

The Provisions agreed on at Oxford in the summer of 1258 did not complete the reform programme. The king's consent to the provisions was published throughout the realm in an English proclamation (October 18th), the first state document to be written in English since the early years of William the Conqueror. The fact becomes significant in the light of what followed. For the earls and great lords, " reform " meant engrafting themselves permanently into the administration at the centre : the hearing of local complaints was a necessary, but temporary, act of grace, to be replaced as soon as possible by the normal processes of law. But for the free men in the shires, whether of knightly or lesser rank, for the merchants in the cities and boroughs, and for the poorer clergy, reform of the central government was a remote affair and the hearing of complaints only a beginning. It was these men, for whom English was the mother tongue, whom it was necessary to placate by the October proclamation. The year, it should be added, had proved an exceptionally promising one for the growing crops, but an autumn of ceaseless rain put paid to any hope of saving the harvest. Corn had to be imported from Germany and Holland, and those with no money to buy it died. The country gentlemen who, for the third successive season, watched their corn rotting in the fields grew impatient as nothing seemed to be done to remedy their grievances with regard to local administration. It was the pressure of this class that induced the magnates to agree, in the February Parliament of 1259, that local reforms should apply with equal force to baronial estates and officials as to royal sheriffs and bailiffs. Not surprisingly, a second stage of reform was reached by the autumn of 1259. Under the momentary patronage, oddly enough, of the king's son, Edward, a group of men referred to as the " community of the bachelry of England ", intending, it seems, to represent the gentry against the baronage, successfully pressed (October 13th) for the acceptance of further, legislative, provisions, which had evidently been under discussion since the summer of 1258. These are known, again from their place of issue, as the Provisions of Westminster.

The burden of these provisions is remarkably anti-baronial. Their limitations on seigniorial jurisdiction are more numerous and expressed more forcibly than can be said of any document of royal origin, even from an autocratic king like Henry II or John. Lords holding courts were not to demand the attendance (" suit ") of their tenants unless (i) they held their tenements by a charter which specifically required it, or (ii) they or their ancestors had been wont to perform suit of court prior to 1230. Where (as in many cases) a subordinate fief had been split up through a failure of male descent, only that part inheriting the special rights and position of the eldest by descent should perform suit of court. The rightful heir of a feudal estate ought not to have to bring an action of mort d'ancestor

272

against his lord before being allowed to succeed to his property, and if the lord forced him to do so without cause, the tenant ought to recover damages. No one save the king and his servants should have power outside his own fief or on the king's highway to distrain upon a man's goods and animals. The rules which Magna Carta had prescribed for feudal lands held in custody during the minority of the heir ought to apply equally to non-feudal estates held in free socage. Most strikingly of all, perhaps, no one save the king should hear in his court a plea of false judgment, " since pleas of this sort belong specially to the Crown and the dignity of the king ".

Yet though such provisions set an anti-baronial tone and were surprisingly favourable to royal prerogative, there were also limitations on the activities of royal officials. Men with lands in many different hundreds must not be forced to attend the sheriff's tourn in each single hundred, but only in that in which they normally resided. Justices were not to impose fines on villages which had not sent all their adult menfolk before sheriffs and coroners to attend inquests into unexplained death, so long as sufficient witnesses had been forthcoming. Moreover, during the famine great numbers of destitute people had been wandering through the countryside in search of food, and many had died of starvation in a strange neighbourhood, far from their homes. Sheriffs and coroners, carrying out their orders with no imagination, had been unfairly reporting whole groups of villages for not accounting for these deaths, and the murder fine had been imposed. In future, death by misadventure was not to occasion the murder fine, which must be limited to cases of criminal killing.

Thus far, the reform programme had been carried through with astonishing unanimity. Much valuable and necessary work had been done. It seems that the barons envisaged a twelve-year period (1258-70) during which reforms were to be, so to speak, experimental. Provisions made during that time which had proved their worth in action would thereafter become the law of the land. In any case, they probably argued that King Henry would have died before twelve years had passed, and there would no longer be any need for a state of emergency. In fact, the period of wholehearted and enthusiastic reform lasted barely two years. Unity broke down chiefly for three reasons : (1) personal enmity between the king and de Montfort ; (2) divisions among the baronage, partly caused by the fact that, for all his powers of leadership, his equals did not find de Montfort an easy man to co-operate with ; (3) the practical difficulty experienced by the Fifteen and the depleted Twenty-four in governing the country when they themselves were divided or dispersed, while the king, from whom all acts of government still proceeded, could pursue a single line of policy.

The mutual enmity of the king and Earl Simon came to a head at the end of 1259 when at long last a final treaty of peace was made between England and France.[1] The main provisions of this Treaty of Paris (December 4th) were that Henry III renounced all claims to Normandy, Maine, Anjou and Poitou, but retained, subject to homage to the King of France, the dignity of Duke of Aquitaine, the region of Gascony and the city and district of Bordeaux. Between Gascony and Poitou lay the district of Saintonge, vital for Gascon defence. In 1259 it was held by Louis IX's brother Alphonse as part of his county of Poitou. It was agreed that on his death Saintonge should revert to the English Crown. Count Alphonse also held, in right of his wife (a great-grand-daughter and in this case heiress of Henry II), the border region of Agenais ; when the countess died, it too was to revert to English possession. Finally, Louis IX generously and unwisely transferred to Henry all his rights in the rich dioceses of Cahors, Périgueux and Limoges. Apart from this concession, which gave rise to frequent disputes, the Treaty of Paris was extremely statesmanlike. It was all the more unfortunate, therefore, that Simon de Montfort chose to delay its ratification until a private dispute regarding his wife's dower could first be settled. As the king's sister, the Countess of Leicester was one of the English royal personages required to surrender rights and claims under the Paris treaty. As the former wife (by her first marriage) of Richard the Marshal, Earl of Pembroke, she had a claim, unsatisfied after twenty-five years, to a share of the vast Marshal estates. As the wife of Earl Simon, she had a husband who would champion her cause even at the expense of a break-down in the treaty negotiations. Eventually a compromise was reached ; Eleanor subscribed to the treaty, which was then duly published. But the incident added to the rancour between de Montfort and the king.

Baronial disunity had shown itself as early as February, 1259, in a quarrel between de Montfort and Richard, Earl of Gloucester.

[1] See the map on p. 165.

This may not have endured, but it is clear that in the next few years the baronage was far from being the single-minded community envisaged by the Provisions of Oxford. The most significant development, hardly noticed at the time, was that a powerful group of marcher lords, led by Roger Mortimer of Wigmore and Radnor,[1] began to come out more and more strongly in opposition to de Montfort personally and ultimately to the reform programme itself.

Earl Simon, however, was not yet sole leader of the baronial party. Despite their differences, the magnates who supported reform were able to keep the initiative until early in 1261. By this date the king had begun to manoeuvre openly for the recovery of his full royal authority. He had been able to dispatch John Mansel[2] to the papal court, where (April, 1261) he obtained a Bull from Pope Alexander IV releasing the king from his solemn oath to abide by the Provisions of Oxford. At home the king publicly denounced Simon de Montfort as a disturber of the peace. The last remnants of central control by the Twenty-four and Fifteen disappeared in the summer when the baronial Justiciar and Chancellor were dismissed without the baronage as a body rallying to their support. Philip Basset, a baron of Wessex on whose loyalty Henry could depend, was made Justiciar with powers like those of Hubert de Burgh, combining an oversight of the judiciary with control of royal castles. Yet the king and Philip Basset did not rule the whole kingdom. Royalist sheriffs had charge of some shires, but in many others there were local knights acting in the baronial interest as " wardens ", in accordance with the Oxford provisions. Each side tried to measure its strength in the country by summoning three knights from every shire to meet to discuss the affairs of the realm (September, 1261), at St. Albans in a baronial assembly, or at Windsor in a rival royal one. As many as 150 tenants-in-chief whom Henry now believed to be on his side were summoned to bring their knight-service in the king's defence. A long discussion held at Kingston in October ended in most of the baronial leaders making their peace with the king, though without accepting his terms outright. De Montfort considered that his English colleagues

---

[1] The Briouze lordship of Radnor came to Mortimer through his wife Maud, a daughter of William of Briouze, grandson of King John's favourite and subsequent enemy.

[2] Nephew and protégé of the councillor.

had let him down, deserting the cause of reform which they had sworn to uphold. It was, he said scornfully, the English way to lead a man into a tight corner and then leave him there and turn tail. He sailed for France in disgust.

The year 1262 saw the highwater mark of the reaction in Henry's favour before reform turned to open rebellion. A new Pope supported him even more emphatically than his predecessor. De Montfort was out of the country. Yet, instead of consolidating his position at home, Henry foolishly crossed to France to discuss with King Louis problems arising from the Treaty of Paris and to rake up all his old complaints against de Montfort. While abroad, he succumbed to a serious epidemic and the rumour spread that he had died. In November, Llywelyn of Wales, provoked by marcher encroachments, launched a general attack upon the English border fortresses. Earl Richard of Gloucester had died in July, and the fittest man to restore order on the Welsh march, the king's son Edward, returned from jousting in Gascony only in February, 1263. Some opposition to Edward and his father, reckless, personal, and unexplained, seems to have arisen among a group of younger barons of the march. They called Earl Simon to their aid. Their action and the earl's arrival in April stirred into fresh life the support for the reform movement still deeply felt in many parts of England, in the towns as well as in the rural areas.

The civil war which now seemed inevitable was in fact postponed for twelve months. Neither the king and the openly royalist barons on the one hand nor de Montfort and the hard core of the old baronial movement on the other were prepared for war, and two attempts were made to settle their differences by submitting them to the arbitration of the saintly and much-revered King of France. Henry had no quarrel with the legislative Provisions of Westminster, which he had in fact re-issued in January, 1263. His case was that the Provisions of Oxford of 1258 had unlawfully deprived him of the right to appoint his own ministers ; that the Pope had absolved him from his oath to observe them ; and that in any case they were contrary to his own coronation oath. The barons ignored the papal dispensation and put most weight on the king's solemn oath of 1258 and his subsequent breach of it. They also restated, in some detail, the reasons why reform was necessary and accused the king of acting against Magna Carta. Louis, who combined a very strong sense of justice with an exalted notion of kingship, pronounced, by the Mise of Amiens [1] (January 23rd, 1264), unconditionally in Henry's favour.

The judgment was rejected by Earl Simon. In April, the town and castle of Northampton, a baronial stronghold, were captured and sacked by Prince Edward, and little more than a month later the royalist army, anxious to prevent de Montfort from cutting its communications with France, engaged the earl's forces at Lewes in Sussex. The baronial host was marshalled along the crest of the down which rises north-west of the borough. Added to this advantage of ground, the barons, though fewer in number, seem to have had more weight in armour and first-rate mounted troops. Their left wing was made up of an enthusiastic, if undisciplined, throng from London, where the majority was devoted to the cause of the reform movement. This wing was opposed by Prince Edward. In the centre were the two chief baronial leaders, the young Earl of Gloucester, Gilbert of Clare, in the van, Earl Simon himself commanding the reserve. Appropriately enough, they faced the king, who had raised his great dragon standard in front of the Cluniac priory outside the town wall. The baronial troops on the right were under two of de Montfort's sons, Henry and Guy, and were marked by knights—many of them foreign—led by the king's brother Richard, Earl of Cornwall and King of Germany.

The first phase of the engagement was the complete rout of the Londoners by Prince Edward, who, however, carried his pursuit so far that before his return the battle had been lost and won. The royalist left fared badly. After many of his men had been killed or captured, King Richard shut himself up inside a windmill. In this plight the would-be emperor, " semper Augustus ", became not surprisingly a target for boisterous humour :

> The king of Almain thought to do well
> He seized the mill for a castél ;
> With sharpened swords they ground the steel ;
> He thought the sails were a mangonel.[2]

With their left wing broken, the royalists were pressed back to the shelter of the priory. The king, despite his fifty-six years, fought bravely and was badly wounded, but several of the greatest magnates

[1] " Mise " = (here) " arbitration " or " agreement ".
[2] Modernised from T. Wright, *Political Songs* (Camden Soc., 1839, p. 69). Almain = Germany ; castél = castle ; mangonel, an engine for throwing stones.

on his side, including the Earl Warenne, fled to the coast and found ships to take them to France, where they joined Queen Eleanor. After this, surrender was unavoidable. Earl Simon's victory has been called " bloodless ", but in fact the London levies and the royalist infantry [1] suffered heavy casualties, including many killed.

Pending a permanent settlement, the governance of king and kingdom was assumed by three " electors " (Earl Simon, Earl Gilbert of Gloucester and Stephen Berksted, Bishop of Chichester) who in theory represented the community of the baronage. Chosen by and subordinate to them was a council of nine, at least three of whom were to be always with the king and through whom the day-to-day work of administration was to be carried on. If government by the king with the compulsory advice of the Fifteen had proved unworkable, then this new " forma regiminis " would certainly function only so long as the king remained a prisoner and de Montfort in effect dictator. Yet the earl, if he overrode English custom in this revolutionary way, can be acquitted more easily than most ambitious men of the charge of dictatorship. He wanted a return to the hopeful co-operation of 1258 and was not willing to recognise that the bitterness and divisions of the intervening years had made that impossible. He was able, it is true, to rally the townsmen and peasantry to the defence of their country when Queen Eleanor threatened to invade England in support of her husband. He held Parliaments in June, 1264, and January, 1265, to which he called knights to represent the shires and (in the latter) two burgesses each from a number of cities and boroughs. This was an intelligent and fruitful recognition of the growing political importance of the gentry and the merchants. But a detailed examination of the January Parliament reveals not the strength but the weakness of de Montfort's position. His support came overwhelmingly from the middle classes and the clergy (including nearly half the English bishops). Only eighteen barons and four earls (in addition to himself) were summoned as definite adherents of the new regime.

The peace agreed on at the close of this Parliament (March 8th) was in no sense a political settlement. The king remained a prisoner of the three electors and the council of nine, to whose rule Prince

---

[1] These probably included light-armed, unarmoured highlanders from Badenoch, brought to this south-coast battle by John Comyn the Red, who fought on the king's side.

Edward was forced to swear obedience. His lordship of Chester was transferred to de Montfort, and even his other lands and castles were to be withheld from him for five years as security for his good behaviour. To continue the virtual suspension of the monarchy for so long would hardly have been easy for de Montfort even if his party had still represented a majority of the baronage. But in fact he was losing his hold over the loyal band who had won the fight at Lewes. In the early summer of 1265, renewed threats from the Prince of Wales brought the electors and their royal captives to the Severn valley. There, in May, Earl Gilbert changed sides and allied himself to the royalist marcher lords, Roger Mortimer and his friends, whom de Montfort had rashly left at liberty. On May 28th Prince Edward himself escaped from custody and rode to Ludlow where Mortimer and Gloucester joined him. Together, they raised the marches for the king.

Simon de Montfort was at this time the best general of any man in England. Had he moved eastward into the midland shires where sympathies were strongly baronial, and where he possessed at Kenilworth the most up-to-date fortification on English soil, Edward's task would have been extremely difficult. Instead, he was strangely irresolute and made the tactical error of entering Wales to make peace with Llywelyn. Meanwhile the royalists captured Gloucester castle and occupied the valley of the Warwickshire Avon. A diversion in their rear by the younger Simon de Montfort (the earl's second son) enabled his father to cross the Severn and reach Evesham. His army was small, tired and hungry. On Tuesday, August 4th, it was overwhelmed by the fierce onslaught of men for whom the very name of Montfort had become a byword for treason. The earl himself was killed and his body brutally dismembered. The motives of many of his enemies were not admirable, but a Montfortian victory would not have established a new and permanent constitution. The French nobleman has rightly become one of the great heroic figures of English history through his steadfastness, honesty of purpose and devotion to an ideal. He succeeded for a space in uniting baronage, gentry, townspeople and even simple villagers in the belief that the reform programme, observed in every point, would guarantee justice and the triumph of true religion. To his opponents, less intellectual than the Montfortians but not necessarily weaker in political sense, reform of the realm as an ideal had become not only impracticable but also unattractive. The monarchy could be hedged about with checks and safeguards, but it could not be dispensed with. The baronial movement has been called " the first deliberate and conscious political revolution in English history ".[1] It certainly ended as all other English revolutions have ended, in the victory of the empiricist over the idealist.

Evesham was followed by an understandable reaction. The king was restored to full power, many vindictive reprisals were taken against Montfortians, and there was much confused confiscation of their property. It was due to the statesmanship of the new papal legate, Cardinal Ottobuono Fieschi, helped by the King of Germany's son, Henry of Almain, that the reaction was not more prolonged and savage. Montfortian rearguards were still holding out in Kenilworth and (under the young Simon) in the Isle of Axholme, between Lincolnshire and Yorkshire. The long siege of Kenilworth (June-December, 1266) allowed passions to cool, and the final peace was made on the basis of the surrender terms for the Kenilworth garrison, drawn up largely by the legate, and known as the " Dictum of Kenilworth " (October 31st, 1266).

The Dictum made it clear that the king's authority was now restored in full, and that the Crown was to recover its rights and property unless those who enjoyed them could show a reasonable warrant. There was, moreover, to be an end of summary justice : " all shall seek and stand to justice in the king's court *by writ*, as was the custom before the time of disturbance ". Nevertheless, the king was asked, significantly, to appoint as judges and ministers men who " will settle the affairs of subjects in accordance with the laws and laudable customs of the realm ". He was also urged to observe the liberties of the Church, Magna Carta, and the Charter of the Forest, and was reminded of the oath which bound him to do so. The most acute problem concerned the supporters of de Montfort who, in the revengeful aftermath of Evesham, had been disinherited of their lands which had been granted to royalists. It was solved by a sensible compromise : redemption was to take the place of disinheritance. The great majority of rebels, e.g. those who had fought at Lewes and Evesham, were to be allowed to buy back their lands at five years' value (half the rate at which land was normally sold at that period). Less important rebels could redeem their land at two years' value.

[1] R. F. Treharne, *Trans. R. Hist. Soc.* (1943), 35.

Certain prominent Montfortians, including the commander of the Kenilworth garrison, Henry of Hastings, and the Earl of Derby, must pay seven years' value ; and, indeed, the earl was deliberately ruined by a process of doubtful legality. Though the terms might be hard for those whose chattels had been confiscated and could not be recovered, the Dictum and the milder mood which it symbolised made a general pacification possible. The ardently Montfortian Cinque Ports were reconciled by Prince Edward. The Earl of Gloucester, having been too much of a royalist to stand by Earl Simon, suddenly proved enough of a Montfortian to ally himself to the still mutinous Londoners. At last they too made their peace, in June, 1267, for a fine of 20,000 marks, though not all the citizens had supported the baronial side.

CHAPTER XVII

UNITY AND DEFINITION, 1267-90

1. *Legislation*

IF we search for an appropriate starting-point at which to take up the history of England under Edward I, we shall find curselves carried back five years before his accession, to the great statute enacted in October, 1267, in an assembly at Marlborough in Wiltshire. This Act was a review of the relations between the king and his subjects and of the working of the Common Law. It was so comprehensive that contemporaries wrote of " the constitutions " or " the statutes " of Marlborough rather than of " the statute ", a use of the plural common in our period to indicate any widely ranging restatement of the law. It is an instructive usage, for it warns us that to enact a statute in thirteenth-century England did not mean what it had come to mean within half a century from 1300 and has meant ever since. When the king called together the great magnates of the land, prelates, earls and barons, together with the skilled members of his Inner Council, clerks and judges and the like, and with their advice and assent solemnly enacted that his subjects were to do this or not to do that, his intention was not to make a new law but to pronounce the old, to state explicitly what the force of existing custom or the ruling of divine law provided for in particular instances. There might, it is true, be conflict between English custom and divine or " natural " law, as, e.g. on the question of bastardy. The Church, claiming to interpret divine law, held that children born out of wedlock were made legitimate if their parents subsequently married. The Statute of Merton (1236) proclaimed the harsher rule of English feudal custom, that such children must always suffer the legal disabilities of bastardy. But more commonly a statute was uncontroversial. In the absence of any official code of English law, statutes made the law clearer, " declared " it, with the maximum of solemnity and publicity. It is largely by his use of this device of the statute, and also by his development of the assembly caiied

Parliament in which statutes were normally enacted, that Edward I has compelled the admiration of posterity and justified the received opinion of historians that he was the greatest king of medieval England.

The Statute of Marlborough was a starting-point for the unification of England after the civil war. It confirmed the charters of liberties—Magna Carta and the Charter of the Forest—and it re-enacted the Provisions of Westminster of 1259 regarding suit of court and the other matters about which the community of free men felt most strongly. Thus it reconciled the reform programme's numerous sympathisers to the restored monarchy of Henry III and, still more readily when the old king died in November, 1272, to the rule of his son Edward. It was clear that a new atmosphere prevailed when, in an especially full Parliament at Hoketide, 1270, it was agreed to grant the king a general tax of one-twentieth of movable property, the first tax of this kind which Henry III had been able to levy since 1237. It was designed primarily to enable Prince Edward to join the King of France on crusade.

King Henry had never abandoned his desire either to go on crusade himself, or at least to send a strong military contingent. He wished greatly to emulate St. Louis of France in devotion to the Christian religion. But in striving towards saintliness he achieved only a self-centred piety. The best-known story of King Henry's devotion tells how he held up the important negotiations for the Treaty of Paris (1259) for two days because he insisted on hearing Mass in every church between his lodgings at St. Germain-des-Prés and the French court. King Louis countered this by ordering all the churches to be bolted and barred until Henry had ridden past. Not surprisingly, Henry was among the first to arrive on the third day, but blandly refused to proceed to business with a ruler whose capital city had obviously been placed under an interdict! The story may well be true. If so, it suggests that Henry had a sense of humour. But coupled with what we know from unquestionable sources of his habit at times of crisis of going off on a pilgrimage (e.g. to the supposed relic of the Holy Rood preserved at Bromholm priory in Norfolk), it may lead us to suspect that for his contemporaries the king's piety was more irritating than admirable. The most striking outward expression of his religious feeling was not a popular memory of justice and charity shown to his people, but a

marvellous building of stone, wood, and glass—the choir of Westminster Abbey, including the shrine of Edward the Confessor,
Henry's patron saint. The king's architect was Master Henry de
Reyns, who probably took his surname from Rayne in Essex, near
Bishop's Stortford. The work was under his direction from 1245 to
1253. The greater part of the new abbey church from the choir eastward, including the crossing and north front, was completed by 1269.
The nave was finished in the same style a century later. It is
generally agreed that Westminster Abbey is English work, though
its designer undoubtedly derived inspiration from the new French
cathedrals of Rheims (finished 1241) and Amiens (1248-69).[1] We
must be grateful to King Henry for having conceived this wonderful
monument, even though, characteristically, he was not able to pay
for it.

Edward was absent for four years (1270-4). First he commanded
crusading armies at Tunis and Acre, prosecuting a fruitless campaign
against the Mameluke Sultan of Egypt, Bibars, who controlled
almost the entire coast of the eastern Mediterranean. Afterwards
(1273-4), he was busy in Gascony, securing its southern frontiers by
treaties with Aragon and Navarre and attempting to pacify Gaston
of Béarn, who had revolted against the Duke of Aquitaine's authority
and appealed from the ducal court to the King of France's court
(the *parlement*) in Paris. Edward returned to England on August
2nd, 1274, and was crowned at Westminster seventeen days later.
Almost [2] at once (October, 1274) he embarked upon an enquiry
which penetrated minutely into every detail of local government and
embraced every class from earls to villeins. In most shires fresh
sheriffs were appointed. Groups of counties were formed into
circuits, in each of which certain trusted royal servants rode from
place to place taking evidence from juries appointed to represent
every hundred and borough and (in certain shires) every village.
The jurors were required to answer some forty questions. To the
resultant sworn " verdicts ", written on rolls of parchment, each

[1] See W. Lethaby, *Westminster Abbey and the King's Craftsmen* (1906)
and *Westminster Abbey Re-examined* (1925) ; F. M. Powicke, *Henry III
and the Lord Edward*, ii. 571, n. 1 ; John Harvey, *Biographical Dictionary
of Medieval English Architects* (1954), under " Reyns ".

[2] The following pages are based largely on Helen Cam, *The Hundred
and the Hundred Rolls* (1930), and T. F. T. Plucknett, *The Legislation of
Edward I* (1949).

juror fixed his own seal, hanging on a tag. As the months passed, the royal commissioners accumulated on the backs of their pack-horses vast quantities of these sealed replies. " The bundles of rolls made a great impression on the minds of the countrymen. In later years, when they spoke of the searching inquisition that they or their neighbours had undergone, in the winter after the king came back from the Holy Land, they called it the Ragman Quest, because of those rolled-up verdicts with their dangling seals." [1]

The enquiry of 1274-5 was made with two objects in mind. (1) The king wished to find out the extent of encroachment by private persons upon the rights and property of the Crown, so that, in accordance with the Dictum of Kenilworth, the appropriators should either show that they had a sufficient warrant for their possession of such royal rights or, if not, restore them to the Crown forthwith. The constant iteration of the question *Quo waranto ?*—" by what warrant ? "—has led to the whole process being called the Quo Waranto enquiry. This aspect was undoubtedly important. The king was determined that no one should exercise royal jurisdiction or enjoy the possession of royal land or other property unless it could be proved that an earlier sovereign had granted him such privileges. Moreover, he and his judges were disposed to the view that the sole effective proof was a royal charter in which the liberties granted away by the king were specifically named. Many lords held liberties which their ancestors had possessed since time immemorial ; no charter had ever been obtained for them. A famous story is told of one great magnate, John, Earl Warenne, lord of Lewes in Sussex. He is said to have replied to the justices' *quo waranto ?* by producing in their midst an ancient and rusty sword, saying : " This, my lords, is my warrant. My forebears came with William the Bastard and conquered their lands with the sword, and with the sword shall I defend them against any who may wish to usurp them." The earl's history was sound enough : the Warennes had indeed come over with the Conqueror. But his boast sounds a little ironical when one remembers that only ten years before, when the king was fighting desperately in the earl's own town of Lewes, Warenne had been among those who had fled to fight another day. Whether or

---

[1] Cam, *op. cit.* 45. Professor Cam explains that " ragman " was the nickname given to any piece of parchment with a fringe of loose tags hanging from it.

not the story is true, he was in fact required to argue his case before the royal justices, who were at last satisfied by his demonstration that he and his ancestors had enjoyed certain liberties " from a time of which there is no memory ".   Lesser lords might prefer to be in the position of Theobald Bussel or Bushel of Devonshire, who could produce a charter of Henry III to justify his holding of the assize of bread and ale in Newton Bushel and his fair at Highweek.   Other typical privileges which formed the subject of royal scrutiny were the " return of writs "—i.e. the right to receive the king's writ and act upon it independently of the sheriff—the holding of hundred courts, the taking of view of frankpledge, seizing wreck of the sea, and keeping gallows to hang thieves caught red-handed.

The Quo Waranto enquiries continued for more than a decade. By 1290 the king realised that he had pushed the matter as far as baronial opinion would allow.   The process was therefore concluded in this year by a statute, the Statute of Quo Waranto, which marked a compromise between a wholesale reduction of private franchises and the desire of prelates and barons to retain all their ancient liberties intact.   Under the statute, franchise holders, if they could prove possession since time immemorial, or, in technical language, " by long user ",[1] were entitled to obtain a royal charter of confirmation, which would henceforth constitute their only warrant.   Those who held by an earlier charter might retain just so much as it specifically mentioned.   In view of the vagueness of older documents and the severity of the royal judges with whom their interpretation exclusively lay, this provision meant in practice a gain for the Crown.

(2) The " Ragman Quest ", however, was not solely concerned to stop the whittling away of royal rights by private persons.   The king was prepared to give attention to all manner of complaints against sheriffs, coroners, escheators, and bailiffs who had abused their authority.   In spite of what the Dictum of Kenilworth had had to say on the need to obtain justice by writ, the simpler procedure whereby an individual could lodge a *querela*, or a bill of complaint, proved equally acceptable to the judges of Edward I.   In 1274-5 the commissioners collected hundreds of accusations of petty tyranny and misbehaviour, both in the form of jury " verdicts " and of private bills.   It follows inescapably from a study of this volume of

---

[1] The limit of memory was defined as the first coronation of Richard I (1189).

discontent that there were grave defects in the Angevin system of local government. In so far as the maladies could be cured by modifying the system, the king and his council made a conscientious attempt to do so by the great Statutes of Westminster I (1275) and II (1285) and the Statute of Gloucester (1278). Out of fifty-one chapters in Westminster I " some twenty-four deal with local government, and most are so nearly concerned with the type of offence reported in the Hundred Rolls that it is impossible to believe that there is no connection." [1] Westminster II was a vast, comprehensive statute, a considerable part of which again attacked the problem of abuses in local government.

Much of the evil complained of by local gentry and villagers lay not in the system but in men like themselves who while in office took bribes, brought influence to bear upon jurymen, embezzled Crown revenues, or levied extortionate fines and amercements. This problem Edward I never solved. No judicial proceedings resulted directly from the exposures of 1274-5. Yet King Edward takes first place among those medieval English kings who have visited sudden and condign punishment upon an entire group of corrupt and unjust ministers. From 1286 to 1289 he paid a prolonged visit to Gascony. His return in December, 1289—like those of Henry II in 1170 and 1178—released a pent up flood of complaints against the misconduct of justices, exchequer officials, sheriffs, and bailiffs. The charges touched men in the highest places of government. A special judicial commission was appointed to try the accused. It included one nobleman, the Earl of Lincoln, whose career of service to the Crown was unsullied ; but most of its members were non-aristocratic royal servants whose actions at other times will not always bear close scrutiny, and whose best claim to innocence in 1289 was their alibi of having been in Gascony with the king. Prominent among them was the king's close friend, Robert Burnell, a genial clerk whom Edward had made Chancellor in 1274, and whom he would have made Archbishop of Canterbury if the scandal of his highly unpriestly private life had not made this obnoxious to the Papacy.[2]

Between the close of 1289 and the beginning of 1293, scores of royal officials were brought to trial on bills of complaint tendered by

[1] Cam, *op. cit.* 226.
[2] Burnell had to be content with the rich bishopric of Bath and Wells.

individual accusers. No fewer than ten of the justices were convicted and dismissed. Fines and imprisonment in the Tower were sufficient to deal with the majority. Indeed, the extremely heavy fine imposed on Ralph Hengham, Chief Justice of the King's Bench, seems to have been intended to make an example of him rather than to constitute a just punishment, for the irregularities of which he was accused had been prompted by his desire to help poor suitors. Before the commission met, his colleague, Thomas Wayland, Chief Justice of Common Pleas, fled to sanctuary with the Franciscans of Babwell in Suffolk—which for a contemporary satirist promptly became the "Well of Babylon". Sooner than face trial he forswore the realm. Making an exit which, whether salutary or not, was certainly dramatic, he journeyed to the coast on foot, bearing a cross, and taking ship at Dover was never heard of again. For notoriety in misdoing Wayland was probably surpassed by the Chamberlain of the Exchequer, Adam of Stratton. Adam had gained financial experience by service in a great baronial household, and would appear to have profited by studying a contemporary treatise on estate management which had the effrontery to tell its readers how accounts could be dishonestly manipulated. What particularly shocked his contemporaries was that he openly lent money at high interest, a contravention of Canon Law barely to be tolerated among Christians unless they came from Cahors in the Midi,[1] or at least kept their usury decently concealed. In 1292, Stratton's house in London was found to contain over £12,000 in cash ; but he was in fact convicted and ruined, not for prospering in a nefarious business, but for tampering with, and even forging, legal documents.

Edwardian legislation in the field of local government, chiefly embodied in the two Statutes of Westminster, formed but a small part of the impressive series of enactments in which, year after year between 1275 and 1290, the laws and customs regulating almost every aspect of national life were skilfully scrutinised, modified, augmented, above all defined, in the interests of good government. In this activity Edward I was neither an innovator nor in advance of his age. In France St. Louis, in Castile Alfonso X (1252-84), to name only rulers with whom Edward had close personal relations,

[1] The *Caursini* or men of Cahors were among the most prominent Christian money-lenders of the period.

had been responsible respectively for administrative measures and for publishing definitive codes of law which marked a new stage in the political history of their two kingdoms. Edward I resembled his great-grandfather Henry II not only in his lawyerly approach to problems of government but also in being a notable adapter. The *Quo Waranto* inquests showed this quality, for they copied on a larger scale the enquiries carried out by Henry III, especially those of 1255. The Edwardian capacity for adaptation is nowhere more evident than in his law-making. It may be easier to gain some idea of the content of this legislation if we consider it under the four headings of feudal relations, criminal justice, the Church and the merchants.

(1) *Feudal Relations.* The century before Edward I's accession had witnessed a major transformation in the character of English feudalism. The old rules of homage and fealty, the feudal incidents, above all the fundamental tenurial structure of feudalism dependent on knight-service and serjeanty, still held the field and had, indeed, been elaborated. But they were already anachronisms, preserved as men will preserve a set of known and familiar rules when the need for change is not yet urgent and when the changes needed are by no means clearly appreciated. In the first place, the feudal relationship between lord and vassal was rapidly becoming merely a matter of legal form and cash payments. The typical thirteenth-century landholder was the tenant of many lords, and was as glad to hold land in free socage as by knight-service—often gladder, because the feudal incidents formed a real burden on a small estate. At the same time, no one wished to abolish the incidents, for the majority were lords as well as tenants, owing to the fact that by feudal rules the man who alienated land to another must retain some right, a lord's right, over both the land itself and its new tenant. Yet buying and selling and subinfeudation were going on constantly, and the lords of great estates found it increasingly difficult to keep trace of their lesser free tenants and of the multitude of small payments owed to them by way of feudal incidents or commuted services.

There were other and perhaps more striking changes in the English feudal landscape. In 1272, very few of the great baronial families of the Conqueror's day survived. There had been some tendency for the class of greater magnates to diminish and for their estates to grow correspondingly larger. The Crown benefited from this tendency. During the twelfth century the kings may be said to have parted with landed property faster than they gained it. In the thirteenth, however, the extinction of a number of old families brought land back to the Crown. Henry III, e.g. was still able to keep many rich escheats in his own hand even after granting a number to the hated " foreigners ". In 1237, John of Scotland,[1] the last Earl of Chester not of English royal blood, died without leaving a son. The king bought out the coheiresses and made the palatinate into a lordship for Prince Edward. In 1245, as we have seen, the vast estates of William the Marshal were split up, but the greater part went to men who were already landowners on the largest scale, e.g. Roger Bigod, Earl of Norfolk. We have also seen how the Bohun earls of Hereford and the Clare earls of Gloucester possessed enormous tracts of land, and the same may be said of the Warennes of Lewes, earls of Surrey and great landlords in Yorkshire, and the family of Forz (*de Fortibus*) which held the earldom of Aumâle, comprising the Isle of Wight, and also Craven and Holderness in Yorkshire.

It is now generally recognised that Edward I did not set out to " destroy feudalism " by legislation or any other means. The fact was that feudal relations had become excessively complicated, and the king and his Council were determined to restore order and tidiness. For example, the amount of aid payable in any one year from a single knight's fee was fixed by Westminster I at 20s. At the same time, the king continued his father's policy of treating all landholders above a certain level of income as though they were of knightly status, even when they had not taken the arms of knighthood. Not only was the Assize of Arms of 1181 enforced by Chapter Six of the Statute of Winchester (1285) in such a way that all who held land to the value of £15 were required to maintain the horse and equipment of a knight. On the occasion of several military campaigns prior to 1272 men with land worth £20 a year were compelled to accept knighthood or else pay a fine which amounted to a knight's obligations. Moreover, aids were to be paid by tenants in free socage as well as by strictly feudal tenants. By this process of " distraint of knighthood " the rigid system of knights' fees which had served in the twelfth century was replaced

[1] Nephew of Earl Ranulf of Blundeville (d. 1232) ; above, p. 243, n. 1.

by a more flexible system of military obligation based on wealth derived from every sort of tenure, feudal and otherwise.

The incidents of wardship and marriage, and the problem of default of service by a tenant, were treated in the Statute of Gloucester as well as in Westminster I and II. In respect of wardship and marriage, the statutes were in the main conservative, restating the customary feudal rules in all their harshness. Yet there was some attempt to prevent wards and their lands being exploited commercially to their own injury cr disadvantage. Where a tenant failed in his service, a remedy was given to the lord who could show that there had been continuous default for two years. In such a case the lord could recover the tenement. This was of especial benefit to the many smaller landholders who had granted away their estates in return for the " services " of a money rent or an allowance of food and clothing.

There remained, finally, the central problem of legislating in the field of feudal relations : the regulation of the transference of land from one holder to another. Two extremely important statutes attempted, one successfully, the other with rather less than success, to deal with this problem. To take first the less effective statute, the first chapter of Westminster II enacted that whenever a lord had granted away part of his estate on certain conditions, he or his heirs should recover the land so granted if these conditions were not duly fulfilled. For example, a father, William, might settle some property on his daughter, Isabel, at her marriage. It would be the intention of the grant that the estate, the *maritagium* or " marriage portion ", which passed to the daughter should be used to support her and her children, and perhaps the children of her eldest son. Now suppose the daughter dies childless. If her husband, Robert, then retains the land, he is clearly robbing the father and defeating the object of the grant. Or suppose Isabel has a family, but her eldest son dies without heirs of his body. Again, if Robert, or any person who happens to be his heir without also being the heir of Isabel, retains the estate, then either William or whoever happens to be his direct heir will be kept out of his property.

Another form of conditional grant was that which a father, Walter, might make to a younger son, John, who would otherwise be left without any provision because of the rule of primogeniture. The purpose of such a grant would be fulfilled if the estates which composed it supported John and his family, his heir and his family, and so on, perhaps for three generations. There may have been a tacit understanding that John's third male heir in direct descent would be able to treat the property as his own to alienate as he pleased. But if there were only two or three generations in succession to Walter, the original donor, and the junior line then died out, it was equally understood that the property should revert to the main line of the family, represented by Walter himself and his heirs. A grant made with these conditions or limitations was said to be *entaillé* (" cut ") or " entailed " : the property was an " estate-tail " or " fee-tail ", as opposed to an ordinary estate or " fee-simple ", which passed freely from eldest son to eldest son or could be alienated by its owner in any generation.

At first, when a *maritagium* or an entail was granted by charter, it was thought sufficient to settle the estate " on Isabel and the heirs of her body " or " on John and the heirs of his body ". But during the thirteenth century the courts developed a perverse interpretation of these simple phrases. Instead of limiting the gift to X and the heirs of his or her body they held that, so long as X *had* such heirs the estate at once became the outright property of X to dispose of as he or she pleased. Chapter I of Westminster II, *De donis condition-alibus*, took up the question of conditional grants with the object of calling a halt to this perversity. It enacted that in future the precise terms of a grant were to be strictly adhered to. Owing, however, to bad drafting uncommon in an Edwardian statute, the explanation which followed this simple decree failed to make it plain whether a *maritagium* or an entail should benefit more than a single generation in succession to the donor. In the following reign, one judge, claiming to know what the drafter of *De donis* really meant, said that a conditional grant must be allowed to benefit four generations from the donor. But though this view was very probably correct, no authority was given to it. *De donis* seems, on the contrary, to have discouraged the formation of enduring entails and encouraged instead the free transfer of landed estate.[1]

The second piece of land law dealt with subinfeudation. This was the statute promulgated in the protracted Easter Parliament of

[1] This is based on the full and lucid account of the background to and meaning of *De donis* given by Professor Plucknett, *Legislation of Edward I*, 125-35.

1290 and known from its opening words as *Quia Emptores* (" whereas the buyers . . ."). Its solution of the complexities produced by excessive subinfeudation was simple and drastic. " Henceforth every free man shall be allowed to sell his land or tenement or any part thereof at will, so that the person enfeoffed with it (i.e. the buyer) shall hold the land of the chief lord of whom the seller of the land formerly held it, and by the same services and customs." In other words, the intermediate stages of the feudal pyramid are abolished. There are to be only " chief lords " and tenants, and since the Crown is the ultimate chief lord of all land and never dies, the statute will in time make every landholder the direct tenant of the Crown. But it would be wrong to suppose that the statute was designed particularly to benefit the Crown : after all, it would be many generations before all traces of subinfeudation disappeared, and the Church was an intermediate lord who also never died. By facilitating the transfer of land, *Quia Emptores* was of advantage to the entire landed class, and there are no grounds for doubting the statement of its preamble that it was enacted " at the instance of the magnates of the realm ".

This account of King Edward's law-making in the field of feudal relations has been unavoidably technical, and the generalisations to which such a brief survey must be reduced make somewhat dry reading. We should try to offset this as far as possible by remembering that for the king himself and for the nobles and country gentlemen of his age the rules of feudalism were the very stuff of their being ; that statutes such as *De donis* and *Quia Emptores* might make all the difference in the world to a widow's enjoyment of old age, to a girl's prospects of marriage, to the head of a family's hopes of improving or maintaining his ancestral estates for the benefit of his son and grandson. As for the king himself, at the very centre of this complex of feudal laws, it may be worth while to conclude with a brief illustration of how, in Sir Maurice Powicke's words,[1] " King Edward was playing with, not against, feudalism ". Earl Gilbert of Gloucester, on marrying the king's daughter Joan in 1290, surrendered the bulk of his estates to the king and received them back to hold jointly with his wife on certain conditions. Earl Humphrey of Hereford also married a daughter of the king (1302), and a precisely similar transaction was made with him. In the same year, the childless

[1] *Henry III and the Lord Edward*, ii. 706.

Earl of Norfolk, his estates encumbered with debt, made over to the king his lands, titles, and offices, receiving them back for life only. The Crown paid his debts and had the reversion of his estate.[1] Two years before this, the great earldom of Cornwall, held (1227-72) by Henry III's astute and wealthy brother Richard, King of the Romans, escheated to the Crown on the death of Richard's son Edmund. In the reign of a strong king like Edward I great feudal estates subtracted nothing from the power of the Crown. On the contrary, they could be and were made to add to it.

(2) *Criminal justice.* The Statute of Winchester (1285) and the commissions of " Trailbaston " (1304-7) were the principal Edwardian measures in this intensely conservative sphere. The former applied the principles of the Assizes of Clarendon and Northampton, making the burden of catching the criminal and bringing him to justice rest squarely upon the local community. The punitive quality of the murder fine was paralleled in the new rule that if a murderer or robber was not brought to justice within forty days the whole hundred in which the crime had been committed (or two neighbouring hundreds if it had been on their borders) must pay the penalty and the damages. This was to apply after a six-month period of grace, during which the king would see whether the villages and hundreds ceased protecting the guilty and concealing crimes. If not, then " from fear of the penalty more than from fear of any oath ", as the statute put it, the local communities will be expected to do their duty in this respect. At the same time, the obligation of walled cities and towns to maintain " watch and ward " against strangers at night. already an ancient duty, was re-emphasised. The twenty years which followed were years of war, and crime seems, if anything, to have increased in volume and violence. Under the ordinance of Trailbaston, which first operated from 1304 to 1307, special justices, distinct from the justices-in-eyre, were to tour the country to hear and judge cases of open and violent breach of the peace ; especially to deal with gangs of ruffians (doubtless including deserters and discharged soldiers) who roamed the highways trailing " bastons " or large sticks, beating and robbing travellers.

(3) *The Church.* The general relations between laity and clergy

---

[1] It was granted to a younger son of the king, Thomas of Brotherton, and through his daughter's marriage passed to the ancient family of Mowbray.

in the late thirteenth century seem to have been reasonably harmonious. It was quite otherwise where king and primate were concerned. Instead of his beloved Burnell, Edward I was forced to see the archbishopric of Canterbury occupied in turn by a Dominican, Robert Kilwardby (1273-8), a Franciscan, John Pecham (1279-92) and a noted Oxford teacher, Robert Winchelsey (1294-1313). All were scholarly men, and deeply religious in the best of that word's modern senses. In the conflict of loyalty between Church and State, none was disposed to co-operate with the king in any trespass upon ecclesiastical liberties. Despite this, Edwardian legislation on matters affecting the Church was not anti-clerical. The Statute of Mortmain [1] (1279) is sometimes described as hostile to the Church, and was so regarded by monastic chroniclers of the period. The timing of its enactment was doubtless due to the king's irritation with Archbishop Pecham, but the statute itself merely put into effect, rather more drastically, a baronial petition of 1258. It forbade the acquisition of land by religious corporations : in theory, absolutely, but in practice, except under royal licence. It was not unreasonable that some check should be put on alienation in mortmain, since it meant that the superior lord of the land which had been given to the Church lost the feudal incidents such as wardship, marriage and escheat. Six years later, an administrative order was sent to royal justices in the diocese of Norwich defining the limits of secular and ecclesiastical jurisdiction. While it was made clear that matters like advowson and tithe (if over a quarter of a church's value) were to remain the province of the secular courts, the bishops and archdeacons were left with a wide range of business, e.g. adultery, slander (save in respect of damages), the proving of wills, and even cases of violent assault upon clergymen. This order of *Circumspecte agatis* (" deal cautiously . . .") was in fact soon treated as a statute, the chief authority in this field for more than two centuries.

(4) *The Merchant Community*, and in particular the foreign merchants in England, were helped by the statutes of Acton Burnell (1283) and of Merchants (1285), as well as by part of Westminster II. Here the problem was mainly debts and their recovery. Foreign merchants were useful to the king and (though cordially disliked)

---

[1] *Mortua manus*, lit. the " dead hand ", which, because of the Church's undying possession of its estates, rendered none of the feudal dues such as reliefs.

did more good than harm to England as a whole. The object of these three statutes was to make it easier for the merchant creditor to recover debts. Under Acton Burnell, the mayors of London, York and Bristol were empowered to witness the formal acknowledgment of a debt by the creditor and the debtor, and to add a special royal seal to the bond given by the debtor to the creditor, which also bore, of course, the debtor's own seal. On non-payment of the debt, the creditor could show the bond to the mayor, who would then seize (" distrain ") such of the debtor's chattels and even burgage tenements as lay within his jurisdiction. If the debtor's property was in the countryside, the royal chancery, on presentation of the bond, would instruct the appropriate sheriff to distrain the debtor's goods, though not his freehold land. If the debtor had no chattels from which the debt could be paid, he was put in jail, and the creditor was obliged to keep him on bread and water. Two years later, the Statute of Merchants somewhat modified this procedure. More towns were brought within the scheme, and the debtor was sent to jail as soon as he defaulted. If, during the next three months, he had not sold enough of his goods or burgage tenements to pay off the debt, all his chattels passed to the creditor who was, moreover, given custody of all freehold land owned by the debtor at the time the debt was incurred. In such a case, the creditor was said to hold the land as a " tenant by Statute Merchant ". His obligation to the debtor was limited, as before, to providing him in jail with a diet of bread and water. The effect of these acts was undeniably harsh, yet it must be remembered that debt is always a very serious problem whenever public opinion (as in thirteenth-century England) is on the debtor's side.

2. *Parliament*

To the modern historian, the Edwardian Parliament usually seems more important than Edwardian legislation, the expression of the unity of English society more fruitful than the process by which King and Council defined rights and obligations and the manner in which laws and customs were to be applied. Yet in an historical survey of the reign it seems right to put the law-making before the assembly with which it was normally associated. There is little doubt that for King Edward the statutes constituted an end towards which Parliament was but a means, and not even the sole means. In the statutes, even in those which merely stated hitherto unwritten law, he was providing something new, useful, and constructive. There is no evidence whatever that in calling his parliaments he sought to create a new institution. But the historian must take note of practices which have produced beneficial results even unintentionally. Thus, apart from their intrinsic importance, the sheer bulk and frequency of the Edwardian statutes turned the device of statute from a rarity into a regular method of making fresh laws to meet new problems. So it was with Parliament. Doubtless the king had no idea that his use of Parliament was in any way novel, still less that in the course of his reign Parliament was developing from what has been called " rather an act than a body of persons " into a fixed institution with a fairly well defined membership and the core of an established procedure.

We have already seen how important the Great Council had been under Henry III, positively during the minority and the period of reform, somewhat negatively between 1234 and 1258 as the scene of baronial reluctance or refusal to grant supply. Constitutionally, the Council was simply the *Curia Regis* of the Norman kings when convened at its fullest extent, with king, bishops, abbots, earls, and barons. At two points there was uncertainty about its membership. First, there was a division within the baronage itself, recognised but undefined, between " greater " and " lesser " barons, and it was not certain that every tenant-in-chief of the Crown, however humble his status, had a right to attend. Secondly, the king insisted that he must be free to choose as his advisers whomsoever he considered suitable. Consequently, the king's " Inner Council " or working council included men who were not only not barons, but might not be tenants-in-chief of the Crown at all. True, many such were clerks in holy orders ; but the only clergy who held an unquestioned membership of the Great Council were bishops and certain of the more important abbots and priors. Yet from the king's point of view it was essential that his Inner Council should form part of the Great Council. Historically one was as much the *Curia Regis* as the other, and both were equally concerned with government.

It was to sessions of this Great Council that, during the middle years of Henry III's reign, the words *colloquium*, colloquy, or *parliamentum*, parliament, came to be applied. And it is of the utmost importance to understand that in our period " a session of the King's Council is the core and essence of every *parliamentum* ".[1] At first, therefore, parliament was not a technical term. It was merely a popular word, almost a nickname, used to describe an assembly which was certainly not new. The usage, moreover, was common to England and France. During Louis IX's reign, especially large or " afforced " sessions of the king's court were held with greater regularity than before, and gained the name of *parlement*. There is evidence that in England in the 1240s, in France from *c.* 1250, it was becoming the custom for the king to convene meetings of the Great Council in most years, and, with some regularity, as often as three or four times in one year. There is even a correspondence in the periodicity of French and English parliaments. Most commonly, parliaments met after the feasts of Easter, St. John Baptist (June 24th), Michaelmas, and Candlemas (February 2nd). The Oxford provision of 1258, that there should be three parliaments a year, probably sought to regularise a practice that already existed.[2]

So much for the membership and frequency of Parliament down to the time of Edward I. What of its business ? The barons of 1258 stated that Parliament should " treat of the common needs of kingdom and king ", suggesting (what other evidence confirms) that the widest possible scope was given to parliamentary agenda. Its business was judicial, fiscal, legislative, administrative and political. For the historian of Parliament as an institution, a particular interest attaches to the first two of these fields. It was because Parliament was a court, and because refusal of or consent to extraordinary taxation were signified in Parliament, that the extremely aristocratic Great Council and the extremely bureaucratic Inner Council came in contact and eventually merged with the communal or representative element to form that unique institution, the late medieval English Parliament.

Judicially, the king in parliament was the last resort of the subject who sought justice and failed to obtain it either from a private court or from one of the differentiated branches of the king's court, Exchequer, Common Pleas, or King's Bench. Cases before these smaller courts might be deferred until the next Parliament either

[1] F. W. Maitland, *Records of the Parliament of 1305* (*Memoranda de Parliamento*) (1893), p. lxxxviii.
[2] J. G. Edwards, " Justice in early English parliaments ", *Bull. Inst. Hist. Res.*, xxvii (1954), 39.

because of their gravity or because the legal problem involved was too knotty for a few judges to resolve on their own.   Moreover, any of the king's subjects, as we have seen, could apply to the king for justice where no writ was available to meet his case.   He did so by sending in a bill or petition.   The Common Law courts confined themselves to cases initiated by writ ; and while the justices-in-eyre could hear petitions, they might not be able to give a remedy in every case and were not always available.   Consequently, petitions were received and dealt with by Parliament.   The volume of such business increased enormously during the thirteenth century.   By no means all petitions were concerned to seek judicial remedies. Many merely required administrative action ;   many again were requests for private favours.   Special committees of " receivers " and " triers " of petitions had to be appointed to prevent parliamentary sessions being swamped by the business of remedying complaints and answering requests.   As the practice grew, it must have brought a concourse of people to Westminster, where parliaments were usually, though by no means invariably, held.   There would be members of the secular and ecclesiastical corporations, private citizens of nearly every class, and the lawyers whose professional skill was needed to draw up a petition in businesslike fashion and to argue the case for it before the appropriate committee of the court of parliament.

Nevertheless, though the hearing of petitions and consequent administrative and judicial business took up much of Parliament's time, and were very nearly the only part of which a permanent record was kept in the Rolls of Parliament, they formed but one aspect of the work of parliament as a whole.   A royal ordinance of 1279-80 prescribed that in future no petitions were to come before the king and his Council in parliament unless they had first been heard by the relevant minister of the Crown—the Chancellor, Treasurer or one of the chief justices—and had been found impossible for them to settle independently.   The rule was made " so that the king and his Council shall, without being burdened by other business, be able to attend to the great needs of his realm and other lands ".   From a government standpoint, the judicial business of Parliament seemed in danger of strangling its other business.   Judicial business was certainly important for the subject, but for the king himself Parliament must remain the occasion when he could discuss with his magnates the perennially urgent topics of war, peace and taxation. It must serve as the arena in which the Crown's immemorial need to take the counsel of the wise men of the realm could be satisfied. The view originally put forward by A. F. Pollard, and since elaborated by Mr. H. G. Richardson and Professor G. O. Sayles, that in the thirteenth and fourteenth centuries there were repeated requests for frequent parliaments because parliament's primary function was that of a court of law, has been shown to be erroneous.[1] " The competence of king in council in parliament was not a 'judicial' competence. It was a general competence . . . Parliament was an omnicompetent organ of government at the summit of lay affairs in England." [2]

The folk who thronged to Westminster, Winchester or Glou-cester, or wherever Parliament might be met, in order to present their petitions—unless, of course, they happened to be great magnates —were no more members of parliament than the parties to a law-suit are members of the court which hears it. Dispensing justice assuredly gave to Parliament a universal character : it did not make it representative. If we ask why the parliaments of Edward I came, with ever greater frequency, to be attended by representatives of the shires and boroughs, the answer seems to be that especially for fiscal purposes, and to a less extent for political and legislative purposes, the king required the assent of men who had full power to bind the communities they represented,[3] whether to a levy of taxation, or in support of the king's decision to go to war, or (less certainly in Edward I's time) in approval of a fresh statute.

Local men, usually, though not always, knights, had been required to co-operate with the central government in a representative capacity at least since the reign of Henry II. His Assize of Clarendon ordered the appointment of two law-worthy men from each shire to accompany those accused of crimes to the justices-in-eyre, bearing the record of each case. In 1213 King John appears to have sum-moned four knights from each shire to an assembly at Oxford " to discuss the business of the realm ".[4] In 1226 four knights were to

[1] See the article by Professor Edwards, cited above, p. 298, n. 2.
[2] *Ibid.* 53.
[3] On this subject see J. G. Edwards, " The *Plena Potestas* of English Parliamentary Representatives ", in *Oxford Essays in Medieval History presented to H. E. Salter* (1934), 141-54.
[4] It is doubtful if this council was held, or if it could have contained

be elected by certain shire-courts to explain, in a council to be held at Lincoln, the grievances felt by their counties at the sheriffs' interpretation of Magna Carta. In 1254, when the king was in Gascony and a Castilian attack seemed imminent, the queen and Earl Richard of Cornwall, acting as regents in England, sent the sheriffs a writ (in language alternating between threats and alarm) commanding the election of two knights by every shire, who were to meet the regents in council and state the amount of aid their counties were prepared to contribute. It is not surprising that the Reform Movement of 1258 gave considerable impetus to this practice of calling local representatives to attend Parliament. In addition to the mere administrative convenience of having local representatives summoned for the same date and place as the Great Council, we cannot overlook a deliberate political motive on the part of the reforming barons ; it can be seen especially in de Montfort's measures after the battle of Lewes. That urban representatives (citizens and burgesses) were added to knights of the shire was owing to the imaginative decision of de Montfort, doubtless because of his political necessity, but not the less creditable for that. But we should not think of knights as differing in kind from the humbler, less politically articulate burgesses. Both were in effect attorneys for their communities or *communes ;* and it was of course *communes* (anglicised as " commons ") which they represented, not the " common people " in general. The important point to notice is that even after 1265 parliaments continued from time to time to include local representatives. From 1275 onwards they attended with increasing regularity, though prior to 1327 their presence cannot be said to have been essential for the holding of a full parliament.

Nor were knights of the shire and burgesses the only representatives of lesser communities to be called to Parliament. The lesser clergy, the clergy, that is, below the ranks of bishop and cathedral dean, of abbot and prior, had been recognised as a distinct political entity at least as early as 1254. In that year the regents and council were told that on a matter of taxation the prelates could not speak for the clergy as a whole. Again, in the following year, the lesser clergy who held benefices—that is, ecclesiastical offices from which

---

representatives from the whole of England ; Poole, *Domesday Book to Magna Carta*, 463, n. 2.

they derived permanent incomes—were treated apart from the prelates in the negotiations by which the king sought to apply the crusading " tenth " to the business of Sicily.[1] The contemporary chronicler, Matthew Paris, tells us that the proctors [2] of the beneficed clergy sent a protest to the Pope against the tenth being used for this purpose. In May, 1265, when de Montfort was still in control of the government, a Parliament (never held) was summoned to Winchester in June. To it the dean and chapter of each cathedral church were directed to send two of their number whom they were to elect to represent them, just as the two knights from each county and two burgesses from certain cities and boroughs had been summoned for the first Parliament of that year.

For the next thirty years the lesser clergy (save for chapters of cathedral and collegiate churches) were not directly represented in the king's parliaments. They were, of course, represented in purely clerical assemblies, and during this period the king might well require a grant of taxation to be debated and if possible agreed to in such assemblies. In 1294, however, and again in 1295, the bishops were made responsible for the attendance in parliament of two proctors to represent the parish clergy of each diocese, in addition to representatives of capitular clergy. The step taken in these years became a precedent, and until the close of the fourteenth century the presence of elected clerical representatives was a normal feature of Parliament. The terms used in the summons to describe their function were precisely the same as those used for knights and burgesses. They were to be given " full and sufficient power " by the chapters and diocesan clergy, whose proctors or attorneys they were, to treat, ordain and take action upon what king and magnates might consider needful for the good of the realm.

The Edwardian Parliament, then, was not an assembly of representatives in the modern sense. It was the King's Council afforced in a particularly full and solemn manner, to which, as the occasion seemed to demand, representatives of certain local communities might from time to time be summoned. Now it has been argued that since " their presence was rarely required ", " we can attach no constitutional importance to the presence of the Commons in Parliament before 1327 ".[3] The historian must be on his guard

---

[1] See above, p. 267.   [2] = *procurator*, " agent ", " attorney ".
[3] G. O. Sayles, *Medieval Foundations of England*, 456.

against the fault of anachronism—that is, arguing back from the established institutions of a later age to the intention to create these institutions at an earlier period when all that is in fact recorded is their first dim beginnings.   But anxiety to avoid anachronism should not lead him to adopt the equally dangerous position of denying that later institutions grew from earlier ones, where some degree of continuity is clearly established.   Thus, the fact that most Edwardian parliaments contained no Commons representatives undoubtedly means that their presence was not essential to the *composition* of a thirteenth-century parliament ; it does not mean that when they did come they were insignificant.   The further fact that from 1327 onwards they were invariably summoned to Parliament shows that belief in their essential importance had been gaining ground prior to that date.   Unless, of course, something happened in 1327 which would sufficiently explain the radical difference between a thirteenth-century parliament in which the Commons were not essential and a fourteenth-century parliament in which they were.   But of such an event there is no evidence.

It is true that in the twenty years before 1327 the conflict between Edward II and his barons accelerated the process of calling Commons representatives to Parliament.   But even before the death of Edward I the prelates, earls and barons were no longer confident—as they had been in the earlier thirteenth century—that they represented the whole community of the realm.   It followed that if extraordinary taxation depended, as by custom it did, upon the consent of the community of the realm, then the consent of the old Great Council was no longer sufficient by itself.   As much seems to be evident from our record of the long-drawn-out Easter Parliament of 1290.[1] In this (May 29th) the magnates consented to the grant of a strictly feudal aid (for the marriage of the king's daughter) " on their own behalf, and, *so far as it lay in their power*, on behalf of the community of the whole realm ".   In July, two knights from each shire came to this Parliament at the king's summons, " with full power on their own behalf and on behalf of the whole community of their shires, to advise upon and consent, on the same behalf, to those things which the earls, barons and magnates shall have agreed upon "—

[1] Mr. Richardson and Professor Sayles have shown that the Parliament still in session in the summer of 1290 was the Easter Parliament (*Bull. Inst. Hist. Res.*, v (1927-8), 144).

i.e. financial supply for the king. Almost certainly as a result of afforcing this parliament with county knights, the feudal aid was converted into a general tax of a fifteenth on movables.

It is probable that we are here penetrating to the heart of this matter of Commons representation. The knights and burgesses were the attorneys of their communities, armed with full power to bind the free men of shire and borough to pay a national tax, or, it might be, to demonstrate national solidarity at a time of danger, or to signify approval of legislation. The king was certainly free to legislate without the Commons representatives—the statutes of Gloucester and Westminster II, e.g. were enacted in parliaments where none were present. In our period he could even legislate without the Great Council. But there was a distinct tendency in Edward I's reign for law-making by statute to be linked to meetings of Parliament. Again, when knights and burgesses were summoned, it must not be thought that they were full participants in parliamentary business. They were often summoned after parliament had begun, and dismissed before it ended. Their function was to advise and assent, to hear and carry out what the king with his Council had ordained. Only seldom were they summoned to " treat " or discuss. In short, under Edward I they were scarcely yet " members of parliament " ; rather were they agents without whose help the work of Parliament might be defective.

Since taxation took a central place in the beginnings of the later medieval representative parliament, it will be appropriate as well as useful to conclude this account of unity and definition under Edward I with a brief review of his fiscal policy. In this respect as in others, his reign marks the close of one age and the beginning of another.[1]

We have seen how King John and his servants were fertile in their experiments with fresh taxation and energetic in their efforts to improve the yield of the Crown's fixed revenues. Scutage, levied from the military class, and tallage, paid by the royal demesne (especially by the numerous wealthy towns which were part of the demesne), were still highly profitable in the early thirteenth century. Scutage and aid, both being assessed and paid on the knight's fee, had virtually merged in John's reign, and under Henry III the two

[1] For much of what follows see S. K. Mitchell, *Taxation in Medieval England* (1951).

may together be regarded as the established feudal tax payable by
the military tenants of the Crown.   As such, they were still normally
linked to military expeditions or to the " customary occasions ", the
knighting of the king's son, the marriage of his daughter.   Henry III
was given aid of this type four times.   He also availed himself
fourteen times of his right to tallage demesne.   Without much
profit he levied two " carucages ".   Still this was not sufficient for
the Crown's necessity.   A precedent had been set by Richard I
and John for those general taxes assessed at fractions of a person's
movable property, the nearest approach in our period to universal
national taxation.   This type of levy was without doubt the most
fruitful of all those available to the Crown.   Henry III made use of
it on four occasions and might have used it more had it not fallen
within the category of extraordinary aids which required the consent
of the community of the realm.   It touched everyone possessed of
any appreciable wealth in livestock, equipment, merchandise, furniture, jewellery, and the like.[1]   It was the fiscal counterpart of
distraint of knighthood.

The main point of interest to emerge from a study of Edward I's
taxation is that the levy on movables largely took the place both of
tallage on demesne and of aids or scutages on the knight's fee.
" The astute Edward was able to obtain this much more abundant
levy more frequently than his less capable father took his feudal due,
tallage, even though the tax on movables was not in theory obliga-
tory." [2]   In other words, Edward I knew perfectly well which form
of tax would bring him in most money, and on every occasion when
he could do so converted the obligations of tallage and feudal aid
into this form.   The fact does not merely illustrate Edward's need
for money, or what appeared, even to contemporaries who admired
him, as the grasping side of his nature.   It shows him in a more
creditable light as a ruler in no way afraid to depend on the co-
operation of the community of the realm in the carrying out of his
kingly duty.   The new atmosphere which prevailed after Kenilworth
and Marlborough showed itself not only in the tax of 1270 but also,
more portentously, in a grant made in the Easter Parliament of 1275,

---

[1] Houses, which counted as " movables " on the continent and were
literally movable in twelfth-century England, were not reckoned among
movables in the thirteenth century.

[2] Mitchell, *op. cit.* 361.

which was attended by four knights from each shire and four or six citizens or burgesses from each city, borough and town having a resident merchant community. The king and his heirs were granted a custom of 6*s*. 8*d*. per sack of wool, 6*s*. 8*d*. per sack of 300 woolfells,[1] and 13*s*. 4*d*. per last [2] of hides. This soon became known as the " great and ancient custom ", but if the merchants who apparently prompted the grant of 1275 thought that by so doing they were escaping further royal demands they were mistaken. After 1290 the king was faced by increasingly heavy war expenditure. He levied a tax on movables in that year, and then for three years running from 1294 to 1296. Admittedly the fractions diminished from a tenth to a twelfth, but the country had never before known the tax on movables as a yearly burden, and by 1297 there was widespread opposition to further levies.

At this juncture, Edward's sense of the co-operation of the realm played him false. An army had to be maintained in Scotland, an expedition was required for Gascony, and the king himself was under an obligation to give succour to his ally the Count of Flanders. The honour of the king and safety of the realm alike demanded a national effort. But clergy, baronage and middle classes, already burdened by previous taxation, were now exasperated by the king's high-handed proceedings and by his agents' reckless abuse of the royal rights of " prise " and " purveyance "—i.e. the right to seize animals and goods required for war in return for a promise of future payment and to purchase goods compulsorily at less than the market price. An impressive list has been compiled of the exactions, many of them arbitrary, imposed by Edward I between 1294 and 1297.[3] They included an extra three-year customs duty on wool in 1294, much heavier than the " ancient custom " and almost at once known as the *maletolt* (" evil toll "). Moreover, in March and July, 1297, the king ordered wool in merchants' hands to be seized and sold for the Crown's profit.

The political crisis of 1297 which followed and was very largely caused by this fiscal excess, lies beyond the period reviewed in this chapter and is foreign to its two themes of unity and definition. Discussion of it must be deferred to our account of the long war

---

[1] Skins of slaughtered sheep with the wool on them.
[2] Twelve dozen.
[3] By J. G. Edwards in *E.H.R.*, lviii (1943), 158-9.

which occupied the later years of Edward's reign, and with which it was connected as closely as with taxation. It reminds us that when it came to raising revenue Edward was a true descendant of his Norman and Angevin forebears. Not altogether without cause was he identified in contemporary folklore with *Le Roi Coveytous* of whom Merlin had prophesied in the popular tales of King Arthur. A chronicler puts into the mouths of some noblemen's sons at court a few lines of doggerel which are significant even if apocryphal. " The king covets our money, the queen our fine manors, while the Quo Waranto will make trouble for us all." [1]   Yet it would be quite unjust to Edward I to say that he was avaricious in the true sense. He was no hoarder, and left his son an enormous debt. If this does little credit to his good management, it is certainly no evidence of meanness. Just as to the very end of his life all his strength was thrown into the work on hand, be it the making of laws or the maintenance of what he believed to be his rights in Gascony, Wales and Scotland, so he levied the maximum taxation allowed him by law and custom, and perhaps something over, so that the policies which he had undertaken, largely with the support of his realm, could be efficiently carried out.

The most eminent modern historian of his reign has said of Edward I that he " stands apart in our history. We remember him, but not as a living man who stirs the imagination." [2]   Yet it is also true that Edward I has been the pattern of medieval kingship in a degree of pre-eminence which few other rulers of England have shared. If no intimate portrait was ever drawn by any contemporary who knew him well, this fact itself may be due to the rich and variable nature of Edward's character. What evidence there is suggests that it was strangely compounded of hot temper and sober judgment, of forthright speech and devious manoeuvring, of great courage and determination and at the same time a capacity for changing course unexpectedly.

[1] Walter of Hemingburgh, *Chronicon* (ed. Hamilton, *Eng. Hist. Soc.*, 1849, ii. 7).

> " Le rey coveit nos deneres,
> E la rayne nos beaus maners,
> E le Quo Waranto
> Maketh us alle to do."

[2] F. M. Powicke, *The Thirteenth Century*, 227.

But although contemporaries may have been baffled by the complexity of Edward's personality, they had no doubts about his greatness as a king. The famous description by the Dominican friar Nicholas Trevet, jejune as it is, goes far beyond the formal eulogy which any medieval English king could expect for his obituary notice.

" He was a man of experienced sagacity in the conduct of affairs, devoted since his youth to the exercise of arms, in which he had won knightly fame for himself surpassing contemporary rulers throughout the entire Christian world. He was handsome of figure and so tall of build that he stood head and shoulders above ordinary people. A fine head of hair which in adolescence turned from almost silver to flaxen, grew black in his young manhood and distinguished him in old age when it had become greyish white. His forehead was broad and the rest of his face regularly featured, except that the lid of his left eye drooped, in this resembling his father's appearance. His speech had a stammer, yet he possessed a ready and persuasive eloquence in matters which required discussion. His long arms were in proportion to his lithe body and in muscular strength could not have been more adept at using a sword. His legs were set wide apart and gave him a firm seat on horseback when galloping and jumping. . . . His proud spirit was intolerant of injuries, but it could easily be mollified by a display of humility." [1]

Many flashes of the king's personality enliven the voluminous official records of his reign. He shared the Englishman's love for a graphic use of proverbs to epitomise the sense of a statement or command. In 1304, e.g while siege was being laid to Stirling castle, the Earl of March, commanding troops for the king, let slip through his hands some men of the garrison who had made a sortie. He must, wrote Edward in a stinging rebuke, have been trying to live up to the proverb, " Once the war was over, Audegier drew his sword ".[2] At the same time he wrote to Robert Brus, as yet his ally, praising him for his diligence in the royal service and urging him to complete the work so well begun : " As the cloak is well made ", he concluded, " so make the hood ".[3] We have surely a very authentic expression of Edward I's keenly legalistic sense in another letter, quoted by Sir Maurice Powicke, which belongs to this same year.

" The king has offered to Thomas, son and heir of Sir Hugh Bardolf, a suitable marriage and he has refused the king's offer and answered that he does not wish to be married, and it seems to the king that the answer

---

[1] *Annales* (ed. Hog), 281-2.
[2] J. Stevenson, *Documents illustrative of the history of Scotland* (1870), ii. 467-8.
[3] J. Bain, *Cal. Scottish Documents*, ii. no. 1465.

is insufficient and it may be a bad example for the king and his heirs and all to whom he wishes to do well if heirs in the king's marriage are suffered to excuse themselves and refuse the marriages offered by the king." The chancellor is therefore " to be as stiff and hard towards Thomas in this business as can be without offending the law ; for the king holds the answer of Thomas to be done in despite of him and his crown ".[1]

It was a quality which might under provocation harden into vindictiveness. When Robert Brus made his bid for the Scottish throne and the whole business of subduing Scotland had to be taken up afresh, Edward I's hand fell heavily on the Scots lairds who had rallied to Brus. On June 19th, 1306, the king sent the following order to his lieutenant in Scotland, Aymer of Valence :

" Forasmuch as we have not found in Sir Michael Wemyss either good word or good service and he has now shown in deed that he is a traitor and our enemy, we command you to burn his manor where we stayed, and all his other manors, to destroy his lands and goods and to strip his gardens clean so that nothing is left, for an example to others like him. . . . And as for Sir Gilbert Hay to whom we showed much courtesy when he stayed with us in London recently and in whom we thought we could place our trust, but whom we now find to be a traitor and our enemy, we order you to burn down all his manors and houses, destroy all his lands and goods, and strip all his gardens so that nothing is left, and if possible do worse to him than to Sir Michael Wemyss." [2]

It would be unfair to judge Edward I solely by the events of the last few months of his life. More often than not his contemporaries found him reasonable and magnanimous. We do not need their testimony to tell us that he was conscientious and that few English rulers have shown such a high sense of the duties of kingship.

[1] Quoted from *Calendar of Chancery Warrants*, i. 241, in *Henry III and the Lord Edward*, ii. 706-7.

[2] *National MSS. Scotland*, ii. no. XIV (abridged slightly in translation.)

CHAPTER XVIII

THE OCCUPATIONS OF SOCIETY

1. *The Church from Langton to Winchelsey* [1]

THREE main features characterise the history of the English Church in the century that followed the lifting of the Interdict in 1213. First, and most obviously, we must acknowledge the complete ascendancy of the reform movement. Secondly, it is clear that the importance of the monastic order relative to the other elements in the Church as a whole had suffered a marked decline. The third feature to be noticed provided compensation for the second, as well as being to some extent a cause of it. This was the arrival of the mendicant friars, especially the Dominicans and Franciscans. Finally, some account, however cursory, must be given of the universities. Oxford was the creation of the twelfth century, Cambridge of the thirteenth. But it was not until the period reviewed in this chapter that Oxford University became an indispensable part of the English Church and took a share in its life and work too considerable for even the general historian to dismiss with a bare mention.

(1) *The Ascendancy of Reform.* [2] In our accounts of the Church under Lanfranc and during the twelfth century considerable space was devoted to the activities of the reform movement. It may therefore seem surprising that in the thirteenth century reform was still a vital issue. It might be thought that if the reformers had done their work properly in the earlier period there would be nothing left to reform. Alternatively, if they had failed, it might be supposed that this would have discredited their movement and discouraged the Church from further attempts. But in fact the medieval Church was extremely active, restless and self-critical. Not only was it

---

[1] An excellent general account of this subject is given by Dr. J. R. H. Moorman, *Church Life in England in the Thirteenth Century* (1945).
[2] Much of what follows is based upon M. Gibbs and J. Lang, *Bishops and Reform* (1934), and J. Dowden, *Scot. Hist. Rev.*, vii (1910), 1-20.

seldom satisfied that reforms proposed in the past had been effectively carried out or were being maintained ; there were always before it new problems that cried out for solution, new maladies for which new medicines must be provided.[1]

Prior to the extremely important pontificate of Innocent III (1198-1216), the reform movement within the western Church, though unquestionably dominant and possessing the initiative, was a minority movement. It still struggled to get its views accepted first by the Church as a whole and then by the great mass of the Christian laity. From the time of Innocent III onwards this was no longer true. The actual reforming leaders might still be in a minority, much of what the reform party had striven for in the twelfth century might still be unattained, but the aims and basic assumptions of reform were henceforward accepted without serious question.

The chief of these aims and assumptions remained what they had been at the close of the eleventh century : the centralisation of Church government under a much exalted Papacy ; the freedom of the clergy from lay control and interference ; and the need to raise clerical standards generally through better education, the acceptance of celibacy, and the enforcement of a more ordered way of life. With these aims and all that followed from them the thirteenth-century Church had no real quarrel. There was perhaps rather less agreement with a fourth development originating in the reform movement. This was the belief, expressed in the policies of all the notable thirteenth-century Popes from Innocent III onwards, that the Papacy had a moral duty to supervise and to guide secular affairs where they appeared to affect directly the Christian life of society. In practice this belief was interpreted very widely. It led to papal interference in the politics of the Empire, that is to say, in the German and Sicilian kingdoms, and it involved papal sponsorship of the crusading movement. These were great European questions. There were lesser fields where the belief was at work with notable effect. Thus, when King John surrendered his realm as a fief to Pope Innocent the Papacy certainly did not regard his act as a mere formality. During the whole of the reign of Henry III the Popes

[1] This expression was used by Archbishop Winchelsey in 1297, quoted by H. Rothwell, in *Studies in Medieval History presented to F. M. Powicke* (1948), 319.

exercised in English affairs an influence never enjoyed before or since. As we have seen, during the legations of Guala at the beginning of the reign and of Ottobuono at its end this influence was almost wholly beneficial.

Apart, however, from these extreme implications of papal supremacy, there was complete readiness to accept the programme of the reform movement. The leaders of the Church actively furthered it, while even the most sluggish and indifferent paid lip-service to its ideals. Ecclesiastical reform was now easier because the twelfth-century Popes had successfully established a single government for the entire western Church. It was now possible for reform to be planned by and for the Church as a whole. Such universal reform had really been inaugurated by Pope Alexander III towards the end of his long pontificate in the Third Lateran Council (1179).[1] This gathering was very fully representative of the Church and gave its approval to a large number of canons intended to be binding upon all Christians who acknowledged the supremacy of the Papacy. Pope Innocent III, like Pope Alexander, a lawyer by training, followed the lead of his predecessor in 1215 with the Fourth Lateran Council, a still larger and more impressive assembly. The

---

[1] The Lateran Councils were so called because they sat in the ancient basilica of St. John on the site of the Roman palace of Plautius Lateranus.

MAP VIII. ECCLESIASTICAL MAP OF ENGLAND AND WALES, THIRTEENTH CENTURY (*see opposite page*).

Archiepiscopal sees	‡
Episcopal sees	‡
Religious houses :	
Unreformed Benedictine houses for men .	●
,, ,, nunneries . .	◤
Cluniac	■
Cistercian	□
Tironian	◩
Augustinian canons-regular	◆
Premonstratensian canons-regular . .	◇
Gilbertine house for canons and nuns . .	⌂
Important " Old Minsters " in the diocese of .	
York	+
Pilgrim centres	P
Universities	U

312

MAP VIII

313

Canons of 1179 were re-issued, many of them in an amplified form, and in addition a substantial number of new enactments were published.

The English delegation to the Fourth Lateran Council was strong in influence rather than numbers. It was led by the two primates, Stephen Langton of Canterbury and Walter Gray of York, and included the bishops of Lincoln (Hugh of Wells) and Salisbury (Richard Poore).[1] Gray and Wells probably had no equals in England for administrative experience (gained in the royal service) or for organising capacity. Langton and his pupil Richard Poore had few rivals in the application of learning to practical affairs and in single-minded devotion to the Church. All four held a high conception of the pastoral office. Their country was still in the throes of civil war when they returned from the council, but as soon as peace had been restored they began either to publish or at least to enforce its decrees in their respective provinces and dioceses. It is curious that the lead was taken not by Archbishop Langton but by Richard Poore of Salisbury. Between 1217 and 1222 he issued " the most complete set of all thirteenth-century constitutions ",[2] which either repeated verbatim the Lateran decrees or else were closely modelled on them but modified to suit English conditions. Before 1237 Bishop Poore's constitutions had been used as the pattern for similar legislation in the dioceses of London, Exeter and Canterbury, and had also been made the basis of the Canons issued at the first provincial council of the Scottish Church (1225).[3] The bishops of Coventry and Worcester, both trained scholastics, drew up constitutions independently of Poore's ; but a notable tribute to the excellence of the Salisbury document was paid in 1222, when Langton convened at Oxford a council representing the whole of Canterbury province, and there promulgated the Lateran decrees, not directly as they stood, but largely in the form in which they had been adapted by Poore.

Some modification of the decrees was certainly called for, since English conditions differed markedly in some respects from those prevailing in Italy or elsewhere on the continent. For one thing,

---

[1] Poore was brother of a previous bishop of Salisbury and probably belonged to the family of the great Bishop Roger of Salisbury, Henry I's Justiciar.

[2] Gibbs and Lang, *op. cit.* 108.

[3] Above, p. 239.

much of the council's legislation was directed against heresy, and contemporary England was remarkably free from heretical opinion. Condemning the Albigensians and providing measures for the extirpation of their beliefs appeared an urgent necessity if the life of the Christian Church were to be saved. In view of the nature of Albigensianism this was an aim with which we may feel some sympathy. It is hard to reach any sympathetic understanding of a related aspect of the Lateran decrees, those, namely, which concerned the Jews.

If these decrees had been put into effect in their entirety, they would have made the Jews of the west a community of untouchables. They envisaged a rigid barrier of caste which, as the Franciscans of the time perceived, struck at the very root of Christ's teaching. A few of the bishops in England tried to enforce the rules which ordered a virtual boycott of Jews by Christians and the wearing by Jews of distinctive marks on their clothing. Where this was attempted, however, the Crown at once stepped in to protect the Jews, chiefly because it derived much revenue from the profits of Jewish money-lending. (In fairness to Henry III, it must be added that he concerned himself actively in the conversion of Jews to Christianity, founding a special house for converts in Chancery Lane, London, on the site of the present Public Record Office.) It is a symptom of the conflicting impulses existing within the thirteenth-century Church that one of the bishops most active against the Jews, Roger Black (*Niger*) of London, was also a notable patron of the Franciscan friars, who were among the few Christians to intercede for Jews when they were victims of persecution. The extremes of deliberate persecution do not seem to have been reached very often in England. At the Oxford council of 1222 where the Lateran decrees were published, a young clerk in deacon's orders, converted to Judaism through love of a Jewish girl, was condemned and handed over to the lay authorities for execution. Such incidents were not common. As we have seen, the English solution of the Jewish problem in our period was the entirely negative one of expulsion, carried out by Edward I in 1290.

It was the intention of the Fourth Lateran Council to sum up all the efforts made since the eleventh century to free the clerical order from secular control. It followed, therefore, that one major subject dealt with in its decrees was the election of bishops, abbots and other prelates. The reformers aimed at completely free canonical election of bishops " by the clergy and people "—in practice, by the Chapter of the vacant cathedral church. This aim was never achieved, but it came nearer to attainment in the thirteenth century than at any other time. The method of choosing and making an English bishop became stereotyped in the following manner.

First, as soon as the see fell vacant, the Chapter begged the king for leave to elect (*congé d'élire*). This was recognised to be " the custom of England ", and offered a considerable loophole for royal interference. Leave granted, the Chapter decided to proceed according to one of the three lawful modes of election, " scrutiny " (counting of individual votes), " compromission " (delegation of choice to a small committee), or—rarest of all—" inspiration " (unanimous approval of one candidate). Should the candidate already be a bishop, and therefore " wedded " to another diocese, or should he suffer from some defect such as illegitimate birth, the Chapter could not elect but only " postulate " their choice to the Pope, who, if satisfied that the candidate was suitable, would duly confirm him in office. When the election had been made, the king was requested to give his assent and the metropolitan was informed of the fact of election. Provided, and it was a large proviso, that no hitch occurred, the " elect " then made his homage to the king and was given the " temporalities " of his see, the landed estates, castles, etc. He then proceeded to the three final stages, which were entirely in the hands of the Church. The metropolitan confirmed his election, consecrated him (with the assistance of at least two other bishops) and invested him with ring and staff ; the clergy of his diocese then installed him in his *cathedra* or throne. It was seldom in our period that cathedral chapters were allowed unfettered freedom of election. Yet their rights were respected, the legal forms were seriously observed, and there were few instances where the Crown or the Papacy forced a candidate into a see entirely against the wishes of the Chapter.

Another extremely important part of the Lateran reforms was concerned with the quality and conduct of individual clergymen. The manner of administering the sacraments was defined. A serious effort was made to see that men ordained to the priesthood should conform to an acceptable standard of education. Important churches were ordered to maintain grammar-schools under specially appointed masters. At metropolitan churches there were to be more advanced schools with doctors of theology. Here, again, English conditions made it difficult to enforce the decrees as they stood. In the larger centres of population there already existed reasonable provision for schooling. To equal this in the rural areas proved impossible, because of the difficulties of communication. Moreover, in addition to schools of theology at certain cathedral churches, there was at Oxford a well established " university " (gild) of masters which had attracted many scholars, and the graduates of Oxford were already providing an important leaven of educated clergy in the Church as a whole. The educator in every age is faced by what is essentially a problem of communication. The physical difficulties of communication were probably not the most serious in our period, since its men and women, as we have seen, were hardly ever deterred by distance or the hardships of travel. The biggest obstacle was linguistic. Medieval Europe was a culture which had no living language. The development of the vernaculars was retarded out of reverence for Latin ; but Latin itself was not studied as a language out of reverence for theology.

One contravention of the reforming ideal died very hard in England. The Council of 1215 pronounced severe penalties for priests who kept concubines, and it is significant that the English bishops found it necessary not only to prohibit this practice but also to forbid their clergy to have wives or to marry. Legislation on this subject was only partially effective. It served, indeed, to bring the law into disrepute, for there is little doubt that the attempt to enforce total celibacy on the clergy was premature, having regard to the very high proportion of men in holy orders who possessed no real vocation for Christian ministry.

Perhaps the most fruitful and praiseworthy reforming measures undertaken by the leading thirteenth-century bishops were those by which they sought to raise the standard of this ministry within the individual parishes. Strictly speaking, one priest ought to have the cure of souls in no more than one parish. In fact, very many clergy held several benefices at once. After 1215 this practice of holding " in plurality ", as it was known, was regulated to the extent of being made dependent upon explicit papal permission, or " dispensation ". When permission became almost a mere formality, as it did during the pontificate of Innocent IV (1243-54), a number of the English bishops, among them Poore, now translated to Durham, and Robert Grosseteste of Lincoln (1235-53), attempted to limit pluralism in their own dioceses. Pecham of Canterbury also legislated against it in 1279 and 1281.

Where the bishops found it impossible to call a halt to pluralism, they could at least try to make sure that, if a clergyman did hold more than one benefice involving cure of souls, proper provision was made for the sacraments to be administered and services performed in the church or churches from which pluralist incumbents were absent. This was done by compelling the absentee to put in a properly qualified curate or vicar. In many parishes, again, the office of rector had been appropriated by episcopal permission to some religious house or collegiate church. In such cases, it was of course impossible for the " corporate rector " to reside. The Lateran Council therefore insisted on the appointment of permanent vicars, for whom a decent living must be guaranteed from the income of the church. A number of English bishops were active in the enforcement of this decree. Archbishop Gray of York ordained many vicarages between 1225 and 1250. Successive bishops of Lincoln during the century had a particularly good record in this respect. Hugh of Wells (1209-35) not only ordained some hundreds of vicarages throughout this vast diocese, but was also the first bishop in England to keep a record of his institutions. His good example was followed by his successors, notably Grosseteste, Richard Gravesend (1258-79) and Oliver Sutton (1280-99). The fixing of an adequate minimum stipend went hand in hand with the creation of vicarages. The Oxford council of 1222 considered five marks a year (£3 6s. 8d.) a sufficient income for a vicar ; but there is no doubt that many livings fell on average below this modest figure. It was a vicious circle. The poverty of benefices made pluralism necessary ; the creation of vicarages to combat pluralism made the benefices still poorer.

In the main, the English bishops of the thirteenth century were men of good life, hard-working and conscientious. Few of them were saintly, in the sense in which that word is commonly understood, and even the best of them, such as Langton or Grosseteste or Winchelsey, possessed a severely rational and legalistic outlook, doubtless the product of their long and hard academic training, which tended to overshadow their humanity and charitableness.

During the whole of our period, a prelate of the English Church was expected to fill three quite distinct rôles, each of them important. First and foremost, he must be the pastor of his flock, watching over the people of his diocese and defending his Church against attacks and encroachments on its liberties. Secondly, he was willy-nilly a great tenant-in-chief of the Crown, under an obligation to give his lord counsel whenever required. Finally, he might well be expected to carry out administrative duties for the government. Many twelfth-century bishops had served in the Exchequer, or as justices and sheriffs. The influence of reforming opinion made this practice much rarer in the thirteenth century. While a clerk who had served the king faithfully in high administrative office was almost certain to be rewarded with a bishopric, once he had been consecrated the king could no longer count on his services. It is true that a few bishops, e.g. Peter des Roches of Winchester and Robert Burnell of Bath, did continue to act as justiciars or chancellors after attaining to episcopal office. But for a large number, perhaps for the majority, their pastoral duties came first. This was certainly true of Richard Poore, successively Bishop of Chichester, Salisbury and Durham (1215-37) and of Oliver Sutton, Bishop of Lincoln from 1280 to 1299, whose family, petty gentry of Nottinghamshire, produced in two generations an astonishingly large number of public men—two bishops, an abbot, a judge and a steward of the royal household.[1]

There is no question that the Church benefited greatly in our period from the strong lead given to it by a number of outstandingly able primates. How important academic training had become, and how close were the links between England and the papal *Curia*, may be judged from the fact that the first and last archbishops of Canterbury in the thirteenth century, Langton and Winchelsey, were both university teachers of distinction, appointed by the Papacy and without previous experience of ruling a diocese. Their careers had one other feature in common : both spent some years at odds with the king and even in exile. This is of course a tribute to their strength of character and to the power of the reform movement in the Church. But constructive leadership is difficult for an exiled

---

[1] A sympathetic and extremely full description of the career and activity of Sutton, typical of the best thirteenth-century bishops, is given by Rosalind Hill in the introduction to the *Rolls and Register of Bishop Oliver Sutton* (Lincoln Record Soc.), iii (1954), pp. xiii-lxxxvi.

archbishop. Two primates of the middle years of the century, Boniface of Savoy (1245-70) and John Pecham (1279-92), achieved useful work without straining relations with the Crown to breaking point, though Pecham came very near it. In assemblies convened in 1257 and 1258, Boniface attempted to define more narrowly the respective spheres of Church and State jurisdiction, while between 1261 and 1268 he reached definitive agreement with other bishops of his province over the rights of the archbishop as metropolitan during the vacancy of sees within his province. Pecham, an austerely didactic Franciscan, is chiefly famous for the councils of Reading (1279) and Lambeth (1281). At the first, which he convened without royal licence, he commanded—greatly to Edward I's indignation—that copies of Magna Carta should be posted on the doors of cathedral and collegiate churches. He further ordered the excommunication of all those who secured " writs of prohibition ", that is, orders from the royal chancery prohibiting the hearing of a lawsuit in an ecclesiastical court until the royal judges had decided whether the case was a matter for the Church courts or not. Though he was forced to withdraw these decrees, the Canons published under his direction at Lambeth in 1281 show very clearly that the reforming impulse was still as vigorous in the later part of the century as it had been at the start.

(2) *The Monasteries.*[1] We should hardly be giving too much praise if we spoke of the thirteenth century as the Silver Age of the medieval English monasteries. It is becoming something of a commonplace to compare the monasteries of this period with the colleges of Oxford and Cambridge in the eighteenth and early nineteenth centuries. Provided it is not pressed too far, the comparison can be illuminating. Like the colleges, the monasteries were rich, privileged corporations. They owned a great quantity of land and were patrons of hundreds of parish churches. Again like the colleges, they had been founded for a purpose which it was by no means clear that they were still trying to fulfil conscientiously. Intensely conservative and parochial in their outlook, the abbeys and priories resisted change and disliked the notion of reform. The comparison becomes misleading, however, where relations with

---

[1] The fundamental work on the subject of this and the succeeding section is D. Knowles, *The Religious Orders in England* (1948). A full general account is given by Moorman, *op. cit.* Chapters XVIII-XXVI.

the outside world are concerned. For all their parochialism, the monasteries of our period were public institutions in a sense in which the colleges were not. Their abbots and priors sat in the king's parliaments, collected taxes, and served as judges and ambassadors. Because of monastic obligations of hospitality, the *hospicium* or guest-house of a great abbey and its court-yards and stables were as public as a modern hotel; perhaps more public, for in theory monastic hospitality was free. In hard times poor people depended on the charity of monks and nuns for sheer survival. The religious houses of all kinds filled an enormous place in the life of the country.

We should realise that the religious orders were beginning to pay the penalty of their own success. There were in fact too many monasteries in England, too much property was owned by them, and too many men were admitted to their membership who might have found a truer vocation in the secular Church, and too many women who might have been better employed outside the Church altogether. This was not the fault of the monasteries themselves. They were not transient communities of a generation or two, but permanent institutions with acres of agricultural land and numerous buildings of brick and stone. They were, moreover, by no means entirely negligent of the responsibilities which this entailed.

It was the very permanence and stability of the monasteries that diverted the monks and canons-regular from their primary obligations. It may be said that apart from hospitality and alms-giving, which were incidental, the monks existed for two main purposes: to perform the divine office as regularly as possible, providing a perpetual intercession for the souls of founders and benefactors, and to lead in microcosm the Christian life, self-denying, orderly and communal. The generosity of benefactors had enabled magnificent churches to be built, and because great wealth was available only in the form of land the monks had been forced to become the owners of hundreds of rich manors. The maintenance and extension of their buildings and the management of their estates preoccupied the monks of the thirteenth century to such an extent that they neglected their religious vocation. In most of the wealthier monasteries, the ablest monks turned administrators and engaged in largely secular tasks which took up most of their time.

These " obedientiaries ", as they were called, had charge of the different departments through which the daily life of the house was carried on. At the great East Anglian abbey of Bury St. Edmunds there were nine principal obedientiaries responsible directly to the abbot. These were a prior, sub-prior, sacrist (in charge of the abbey church and its furnishings), cellarer (provisioning), chamberlain (clothing), precentor (directing the choral and liturgical side of the services), two chaplains (apparently the abbot's secretaries), and an infirmarer. There were also an almoner, responsible for charitable gifts, and a guest-master. This list may be taken as typical, though at some houses, e.g. Durham, there was a bursar or treasurer to look after financial affairs.

For some years at the turn of the twelfth and thirteenth centuries the cellarer at Bury was a monk named Jocelin of Brakelond [1] who has left an extremely lively and convincing picture of life in a great Benedictine abbey under the rule of a very remarkable abbot. [2] Jocelin's concern with material things, rents, markets, agricultural estates and the like, has been taken as proof that the spiritual life of Abbot Samson's monastery had suffered some eclipse. As Mr. Davis has pointed out, such an intense interest in revenues is only natural for a cellarer. Yet this fact itself shows that the obedientiary system took professed monks away from the life of prayer and meditation for which the Rule of St. Benedict had provided.

By the close of our period, the monasteries had entirely ceased to be what they had been in the eleventh and twelfth centuries, a main artery in the body of the Church, bearing fresh blood and a vigorous new life into the religion of England. In sharp contrast with earlier ages, the number of monks now promoted to bishoprics was almost negligible. The outstanding monks of the late thirteenth century were famous not for their devotion to religion but because they were extremely capable men of business. Such was Henry of Eastry, Prior of Christ Church, Canterbury, from 1285 to 1331, who built the great central tower of the cathedral and was " one of the most remarkable farmers in medieval history ". [3] It would not be fair to say that the monasteries failed completely to adjust themselves

---

[1] For our knowledge that Jocelin of Brakelond was the cellarer of Bury we are indebted to R. H. C. Davis, *Kalendar of Abbot Samson*, pp. li-lvii.

[2] *The Chronicle of Jocelin of Brakelond concerning the acts of Samson, Abbot of the monastery of St. Edmund*, ed. and transl. H. E. Butler (1949).

[3] Quoted from R. A. L. Smith, *Canterbury Cathedral Chronicle* (1940), by J. R. H. Moorman, *op. cit.* 284.

to a more civilised age. It was the abbeys almost exclusively which provided the chroniclers, the interested observers of contemporary events, without whose works we should have only a fragmentary knowledge of thirteenth-century England. The abbey libraries were still easily the largest in the country, and included works by the great scholars of the day, such as Grosseteste and Thomas Aquinas. A few monasteries, Gloucester, Worcester, Canterbury and Durham, sent monks to graduate at the university. But the old dominance of the monastic order in the life of the Church had disappeared apparently without regret on the part of ecclesiastical leaders and without serious protest on the part of the monks themselves.

(3) *The Friars.* In 1221, while the English bishops were considering how to publish and enforce the reforming legislation of the Fourth Lateran Council, a group of thirteen priests, dedicated to a life of poverty, preaching and the advancement of Christian learning, crossed the Channel in the company and patronage of the Bishop of Winchester, Peter des Roches. They were taken by their patron to Canterbury, where one of their number preached before the archbishop. They were at once received into his favour, and shortly afterwards made their way to Oxford, their appointed goal. These thirteen " preaching friars ", [1] led by Gilbert de Fresnay, were the advance party in England of an order founded a few years previously by Dominic Guzman, an Austin canon of Spanish origin who had laboured for some years at Toulouse and elsewhere in the Midi attempting to combat the Albigensian heresy. St. Dominic conceived his order as an intellectual *corps d'élite*, holding the van wherever battle was joined with ignorance and wrong belief. The strength of his followers derived from a life led in simplicity and poverty, with no more possessions than clothes and books. Their weapons were faith and learning. The south of France, where heresy was strongly entrenched, formed an obvious field for Dominican activity. Elsewhere, it became the object of the order to establish centres in the great universities of western Christendom. At first their intention was not to give but to receive instruction : they went wherever the best masters of theology were to be found. In course of time, however, the Dominicans were able to set up their

---

[1] This was the official name for the Dominicans : popularly they were known from their habit as " Black Friars ", while the Franciscans were called " Grey Friars ", though their habit was brown.

own schools within the universities, at Paris in 1228, at Oxford and other academic centres before the middle of the century. The fruits of this policy in England were seen when their school at Oxford produced three of the most notable theologians of the time, Robert Bacon, Richard Fishacre, and Robert Kilwardby, who became Archbishop of Canterbury in 1274 and a cardinal in 1278.

Little more than three years after the arrival of the preaching friars (September 10th, 1224), a still smaller company—six Italians and three Englishmen, under the leadership of Agnellus of Pisa—landed at Dover, bringing with them for the first time to England the message and inspiration of Francis of Assisi. A first permanent lodging was found for them on Cornhill in the city of London. A number of them soon followed the Dominicans to Oxford, where they were given the use of a house in St. Ebbe's parish, the low-lying south-western quarter of the town. Thereafter, their membership grew swiftly.

The early followers of St. Francis could hardly be said to constitute a religious order within the Church. Hitherto, Christian society had consisted of a clerical and a lay element, of an organised hieratic Church on the one hand and of a wider Church, the whole body of the faithful, on the other. The tendency of the eleventh and twelfth centuries had been all towards sharpening this division. But the early Franciscans could not be placed neatly in a clerical or a lay compartment. Many of them were technically laymen, others were clergy. St. Francis himself never proceeded to the priesthood, but remained in deacon's orders. His message went far beyond ecclesiastical reform. It could barely be reduced to a single rule, certainly not to a monastic rule such as that of St. Benedict, which was intended for small and isolated communities. What he and his followers preached was nothing less than the living of Christ's life anew, here on earth and in their own generation. In fundamental contrast with the Dominicans, the " minor friars "—" lesser brothers "—as St. Francis' followers were known, set little store by the rational conversion of men's minds to belief in the gospel. It was rather their aim to preach the gospel by living it. They called not to a chosen few who felt the vocation to the religious life but to all the world, Christian and non-Christian, for repentance and the total acceptance of the message of the Saviour.

In one respect, the Franciscans and Dominicans coincided

exactly. They directed their preaching where they considered it was most needed, to the men and women of cities and towns. In a few years from their landing, the minor friars had houses in nearly every town of consequence between Thames and Trent, and in 1256 the English province numbered some 1,242 friars in forty-nine houses. The Dominicans, or Black Friars, followed this pattern very closely. Some forty-seven houses had been given them by 1272, out of a final medieval total of fifty-three. Strictly speaking, the mendicants did not " own " the houses they occupied : they aimed to avoid altogether that great stumbling-block of monasticism, the corrupting influence of permanent wealth. The early friars dwelt in mean, unheated buildings with very little furniture. These buildings were bought or rented on their behalf by benefactors and patrons, in whom the property was legally vested.

Moreover, while their purpose was to preach to the laity, they had no wish to do so at the expense of the existing parish clergy. Professor Knowles has explained that in 1215 the parish clergy preached very rarely and were scarcely prepared to meet the decree of the Lateran Council which made annual confession and the sacrament of penance compulsory for all believers. At first, therefore, the bishops and clergy were quite ready to allow the friars to meet these needs. Friction inevitably developed during the century, but at length it was removed in masterly fashion by the bull *Super cathedram*, issued by Pope Boniface VIII in 1300. This left the mendicants free to preach in their own chapels and in public, but forbade them to preach in parish churches without the incumbent's permission. All who wished might ask for burial by the friars in their own cemeteries, provided that a quarter of the dues and legacies were paid to the parish clergy (the complete poverty of Dominic and Francis had been abandoned by 1300). Finally, each bishop must license a certain proportion of friars in every province to hear confession.

Although St. Francis had set his face against learning, as a diversion from the spiritual life very nearly as harmful as owning property, a large, indeed a predominant section of his followers departed from this teaching even in the lifetime of their master. As early as 1229 the Franciscans established a school at Oxford, where no less a person than the Chancellor of the university, Robert Grosseteste, became their first lecturer. The greatest scholar and teacher actually within the ranks of the Franciscans was Adam Marsh who took the habit of the order at Worcester in 1232. Curiously enough, the Franciscans in thirteenth-century England surpassed the Dominicans in the number and eminence of their scholars. Their academic bent was, as might be expected, towards theology. But it often had strongly practical leanings, towards politics, e.g. when in the years 1258 to 1265 the Franciscans were outspoken champions of the baronial plan of reform, and when the " Song of Lewes ", a remarkable statement of political theory in rhyming Latin couplets,[1] was composed in the Franciscan circle at Oxford. It was also possible for one pupil of Grosseteste, Roger Bacon (nephew of the Dominican, Robert Bacon), who was deeply interested in scientific experiment, to become a Franciscan (1255) and yet continue with his studies in " natural philosophy ".

The mendicant friars stood for something essentially new in western European society. The basic picture of the world possessed by educated men and women from the fourth to the twelfth centuries was informed by the pessimism—admittedly a lofty pessimism, but a pessimism nevertheless—of St. Augustine's *De Civitate Dei*. For all that had been best in human culture and achievement society looked backward to the past. The monastic life, whether of the ascetic type associated with the desert hermits or the temperate disciplined communal life of St. Benedict, had its roots in this pervasive pessimism, in a fundamental mistrust of the daily life of man upon earth. The poor friars in the early years of the thirteenth century broke away completely from this pessimism. They sounded a note of hope stronger than any heard since the fall of the Roman Empire, and set an equal value upon the whole of humankind.

(4) *The Universities*. The universities in the thirteenth century undoubtedly formed part of the life of the Church, albeit a highly specialised part which affected directly only a tiny minority of its members. The origins of the medieval English universities are as obscure as those of parliament and for almost the same reason. They were not the result of a single act of foundation, and contemporaries were not aware, during the early period of growth, that wholly new institutions were being brought into existence. At Oxford there seems to have been a school, more elaborate and advanced than a mere grammar school, in the early years of the

[1] Best edited by C. L. Kingsford, *The Song of Lewes* (Oxford, 1890).

twelfth century, perhaps connected with the collegiate church of St. Frideswide and its canons. Even after this church had been converted into a priory for Augustinian canons-regular, the activity of the school probably continued, and in the middle years of the century Master Vacarius, the Lombard jurist whose patron in England was the Archbishop of Canterbury, Theobald of Bec, is thought to have lectured at Oxford on Roman Law.

In the last decades of the twelfth century, the Oxford schools had certainly developed into a genuine *studium generale*, that is, a group of masters properly qualified to teach all the recognised subjects in arts, theology and law, together with students drawn, casually but in large numbers, from every part of England and even from other countries. The Oxford *studium* closely resembled that of Paris, in being essentially a gild or *universitas* (hence " university ") of masters, licensed to teach by ecclesiastical authority. The Oxford curriculum also followed Paris, in consisting of a preliminary arts course, the *trivium*, of three subjects, Latin grammar, logic and rhetoric, followed by the more advanced *quadrivium*, arithmetic, geometry, astronomy and music. The student became a bachelor of arts on completing the *trivium*, and took his master's degree— really a licence to teach—when he had completed the *quadrivium*. It would normally take five years to reach the B.A., and a further three to graduate master of arts. It was only at this stage that the student could proceed to one of the higher studies of canon and civil law, philosophy, medicine, and theology.

In some important respects, however, Oxford differed from Paris, and these differences showed themselves clearly during the thirteenth century. The university of Paris had grown out of the cathedral school and remained largely under the control of the local bishop. It is probable that the bishops of Lincoln, in whose diocese Oxford lay, would have liked to exercise a similarly direct control, but in fact they were never able to achieve this. Instead, the masters of Oxford enjoyed a very considerable measure of freedom from the bishop. The chancellor of the university was not the officer of the bishop but of the whole body of masters, by whom he was usually elected, though the election remained subject to the bishop's approval. The practical consequences of this were extremely important, for it was the chancellor who conferred degrees. The fact that he was a university and not an episcopal official meant that Oxford was a largely autonomous teaching institution. The bishops of Lincoln did not relinquish their authority over the university in our period, but it was on the whole a remote authority, exercised with difficulty by means of periodical " visitations ", which the masters resented and resisted.

By the third decade of the thirteenth century, Oxford university had become a large, well-established and privileged corporation. It has been reckoned that there were in this period some 1,300 students, housed either in lodgings rented from the townspeople or in halls owned by university masters and containing a number of students living together. This huge student body was divided in a rudimentary fashion into " Northerners " and " Southerners ", in accordance with the division into " nations " familiar in the universities of the continent. The two proctors of the modern university derive directly from the " procurators " or representatives of these two nations. The system of halls developed slowly into the college system, which has been characteristic of the university from the end of the fourteenth century to the present day. In 1249, e.g. a bequest left by an Oxford master, William of Durham, was partly applied to the purchase of a building on behalf of the university, and later (perhaps as late as about 1280) this building was assigned to four masters in arts, and gradually grew into University College. Merton College owed its origin to a more definite act of foundation and endowment by the king's Chancellor, Walter of Merton (1264). Balliol College, endowed about 1260 and formally founded in 1282, has already been mentioned. Much less is known of the university of Cambridge in this period. Its history seems to have begun effectively in 1229, when Henry III invited a number of masters and students from Paris to come to England and established them at Cambridge. As far as the mendicant friars were concerned, relations between Oxford and Cambridge were very close in the later thirteenth century.

Something has been said in the previous section about the friars who became distinguished masters at Oxford during the century. The typical master actively engaged in teaching in the schools—the " regent master "—was a secular clerk. Many references have been made to one of the best known of these, Robert Grosseteste, a Suffolk man of obscure origin who was successively student, master and chancellor of the university before becoming Bishop of Lincoln in

1235. Grosseteste's long life (? 1175-1253) coincided with a great influx into western Europe of hitherto unknown works of Aristotle, which at the turn of the twelfth and thirteenth centuries were being translated into Latin from Greek and Arabic. This flood of Aristotelian writing, largely concerned with philosophy and natural science, diverted intellectual effort in the west from the linguistic and humanistic studies which characterised the twelfth century. For a time it even appeared to threaten the supremacy of theology as the chief subject of scholastic study ; but the tremendous work of the Italian Dominican teacher Thomas Aquinas, in his *Summa Theologica*, achieved a synthesis of Greek science and philosophy with the teaching of the scriptures and of the Christian fathers.

In Grosseteste, however, we see a devotion to theology, based very closely on the scriptures, going hand in hand with a keen and acute interest in problems of mathematics and natural science. It is only recently that the full value of his work in these fields has been given the attention and credit which it deserves. If we assume the two necessary parts of scientific method to be, first, the *induction* of general laws from the observation of many particular events, and secondly, the *deduction* of particular occurrences from general principles, then Grosseteste's contribution to the development of scientific method was extremely important, for, as it has been said, he " seems to have been the first fully to understand, expound, and use both aspects of this theory of science ".[1] His insistence on the value of experiment, exemplified in his study of light and the rainbow, strikes a modern note, and so, too, does the great importance which he attached to mathematics in the interpretation of natural phenomena ; though this, of course, was also highly characteristic of Greek thinking. The lead given by Grosseteste was followed by his brilliant if erratic pupil, Roger Bacon (? 1214-92). Dr. Crombie has shown that it would be wrong to say that their work was premature in the sense that all interest in it and record of it were lost in succeeding ages. Their study of light was taken up with great success by Theodoric of Freiberg, a German scholar of the late thirteenth century. Not only was the knowledge of Theodoric's theory never lost, but " the whole Latin medieval tradition of experimental optics begun by Grosseteste was widely known to

[1] A. C. Crombie, *Robert Grosseteste and the origins of Experimental Science, 1100-1700* (1953), 132.

sixteenth- and seventeenth-century writers and formed a point of departure for their own work ".[1] Although the study of the Bible and the fathers unquestionably dominated academic activity in the thirteenth century, we should be quite wrong to suppose that it was an age in which little or no progress was made in science and philosophy, and here the contribution of the university of Oxford was very considerable.

2. *Changes in Country and Town*

(1) *Manor and Village.* Thirteenth-century England did not witness any revolutionary change either in farming methods or in the structure of rural society. We know vastly more in detail about country life in this period by comparison with earlier times, because of the much greater volume of surviving written evidence,[2] in " custumals " (statements of manorial rents and services drawn up for the benefit of a manorial lord), court rolls and other legal records, inquests into land tenure such as those carried out under Edward I in 1279, inquisitions *post mortem*, collections of charters and the like. All this mass of evidence tells us of an extremely active and in the main prosperous agriculture. But its very survival may give us the illusion that activity and prosperity were a new phenomenon in this period, whereas if we possessed equal sources for the twelfth century we might see a gradual continuity from that age to the next.

Nevertheless, the production of more elaborate estate surveys and the writing of manuals on estate management, both a feature of the thirteenth century, show clearly that a deliberate attempt was being made to exploit the land more efficiently. This is borne out by other evidence, e.g. the much greater value of the export duty on wool in the reign of Edward I. Nowadays, we might speak of such a movement as a " drive for greater production ". In the thirteenth century it was all quite unofficial, the largely spontaneous response of individuals to the fresh needs of a larger population at home and a

[1] *Robert Grosseteste and the origins of Experimental Science*, 260. Dr. Crombie's work is fundamental for any study of medieval science. For philosophy at Oxford during this period, see D. E. Sharp, *Franciscan philosophy at Oxford in the thirteenth century* (1930). For Grosseteste's life and career, see *Robert Grosseteste, Scholar and Bishop*, ed. D. A. Callus (Oxford, 1953).

[2] An example of how much knowledge can be gleaned from all this scattered evidence is provided by G. C. Homans, *English Villagers of the Thirteenth Century* (Harvard, 1942).

growing export trade abroad. Yet in many of the records of the period there is undeniably more than a hint of this deliberate striving after greater efficiency, not of course chiefly in the extractive and manufacturing industries, but in working the land and selling its produce in wool, grain, and meat.

Our sources relate chiefly to the economy of big estates, and as we have seen in an earlier chapter, there was some tendency for these to grow even bigger. It will be useful to try to form some idea of the life and structure of an estate of this kind, even though we should remember that the large estate was not characteristic of the whole country. Much of England, including the rich agricultural regions of East Anglia and the east midland plain, contained very many small manors and petty freeholds, whose arrangements might differ markedly from those which prevailed on the broad acres possessed by abbots and earls and other great landowners. The thirteenth-century manor, or group of manors in one ownership, may conveniently be regarded from four points of view, (i) of the lord ; (ii) of his chief official, whether steward or bailiff ; (iii) of the manorial servants and hired·men ; and (iv) of the peasant farmers, the villeins, bound to the manor by legal and economic ties.

(i) *The Lord.* The manor—or manors if he were rich—formed for the lord his principal source of income. To state this obvious truth tells us little about the position of the lord of a manor, still less about society organised within the manorial system. Besides providing him with his livelihood, the manor was the centre of the lord's life, and brought him into direct if not intimate relationship with a multitude of people of widely varied occupations and social position. The lord's life in our period was still what it had been since time immemorial in barbaric society, an extremely *public* life. The centre of the manor was the lord's hall. In the thirteenth century, the hall was still identical, in all essentials, with the hall of Old English kings and thanes, the hall of the seventh-century King Edwin of Northumbria whose familiar warmth and light were compared by one of his noblemen to human life on earth, the hall which figures prominently in the antique barbarian epic of *Beowulf.* Though a lord and lady in the thirteenth century might have a private chamber, this was not a room in which they could pass the day but one to which they would retire for the night. They ate their meals in the great hall in company with the gentlemen of their household and in the presence of the serving men. About 1240, Bishop Grosseteste of Lincoln composed some rules of life (another testimony to his wide interests !) for the guidance of one of the greatest ladies in England, Margaret de Lacy, Countess of Lincoln.[1] The bishop stressed the importance of dining in public and in an orderly manner:

" Make your freemen and guests ", he says, " sit as far as possible at tables on either side, not four here and three there. And all the crowd of grooms shall enter together when the freemen are seated, and shall sit together and rise together. And strictly forbid that any quarrelling be at your meals. And you yourself always be seated at the middle of the high table, that your presence as Lord or Lady may appear openly to all, and that you may plainly see on either side all the service and all the faults. And be careful of this, that each day at your meals you have two overseers over your household when you sit at meals, and of this be sure, that you shall be very much feared and reverenced." [2]

Grosseteste came of humble parentage and was moreover a bishop when he wrote this : he may therefore be painting a somewhat idealistic picture of how a lord's life ought to be conducted. The publicity by which he set such store was becoming a thing of the past in the thirteenth century. The great baronial hall, with cramped and uncomfortable little chambers opening off it, was yielding place to the mansion or manor-house built of sizeable private rooms, in which the lord and his family could live their life away from the bustle of servants and tenantry. It is worth reflecting that the transition from hall to country mansion was perhaps not the least important sign of the decay of the manorial system.

A lord was supposed to take a personal interest in his estates and tenants. On succeeding to his inheritance, he ought to learn the area and capacity of his lands, and cause a proper survey or " extent " to be made showing all the demesne and tenements of which the estate was composed, the rents and labour-services that were owed, the average yield of every manor annually. From this he could judge how much he could prudently spend each year on himself and his household, on the upkeep of the manor, and (not the least of a lord's duties in Grosseteste's opinion) on the dispensing of charitable gifts. The Countess of Lincoln and her great household of knights and valets and other liveried retainers might consume from two to two and a half quarters of grain a day in bread alone, to say nothing of ale. With this amount we may compare the basic

[1] *Walter of Henley's Husbandry*, ed. E. Lamond (1890), 122-45.
[2] *Ibid.* 137.

income which a manorial labourer could obtain from an average small-holding, approximately *one* quarter of grain *a year ;* this, of course, he would need to eke out by working part of the week for wages.

It was thought advisable for the lord to have two copies of his survey made, one for himself and the other for the use of his steward. An unscrupulous steward might cheat his lord as well as exploit the small tenants. The choice of an honest and responsible man was therefore extremely important. In the twelfth century, the steward's office was hereditary on many baronies ; but this does not seem to have been generally the case in the thirteenth. A good lord ought also to get to know all his servants personally and be ready to give an ear to their troubles. He should make sure—and in this we hear an echo of Magna Carta—that if a tenant is adjudged guilty of some misdemeanour and fined, this should be done only by the man's equals and then not too heavily.

A lord of many manors kept high and expensive state. It was not the custom for an earl to allow considerations of expense to limit his activities. He attended the king's court and parliaments, served at his own cost in war, and might well undertake a crusading expedition or the building of a larger, more elaborate castle. His continued sojourn at any single manor would be burdensome and so he travelled about the country, like the king, from one group of estates to another. Bishop Grosseteste advised the Countess of Lincoln to divide her time between her manors in Lindsey, the Vale of Belvoir, Norfolk, Somerset and Hampshire.

" Every year at Michaelmas when you know the measure of all your corn, then arrange your sojourn for the whole of that year, and for how many weeks in each place, according to the season of the year, and the advantages of the country in flesh and in fish, and do not in any wise burden by debt or long residence the places where you sojourn, but so arrange your sojourns that the place at your departure shall not remain in debt, but something may remain on the manor whereby the manor can raise money by the increase of stock and especially cows and sheep, until your stock acquits (= pays for) your wines, robes, wax and all your wardrobe." [1]

The main buying in of imported commodities such as wine, wax and clothing was to be done at two seasons of the year, though the bishop recommends four fairs held at different times, including the great Boston fair of St. Botulph (June 17th), St. Giles' fair at Winchester in September, and the Easter fair at St. Ives (Huntingdonshire.)

[1] Lamond, *op. cit.* 145.

(ii) *The Steward*. The office of steward, appropriate on a great estate, might be performed on lesser manors by the humbler bailiff: a modern comparison might be between a landowner's agent and the manager of a single farm. It was the steward's duty to have a more detailed knowledge than his master of the estate for which he was responsible. He must find out what stock it contained, what was the number of free tenants and "customary" tenants (i.e. villeins), how many ploughs and plough-teams were required to carry out the year's tillage. The author of one manual on estate management believed that one team could plough from 160 to 180 acres a year. This reckoned 308 days out of the 365 when the plough-beasts could be yoked to the plough, with eight weeks off "for holidays and other disturbances". To require forty-four weeks' cultivation every year does not seem to make any allowance for prolonged spells of bad weather.

All the manuals emphasise the importance of frequent and regular visits of inspection by the steward. One treatise recommends a visitation three times a year: presumably this refers to a large complex of manors, for the steward of a few estates could visit much oftener, while the bailiff of a single manor would seldom be absent. A closely related duty was the proper drawing up of accounts. Here the cycle was the same as that of the kingdom: a preliminary "view of account" at Easter followed by a final account and audit after the harvest. In addition to inspection and accounting, the steward was responsible for hiring labour and for seeing that produce was sold off the estate in such a way as to bring in the greatest profit. Produce should be sent to fairs and markets, bargained for and sold to the highest bidder: "it is not to be sold off like lost property", says one writer.[1] The best-known contemporary writer on husbandry, Walter of Henley, gives this advice:

"Sort out your sheep once a year, between Easter and Whitsuntide, and cause those which are not to be kept to be sheared early and marked apart from the others, and put them in an enclosed wood or some other pasture where they can fatten, and about St. John's Day (24 June) sell them, for then will the flesh of sheep be in season. And the wool of these may be sold with the skins of those which died of murrain. . . .

"And if you must buy cattle buy them between Easter and Whitsuntide, for then beasts are spare and cheap."[2]

[1] "It is not chattel of death or of war or sold from the king's pinfold", Lamond, *op. cit.* 93.   [2] *Ibid.* 23.

These writers on husbandry assume that a manorial steward will have considerable freedom to decide the cropping rotation and what seed to use. Walter of Henley, for example, says that seed bought from elsewhere will show better results than seed produced by the ground in which it is sown. This truth, he adds, can be demonstrated if two adjacent " selions " (strips) are sown at the same time, one with native and one with bought seed. The chief crops referred to are winter-sown rye, wheat or a mixture of the two (maslin), and spring-sown oats and barley, grown separately or else together as dredge. The common non-cereal crops were peas and beans.

Altogether, the position of steward and bailiff was a responsible one. " A bailiff is worth little in time of need who knows nothing and has nothing in himself without the instruction of others." But the work had its rewards, and unfortunately the authority wielded by a steward might all too easily be abused for gain. This was especially true of the steward as convener and president of the manor court. A tract on sinners of the time declares

> Among them stewards may be told (numbered)
> That lordings' courts hold.
> For nearly every steward
> The doom that they give is over hard,
> And specially the poor man
> They grieve him all that they can.[1]

(iii) *The Manorial Servants.* General accounts of medieval England often underrate the importance in the manor of the servants and other labourers who spent most of their time working in return for wages.[2] The part played by these men and women was indispensable. Broadly speaking, they may be divided into three classes. First, there were the immediate servants of the hall—grooms and valets, ushers, porters and so forth—with whom we need not concern ourselves here. Secondly, there was in the thirteenth century a class which may well be identical with that of the manorial ploughmen, many of them slaves or freedmen, of whom some 25,000 are enumerated in Domesday Book. Men and women of this class held small holdings allotted to them by the lord out of the demesne.

---

[1] Quoted from Robert Manning of Bourne's poem *Handlyng Synne* (c. 1303) by Homans, *English Villagers*, 320 : the language has been slightly modernised here.

[2] What follows is based mainly on M. M. Postan, *The Famulus : the estate labourer in the XIIth and XIIIth centuries* (*Econ. Hist. Rev.*, Supplement No. 2, no date).

They worked on the demesne partly in return for the holdings, but since these were too small to yield a living for a family, mainly in return for wages. Part of the wages might be paid in kind, by providing free of charge the seed and labour to cultivate an acre of the small-holding and by ploughing it every Saturday with the lord's plough. But part was also in cash, fixed by bargaining. Although wages were important, the connection between landholding and service was close enough for the clerks of the time to use feudal terms when describing these labourers : they were said to be tenants in " base serjeanty ", and their tenements were called " labourers' fees ". Finally, there were labourers of a more modern type, men who worked the whole time for wages, living perhaps in a cottage built on the lord's ground, but not otherwise attached to the manor Probably many of the cottars or cottagers referred to in thirteenth-century sources earned their living by full-time agricultural wage labour.

If the manor's work was performed by the villeins on the one hand and by wage-earning servants on the other, how was it divided ? On the majority of manors, the tasks that were highly-skilled or specialised or continuous throughout the year were in the hands of the manorial servants. This was certainly true of two major operations, ploughing and looking after stock. The lord's plough-man was a skilled specialist. He was in charge of his draught-animals and must be able to repair his implements. It was better to pay good wages to obtain such a man, says one contemporary, than to try to save by hiring an incompetent. Progressive opinion seems to have favoured a plough-team of horses because they worked faster than oxen. But Walter of Henley, who implies this, also says that in practice one must compromise with a team of oxen helped by two horses, since " the malice of ploughmen will not allow a horseplough to go faster than the plough drawn by oxen ".[1]

Shepherds and cowmen were doubtless permanently hired workmen. Indeed, a good cowman was supposed to sleep beside his cows, while a shepherd would also have to keep watch over his flock by night. It is an interesting reflection of the popular pastimes of thirteenth-century Englishmen that we should find quite different authorities for quite different reasons urging that parish priests and other clergy, and also shepherds and stockmen, should not frequent

---

[1] Lamond, *op. cit.* 10-13.

taverns nor go off to fairs and wrestling matches. Among other full-time manorial servants we may mention the dairy-maid, whose most important task was to make butter and cheese; the carter; and the swineherd. There seems to have been no attempt at intensive pig-keeping. The treatises advise that if pigs cannot be fed on mast and other pasture in wood and waste nearly all the year round they should not be kept at all.

(iv) *The Peasant Cultivators.* We are apt to think of the medieval villein, with his holding of thirty acres of arable lying in strips among the open fields, as constituting, with the lord, the very essence of the manor. Yet in fact the peasant farmer existed before the manor, he was to be found in those regions of England where the manor was not the typical form of landholding, and he persisted well into the eighteenth and early nineteenth centuries, when large consolidated farms had long since replaced manors in most parts of the country.

In the thirteenth century, the villein holding his virgate or half-virgate was still bound to his manor by a programme of labour service made up of week-work and boon-work. But there are at least two facts which forbid us to see in this general statement the whole truth about the relations of peasant and manor. First, whatever may have been the position in earlier times, labour services in the thirteenth century did not necessarily form the most valuable contribution rendered by the peasant to his lord. In many cases fixed money rents, the "assessed rents", paid by villeins were estimated to be worth more than the work which they owed. Secondly, on a considerable number of estates labour services had been commuted for cash payments (sometimes called *mal* or *mol*). Commutation was not permanent; it occurred wherever a lord found it more profitable to work his estate with hired labour. Yet labour service had not become quite valueless. The thirteenth century was a time when the supply of labour was relatively plentiful; hence customary labour was dear and hired labour cheap. If labour were to become short, the lords to whom labour service was owed would obviously find it necessary to discontinue commutation and revive the ancient customary week-work and boons.

As a general rule, the work done by villein tenants was the seasonal and discontinuous work such as weeding, haymaking and harvest. The subordinate administration of the manor was also done by them. Most important among the peasant officials were the reeve and the hayward (literally, " hedge-guard "). They were normally elected by the villeins, partly because if either of them defaulted the whole body of the villeins could be held responsible. The reeve was a senior foreman, having a general oversight of the daily round of work done by the villeins, and representing them in their dealings with the lord and his steward. The hayward was an under-foreman, but he also had the highly important duty of supervising the fencing in of hay and corn and taking up the fences to allow pasturing on grass and stubble.

The hay and corn harvests were large-scale communal undertakings, when the entire able-bodied population of the village would be working together in the common meadows and in the various furlongs of the great open fields. At such times the steward was well advised to be good-tempered and use all his skill at cajolery for the sake of winning the crop in time and in good condition. The villagers for their part knew that their bargaining position was strong at such a season. In 1300, nineteen cottars of Elton in Cambridgeshire declared that while they were bound to stack the hay of their lord, the abbot of Ramsey, in the meadows and in his courtyard, they would load the hay on to his carts only out of love at the special instance of the abbot, his servant or his reeve.[1] In other words, the cottars did not wish an occasional practice to harden into custom and then obligation. The seasonal boon-works were commonly made more attractive by the lord's providing food and drink free. There might be gradations of his hospitality, however, and Professor Homans, writing of the harvest boon-work known as " bid-reap ", tells us that the villagers of Barton-in-the-Clay (Bedfordshire) humorously nicknamed their three successive harvest boons " ale bid-reap ", " water bid-reap " and " hunger bid-reap " respectively.[2]

At the same time, it was in the peasants' interest as much as the lord's to see that the harvest was safely gathered. The tenants of a manor in the west Oxfordshire village of Langford must all have wished success to a lawsuit which their lord brought in the court of King's Bench in the late autumn of 1274. In this year the harvest had been poor, a fact that goes some way to explain what seems to have been virtually a case of inter-manorial warfare. It was apparently the custom on this manor for the tenants to keep watch over their cornfields during the autumn nights—presumably after the

[1] Homans, *op. cit.* 263.   [2] *Ibid.* 261.

corn had been cut and while it was standing in stooks. One night a gang of more than thirty men, led, it seems, by some lay brothers of the Cistercian abbey of Beaulieu, which owned the adjoining manor, descended on the men of Langford, armed and "with banners outspread". They chased the Langford men as far as their parish church, smashed their cottages, killed the lord of the manor's horse (worth over £13, as was alleged), and carried away their corn and other property. Besides the dead horse, the damage done was said to have amounted to £20, a grievous loss for a group of poor peasants. In the end, the lord was awarded two-thirds of this sum as damages, but was promptly put in the king's mercy for having falsely accused the Abbot of Beaulieu of conniving at his men's misdeeds ! [1]

The prevailing atmosphere at harvest was one of co-operation, probably much the same as that recalled by Flora Thompson at the north Oxfordshire village of Cottisford during the eighties of last century :

"In the fields where the harvest had begun all was bustle and activity. . . . Old Monday, the bailiff, went riding from field to field on his long-tailed grey pony. Not at that season to criticize, but rather to encourage, and to carry strung to his saddle the hooped and handled miniature barrel of beer provided by the farmer. . . . After the mowing and reaping and binding came the carrying, the busiest time of all. Every man and boy put his best foot forward then, for when the corn was cut and dried it was imperative to get it stacked and thatched before the weather broke." [2]

In conclusion, a brief description of two neighbouring west Oxfordshire villages in the early years of Edward I's reign may help to show how the fully developed "manorial system" could exist side by side with landholding arrangements which defy all efforts to bring them within a tidy pattern of clear-cut manors. In 1279, the small village of Kencot, with two open fields and between them a group of buildings and a tiny parish church, was held of Hugh de Plessy by Roger Doyly for the service of one knight. Hugh de Plessy was tenant-in-chief of Kencot, for he held of the king and paid scutage when it was levied. Roger Doyly was the immediate, and probably resident, lord of the manor, and of the village, for

---

[1] The *Abbreviatio Placitorum* (Rec. Com. edn.), 263, gives a garbled abridgement of this affair. The case is fully reported on the Plea Roll (Public Record Office, K.B. 27/12, rot. 2, Berks).

[2] *Lark Rise to Candleford* (World's Classics edn., 1954), 256-8.

here manor and village and parish coincided almost exactly. The demesne consisted of three *carucates* or ploughlands of arable and one "messuage", that is, a plot which doubtless contained the hall and farm buildings and perhaps orchard and garden. He had two free tenants, William Silven with a sizeable holding of 120 acres or so, and William Ciprian with only thirty acres. There were twelve villeins—nine virgaters, two half-virgaters, and one who held one and a half virgates. Each virgater paid 3s. 9d. a year rent and 6s. in lieu of labour service; the half-virgaters paid at slightly less than half this rate. There was also one cottager with two acres. It is interesting to notice that one of the freeholders, William Ciprian, also held half a virgate as a villein, paying a high rent (5s.) but owing nothing by way of labour service. He was probably a free man who had increased his holding by acquiring land which strictly speaking was held in "villeinage", that is, by an unfree tenure. Such a practice was not uncommon in our period, and in small estates must have hastened the decay of villeinage. Kencot, in short, was undoubtedly a complete manor, but it was already in 1279 moving towards non-manorial conditions.

If we turn to look at the larger village of Langford nearby, we find an arrangement which really defies classification. The biggest single estate here was owned by the Cistercian abbey of Beaulieu in Hampshire, but it did not form a manor in itself : it was merely attached to the abbey's neighbouring manor of Great Faringdon (Berkshire). Most of the abbey's tenants in Langford were villeins, rendering fairly heavy labour service. But there were also some free and semi-free tenants, one of whom held as much as ten virgates (about 300 acres), and was obliged to perform the ancient duty of escorting the king's treasure to the sea (perhaps from Woodstock to Southampton in the days of Henry I and Henry II, when Langford was still a royal estate).

Only about a quarter of the village formed what was actually called Langford manor. This also belonged to the Church, not to a monastery but to the great cathedral of Lincoln. It was assigned as the prebend of one of the canons of Lincoln, and since few of the canons held any one prebend for long, none of them was lord of the manor of Langford for more than a few years. Occupied as he was with his duties at the cathedral or at the university or in the king's service, the prebendary of Langford seldom lived on his manor, though we learn from a record of 1253 that when he did pay a visit he expected to be provided with substantial hospitality, including " fat geese, hens, pigeons and the wherewithal to brew ale ". Though an absentee, he took care to ensure that the manor court was held at the fixed times and that he received its profits.

Besides these two estates, there was an independent freehold of some sixty acres, which preserved its identity from the middle of the twelfth to the middle of the nineteenth century. Its farmhouse and steadings, indeed, survive to this day. This freehold was not a manor : its owner had no villein tenants and must have depended for labour on himself, his family, and hired men. There was also in Langford some land which belonged to a manor located in another village a mile or two distant. Finally there was the rectory or parsonage. In addition to the " great tithe " of corn and some tithes of hay, it was endowed with a considerable acreage of arable, water meadow and permanent pasture. Like the manor, the rectory formed the prebend of a canon of Lincoln, and while the rector held rather less land in the village than his fellow-canon who was lord of the manor, his actual income from tithe and land was appreciably greater.

Langford clearly did not fit into any neat manorial pattern, yet it was not altogether exceptional. Both as a village—a cluster of houses between two great open fields—and as a parish it had a unity, enduring from Anglo-Saxon times to the present day, save that the open fields are now enclosed. But in terms of land-holding, rents, labour services, suit to courts, etc., Langford possessed no unity whatever. One cannot speak of the " decline " of the manorial system in such a village, for it can hardly have been fully manorialised. This is emphasised by the fact that in our period a man from outside the village was busily acquiring arable, meadow and grazing in Langford from nearly all the estates we have mentioned, enclosing the land so acquired and retaining it as his separate property. There is little doubt that his business was sheep rearing on a fairly large scale. The point of special interest is that this persistent and enterprising outsider was able to carve a farm of an essentially modern type out of a thirteenth-century open field village.

(2) *The Towns.* The general prosperity of the age was reflected very strongly in the life and development of the English towns. It is true that the reigns of Henry III and his son do not compare with

those of the first three Angevins in the total of towns newly founded or given for the first time the corporate privileges of a borough. But the expansion of trade which had created the new towns of the twelfth century continued without a break until the early decades of the fourteenth. Individual towns grew in size, and the whole importance of the urban element increased in relation to the rest of the country. During the thirteenth century the movement towards self-government proceeded steadily. It was accompanied by a tendency for a fairly sharp class division to arise in the larger cities, e.g. at York and Lincoln and, most noticeably, at London. The right of the burgesses to collect and account to the king for the *firma* or compounded rent of their borough had been effectively won at the end of the twelfth century. With this the right to elect their own bailiffs or reeves was closely connected, and by the end of King John's reign it had been secured in most towns of any importance.

The next step was taken under the influence of contemporary urban development in France and Flanders. In its earliest phase, it took the form of organising the burgesses into a sworn association, a *communa* or commune, with a governing body composed of a mayor and echevins. It is a testimony to the foreign origin of this arrangement that both " mayor " and " echevin " are French words. At a somewhat later period, it became normal to describe the important town councillors as " aldermen ". But until the second half of the thirteenth century, " alderman " was applied not merely to any senior member of a town council but more narrowly to the burgess who, by himself, or perhaps jointly with a fellow, held governmental authority under the king or other lord of the borough. Communes of the continental type were discouraged by the Crown, and—under that name, at least—never seem to have taken hold in the towns of England. But the influence of the communal idea may undoubtedly be seen in the second phase of the movement towards burghal self-government, which was reached fairly generally during the opening decades of the thirteenth century. This stage was the election, often actually at the king's behest, of a body of " jurats ", sworn councillors, usually twelve or twenty-four in number. Their function was to advise and assist the town's governing officers, who in most places were still known by the older style of aldermen or bailiffs, though the imported title of mayor was gaining ground rapidly. The development of these early town councils may be found before 1215 at London, Ipswich, Shrewsbury, Lincoln, Gloucester, and Northampton, and, almost certainly before 1272, at Leicester, Oxford, Cambridge, Great Yarmouth, Winchester, and Exeter. Along with the setting up of councils went the use of a common seal. Here again, we have early record of the leading towns possessing common seals, York and Oxford about 1190, London,[1] Gloucester, Ipswich, and Lincoln in the first two decades of the thirteenth century. The fact that early borough records have survived so haphazardly and in such small quantities may well disguise a general progress of corporate feeling and activity reaching down even to the comparatively small towns. It is only casually, e.g. that we learn that Barnstaple, a Devonshire borough of secondary importance, employed a common seal as early as 1210, and that the men of Bedford, whose town was by no means in the forefront of commercial centres, had formed themselves into a commune before 1194.[2]

It is likely that the mayor and jurats represented even from the first the interests of the more substantial citizens. When the councils of Twelve and Twenty-four were described as consisting of " the more discreet and better men of the town ", what was really meant was that they were the men who had the biggest stake in the town's prosperity. Some of them were very rich men indeed. When, for example, in 1238 Simon de Montfort laid a heavy tallage upon his borough of Leicester, Simon Curlevache, one of the two aldermen—in effect, joint-mayor—contributed 500 marks (£333 6s. 8d.) out of his own pocket and yet could afford to remain alderman.[3] William of Holgate, mayor of Lincoln from 1267 to 1273, was said to be " a great lord and power in Lincoln " ; at his own expense he had houses built at Boston for use at St. Botulph's Fair, using Lincoln stone which he caused to be quarried, hewn and shipped for the purpose.[4] From time to time the authority of these great merchants was contested by the general body of the citizenry. This was naturally the case at a time of political and social upheaval, such as the period 1258-65, when there was a severe struggle for

---

[1] It is doubtless an accident that we have no twelfth-century record of a common seal for London.

[2] J. Tait, *The Medieval English Borough* (1936), 236 ; F. M. Stenton, *Publications of the Bedfordshire Historical Records Society*, ix (1925), 177-80.

[3] Mary Bateson, *Records of the Borough of Leicester*, i (1899), p. xliii.

[4] J. W. F. Hill, *Medieval Lincoln* (1948), 212.

power in London between the mayor, sheriffs, and aldermen on the one hand, representing the wealthier merchants and tending to be royalist in sympathy, and on the other hand, the lesser citizens, small traders, shopkeepers, and artisans who, as we have seen, were among the most fervent admirers and adherents of Simon de Montfort. There was a similar cleavage of interest at Lincoln in 1290 when, on the complaint of the citizens, the government of the city was for a time taken out of the hands of the few rich merchants who had exercised it hitherto and entrusted to a custodian responsible directly to the king.[1] This tendency for town government to become concentrated in a small oligarchy grew more and more pronounced during the thirteenth century. It may be associated with the gradual merging of gild-merchant and civic corporation which Gross, the historian of the English merchant gilds, found to be characteristic of the fourteenth century.[2]

Well before the close of our period, the prosperity of the great wool-exporting and cloth-making towns of eastern England had been adversely affected by a remarkable industrial revolution.[3] Prior to the thirteenth century, the first four main processes of preparing cloth from raw wool, (i) carding or combing, (ii) spinning, (iii) weaving, and (iv) fulling—that is, shrinking, scouring and felting the cloth—had all been carried out either by manual power or else directly (as in fulling) by human hands and feet. It followed, therefore, that the best locations for cloth-making were the towns where it could at once be marketed or exported. Hence, in the twelfth and for the first half of the thirteenth century, the centres of English cloth-making were the market towns of the eastern midlands, and seaports of the east coast. Such were York, Beverley, Louth, Lincoln, and Leicester in the north of this region, and Stamford, Northampton, Norwich, Oxford, and London in the south. Professor Carus-Wilson has shown that there existed at Leicester in the middle years of the thirteenth century, " an industry highly organised on a capitalist basis in a town specialising in cloth-making ".[4] The dyers of Leicester employed weavers and fullers

---

[1] *Medieval Lincoln*, 213-14.

[2] C. Gross, *The Gild Merchant* (1890), i. 72-6, 159-61.

[3] For this, see E. M. Carus-Wilson, " An Industrial Revolution of the Thirteenth Century ", *Econ. Hist. Rev.*, xi (1941), 39-60 ; also the same writer in *Cambridge Economic History*, ii (1952), 409-13.

[4] *Econ. Hist. Rev.*, xiv (1944), 47.

to process raw wool before supervising the final stages of dying and shearing. Moreover, they did their own trading at Boston Fair. This concentration of the textile industry in the towns of eastern England was made possible, indeed, almost inevitable, by the fact that the processing was done by hand. The wool and cloth merchants gathered at the best centres for marketing and exporting, and the weavers and fullers simply followed them. The business of selling, in other words, determined the siting of the industry.

The revolution of the thirteenth century was caused by the introduction into England of fulling by water-powered machinery. The apparatus was popularly called a " fulling mill " (" tucking mill " in the west country, " walk mill " in the north and in Scotland), although the word " mill " was here used merely in the loose sense of a mechanical contrivance. Once mechanical fulling had become widespread, the siting of the cloth industry was no longer determined by selling but by production. Cloth-making moved to the valleys and dales of the west country and the Pennines. In this region of fairly high rainfall and steep hillsides water power was abundant and could be got without serious difficulty. A channel was taken off some swift-flowing river or stream, leading the water to a wheel whose axis was extended into the mill building. Here, projections on the revolving axis alternately raised and let fall heavy wooden hammers. The cloth was placed beneath in a trough of water and fuller's earth, and was beaten by the power-driven hammers as well as, and certainly much quicker than, had been possible by the primitive " walking " of human feet.

Although the first fulling mill known in England—at Temple Newsam, near Leeds—is on record as early as 1185, it was not till the middle of the thirteenth century that the new method had begun seriously to threaten the supremacy of the towns of the eastern lowlands as the headquarters of English cloth-making. Thereafter, however, there was a steady shift from east to west and from town to country. The new industry was widely scattered and always remained more rural than urban in character. The fulling-mill made it cheaper to carry out all the processes of the industry in the Cotswolds and the West Riding, even though this meant transporting the finished cloth by boat and packmule to the old-established market towns and seaports. But although the eastern towns kept their importance as centres of trade throughout our period, there is no doubt that the migration of their one large-scale and characteristic industry appreciably diminished their total wealth and prosperity.

Of the towns of thirteenth-century England practically no physical trace now survives save for the cathedral, monastic or other churches, in which, it may be, an age remarkable for its creative enterprise reached the very summit of its achievement. Great architecture was by no means a monopoly of the towns, but we may fittingly conclude this section on urban life with a brief reference to some of the cathedral churches which, while all in their different ways glorifying God, contrived in addition to bear particular witness to a city's wealth and civic pride and to distinguish its individuality.

The entire period covered by this book was one of extremely active cathedral building. In order to understand the progression of this great architectural effort, it should be realised that the almost invariable rule in constructing a medieval church was to begin with the choir which formed the housing of the principal altar at the east end. The normal cathedral church in England was cruciform in plan, and after completing the choir the next stages were to construct the north and south transepts and then proceed to the nave, usually the largest part of the church, and the only part completely open at all times to the laity. It is broadly true to say that the first half of our period, down to about 1190, was one in which a fairly sustained effort of building had completed the choirs and in very many cases also the crossings and naves of the English cathedrals. From 1190 to 1300, very approximately, this process began again. The styles of the earlier period were no longer found satisfying, and so we see the demolition (here and there, accidental destruction) of the eastern arms of cathedrals and their replacement by entirely new choirs, retrochoirs and Lady Chapels, designed in the Early English and (from about 1250) Decorated styles. Generally speaking, naves were not rebuilt at this period. Many twelfth-century naves were large and of massive construction. To rebuild them would have been an enormous expense, and from a liturgical viewpoint they were the least important part of the church.

The artistic genius of the age was far from confined to the architectural design. The master masons found sculptors, carpenters, and contrivers of other kinds of enrichment whose work could easily match their own. Towards the end of our period, the carvers turned to greater realism in their portrayal of the human figure and of other living forms. A wonderful instance of this naturalism may be found in the chapter-house of Southwell Minster in Nottinghamshire, which dates from 1293 to 1300, years when the country was deeply embroiled in war with France and Scotland. At Southwell, the stone-carver was allowed to embellish capitals, tympana, bosses and so on with a marvellously rich proliferation of foliage, maple, hawthorn, mulberry, bryony, and many plants observed from nature yet all subordinated to a disciplined design.[1]

One of the earliest examples of the great first period of Gothic rebuildings was produced appropriately enough at Canterbury, which was devastated by fire in 1174. A French architect, William of Sens, planned and began the new cathedral with a distinctively French feature : a " chevet ", that is, a curved east end or apse with small chapels opening off it. He was incapacitated by injury in 1177, and the work was completed by his assistant, William " the English-man ". The cathedral of Wells was reconstructed even more thoroughly in this period : choir, transepts and nave were finished between 1174 and about 1200, while the magnificent sculptured west front, the peculiar glory of Wells, was probably the work of the master mason, Thomas Norreys, and of the sculptor, Simon of Wells, in the period 1230-50.

The great minster church of Lincoln was also rebuilt at the turn of the twelfth and thirteenth centuries, under Master Geoffrey de Noiers and Master Richard the mason. The choir dates 1192-1200, and the remainder of the church was completed during the next fifty years or so, an elaborate west front being superimposed on the Norman work of Bishop Remigius (1072-92), and an enormous twelve-sided chapter-house erected to the north of the choir, modelled on a slightly earlier circular one at Worcester and probably built by the same master-mason. " At Lincoln ", it has been said,[2] " we have the supreme type of Early English cathedral. . . . We must, of course, reconstruct in the mind's eye the three spires of which the minster has been robbed : the central one, the highest work of man ever erected in (England). If we do this we shall see that everything is of one piece : the whole great church from east

---

[1] See N. Pevsner, *The Leaves of Southwell* (1945).

[2] J. Harvey, *The English Cathedrals* (1950), photographs by H. Felton, 37.

to west and from north to south, the subsidiary chapels and the
chapter-house, is beating against the sky with its spires, its spikes,
its pinnacles. The lancet windows in the gables, the tall lights in
the great tower, all are steadily and insistently surging up to heaven.
And inside, the shafts, the vaults and the pale flames of the windows
are doing the same."

Among the purely Gothic cathedrals built according to a single
design, Lincoln is the most inspired and satisfying ; but the beauty
of Salisbury may perhaps be appreciated more immediately, and if
all the elements of a medieval cathedral church are considered together, Salisbury has no equal for unity of design. This architectural triumph was made possible when the reforming and scholarly
bishop, Richard Poore (1217-28), obtained leave to transfer his see
from the inconvenient hill-site of Old Sarum down to the banks of
the River Avon (1220). Here there was ample space for new church,
cloisters, chapter-house and lodgings for the canons, and full
advantage was taken of it. Work on the cathedral began with the
Lady Chapel, with its marvellously slender shafts. It progressed
steadily westwards from 1220 until 1284, but much the greater part
(in fact, all except the west front, tower and spire) was finished within
the first forty years. The canon of Salisbury, who was master of
works during this period, was an influential royal clerk from Norfolk
named Elias of Dereham. That he was an artist as well as an
administrator is clear from the fact that he helped to design the
shrine of Thomas Becket at Canterbury prepared for the martyr's
translation in 1220. He may therefore have influenced the design
of Salisbury. But the main credit for the creative architectural work
at Salisbury should probably be given to another East Anglian,
Nicholas of Ely, who is known to have been resident master-mason
at the cathedral during and after the time of Bishop Poore.

THE CONQUEST OF WALES

THE Edwardian conquest of Wales was not a single act of military aggression, prompted by deliberate policy. If it did not happen by accident, it was none the less unpremeditated and gradual. Moreover, since it left out of account those parts of Wales held by the marcher lords, the conquest was not even a definitive solution of the problem of Anglo-Welsh relations. There is no question that the English king was determined to define the rights of himself and of those subject to him. But in the case of Wales it seems highly doubtful whether he would have pushed his policy of definition to the extreme of conquest if Llywelyn ap Gruffydd and, later, his brother David, had not given him formal and obvious provocation.

It was customary at the time of Edward's accession that a new king of England should receive the homage of the rulers of Scotland and Wales. We have seen how, in the thirteenth century, the separate homages of many Welsh princes had been replaced by the homage of the ruler of Gwynedd acting as their recognised feudal suzerain. In 1270 only Maredudd ap Rhys, lord of part of Ystrad Tywi (the Towy valley) and lineal descendant of the great Lord Rhys who died in 1197, stood outside the hegemony created by the two Llywelyns, and made his separate homage to the English king. From the Welsh standpoint, the change may be seen to have brought the régime of Gwynedd a long way towards the centralised feudal state exemplified elsewhere in Britain and on the continent. For the English monarchy, however, the predominance of Gwynedd, which it had freely recognised, meant that the relationship of its prince to the Crown would need to be more clearly defined. The homage of the prince, as the outward symbol of the relationship, became not less but more important than ever before.

Llywelyn was at the height of his power when Henry III died, and his mood was clearly not pacific. He was at loggerheads with

Earl Gilbert of Gloucester, whose castle of Caerphilly in Glamorgan he had sacked in 1270. It was only to be expected that the earl, in self-defence, should rebuild. But the new work was begun on a massive scale, and the castle appeared as a standing threat to Llywelyn's position in the country immediately to the north and west. He was prevented from attacking it again only by a promise that the new fortress would be handed over to the English king; but the promise was never carried out, and the two most powerful lords west of the Severn remained at enmity. Llywelyn may also have been suspicious of the activities of King Henry's younger son, Edmund of Lancaster, who had been granted the Crown castles and lordships in Wales, and was administering the districts of Carmarthen and Cardigan as shires on the English model.

These facts may go some way to explain why, on Edward I's accession, Llywelyn ceased to pay the 3,000 marks required annually under the treaty of Montgomery, and refused to take the oath of fealty demanded, in the king's absence, by the council of regency. He was no more conciliatory when Edward returned. His absence from the coronation was a piece of rudeness which Edward might have overlooked; his persistent refusal of homage, however, was politically unwise and could not be ignored. Nevertheless, the king decided on military action only after these bad relations had been greatly worsened by two unconnected incidents. In the first place, Llywelyn had resumed the ancient quarrel of Gwynedd with Powys by attacking Gruffydd ap Gwenwynwyn, in the spring of 1274, and depriving him of the western parts of southern Powys, including the strategically important district of Arwystli. Towards the end of the year he drove Gruffydd into exile in England, where he made common cause with Llywelyn's brother David, who, perhaps with rather more justification, had been similarly treated. According to Llywelyn, it was for him alone to discipline these subordinate chiefs. But Edward I could not agree that the treaty of Montgomery had nullified a Welsh subject's right to appeal to him as ultimate feudal overlord. Warfare on several parts of the march in the summer of 1275 brought the king to Chester in September to receive Llywelyn's homage, but again he refused it, this time with the support of a large assembly of lesser Welsh princes. The second aggravation was one in which Llywelyn seems more sinned against than sinning; yet even here there was provocation for Edward of a personal kind. Before the battle of Evesham, Simon de Montfort had agreed that the Prince of Wales should receive his daughter Eleanor in marriage. Now, ten years later, Llywelyn arranged for her to be escorted from France by one of her brothers, Amaury. Quite apart from his feelings towards Earl Simon, the king's anger had been freshly roused against another of his sons, Guy de Montfort, who on March 13th, 1271, had brutally and foolishly murdered Henry of Almain, Edward's cousin and close friend, in a church in Viterbo. The bridal convoy was therefore intercepted off the Scilly Isles, and Eleanor de Montfort placed in custody in Windsor Castle.

The king announced his intention to make war on Llywelyn in the Michaelmas Parliament of 1276. His preparations were leisurely, even by thirteenth-century standards, but they were extremely thorough. The feudal host met the king at Worcester on July 1st, 1277. One of the Llywelyn's supporters had already been put out of action before this date. Rhys, the son of Maredudd ap Rhys and since 1271 his successor as lord of Ystrad Tywi, had surrendered his ancestral castle of Dryslwyn to the royal forces on April 11th. The southern objective in the late summer was therefore Cardigan, which Llywelyn had seized from Earl Edmund of Lancaster, and appropriately enough the earl was made commander in this area. His progress was rapid, and within a month he had reached Aberystwyth. In the meantime, Edward himself moved with the main army by way of Shrewsbury to Chester. Here a fleet supplied by the Cinque Ports joined him, partly to secure his march along the north coast, partly to blockade the Welsh in the mountain triangle of Snowdonia. At that date, the coastal strip from Chester to Rhuddlan was covered by a dense growth of wood. Through this a broad marching tract was cut by squads of specially hired workmen. It was not until August that the king reached the mouth of the Conway. His complete command of the sea enabled him to send a force to hold the isle of Anglesey. Its corn harvest, instead of feeding Llywelyn and his men in Snowdonia, was reaped for the invading army. As Sir John Lloyd has said, Edward I realised that to defeat the Welsh of the north, Gwynedd must be treated as a natural fortress, to which a formal siege should be laid. He therefore observed the rules of siege-warfare—patience and the blocking of supply—and early in November was duly rewarded by Llywelyn's surrender.

In 1277 Edward was not bent upon conquest. His first Welsh war was concluded not by a royal decree but by an agreement, sealed at Aberconway, or Conway, on November 9th. The settlement reduced Llywelyn to being lord of Gwynedd merely, and not even of the enlarged Gwynedd which included the Four Cantreds between the Conway and the Dee. The upland pair of the four, Rhufoniog and Dyffryn Clwyd, were granted to Llywelyn's brother David; the coastal pair, Rhos and Englefield (Tegeingl), were annexed to the Crown. Severer still from Llywelyn's point of view, although he kept the title of " Prince of Wales ", his feudal suzerainty over the lesser princes of the country was abolished, save in five minor instances. Instead, King Edward was to receive their homage direct, in addition to Llywelyn's own homage for his much curtailed territory. Finally, Llywelyn now surrendered whatever claims he might have had to the custody of Carmarthen and Cardigan, two of the key strongpoints of South Wales. Edward made some return for these concessions. Eleanor de Montfort was released, and married Llywelyn in Worcester cathedral on October 13th, 1278, in the presence of the king and his queen, Eleanor of Castile. With the four most prominent Welsh rulers, Llywelyn and David of Gwynedd, Gruffydd of Powys, and Rhys of Dryslwyn, all apparently on the best of terms with the king, there seemed a very reasonable prospect, in 1278, of a lasting peace between the English and the Welsh.

The friendliness of Edward I and the Welsh princes was a façade, pleasing to the eye and by no means jerry-built, but a façade for all that. Behind it was the starker reality of military defeat and occupation. The foundations were being laid of a tighter and more thoroughgoing control over Wales than her people could have believed possible. Six months after the peace of Aberconway, the king had begun to build the first of the great stone castles which stand yet as powerful witnesses to his conquest of Wales. Rhuddlan and Flint in the north, Aberystwyth and Builth in the south, were pushed forward rapidly in the summer months from 1278 to 1281. The construction of these huge fortresses, of a type quite different from any previous military architecture in Britain,[1] removed at one stroke the chief military weakness of English kings engaged on campaigns in Wales. Hitherto, their main bases of attack, Chester,

[1] Except perhaps for Caerphilly. See below, p. 366.

Shrewsbury, Worcester, and Hereford, had been set too far back from Welsh territory, and lines of communication had therefore been extended and highly vulnerable. Edward I advanced and shortened this line of defensible bases.

The sureness of touch which the king always displayed in military matters was not equalled in his administration of Wales after 1277. In the peace of Aberconway, it was as though he had confronted Llywelyn with a *Quo Waranto?* and had found his answer insufficient. The consequent judicial aspect of the settlement was more important for the immediate future than the military occupation. Judicial commissions were issued in 1278 to groups of Englishmen and Welshmen, who were empowered to hear and determine pleas of all kinds throughout the greater part of the country, save in Llywelyn's own land of Gwynedd and in the marcher lordships of Gloucester and Hereford. The judges were instructed to apply the law, Welsh, English, or marcher, appropriate to the locality of the case and to the litigants. It was understood that Welsh law prevailed when Welshmen alone were concerned, but serious doubt arose where cases involved Welsh princes and marcher lords, and with regard to Welshmen dwelling in marcher territory and English lords who held lands in Welsh Wales. The king's intentions were praiseworthy, and we need not doubt his sincerity in believing that Aberconway merely confirmed an ancestral right to dispense justice in the parts of Wales. But the commissioners of 1278 were administering justice in a manner which to the Welsh was both novel and unpleasing. The dislike they felt for its alien character was aggravated by the harshness of the new administrators. Cardigan and Carmarthen, now definitely made into shires of the English type, were surrendered by Edmund of Lancaster in return for English estates and placed under a Shropshire baron, Bogo de Knovill, as Justiciar of West Wales. He governed oppressively for a year, and was replaced by Robert de Tibetot (Tiptoft), who, though not so rough a man, was too efficient to be popular. In the north, Reginald Grey, another marcher baron, became Justiciar of Chester with jurisdiction over the parts of North Wales directly subject to the king.

The activity of the new justices and their growing unpopularity among the Welsh people do not by themselves explain the depth of dissatisfaction at the king's rule from 1277 to 1282. The most unsettling factor was the question of appeals to a higher jurisdiction.

Edward I's solution of the problem in Wales was drastically simple. Perhaps because of this, he underestimated its explosive quality when he came to deal with the kings of France and Scotland. What happened in Wales may be told very briefly. Llywelyn claimed against Gruffydd of Powys the territory of Arwystli, the land about the headwaters of the Severn. Geographically, Arwystli was part of southern Powys, but it had ancient connections with Gwynedd, as its inclusion in the diocese of Bangor bore witness. After 1277, Llywelyn and his opponent were both equals before their lord the King of England, but they disagreed on the manner in which their dispute should be settled. Llywelyn held that since Arwystli was purely Welsh, the case should be tried there by the laws of Hywel Dda. Gruffydd for his part preferred to regard himself as a marcher baron, and urged a trial by the law of the march. The fact that appeal lay to Edward I meant that in the last resort a law alien to Welsh tradition would be brought to bear, for it was unthinkable that the king, with his intensely legalistic outlook and his training in the feudal-cum-Roman legal concepts of western Europe, would settle an important lawsuit merely by reference to what he regarded as inferior tribal custom. Because the problem was new, a special commission was issued, at the end of 1280, to the Bishop of St. David's (Thomas Bek), Walter of Hopton, a professional judge, and Reginald Grey. They were instructed to enquire " by what laws and customs the king's ancestors were accustomed to rule and judge a prince of Wales and a Welsh baron of Wales ". Their findings are not known, but it is certain that Montgomery was fixed as the site of a final hearing, and to this Llywelyn agreed. The Prince of Wales deserves credit for his restraint during these tedious delays and offensive inquisitions. A few years earlier, he would have settled the matter promptly enough by descending upon Arwystli with fire and sword and driving Gruffydd into exile. Now, in the winter of 1281-2, he kept the king's peace, and waited for the issue of a writ which would enable him, like any other tenant-in-chief, to seek justice from the royal judges in the king's court.

His brother David did not keep the king's peace. On March 21st, 1282, the night before Palm Sunday, he seized the castle of Hawarden on the Dee estuary by a surprise attack, and in the next few days laid siege to Flint and Rhuddlan and rode south through the mountains to encourage a widespread revolt among the Welsh.

His own motives may have sprung from personal grievances at the interference of royal officials in his lordship of Denbigh and elsewhere; but his capture of Hawarden touched off an explosion of resentment undoubtedly very general among the people of middle and south-west Wales, so that his piece of bravado quickly became a national movement. Only thus can we explain how the new castle of Aberystwyth and two lesser fortresses, Llandovery and Carreg Cennen (Carmarthenshire), were at once stormed and destroyed. All the southern Welsh rulers joined the rising save Rhys ap Maredudd of Dryslwyn. On June 17th, their men ambushed a force under the Earl of Gloucester at Llandeilo on the Towy. The engagement ended in a severe defeat for the earl, who sustained heavy casualties. He was unable to prevent Llywelyn, who had by this time come out in support of his brother, from ravaging the valley of the Towy and moving freely in South Wales.

By the late summer, the king had recovered not only from the completely unexpected shock of a Welsh rising but also from the setback of Gloucester's defeat. The feudal host was summoned, as in 1277, and the forty days' service which it owed at its own expense ran from August 2nd to September 11th. During this period the two commanders who had replaced the discredited Gloucester, William of Valence, lord of Pembroke, and the Justiciar Robert Tibetot, recovered the whole of Cardigan save for Aberystwyth itself. Farther east, the Earl of Hereford operated in his own country of Brecknock, Roger Lestrange in the region of Builth, and Roger Mortimer from Montgomery. The main offensive was launched once again in the extreme north, where the king took personal command. He guarded his army against a flank attack by despatching a force up the Dee to overrun and hold down David's two cantreds. As in the first campaign, the main body marched from Flint to Rhuddlan. At Rhuddlan the king struck inland, moving up the River Clwyd to Denbigh, which fell in the middle of October. The Four Cantreds and the lands to the southward were granted to a few English magnates who had served Edward I well in this and other wars. The Earl of Lincoln got Rhos and Rhufoniog. Reginald Grey was made lord of Dyffryn Clwyd and its castle of Ruthin, and founded the historic baronial family of Grey de Ruthin. The Earl Warenne was given the lordships of Bromfield and Yale in the middle Dee valley.

355

The war was now virtually confined to Snowdonia, but still the Welsh were far from subdued. In the autumn the king sent one of his most trusted henchmen, Luke de Tany, to seize and hold Anglesey. Scores of boats were collected and pontoons prefabricated at Chester in order that a floating bridge could be built across the Menai Strait at Bangor. Luke de Tany's instructions were to supervise the erection of this bridge and then guard it, but on no account to cross it in force until the king could advance from Aberconway to meet him. At this stage, the Archbishop of Canterbury, John Pecham, affronted the king by an attempt to make peace, undoubtedly well-meant but inept and tactless in execution. A truce was arranged, but it is clear that Edward was not prepared to make peace except on terms of Llywelyn's complete surrender. The Prince of Wales, he proposed, might become an earl in England; his restless brother should go on crusade; but neither was to have any land, or bear rule, in Wales. Of course Llywelyn could not accept such terms. He and his family were a part of Wales. He believed that he ruled Gwynedd freely, not as the English king's tenant but as a descendant of Brutus, who, as every thirteenth-century schoolboy knew, had come from Troy in ancient times to be the first king of Britain.[1] In spite of the archbishop's strictures on the wickedness of the rebellion, Llywelyn firmly believed in the essential justice of his cause, which he identified with that of his people. Nevertheless, Pecham took the negotiations earnestly enough to brave a personal visit to Llywelyn's court, but while he was thus vainly going to and fro between the opposing camps, the Anglesey garrison suffered a severe setback. Luke de Tany had impatiently crossed his bridge of boats before it was finished, in disobedience to the king's orders and in defiance of the truce. His small band of cavalry was attacked and routed by the Welsh, and he himself and many of his companions were drowned trying to regain the Anglesey shore.

This minor but striking triumph put new heart into the Welsh resistance. Llywelyn, momentarily relieved of danger in his rear, went south to give encouragement to the men of Brecknock and the upper Wye valley. Here John Giffard had recently replaced Roger Lestrange, who had been transferred to Montgomery on Mortimer's

---

[1] For the landing of Brutus of Troy at Totnes and the naming of Britain after him, see Geoffrey of Monmouth's historical romance, *Historia Regum Britanniae*, ed. A. Griscom and R. E. Jones (1929), 249.

death.   On December 11th, Llywelyn's army was stationed a little distance to the west of Giffard's headquarters at Builth, covering a bridge over the River Irfon (Orewin).   While their leader was absent,[1] they were surprised and scattered by an English force of cavalry intermixed with archers, who, unknown to the Welsh, had forded the Irfon some way above the bridge.   It seems that Llywelyn was hurrying back, unattended, to rejoin his followers when a Shropshire trooper, Stephen Frankton, chanced on him and slew him without knowing who he was.

The sudden death of their great prince dispirited the Welsh as quickly as the routing of Luke de Tany had fired them with fresh enthusiasm.   At once the king pressed his advantage.   Disregarding the winter season, he continued his campaign to encircle Snowdonia and starve David into submission.   Five hundred crossbowmen were brought from Gascony, and with them came several Gascon notables, the counts of Armagnac and Bigorre, the lord of Bergerac, the *captal*, or lord, of Buch, and Arnold of Gabaston, whose son Peter (" Piers Gaveston ") was in later years to become the evil genius of the king's son Edward of Carnarvon.   Luke de Tany's post was given to Otto of Granson, perhaps the closest of Edward's many Savoyard friends.   These reinforcements stiffened the Anglesey contingent, and within a short time Otto of Granson had succeeded in occupying Carnarvon and Harlech.   Leaving the coast, the king advanced in January, 1283, to Dolwyddelan, half way between Harlech and Aberconway, and by capturing the castle there completed his blockade of the Snowdon massif.   David became a mere fugitive, hunted from one group of mountains to another.   At last, in June, some fellow Welshmen betrayed him to the king.   He was tried by his peers, the barons of England, in a great parliament summoned to Shrewsbury for Michaelmas.   Here he was convicted as a traitor and hanged.   The heads of himself and of his brother Llywelyn were taken to the Tower of London to be displayed at the ends of lances.

In the war of 1282-3, Edward I aimed at the conquest of Wales and the post-war settlement was on an entirely different footing from that of 1277.   It was a symbol of the new situation that the king at this time took possession of an ancient relic sacred to the Welsh, the

---

[1] It is possible that Llywelyn was lured away by a treacherous invitation to a parley.

Cross of Neot or Neath. The Statute of Wales was promulgated at Rhuddlan on March 19th, 1284.[1] By it the whole of Wales was made subject directly to the Crown, except those areas which were already marcher territory either of long standing or by reason of the king's own grants in 1282. The eastern part of the Four Cantreds was turned into a new shire, Flint, with its own sheriff subordinated to the Justiciar of Chester. Gwynedd became three new shires, Anglesey, Carnarvon, and Merioneth. They were subject to a Justiciar for North Wales (Otto of Granson), whose headquarters at Carnarvon included a special exchequer of North Wales subordinate to the Exchequer at Westminster. Robert Tibetot continued as Justiciar for West Wales, his territory of Carmarthen with Cardigan being now contiguous on the north with the new royal district of Merioneth. Granson was succeeded in 1295 by John of Havering, who, five years later, after Tibetot's death, was appointed Justiciar for the whole of royal Wales. In 1301 Wales and Chester were granted to the king's son, Edward, who had been born at Carnarvon one month after the Statute of Wales had been published. At the time of his birth, the baby had an older brother, Alfonso, still alive, and the famous story of Edward I presenting his latest child to the Welsh people as their prince, " one that was born in Wales and could speak never a word of English ", is apocryphal.[2] Nevertheless, the bestowal of the title of Prince of Wales on the Welsh-born Edward of Carnarvon in 1301 was more than a gesture ; it did go some way towards reconciling the Welsh to the direct rule of the English Crown. The Statute of Wales contained one other feature of the first importance, namely, the virtual substitution of English criminal law for the laws of Hywel Dda. Thus, the kindred-group was no longer to be responsible for doing justice upon its own members. It still retained the function of presenting members who had committed offences to the appropriate authority ; but even in this restricted sphere, its responsibility was practically submerged with that of the commote, which in this respect was brought into line with the English hundred. But Welsh law and custom were not wholly abolished : " civil law ", it has been said, " remained essentially Welsh ".[3] The chief changes lay in administration, for

---

[1] Hence it is often called the Statute of Rhuddlan.
[2] Hilda Johnstone, *Edward of Carnarvon* (1946), 6-7.
[3] Powicke, *The Thirteenth Century*, 437.

the new bailiffs, sheriffs, shire courts and regional Justiciars represented a large measure of anglicisation.

Before it was possible to make Edward of Carnarvon Prince of Wales, the peace of 1284 had been challenged by three disturbances on Welsh soil, two of them serious. In 1287, Rhys ap Maredudd, having supported Edward I loyally in his second Welsh war, broke into open revolt. His career had been played on a smaller stage than that filled by Llywelyn ap Gruffydd, but he had enough pride, as a descendant of the great Lord Rhys, to wish to cut a respectable figure upon it. It irked him to be summoned to plead a suit in the shire court of Carmarthen, and it was mortifying that what he considered to be his rightful claim to the castle of Dynevor, the ancient seat of the rulers of Deheubarth, had been rejected by the king. The flame of his rebellion burned fiercely but was soon extinguished. At first the Justiciar Robert Tibetot was able to keep it in check, largely with the forces already available to him in South Wales. Rhys was now to pay for his loyalty to the English side during the greater part of the Edwardian campaigns, for few of the Welsh outside his own lordships in the Towy valley and Emlyn came out in his support. Indeed, when the Earl of Cornwall (acting as regent in the king's absence in Gascony) gathered an army at the end of the summer, it included considerable numbers of Welsh infantry from the north, in addition to troops from the marches and the English midlands. Rhys's castle of Dryslwyn was captured early in September, after a huge siege-engine, which required some forty to sixty oxen to haul it, had been set to work lobbing heavy stones at the walls. The revolt had crumbled before the end of the year, thongh Rhys was at large until 1291, when he was taken to the king at York and executed.

There was a graver danger to Edward and to the peace of his realm in a private war which flared up in 1290 between the earls of Hereford and Gloucester. Gloucester's reputation had suffered seriously in the Welsh wars ; Hereford had some reason to feel aggrieved in the fact that when some of his own tenants in Brecknock joined Rhys's rebellion, it was Gloucester who was ordered to take action against them. The immediate cause of the quarrel was a dispute over grazing rights in the wild, mountainous country of the Brecon Beacons, which formed the march between Brecknock and Glamorgan. There is little doubt that the wayward and impulsive

Gloucester was the aggressor in this affair. His men certainly continued to ravage Hereford's lands in defiance of a royal prohibition. Gloucester took his stand as a marcher lord, objecting that the king's writ did not run in Glamorgan, and that in waging private war and seizing for himself a third share of the booty taken from Hereford's men he was merely observing the accepted custom of the Welsh marches.

The king intervened personally in the autumn of 1291, at the end of a remarkable display of patience. On September 29th a full meeting of the Great Council was summoned to Abergavenny, at the entrance to Brecknock. It had before it evidence on the facts of the dispute supplied by a powerful judicial commission which had sat at Llanthew near Brecon in the previous March. J. E. Morris and, more recently, Sir Maurice Powicke have emphasised the importance of the affair as a test case.[1] The judges at Llanthew had found marcher opinion ranged almost solidly against the king's claim to adjudge a dispute between barons of the march unless the business were conducted in accordance with the customs of those parts. The judges replied that, " in the common interest ", the king through his prerogative authority was in many cases above the laws and customs in use within his realm. The presence of the king himself sitting in Parliament at Abergavenny impressed even upon the stubborn lords of the march his determination to exercise his supreme judicial authority. After a thorough hearing, the Parliament declared both earls guilty of contempt of court and of contumaciously disobeying the royal prohibition on private war. Formal sentence was given at the next Parliament, which met at Westminster in January, 1292. The earls were committed to prison—from which they were quickly released after paying fines—and condemned to lose their privileges in Glamorgan and Brecknock. Their very lands were confiscated, though only temporarily. It was a signal humiliation. Gloucester was the king's son-in-law, one of the greatest lay magnates of the realm, who twenty-seven years before had actually ruled England as de Montfort's colleague. But for his defection from de Montfort, Edward might never have been able to restore his father to power. Hereford was also an extremely influential baron. As Constable he had done his duty ably in the Welsh wars, and in his dispute with Gloucester he had been the innocent party.

[1] *Welsh Wars of Edward I*, 220-39 ; *The Thirteenth Century*, 329-30.

He had, in fact, some grounds for complaint at his sentence, and his resentment was made dramatically evident a few years later. It was a dangerous moment for Edward I, yet it was vitally important for the monarchy that on this occasion his will should prevail. Now that Wales had been subdued, the marcher lords must not be allowed to become a law unto themselves, and take the place of the princes of Gwynedd and Deheubarth. Now that defence against the Welsh could be conducted within Welsh territory, there was no reason for the marcher lords to be treated differently from the rest of the English baronage.

The purely Welsh rising of 1294 differed in kind from the quarrel of Gloucester and Hereford, and was more intense and widespread than the revolt of Rhys ap Maredudd. It took the government entirely by surprise and arose simultaneously in Gwynedd and West Wales, and in Brecknock and Glamorgan, where the humbling of the earls may have taught the native Welsh a lesson which the king had not intended. Edward, in 1294, was busy with plans for a great war against Philip IV of France, to be fought on two fronts, Gascony and Flanders. As part of these plans he had summoned Scots and Welsh to his service. Arms had been distributed among the Welsh before they had left their native districts. Instead of using them against the king's enemies, they rallied to the young noblemen of their own race who had protested against compulsory military service across the Channel. At first the chief leader was a certain Maelgwn, about whom little is known. He roused the men of West Wales and captured Cardigan castle, which the king had held successfully in the war of 1282-3. The other southern leaders are likewise known only by their names. Morgan brought out the Earl of Gloucester's tenants in Glamorgan, Cynan those of Hereford and John Giffard in Brecknock and Builth. But the greatest danger lay in the north. Here the leading spirit was Madog ap Llywelyn, the scion of an ancient but dispossessed family of Merioneth. The rising was timed for the day (September 30th) on which the Welsh levies had been summoned to Shrewsbury to go to France. Bere and Denbigh were attacked, while—greatest achievement of all !—Carnarvon itself was captured and destroyed.

Some of the king's forces had already sailed for Gascony, but the main strength of his army was still in England and was turned against the Welsh with astonishing promptitude. For the third time in less than twenty years, the king marched from Chester into North Wales. Other bases were Cardiff (under the Earl of Gloucester), Brecon, and Montgomery, where a strong force of cavalry and archers was operating under the Earl of Warwick, William de Beauchamp. Edward's army contained a preponderance of infantry. It moved first into the Vale of Clwyd, and then to the coast, arriving at Aberconway in time to keep the Christmas feast there. It is odd that so little is known in detail about Edward's movements during the next few weeks. All that is certain is that in January, 1295, he pushed on from the Conway towards Bangor, and that while his soldiers and baggage train were strung out along the narrow coast road the Welsh laid a brilliant ambush and destroyed the army's food and equipment. The setback was severe enough to bring the king's winter campaign to an end. Madog was able to divert his forces to mid-Wales. Here, however, he met with disaster. It seems that his men had raided across the Severn in the region between Oswestry and Shrewsbury, and were promptly pursued as they returned to Wales by the Earl of Warwick. The earl overtook them (March 5th) while they were halted in the small plain of Maes Moydog,[1] about a mile and a half north of Castell Caereinion (Montgomeryshire). The English attacked in the dark, drawn up in a line in which one crossbowman alternated with two mounted men-at-arms. The Welsh dug the butts of their spears into the ground to turn aside the cavalry charge, but were overwhelmed by the massive fire of the crossbows. Very soon the remnant of Madog's force was fleeing westward, and many were drowned in the Vyrnwy and Banwy rivers, swollen after months of rain. The fight at Maes Moydog ended the rebellion. During the last twelve years of his reign, Edward I was troubled by no more resistance from the Welsh. Whether they were reconciled to his rule is hard to say. There was no national rising of the Welsh in the century which divided Madog ap Llywelyn from Owen Glendower. But we should remember that the system of massive fortresses which Edward I erected in Wales held the country in an iron grip.

The Welsh wars precipitated a revolution in English military

[1] The locality of the battle has been established by J. G. Edwards in *E.H.R.*, xlvi (1931), 262-5 ; see also, for the whole campaign, the same writer's article, *ibid.* xxxix (1924), 1-12.

organisation.[1]   The war of 1277 made use mainly of the accustomed feudal levies, and they were found wanting.   By a process which we have seen at work already in the reigns of Richard I and John, the feudal host had been reduced in effective strength to only a fraction of the total which, nominally at least, had been available to Henry I or Henry II.   The change may have been less apparent than we suppose, for the Conqueror and his twelfth-century successors could never have hoped or wished to call out for one campaign every one of the 5,000 or 6,000 knights whose service was owed by the conditions of their tenure.   But there is no question that the cost of fully-equipped knights rose steadily in the thirteenth century and outstripped the rise in the value of the land assigned for their maintenance.   Weapons were more elaborate, and much heavier protective armour made necessary a stronger, more expensive *destrier*, or charger, which in 1277 might cost from 60 to 120 marks to buy, as well as being costly to feed.   Consequently, when the king called out the feudal host, he obtained not an army of several thousand heavy-armed cavalry but, instead, a few hundred barons and knights equipped at the full rate, each of whom would bring with him two or three troopers or " serjeants-at-arms ".   These men were more lightly armed and armoured, and their weaker horses were protected not by chain-mail but merely by coats of boiled leather.

The upper ranks of this small but up-to-date cavalry force, the earls and greater barons (especially, in a Welsh war, the marcher lords), served for no pay, as their ancestors had been bound to do, at least for the customary forty days.   But already in 1277 the king had realised that more efficient service could be obtained if he contracted to pay men for a definite term, even those who owed him feudal service.   Such men were not mercenaries in the old sense, but military vassals whom the king had invited to serve " at his wages " in order to fight a particular war or campaign.   As Morris has written, " pay produces discipline, and naturally leads to a subordination of commands ".   The Edwardian armies of 1282-3 were better organised than in 1277 largely because a higher proportion were under contract to fight for pay.   The feudal host was still summoned in the old way, but in fact the greater part of the

[1] A clear account of this revolution is given by J. E. Morris in his *Welsh Wars of Edward I*, Chapter II.

feudal levies became paid troops, grouped into squadrons commanded by " bannerets ", normally distinguished tenants-in-chief, whose authority was symbolised by the right to fly a square banner. In addition to the feudal host transformed in this manner, large numbers of infantry were also employed, especially in 1282-3 and 1294-5. Here again there were improvements. The levies of free men from the various shires were not only paid wages—some form of payment had doubtless long been customary—but were divided into battalions of 1,000, companies of 100, and lesser groups of 20, each under distinct commanders. The chief weapons of the infantry were the spear and the long-bow, a powerful weapon drawn across the body, which in Edward I's reign was at last replacing the relatively feeble short-bow drawn into the chest. It is interesting to notice a close relationship between the arena of war and the shires called upon to provide infantry service. In the Welsh wars the heaviest burden fell upon the march counties from Gloucestershire to Lancashire. Contributions were also demanded from Nottinghamshire and Derbyshire, probably (as Morris suggested) because of the proficiency of the Sherwood Forest men at poaching. Finally, there were the specialist crossbowmen, recruited almost entirely from Gascony and Ponthieu. Because it required long training to use their weapon effectively, the crossbowmen were necessarily professional soldiers in receipt of high wages (6*d.* a day, or as much as an eighth of the daily pay of a banneret).

The generalship of Edward I personally is beyond doubt, and he was well served in this capacity by several of his barons and officials, notably Otto of Granson, the Earl of Warwick and Robert Tibetot. It is in his wars in Wales that the king's sense of strategy and his coolness in emergencies can be seen at their best. Their historian has told us that the Welsh wars taught three lessons of fundamental importance. The first was the need for command of the sea ; it is clear, indeed, that Edward already understood this in 1277. Secondly, the value of supplementing and to a large extent replacing the old feudal host by a system of paid troops became more and more apparent

---

MAP IX. ENGLAND AND WALES IN THE THIRTEENTH CENTURY
(*see opposite page*).

Chief towns and ports are shown, and also the road system, based on the Gough map of *circa* 1300. The Welsh shires are shown as existing after the Statute of Wales, 1284. The letter (C) denotes Cinque Port.

MAP IX

365

from 1282 onward. Finally, we must note the lesson of Maes Moydog, the tactical advantage of interspersing archers among cavalry in open battle. All three lessons were applied in the war against Scotland.

We may doubt whether the Edwardian conquest of Wales would strike the imagination as forcefully as it does had it not been rounded off, with a thoroughness never achieved in Gascony or Scotland, by an elaborate system of castles and new towns. Winning the war had not been cheap : in 1282-3, the cost of troops alone came to over £60,000. It was equally certain that no expense would be spared to keep the peace. We have noted that in the spring of 1278 new stone castles had begun to rise at Rhuddlan and Flint, while two others, Aberystwyth and Builth, were commenced in the course of the same year. Conway, which was building from March, 1283 until 1293, and the contemporary castles at Carnarvon and Harlech, all formed part of the general pacification after the overthrow of Llywelyn and David. Beaumaris in Anglesey, which of all the Welsh castles shows perhaps the most consummate architectural mastery, belongs to the last phase of Edwardian building. It was begun in 1295 after Madog's revolt had been suppressed. Some idea of its scale may be grasped from the fact that at one time 400 masons, 200 quarrymen, 30 smiths and carpenters and some 2,000 unskilled labourers were employed on the work, and that their equipment included 160 carts and wagons and 30 boats to carry stone and sea-coal. The novelty of these castles consisted partly in the enormous scale of their conception, but more especially in the bold abandonment of the old motte-and-bailey lay-out, even in its more developed form, and the substitution of a symmetrical plan of concentric " curtain walls " defended at regular intervals by stout towers, whose loop-holes were directed in such a way that the archers within could cover all the approaches to the castle at once. The concentric plan is well seen at Caerphilly, and at one time this Glamorgan castle was thought to be the earliest example of the type known. But it seems more probable that in its final form Caerphilly is later than the great castles of the north. All the northern castles were conceived as joint military and urban settlements. Adjacent to each castle there was founded a " free borough ", peopled by incoming English merchants, who were usually granted the liberties of Hereford. Taken together, they represent the greatest piece of urban and commercial enterprise in medieval Wales.

The symmetrical perfection of their design and the fineness and sharp precision of their execution place the Edwardian castles of Wales in a different class from any secular buildings constructed in Britain before their time, or for long afterwards. It is owing principally to the painstaking and wide-ranging researches of Mr. A. J. Taylor [1] that we are able at last to give proper credit for these works of genius to a Savoyard master-mason, James of St. George, who had gained his first experience of large-scale building by assisting his father on the new (fortified) town of Yverdon, at the head of Lake Neuchâtel. Master James of St. George combined, as was customary in medieval times, the functions of architect or designer with those of master builder. He is known to have been responsible for Flint, Rhuddlan, Aberystwyth, Conway, Harlech, and Beaumaris. He can be connected with Builth and Denbigh, and with the re-fitting of Dolwyddelan. Carnarvon castle, impressive though it is, differs too markedly in design from the rest to be assigned confidently to the same architect. We should remember that Edward I employed a number of other excellent master masons on his Welsh projects, among them Master Walter of Hereford. But it is thought that the town wall of Carnarvon, itself a superb piece of design and workmanship, may have been constructed by St. George. In the year when Carnarvon was begun (1285), Master James was already described as " master of the king's works in Wales ", and from 1290 he held along with this appointment the important post of Constable of Harlech castle. His exceptionally high regular wages and the scale of his other rewards, among them a manor in England, are clear proof of the esteem in which he was held by the king, who, with the aid of his specialist knowledge, " was enabled to create within a single quarter of a century, a group of castles and castellated boroughs hardly surpassed by any comparable group of buildings in Europe ".[2]

---

[1] " Master James of St. George ", *E.H.R.*, lxv (1950), 433-57. J. E. Morris was aware that James of St. George was the architect of several of the Welsh castles, though he did not know of his Savoyard origin. It is almost certain that Master James came from St. Georges-d'Esperanche (dép. Isère, France).

[2] Taylor, *op. cit.* 452.

CHAPTER XX

THE FRENCH WAR AND THE STRUGGLE FOR
THE CHARTERS

1. *Gascony and the Flemish Alliance*

IN the twelfth and thirteenth centuries, the seas round the coast of
Britain and France formed a wild border region. It was not wholly
lawless, but what law there was parodied, in cruder and starker
fashion, the relatively civilised custom of the land. Piracy and other
kinds of violence were endemic. They gave added danger—as though
more were needed—to the inevitable hazards of navigating coasts un-
charted save in a pilot's memory and to the peril of sudden storms from
which, even in summer, the tiny ships of that age were never free.

We must presume that for men of the time the rewards of
seafaring matched these dangers. The seaport towns of southern
England, from Bristol round to East Anglia, grew rich on the trade
in wine from Normandy, the Loire valley and, above all, Gascony.
The east coast ports naturally tended to concentrate on the equally
lucrative business of exporting wool and leather from England to
Flanders and Brabant. Trading was composed of a great number of
ventures on the part of individuals and small groups. A single
merchant, or perhaps a group of merchants, might own a ship and
appoint a master for her. The master would sign on a crew of
seamen, to whom wages would be paid at an agreed rate (usually
according to distance). But a considerable part of the ship's
company would consist of men who joined at their own expense, had
some share in her main cargo, and would normally expect to do some
trading on their own account in whatever ports the ship visited. In
these circumstances, it is not surprising that there was much scope
for individual enterprise—and selfishness—and that discipline was
either lax or rough-and-ready. The " Laws of Oléron ",[1] the

[1] Oléron is an island in the Bay of Biscay, off the mouth of the Charente,
a common place of shelter and assembly for shipping.

customs followed by merchants and seamen engaged in the Bordeaux trade, dating in their earliest form from *c.* 1200, contain rules for a crude but perhaps effective discipline. For example, " if the master smite any of the mariners, the mariner ought to abide the first buffet, be it with fist or flat with his hand, but if he smite any more he may defend himself ; and if a mariner smite the master, he must pay five shillings or else lose his fist, at his own choice ".[1] Or again, a ship's company was free to execute a pilot whose negligence had caused the loss of their ship, if he could not pay compensation in full. Pilotage was necessary over long distances because the art of navigation was so imperfect. Wherever possible, ships steered on " courses "— from one well-known landfall to another—divided into " kennings ", that is, the distance between two headlands or other landmarks within sight of each other. A ship sailing from Bordeaux to the south coast of England had local pilotage as far as Guernsey, and to Scotland as far as Yarmouth, paid for by the Bordeaux merchants.

The seafaring community displayed the caution common to men who are constantly faced by great risks. To this apparent contradiction, we should add another. The merchants were both gregarious and torn by rivalry, often intensely bitter, which made itself felt between nations, regions, groups of ports, even between ports which were neighbours to one another. This hostility became more serious during the thirteenth century both because the volume of trade expanded enormously and because the loss of Normandy made the Channel a frontier dividing unfriendly monarchies. Gascony, however, was still ruled by the English Crown and was tied to England not only by the legal bond of vassalage but by a commercial link in which many Englishmen and the majority of Gascons had a direct interest. Yet Gascony was part of the duchy of Aquitaine, and the duchy was a fief held of the King of France, a fief, moreover, to which the French kings of the late thirteenth century were paying ever closer attention.

We should remember these circumstances when we try to understand why it was that a fierce sea battle in 1293 inaugurated a new phase in Anglo-French relations. For the first time in over a generation war took the place of peace. For the next forty years relations remained bad or actually grew worse, until in the fourth decade of the fourteenth century the English king's military activity

[1] *Black Book of the Admiralty*, ed. Sir Travers Twiss, i. 104-5.

south of the Channel became a full-scale war between England and France which lasted, with long intervals of truce, for more than a century. In a sense, what we call the " Hundred Years' War " began on May 15th, 1293, when a fleet composed of ships from the Cinque Ports and from Bayonne in Gascony engaged the merchantmen of Normandy and Poitou off Cape Saint-Mathieu (Mahé), in the extreme west of Brittany. The Normans were alleged to have flown the red pennant or *baucan*, indicating that no quarter need be given or expected. After breaking up their fleet with much loss, the Gascon and English mariners sacked the town of La Rochelle. The King of France, Philip IV, at once demanded the arrest of the Gascon offenders and full compensation for the injuries inflicted on his merchants. Edward I claimed that his own subjects had only acted in accordance with maritime custom, and that the defeat had been suffered " in fair fight ". But the influential lawyers in the French royal council " welcomed the opportunity to follow up the legal penetration of the duchy of Aquitaine in the *parlement* of Paris by its annexation to the French Crown ".[1] Edward was therefore summoned to Paris for October 27th, to answer the complaint against him, and when he refused was threatened with the loss of the duchy. Negotiations followed, conducted on the English side by the king's brother, Edmund of Lancaster. He was deceived by the French negotiators into believing that if Gascony were handed over to the Constable of France the " occupation " would be merely temporary and nominal, and that the agreement of Edward (a widower since the death of Eleanor of Castile in November, 1290) to marry Philip's sister Margaret would cancel the sentence of confiscation. Quite the opposite was true. On May 19th, 1294, Edward I was formally condemned to lose his fief, and French troops and administrators proceeded to take over the government of Gascony.

All this was the harder for Edward I to bear because since his accession he had devoted much time and thought to Gascony and its problems. In 1273-4 he had tried to pacify the obstreperous Viscount of Béarn, and he had embarked on an enquiry into ducal and other customs which compared with the English Quo Waranto inquests. In the treaty of Amiens (1279) with Philip III, and in the second treaty of Paris (1286) with his son, Philip IV, Edward had

[1] F. M. Powicke, *The Thirteenth Century*, 646.

successfully pressed his claim under the first treaty of Paris (1259) for the lands which were due to pass to him at the death of Count Alphonse of Poitou, which took place in 1271. Moreover, the English king freely employed his ablest and most confidential counsellors in Gascon affairs, e.g. Robert Burnell the Chancellor and the Savoyards, Otto of Granson and John of Grilly, in 1278, when Gaston of Béarn was finally reconciled and ceased to make a nuisance of himself.

Nor did the king spare himself in the government of Gascony. After his visit to Paris to conclude the treaty of 1286, he spent nearly the whole of the next three years in the duchy. This prolonged sojourn culminated in the issue (1289) of a comprehensive set of ordinances regulating Gascon administration. The duties of the two chief ducal offices, the Seneschal of Gascony and the Constable of Bordeaux, were clearly defined. The Seneschal (John of Grilly, 1279-87, succeeded by an Englishman, John St. John) was in general charge of administration and the dispensing of justice. He must hold regular assizes in every division of the duchy, and he was given a large staff of subordinate officials, including a deputy or " subseneschal " and trained legal advisers to attend the judicial sessions. The Constable was in origin a military commander, and was responsible for the upkeep and defence of the duke's castles. But in the late thirteenth century his duties were chiefly fiscal. He received and accounted for the ducal revenues, some £17,000 a year, of which the wine custom of Bordeaux formed by far the greatest part. Like the Seneschal, the Constable was assisted by various permanent subordinates ; and both officers were paid fixed and generous salaries, allowed out of the Bordeaux customs.

One striking feature of Edwardian rule in Aquitaine was the foundation of over 100 " new towns ", and the active conversion from waste to intensive cultivation with which this urban development was closely connected. The towns are usually known collectively as *bastides*. The word *bastide* means an isolated fortress, and its use here suggests that Edward I was busy repeating in Gascony on a larger scale what Richard I had done in the Norman Vexin a century earlier. But it would be nearer the truth to regard the *bastides* primarily as new urban communities in which colonies of agriculturists, wine-growers and traders were placed, often with the reluctant agreement or downright hostility of local potentates.

The strangers would need some rudimentary protection, a ditch and rampart of earth. But the *bastides* located under or within a first-class military fortification formed a minority of the whole. The main purpose of these new towns was to meet a demand for the opening up of forest and other waste ground so that more corn and vines could be cultivated. They cannot therefore be regarded as equivalent in every respect to the new boroughs of Wales, which were an integral part of a system of military occupation and defence. But clearly the same combination of method and desire for development underlay both enterprises.

In Aquitaine as in Wales, the problem of appeals from lower to higher courts was unsolved and explosive. It was more complicated in Aquitaine because the duchy was both a part of France (though in a manner as yet undefined) and joined to the English Crown. For Gascons, there was a choice of supreme lords and ultimate courts of appeal, a choice between the *parlement* of Paris and the parliaments of Edward I. The French kings, especially Philip IV (1285-1315), lost no opportunity of applying the doctrine that Gascony was simply a fief like any other, held by a vassal who merely happened elsewhere to be an independent king. It followed that all subjects of the duke were subjects of the French Crown, and if they failed to get justice from the duke their next recourse should be to the court at Paris. At first Edward did not deny this argument in principle, but he objected to the manner in which it was applied in practice by the French king's agents and to their constant interference in Gascon affairs. At a later stage, however, Edward seems to have given some encouragement to a counter-principle, too subtle to carry much weight, that since Aquitaine had before 1259 been an " allod ", that is an estate held freely under no conditions of service whatever, the first treaty of Paris could not have turned the duchy into a true fief, but merely signified the duke's personal vassalage in respect of Aquitaine.[1]

It was with a clear conscience and a strong conviction of his right that Edward I, in the early summer of 1294, decided to oppose by force the French occupation of Gascony. He formally " defied " King Philip in June, and summoned the feudal host for service overseas in September. The bulk of Edward's military service on this occasion was obtained by recruiting paid knights and troopers

[1] Powicke, *op. cit.* 313.

by means of individual contracts with prominent barons, and infantry through the agency of special " commissioners of array ", substantial local landowners who had the whole responsibility of raising men in their shires or districts. Some at least of the money required to pay for this force was obtained by taking fines from those feudatories who preferred to pay money rather than serve personally or have the trouble of finding others to serve on their behalf. As we have seen, the Welsh revolt forced the king to abandon his plan for a full-scale campaign in Gascony. John of Brittany, his nephew and one of his most loyal adherents,[1] was able to take a limited number of troops to Gascony in October to join forces with John St. John. But not until 1296, when Edmund of Lancaster and the Earl of Lincoln sailed to Aquitaine, was any substantial army added to the inadequate forces on the spot, and even then no headway was made. The English were faced by determined and capable opponents. The French commanders were the king's brother, Charles of Valois, and Robert, Count of Artois, a tough and experienced warrior who had seen much service in Tunis, Sicily and Navarre. In the campaigns of 1295 and 1296 the French had much the best of the fighting, and this in spite of the fact that Gascon feeling was overwhelmingly on the side of Edward I. By the time a truce was reached in October, 1297,[2] the English hold on Gascony had been reduced to Blaye and Bourg, north of the Gironde, and the district around Bayonne in the far south.

It was part of Edward's strategy to revive the policy of encircling alliances used with varying success by Richard I and John. Treaties, inevitably accompanied by generous cash subsidies, were made in 1294 and 1295 to secure the actual assistance or the friendly neutrality of the counts of Bar, Brabant, Gelderland and Holland, all rulers who held their counties as fiefs of the Empire. The King of Germany himself, Adolf of Nassau,[3] was brought into the scheme of alliances in August, 1294. He proved a broken reed. His position in Germany was extremely insecure, and in August, 1297, when his help would have been most useful, he was compelled to withdraw from his undertaking to give military support. Alliances with these

[1] He was the second son of John, Duke of Brittany (1285-1305), and great-grandson of Peter Mauclerc, for whom see above, p. 265.

[2] See below, p. 381.

[3] Adolf was never crowned emperor, and in 1298 fell in battle against his rival, Albert of Habsburg.

imperial principalities formed a prudent security measure : it was of much greater moment for Edward I to detach the Count of Flanders from his liege lord the King of France. In principle this was not difficult, for the count, Guy of Dampierre, though a Frenchman on his father's side, had been scurvily treated by Philip IV and was at odds with his nephew the Count of Hainault who was King Philip's protégé. But Count Guy was not very forceful nor independent, and in fact it was not until January, 1297, that a French invasion of western Flanders prompted him to make a firm alliance with the English king. The main conditions were that Edward of Carnarvon should marry the count's younger daughter Isabella (his elder daughter was a prisoner of Philip IV), that the count should receive a large subsidy, and that an Anglo-Flemish military effort, at least as substantial as any planned for Gascony, should be made against Philip in Flanders.

Two further features of this system of Netherlands alliances call for notice. First, it was linked by Edward I to a strategic seizure of the entire English wool trade. Wool exports were directed into certain fixed channels in order both to provide the Crown with the maximum revenue and to discomfit its enemies. Thus English wardrobe officials were given a general oversight of the trade, and all wool must be exported through a single appointed port overseas, at first Dordrecht in Holland, afterwards (1297) Mechlin, and then Antwerp, both in Brabant. Wardrobe control made difficult any evasion of the 1294 *maletolt* of 40s. per sack,[1] and the single export channel ensured that, unless it were smuggled, wool would not get through to the wealthy merchants of Ypres, Ghent and Bruges who, since they were at feud with their count, took the part of King Philip. Secondly, the alliance with Flanders, which amounted to the seduction of a vassal from his lawful lord, brought about a change in papal opinion, and perhaps in clerical opinion generally, on the righteousness of Edward's cause. As the Pope, Boniface VIII, wrote later, after Edward had gone to Flanders, " if he had come into Gascony, which is his own land, to defend or recover it, that would have been a different matter ". Today, Edward's realism strikes us as mere common sense ; but the Pope's view that a war should be confined to the area of the dispute which originated it was closer to the spirit of the thirteenth century.

[1] See below, p. 378.

2. *The Struggle for the Charters*

By 1297, King Edward had little to show for three years' warfare except a gigantic and steadily mounting bill for its cost. It has been reckoned that the Gascon war cost over £400,000. It was therefore more than four times as expensive as the most serious of the Welsh wars, in 1282-3, even when the cost of the Welsh castles is included. Gascony, it is true, if only it could be recovered, might pay a large share towards its own defence : the king's revenues in Wales, by contrast, barely paid the wages of his garrisons. Nevertheless, the greater part of the expense, including the huge subsidies to Flanders and the rest, must be borne by England. The king and his realm were in complete agreement on the necessity of resisting the encroachments of Philip IV. It is therefore all the more instructive to see how the king's financial and military demands, growing steadily more burdensome from 1294, brought forth from a fundamentally co-operative community of the realm a constitutional movement similar in type to those which had aimed at restraining King John and King Henry III.

The events of 1297 and after will be more readily understood if we bear in mind that the king had antagonised three distinct groups, the clergy, the merchants engaged in wool and leather export, and the lay landholders, barons and gentry. We must also remember that open Scottish resistance to Edward I began in 1294, calling for an invasion of Scotland two years later and the establishment of an English garrison and administration under the Earl Warenne. All these factors were at work simultaneously, but for the sake of clarity it will be best to take them in order, reserving the Scottish question for the next chapter.

(1) *The Clergy.* During the thirteenth century, the clergy had had to accustom themselves to two main types of taxation, papal and royal. Both types were levied on income, with increasing frequency and at increasingly high rates. It is true that many of the higher clergy, the bishops, for example, and certain of the abbots and priors, were extremely wealthy, though we should remember that much of their wealth consisted of landed estates classed as secular baronies or fiefs and therefore subject to the full weight of secular taxation in aids, scutage and the like. Even so, their income from " spiritual " sources, tithes, prebends, dues payable by the diocesan laity and

375

clergy, was very considerable, and they could hardly expect it to be ignored by the Crown as a source of revenue. The lower clergy depended on spiritual sources for most of their income : tithes, parochial dues and customary offerings, such as " mortuaries " (that is, gifts left to their parish church by the deceased in order that prayers might be said for their souls), and occasional alms. Their prosperity was closely geared to that of the country as a whole, and they probably had better cause for grievance against the double burden of taxes paid to the Papacy and to the Crown ; though again we should remember that bishops and abbots had larger obligations of charity, and would normally be patronising expensive cathedral or monastic building projects. The lower clergy made no attempt to deny their duty to pay both papal and royal taxes, but protested that they were too heavy and levied too often.

Between 1274 and 1301 [1] the English clergy contributed to two major levies of papal taxation, each consisting of a tenth of income over six years. In the same period, the king obtained from them eight taxes, ranging from as little as a thirtieth to as much as a half of income. For clergy, as for laity, the years from 1294 to 1297 were the most burdensome. During the period 1291-7 the clergy were already paying annual tenths to the Pope, based on a fresh and higher valuation of their income. When, in the autumn of 1294, the king addressed the Convocation of Canterbury province and made the unprecedented demand for a half of clerical income assessed on this new valuation, there was consternation and a widespread attempt at resistance. The Dean of St. Paul's, William de Montfort, died of shock in the king's presence. The Church as a whole was without a strong leader, for Robert Winchelsey, Pecham's successor as archbishop, had been but newly consecrated in Rome and before he could return to England the prelates had agreed to the tax. The lower clergy's proctors followed suit only after being threatened with outlawry and being promised that benefices worth less than 10 marks ($£6$ 13s. 4d.) a year should be exempt. This huge tax should have brought the exchequer about $£105,000$, and it is known that within a year some 75 per cent. had been collected. Yet in November, 1295, despite Winchelsey's protests, the king successfully demanded a further tenth of income, this time from benefices worth only $£4$ and upwards.

[1] This account largely follows H. S. Deighton, " Clerical Taxation by Consent, 1279-1301 ", *E.H.R.*, lxviii (1953), 161-92.

These English clerical taxes to finance the war found an exact parallel in France. By 1296, Pope Boniface VIII, indignant at the spiritual wealth of two rich kingdoms being used for purely secular ends, was driven to declare, in the famous Bull *Clericis Laicos* (February 24th), that in no circumstances should the clergy pay taxes to lay rulers without papal permission. Neither Edward I nor Philip IV was prepared to tolerate such a categorical prohibition, though both realised that argument rather than force was required to turn the flank of the papal attack. The clergy themselves, faithful to their kings and noticeably nationalist in feeling, were by no means agreed on the wisdom of *Clericis Laicos*, and faced an acute crisis of divided loyalty. From this crisis the French clergy were released first. The Anglo-Flemish alliance of January, 1297, was a direct threat to Philip's realm, and in February the Pope sent a letter to the Archbishop of Rheims allowing that in " perilous necessity " the clergy might pay a tax to their king, and that the king should judge what constituted such necessity.

This did not solve the dilemma for the English clergy, who in any case knew nothing of the Pope's letter. In November, 1296, the clergy of Canterbury province assembled at Bury St. Edmunds where, at the same time, a lay Parliament was also in session. The king, having got a subsidy from the laymen, asked the clergy for a fifth, but they could not agree whether to grant a tax or not. A further meeting was held at St. Paul's at Christmas. Archbishop Winchelsey expounded the king's need, and also explained the effect of *Clericis Laicos*. He called on those present to give their decision clearly. It was decided to refuse the king's request. The king's answer was prompt and drastic. He placed the entire clergy outside his protection. The first writs to this effect were issued to the sheriffs on January 30th, 1297, and on the same day the Earl of Lincoln was soundly defeated by Robert of Artois at the *bastide* of Bellegarde, near Bayonne. The coincidence was not lost on Church chroniclers, but King Edward remained unmoved. He let it be known that the outlawry would be lifted if the clergy paid him a fine amounting to a fifth of their income, the precise figure which they had refused to give in taxation. If not, the outlawry would be made permanent.

During Lent, a number of individual clergymen in the southern province accepted these terms and paid their fines, while the entire northern province, mindful of the danger from Scotland, submitted as a body. A second meeting of the Canterbury clergy was held at St. Paul's on March 21st. Again Winchelsey made an impressive speech, but this time it indicated a significant withdrawal. Speaking for himself, he could not pay the tax in defiance of papal prohibition, nor the fine, which he regarded as mere equivocation. But he advised each individual clergyman to act according to his conscience. It was easier for an archbishop to defy outlawry than a humble parish priest; and he would not punish those who decided to submit. There followed a fairly general surrender of the clergy. Though it had cost him five months' struggle, the king had his tax. Moreover, in July the Primate heard of the Pope's modification of *Clericis Laicos* in respect of the French clergy, and his application of the doctrine of " perilous necessity ". The king was wisely conciliatory. He restored the archbishop's confiscated estates, and on July 14th, in Westminster Hall, he and the Primate were formally and publicly reconciled. Edward could now feel that one wing of the opposition had been virtually eliminated.

(2) *The Merchants.* The merchant community was in a much weaker bargaining position than Church or baronage because the greater part of overseas trade was in the hands of foreigners with whom the king could deal at will. Nevertheless, the native merchants did make some protest against the abuses of royal taxation. In July, 1294, they had granted the *maletolt* for two or three years, at the rate of 40s. per sack, instead of the " ancient " custom of 6s. 8d. In Lent, 1297, the king ordered that all wool belonging to foreign merchants should be seized and sold for his own use. His servants, unknown to their master, interpreted this order to include all those English traders rich enough to be exporting more than five sacks. These men were allowed to export up to five sacks after paying the *maletolt*, but all wool in excess of five sacks was seized. The native merchants, led apparently by one Thomas de Schelmingg of Sandwich, lodged an effective protest at this arbitrary decision by wardrobe officials. Having heard their complaint, the king agreed that the prise of wool should not affect English merchants as long as they paid the full 40s. customs duty. It was a notable minor victory over administrative sharp practice.[1] The wool trade apart, the townsmen tended in the matter of taxes to take their cue from the barons and

[1] G. O. Sayles, in *E.H.R.*, lxvii (1952), 543-7. Thomas may have taken his name from one of the places called Shelving not far from Sandwich.

knights, and in 1294, 1295 and 1296 granted a sixth, a seventh and an eighth of movables respectively. They had some cause for complaint in that their payment of higher fractions than the country landowners seems to have been an innovation of this period. There was, moreover, a tendency for the king to persuade London separately to pay a tax, and then expect all the other towns to follow suit.

(3) *The Landholders.* Here the king found a more intractable problem, and eventually met his match. From 1294 to 1296, he had been duly granted in Parliament taxes on movables of a tenth, an eleventh, and a twelfth. But in January, 1297, two great magnates, Humphrey de Bohun, Earl of Hereford and Constable, and Roger Bigod, Earl of Norfolk and Marshal, opposed the king's projected expedition to Flanders and refused to lead a second army to Gascony without him. The Marshal's place in battle was with the king, and in 1294 Edward had so offended Bigod by sending him to command in South Wales that he had promised not to repeat the solecism. Consequently, Bigod's refusal in 1297, as described in Walter of Hemingburgh's famous account, is not surprising.

" I shall go with you willingly, my lord king, riding before you in the van, as is my duty by hereditary right."
" And you shall also go with the rest, even without me ", said the king. To which the earl answered, " I am not bound nor is it my wish to undertake the expedition without you." Angered by this, the king is said to have exclaimed in these words, " By God, my lord earl, you shall go or hang ". " By the same oath, my lord king, I will neither go nor hang." [1]

Edward [2] thought he had the measure of his opponents, and went ahead with his plans for a summer campaign in Flanders. He judged his men well enough, but (as Professor Rothwell has said) he misjudged the situation. He made light of the new threat gathering in Scotland, and his belief that Philip IV could be effectively defeated in the Netherlands proved for some years to be unjustified. On July 16th, in a great ceremony in Westminster Hall, the reconciled archbishop and the other magnates of the land took the oath of fealty to the king's son and heir, Edward of Carnarvon. Hereford and Norfolk politically took the oath with the rest, but their opposition

[1] Ed. Hamilton, ii. 121 (my translation).
[2] For what follows, I have depended chiefly on J. G. Edwards, " Confirmatio Certarum and Baronial Grievances in 1297 ", *E.H.R.*, lviii (1943) ; H. Rothwel " The Confirmation of the Charters, 1297 ", *ibid.* lx (1945) ; and V. H. Galbraith, *Studies in the Public Records*, 143-50.

had in fact hardened during the spring and early summer, and they now cast aspersions on the value of the Count of Flanders as an ally. When the king let it be known that at the end of July a group of magnates meeting in his private chamber had granted a tax of an eighth and fifth of movables, that is, at the high rate of 1294, the two earls protested at the bar of the Exchequer (August 22nd). The grant, they said, had not been made by the community of the realm : it was a " tallage at will ", than which nothing was more calculated to reduce a man to servitude. If the eighth were taken, it would lead to the disinheritance of free men and their heirs. Indeed, it is clear that the government had some misgivings on the point, for the collectors of the tax were to be men who knew how to " speak to the people in the nicest and most polite manner possible ", and ten days before the earls' public protest the king found it necessary to issue a manifesto in the shires setting forth his own case.

The earls accompanied their personal protest by a schedule of grievances, the *Monstraunces*.[1] Its main points were as follows. Military service was not owed in Flanders, and in any case could not be performed, nor an aid offered, by men impoverished by tallages and prises. (It is to be noted that " tallage " was here used tendentiously to make the recent taxes on movables seem like the arbitrary feudal tallage on demesne.) The *maletolt* burdened the whole community (doubtless the merchant exporters passed some of its cost on to the grower by paying less). People had been arbitrarily deprived of their liberties, Magna Carta and the Forest Charter seriously infringed. Before he received official notice of the *Monstraunces*, the king's reaction to the opposition seems to have been to pretend that it was so irresponsible and unrepresentative as not to be worth considering. When the document was formally presented to him at Winchelsea, probably on August 20th, as he was about to embark for Flanders, his reply was that he could only give a proper answer with his whole Council, which was not then with him. In August the clergy had recovered from the outlawry and had again taken their stand on *Clericis Laicos*. The king read them a lecture, polite but firm, on the doctrine of " necessity ", which might have been produced by a canon lawyer. It seems to have been effective, for apparently the clergy, or some of them at least, agreed to pay a

[1] J. G. Edwards, *op. cit.*, favours this term (found in the French version of the grievances) and is followed by Professor Galbraith.

tax amounting to either a third of the value of their temporal property or else a fifth of their whole income.

Fortified by this and by the seizure on July 30th of 8,000 sacks of wool (to be paid for out of the eighth when it was collected), the king sailed for Flanders on August 22nd with what force he had been able to muster. Because of the refusal of the Constable and Marshal to perform their offices, the army had been organised by two lesser barons, more faithful to the king, Thomas of Berkeley and Geoffrey de Geneville. In cavalry, it consisted very largely of the king's own household troops, between 475 and 550 horse. By contrast " the maximum cavalry force supplied by the general body of his subjects amounted to 200 ".[1] There were also a few Irish knights and some Scotsmen, captured while in arms against the king and released on condition of fighting for him in Flanders. Besides the cavalry, there were over 7,000 infantry, mostly archers from Wales. Though J. E. Morris's description of the cavalry as " a very fair force " may be justifiable, it is easy to see why the Flemings, expecting their English ally to make a full-scale military effort, found Edward's army disappointingly inadequate. In view of the prosperity of the Flemish, who considered it a famine if the common folk were reduced to eating bread made from oatmeal, it is not surprising that Edward's motley and undisciplined collection of English, Scots, Irish and Welsh, the last bare-legged and quite unarmoured, was dismissed by a contemporary observer in Ghent as " an army of no great size ".[2] Instead of taking the offensive, Edward remained inactive at Ghent. On October 4th, he made the first of a series of truces with the French which was in fact to continue until the firmer agreement of Montreuil (June-August, 1299), as the result of which Edward married King Philip's sister Margaret.

Before there was any easing of Anglo-French hostility, and long before the king himself returned to England (March, 1298), the opposition at home had wrung from him what seemed for a time at least to be very notable concessions. By the *Monstrances* and by their protest against the unofficial eighth, the earls of Hereford and Norfolk had made themselves the spokesmen of a considerable movement, which the king and the council of regency tried to

[1] N. B. Lewis, " The English Forces in Flanders, 1297 ", in *Studies in Medieval History presented to F. M. Powicke*, 314.

[2] *Annals of Ghent* (ed. and transl. Hilda Johnstone, 1951), p. 4 ; cf. p. 28.

discredit by comparing it with the Montfortian rebellion of 1264-5. Sheriffs, constables and mayors were ordered to prevent and prohibit seditious " congregations and conventicles ". Despite the order, the earls and the barons who supported them did hold an unofficial " parliament " on September 21st, ominously enough at Northampton.[1] If the famous document known as *De Tallagio non Concedendo* (" Tallage not to be granted ") belongs authentically to 1297, it probably represents a baronial programme put forward at the Northampton assembly. If so, the opposition, or a part of it, had become extremely radical in its demands. No tallage or aid—that is, in effect, no taxation whatever—was to be levied without the consent of the great magnates, lay and ecclesiastical, and of the knights, burgesses and other free men of the realm. No prises were to be made without the consent of the owner of the goods seized. No duty was in future to be imposed on the sack of wool " by occasion or in the name of the *maletolt* ". *De Tallagio* is so uncompromisingly free from any reservations of royal prerogative, its negatives are so categorical, that it is impossible to believe that Edward I would have accepted it even as a basis for discussion. That it should ever have been thought to be a statute now seems quite fantastic, although counsel and judges in the Ship Money Case (1637), long before the days of critical historical scholarship in England, did in fact hold that belief. Whether or not *De Tallagio* represents the extreme views of the opposition, whether or not it is even the product of 1297, its far-reaching terms are markedly different from what the insurgent earls and their followers actually obtained.

The constitutional crisis was resolved—for a year or two, at least —in the Michaelmas Parliament. The mediation of Archbishop Winchelsey seems to have saved an ugly situation from becoming worse, for the opposition came to the Parliament with a force of armed men, and the council of regency for its part had summoned loyal barons and knights to appear under arms. By October 10th it had been found possible to reach a formal agreement. Letters patent were issued by Edward of Carnarvon (re-issued by his father at Ghent on November 5th) confirming Magna Carta and the Forest Charter " in all their points ". The Charters (themselves re-issued as letters-patent on October 12th) were to be sent to every cathedral church and read aloud to the people twice a year. The bishops were

---

[1] Above, p. 277.

to excommunicate any who refused to do this or infringed the terms of the Charters. The severe exactions of the last three years were not to be made a precedent, and in future such extraordinary taxation would depend on the " common assent of the whole realm ". The 40s. *maletolt* was rescinded. On the other hand, the ancient and accustomed aids (those taken on the accepted occasions) were reserved to the king, who also kept the right to levy the " ancient " custom of 6s. 8d. on the sack of wool granted in 1275.

Considered without reference to *De Tallagio*, the concessions of October 10th were very considerable, and met the grievances of July-August closely at nearly every point.[1] The king had been compelled to face unpleasant facts. It had proved impossible to collect the eighth, and this political setback had been followed by a serious military reverse ; on September 11th Warenne's army had been overwhelmed at Stirling Bridge and the English administration in Scotland had collapsed. Some concession was therefore unavoidable. We may judge that the opposition felt satisfied from the fact that in the Michaelmas Parliament a ninth of movables was granted in place of the discredited eighth.

The particular interest of the years from 1297 to 1307 lies in the fact that the extent of royal prerogative was under dispute while a popular king was on the throne, pursuing a popular nationalistic policy. What may still fairly be called the " accepted opinion " of historians, deriving ultimately from William Stubbs's *Constitutional History of England*, holds that the confirmation of the Charters of 1297 was sufficiently permanent and effective to solve the central problem of the constitution. This view has lately received a serious challenge.[2] Professor Rothwell has argued that the crucial event of the closing years of Edward I's reign was not the confirmation of the Charters in 1297, but the fact that between that date and 1307 the opposition to the Crown realised that the Charters, even with the additions of 1297, were insufficient to control royal prerogative. Thus, by 1311, in Dr. Rothwell's expressive phrase, " the Charters remain in the pharmacopoeia, but they are no longer the sovereign remedy ".

---

[1] This is shown clearly by Professor Edwards, *op. cit.* 162-8.
[2] H. Rothwell, " Edward I and the Struggle for the Charters, 1297-1305 ", in *Studies in Medieval History presented to F. M. Powicke*, 319-32.

Now there is no question that the political atmosphere of England changed for the worse in 1297. Much of the baronage remained unco-operative, even recalcitrant, in face of the Scottish danger. Yet baronial leadership was weakened and events south of the Channel took a turn definitely favourable to Edward I. The Earl of Hereford died in 1298 and we have already seen how his young son and the Earl of Norfolk, who had been one of the opposition leaders in 1297, became more dependent on the Crown in 1302, surrendering their estates and receiving them back as grants for life.[1] On July 11th, 1302, the cavalry of France, under the renowned Robert of Artois, was cut to pieces at Courtrai by "the weavers, fullers, and the common folk and foot soldiers of Flanders ", Count Robert and many other French notables being killed.[2] This altogether unexpected reverse made Philip IV ready to negotiate, and in May, 1303, the third treaty of Paris secured a peace, albeit uneasy, for some twenty years. Gascony was restored to Edward I as a fief under the terms of the treaty of 1259, and was made over to his son Edward, who at the same time received Philip IV's daughter Isabella in marriage.

Removal of the French threat meant that Edward I could try to " live of his own " instead of raising taxes. He undertook to do so, indeed, as early as 1298, but the war with the Scots imposed such a strain on this laudable intention that living of his own continued to mean the taking of prises, often in the most arbitrary manner. In 1299 the king explicitly went back on his promise to keep the Forest Charter. As a result the magnates in the especially full Easter Parliament of 1300 compelled the re-issue of Magna Carta and the Forest Charter not in the form of mere letters-patent (as in 1297) but in solemn charter form with an impressive array of witnesses, including eleven prelates, eight earls, and twenty-two major barons. At the same time, the king was forced to accept twenty "Articles upon the Charters " (*Articuli super Cartas*). These provided, among other things, that three " good men ", knights or others, were to be elected in every shire, fully empowered by the Crown to act as justices to hear and determine complaints of the infringement of the Charters. The jurisdiction of the Steward and the Marshal, largely

---

[1] Above, pp. 293–4.
[2] For accounts of this extremely important battle, see *Annals of Ghent*, 28-32, and Charles ffoulkes, " A Carved Flemish Chest ", in *Archaeologia*, lxv (1914), 113-28.

military in scope and consequently widely exercised in wartime, was to be severely restricted. Shires which wished to do so might elect their own sheriffs. Above all, prise was to be taken only by official purveyors of the king who could show a warrant bearing a royal seal. Less than a year later, the opposition in the Parliament of Lincoln (January, 1301) followed this up not only by a further demand that the Charters should be observed but by trying to ensure that royal ministers who had offended against the Charters should be brought to justice by auditors " not suspect in the eyes of the prelates, earls and barons". On this point Edward, having made some concessions, would not budge. " The lord king ", he answered, " is willing to provide a remedy, but not by such auditors ". He was equally obdurate in the matter of alleged infringements of the Forest Charter.

These parliaments of 1300 and 1301, in which the concessions of 1297 were tacitly ignored, Dr. Rothwell believes to have marked the turning point. The Articles upon the Charters had concluded by saving the right of the Crown, and prise became merely a question of the misuse of the prerogative and was no longer challenged in principle. In 1303 the king defied the spirit though not the letter of the confirmation of 1297 by negotiating a new custom with the foreign merchants. He would have broken the letter also by a similar arrangement with the English merchants, but they stood firm. Two years later, he obtained a Bull from Pope Clement V which released him from his obligations of 1297 altogether, though it must be added that he never acted on this dispensation. Yet far from being finally subdued, the baronage entered upon the next reign in a truculent and suspicious mood, armed with a freshly-composed and more narrowly binding coronation oath for the new king, and very soon forcing upon him a constitutional programme which echoed, though it went much beyond, the Articles of 1300. The personality of Edward of Carnarvon will hardly by itself explain all these facts. The struggle fought in 1297 had given the baronage fresh assurance, but it had also forced the Crown into new interpretations of the prerogative. In consequence, the last decade of the reign of Edward I brought about no permanent constitutional settlement but provided nevertheless some very substantial precedents.

CHAPTER XXI

THE ANGLO-SCOTTISH WAR

WE have seen that the thirteenth century was an age of legal definition. It was inevitable that Anglo-Scottish relations should become
an object of this prevailing activity; it is only surprising that,
following Falaise (1174) and its cancellation (1189), the first serious
attempt to define them anew was not made for another hundred
years.

English and Scottish opinion differed on the meaning of the
homage performed by a king of Scotland to a king of England. The
Scots held that homage was due for lands held of the English Crown,
which apparently included Lothian. It was not owed for the kingship of Scotland. As much is clear from the following facts. In
1216, when Alexander II was supporting the Magna Carta barons
he did homage to Prince Louis of France, then regarded by the insurgents as prospective King of England, " for the land of Lothian".
In 1237 Alexander obtained the cancellation of the treaty made in
1212 between his father and King John, which he clearly felt to have
imposed too great a degree of submission upon the Scottish monarchy.
Thirdly, the Scots account of Alexander III's homage to Edward I
(October 29th, 1278) differs markedly from the English. According
to it, Alexander declared : " I become your man for the lands I hold
of you in the kingdom of England, for which I owe you homage ;
saving my kingdom." Then the Bishop of Norwich, William of
Middleton, said, " And be it saved to the King of England if he have
the right to homage for it." And the king speaking clearly answered,
" No one has a right to homage for my kingdom of Scotland save
God alone." This account receives some confirmation from the
further fact that before 1261 a petition is known to have been made
to the Papacy on behalf of King Alexander, seeking the right to
receive anointment.[1] It was felt that the absence of this rite from
the Scottish enthroning ceremony laid him and his ancestors open
to the charge of not being kings in the fullest sense.

[1] Marc Bloch, *Scot. Hist. Rev.*, xxiii (1926), 105-6.

It is equally clear that the English Crown pressed for recognition of its feudal superiority. The treaty of 1212 (though destroyed in 1237) must have borne this interpretation, and Henry III reserved his right to reconsider matters between the two kingdoms dealt with in 1212 but not in 1237, i.e. the question of superiority. The English version of what happened on October 29th, 1278,[1] simply states that Alexander III did homage to Edward I " against all men ", and that Edward reserved his right to speak of homage for the Scottish kingdom whenever he wished. That even on the English side there was a belief that the relationship of the Crowns was personal rather than territorial is suggested by a clause in the settlement which Simon de Montfort forced Henry III and his son to accept on March 8th, 1265. The king and his heir were to do their best to get the settlement accepted " throughout (*par*) Ireland and Gascony, by the King of Scotland, and throughout all the lands subject to the King of England ".[2]

The sudden death of Alexander III in 1286 made no immediate change in this ambiguous position, but it at once threatened Scotland with a political crisis more serious than that of 1255. The king's successor was his grand-daughter Margaret, the only child of Margaret of Scotland and Eric II of Norway, three years old and sickly. It was bad enough that the throne's proper occupant was out of the country and her survival problematical. It was a worse danger that in the event of her death the succession was anything but clearly defined. In this emergency one of two things might happen. The few magnates who had good claims to the throne might mobilise their factions and resort to civil war, so that if the " Maid of Norway " lived they would have control of the government, while if she died they could enforce their claims. Alternatively, the Scottish nobles might try to preserve the unity of their country, appealing for help and support to the King of England, then at the very zenith of his power and prestige. It is to the credit of the community of the realm of Scotland that it chose the second course.

Six guardians of the realm were elected : for the country north of Forth, William Fraser, Bishop of St. Andrews, Duncan, Earl of

[1] Wrongly dated September 29th on the Close Roll (*Cal. Close Rolls, 1272-1279*, 505), and wrongly said to be of date 1279 in F. M. Powicke, *The Thirteenth Century*, 595.

[2] *Foedera*, I. i. 451. Not " Scotland, ' and other lands subject to the King of England ' ", as in Powicke, *Henry III and the Lord Edward*, ii. 489.

Fife, and Alexander Comyn, Earl of Buchan ; for south of Forth, Robert Wishart, Bishop of Glasgow, James the Stewart [1] and John Comyn " the Black ",[2] lord of Badenoch and part of Nithsdale. With the doubtful exception of the Black Comyn, these six included no one with a good claim to the throne ; doubtless their influence was the greater on that account. Despite a serious depletion of their number by the murder of the young Earl of Fife in 1288 and the Earl of Buchan's death in 1289, the guardians went ahead with their task of bringing the Maid of Norway home and providing for her future. To seek the help of King Edward was only prudent, and the price which he demanded, namely, a marriage of the Queen of Scots with his own son and heir Edward of Carnarvon, was one which on certain conditions the Scots were quite willing to pay. In March, 1290, twelve bishops, twelve earls, twenty-three abbots, eleven priors and fifty barons of Scotland, assembled in parliament at Birgham (Berwickshire), announced their assent to the proposal, and in the following July the terms were formally set out in the Treaty of Birgham, ratified by Edward at Northampton on August 28th. Besides the marriage, the chief stipulations were that the kingdom of Scotland should remain " separate, apart, and free in itself without subjection ", preserving intact its own liberties and customs. No Scottish parliament was to be held, and no Scottish litigant was to be forced to plead, outside the realm. No taxation was to be levied in " tallages, aids or *maletolts* ", other than what was customary

[1] Since the title of Steward had become a surname in this family before 1300, its more familiar and historic form of Stewart will be used in this chapter.

[2] Son of John Comyn the Red, mentioned above, pp. 247, 249.

MAP X. SCOTLAND AND THE NORTH OF ENGLAND, TO ILLUSTRATE THE ANGLO-SCOTTISH WAR (*see opposite page*).

Main routes shown thus . . . . . ══

Places or districts which were the seats of earldoms shown thus . . . . BUCHAN E

Names of influential families . . . . *(COMYN)*

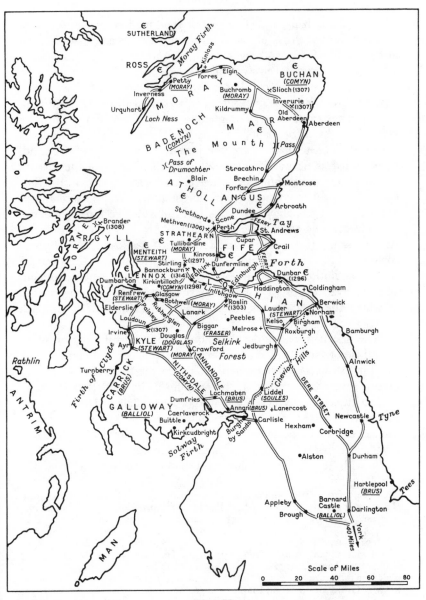

MAP X

389

The guardians had had a fine seal of the kingdom struck for their use, bearing the cross of St. Andrew and the legend "Andrew be leader of the Scots and their fellow-countrymen". This was to stay in use till the queen's arrival.

The hope of a peaceable settlement and union of the Crowns envisaged by the treaty of Birgham was extinguished in the autumn, when the news came that on September 26th the young queen, while being brought to Scotland, had died in Orkney. The Scots lords began at once to manoeuvre for power. The King of England, preoccupied as he was by his wife's death and trials of the corrupt ministers, embarked on yet another characteristic process of definition. He had lately vindicated his lordship over Wales by conquest, and it is hard to believe that this fact did not give him confidence and a precedent when he came to deal with the Scottish problem. At the same time, the years 1290-1 in Anglo-Scottish history correspond to 1277 in Anglo-Welsh history, not to 1283. Edward I wanted definition, not conquest. But as in Wales, so in Scotland. he took advantage of his opportunity to create a wholly new situation in which the balance was tilted heavily in favour of the English Crown.

The first task was to decide who was the rightful King of Scots. King Eric of Norway, Count Florence of Holland, and eleven Scots and English barons put forward claims to the throne, but here we need consider only two competitors, John Balliol and Robert Brus.[1]

Brus was eighty years of age, lord of Annandale in Dumfriesshire and Hartlepool on the coast of County Durham. In England he had served as a judge, acting from 1268-9 as the first Chief Justice of King's Bench. He had fought and been taken prisoner at Lewes, along with the fathers of his rival Balliol and John Comyn the

---

[1] Apart from Brus and Balliol, the most serious claimants were John Hastings, a great-grandson of Earl David of Huntingdon by the junior line, and the Count of Holland, great-grandson of William the Lion's eldest sister Ada. The count based his claim on a document (which he failed to produce) purporting to show that David of Huntingdon had surrendered all his claims ·and those of his heirs to the Scottish throne to his brother William the Lion, thus giving Ada and her heirs best claim should the direct male line fail. A copy of the Count's document has recently been discovered by Mr. Grant Simpson and is printed in the *Scot. Hist. Rev.*, xxxvi (1957), 111-124. I am grateful to Mr. Simpson for showing me how strong Count Florence's claim must have seemed in 1290; but, in the event, he failed to produce the document in Edward I's court.

guardian. He had one claim to the Scottish throne which dated from as long ago as 1238, when Alexander II, still childless and about to make an expedition to the isles, had recognised Brus as his heir. But that had been in exceptional circumstances, and the birth of the future Alexander III might be thought to have cancelled his father's declaration. Brus's alternative claim was more substantial. Since the direct royal line had failed, the best hereditary claimants were the descendants of William the Lion's brother, David, Earl of Huntingdon. Earl David's only son, John of Scotland, had died childless, and his heirs were his three sisters, Margaret, Isabel, and Ada. Robert Brus was the son of Isabel, and therefore great-great-grandson of King David I.

John Balliol of Barnard Castle, the other serious claimant, was a considerable landowner in Northumberland and Durham. His claim to the Scottish throne derived solely from his descent from Earl David of Huntingdon. His mother, Dervorguilla, was in her own right lady of Galloway, being one of the daughters of Alan of Galloway, who died in 1234.[1] Dervorguilla's mother was Earl David's eldest daughter Margaret. Balliol therefore was great-great-great-grandson of King David I.

The two claims were closely balanced. Both depended on female descent, but whereas Brus was separated from the male line by one woman only, Balliol was separated by two. Moreover, Brus was one whole generation nearer to King David than Balliol. But if seniority counted for more than " nearness of blood ", then Balliol, the grandson of an elder daughter, had the better right than Brus, the son of a younger daughter.

Descent alone was not the only consideration. Scottish opinion was bound to be influenced by divisions among the magnates and by the vastly greater prestige enjoyed by Brus, who belonged to the generation of Henry III and had long held lordship in Scotland. Balliol by contrast seemed an Englishman. He became lord of Galloway only in the very year of the dispute, when the lady Dervorguilla died. Yet he had powerful friends. Two of the guardians supported him, the Black Comyn, who was his brother-in-law, and Bishop Fraser of St. Andrews. The immense influence of the Comyn family in all its ramifications was ranged on his side.

---

[1] Above, p. 248. Dervorguilla was the youngest daughter, but had acquired the rights of her older sisters.

The other two guardians, however, James the Stewart and the Bishop of Glasgow, gave their backing to Brus. Moreover, a party among the earls of Scotland, led by Donald, Earl of Mar, came out strongly in Brus's favour. This party claimed to represent the "Seven Earls of Scotland", that is to say, the mormaers of the seven provinces into which Scotland was traditionally divided. There were, of course, many more earls than seven in 1291; the phrase described a constitutional concept rather than a precise number of actual magnates. Undoubtedly, by custom, the earls played an important part in the inauguration and enthronement of the Scottish kings. It was a part which had been freshly emphasised in the thirteenth century, after being depreciated by the Norman-trained kings of the twelfth. But the claim made in the petition of 1291, that, in addition to placing him on the Stone of Destiny and bestowing upon him the honours of kingship, they could actually "make a king" seems either ill-founded or misleading. The petition, in any event, is so much a piece of special pleading for the Earl of Mar that it cannot safely be regarded as the authentic statement of the Seven Earls. There is no question, however, that Brus was widely supported among men of influence. His own son, Robert, was Earl of Carrick in his wife's right, and was shortly (1292) to resign the earldom to his son, the future King Robert I. Thus was the ancient feud of Galloway between the unruly sons of Fergus reborn in the rivalry of Balliol and Brus.

In the circumstances, a decision between the claimants could be made only by the arbitration or the judgment of Edward I. Edward was determined that it should be judgment, and that as a first step the land and castles of Scotland should be handed over to him and his feudal superiority admitted by all parties. He instructed the English monasteries to send him excerpts from their chronicles which would demonstrate the suzerainty of England over Scotland. Relevant records in Edinburgh castle were brought to Berwick; they included clothes, relics, and valuables, though "how these latter could bear upon the question at issue does not seem clear".[1] In their eagerness for a decision, Balliol, Brus and the rest made their submission to Edward as "superior lord" in a document dated June 4th, 1291. It is not easy to see what else they could have done; the alternative would have been war, which no one seems to have

---

[1] J. Maitland Thomson, *The Public Records of Scotland*, 4.

contemplated. Copies of the submission were despatched to the cathedrals and principal monasteries of England to be preserved as a perpetual memorial. There was to be no more ambiguity. Yet, at the same time, the king undertook to demand from future Scottish rulers nothing but homage and the rights incidental to it.

The community of the realm of Scotland—possibly the non-competing magnates, almost certainly the knights, gentry, burgesses, and (probably well to the fore) the clergy [1]—wished Edward I to act not as a judge but as arbiter. They were not prepared to go so far as the competitors [2] and demurred to the recognition of the king as superior lord. They knew of no precedent for this recognition, which they clearly felt to be prejudicial to the terms of the Treaty of Birgham. But at this moment the power rested with Edward. The petition of the community was disregarded. A court was set up consisting of 104 auditors, under the king himself, as judge not arbiter. This impressive tribunal was deliberately modelled on the *centumviri*, the court of 105, employed in the Roman republic to deal with questions of succession to property. [3] Twenty-four of the auditors were of King Edward's Council, and Brus and Balliol each nominated half the remainder.

The court sat at Berwick from August 3rd to 12th, 1291 and again from October 14th to November 17th, 1292. Some of the finest contemporary legal skill was available to it, and its proceedings were very fully recorded, chiefly by an expert Yorkshire notary, Master Andrew of Tong. The two main questions which it considered were (1) Was the kingdom of Scotland to be treated as a feudal barony, which on a failure of male heirs would be divided equally among the female heirs, save only that the eldest heiress would enjoy the " honours "—the chief castle, title, chief lordship, etc. ? (2) Irrespective of whether the kingdom could be divided, who had the better claim, Brus or Balliol ?

[1] The composition of the " community " is nowhere defined. The *Annales Regni Scotiae* (ed. Riley, pp. 241-2, 244-5) state that, while a petition was presented " in the name of the community ", nothing was put forward " by " or " on behalf of " the bishops, prelates, earls, barons, magnates and nobles. This does not necessarily exclude the bishops, earls, etc. from the community ; it may mean that instead of group petitions only one collective petition was presented.

[2] It should be remembered that only six out of the thirteen competitors could be described as Scotsmen.

[3] G. Neilson, *Scot. Hist. Rev.*, xvi (1919), 1-14.

On Balliol's side, it was urged that Scotland was a barony. It could and should be divided among the descendants of Earl David (who included one other competitor, John Hastings, besides Balliol and Brus), so long as Balliol, as descendant of the eldest heiress, got the throne and royal power. Brus, on the other hand, was opposed to dividing the realm, but claimed that Scottish custom preferred nearness of blood to seniority of line. When, however, the court decided that Balliol's seniority gave him the better right, Brus shifted his ground and demanded a division of the kingdom, so that if he did not get the throne he would at least have a third of the royal estates. Early in November the issues were put before the whole of King Edward's Council, including the twenty-four English auditors but excluding the eighty nominees of Balliol and Brus. This body decided that Scotland was impartible and that Balliol had the better right. The Scottish auditors agreed with the verdict. The king gave judgment to this effect on November 17th, and on the 18th Balliol swore fealty to Edward I as superior lord of the realm of Scotland. On St. Andrew's Day he was installed as King of Scots on the Stone of Scone.

Though Balliol had little prestige in Scotland, and not much strength of character, all might have been well between the two kingdoms if Edward I had not insisted that feudal superiority over Scotland meant " direct lordship ", including the right to hear appeals from Scotland in his own court. The competitors in 1291 had admitted " superior lordship ", but not " direct lordship ". This was a gloss which Edward had dishonestly caused to be inserted in the official record of the proceedings at a later date. No Scottish ruler before Balliol had ever admitted that judicial appeals could be made from his court to the court of the King of England, and no such appeals had ever been made. On this matter of vital importance, Edward I may have sincerely believed in his right. But in his interpretation of that right, there is no doubt that he deliberately produced a wholly new and unprecedented situation.

The question of appeals was raised within a few weeks of King John's enthronement. A Berwick merchant, Roger Bartholomew, probably at the instigation of Edward or his advisers, appealed to Edward at Newcastle against an adverse judgment passed on him in the previous May by the Scottish justiciars. Judgment was given in his favour within fifteen days, an astonishingly short time. King

John objected to the appeal on the grounds that by the Treaty of Birgham Edward had clearly agreed that no Scot should have to plead a case outside the realm of Scotland. To this Edward answered that the treaty had ceased to apply·; he would no longer be hampered by promises made in 1290. King John's objection has been dismissed as " ingenious ",[1] yet it seems beyond question that in repudiating Birgham and then persuading the Scots king to do likewise (January 2nd, 1293), Edward I was breaking the spirit and the letter of the understanding between the two kingdoms. If it had seemed important to the Scots in 1290 to guarantee their independence in the event of Edward of Carnarvon becoming king, it could not have ceased to be important in 1292 with John Balliol on the throne. King John's assent to the cancellation of the Treaty of Birgham " signed his own doom ". Though a number of his subjects proceeded to take advantage of the new opportunity of appealing from his judgments to the court of Edward I, the Scots as a nation could not tolerate it. John himself, by allowing appeals, had virtually parted with his kingship.

Since the death of Alexander III all had been characterised by doubt, hesitation and delay. Now for three years events moved swiftly and, as it seems, inexorably towards war. King John's position was not enviable. On the one hand, relations with his masterful overlord reached breaking point over an appeal more complicated and vexatious than Roger Bartholomew's. It was lodged by Macduff, the younger son of a former Earl of Fife. During 1293 Edward I twice summoned the King of Scots to London to answer for his adverse judgment against Macduff. He ignored the first summons. When he obeyed the second, he was put in mercy for contempt, and after first denying the competence of Edward's court was compelled to submit under threats. He then made a fresh homage to King Edward as his man for the kingdom of Scotland. A set of rules was drawn up to regulate appeals, which if they had been strictly observed would have reduced King John to a position of less judicial independence than a typical English baron.

North of the border, on the other hand, King John's own subjects harassed him and overruled his commands. He " opened not his

[1] H. G. Richardson and G. O. Sayles, in *Scot. Hist. Rev.*, xxv (1928), 308-9.

mouth, being like a lamb among wolves ", wrote one contemporary. In 1294, as we have seen, Edward I mobilised the resources of England and Wales in the defence of Gascony. From Scotland he demanded military service of the King of Scots, ten earls, James the Stewart, and fifteen barons. It was a similar demand which had touched off the Welsh revolt, and the Scots were now determined to profit by the Welsh example. In a parliament at Stirling (July, 1295)[1] a council of four bishops, four earls and four barons was elected to take over the government. Edward's representatives were driven from the country. Brus the competitor had recently died, and his son and grandson, who refused to adhere to the new régime (dominated by the Comyns), were deprived of their estates. An alliance was made with the King of France, to be cemented by the marriage of King Philip's niece, Joan of Valois, to King John's son Edward Balliol.

King Edward's answer to this defiance was to invade Scotland in the spring of 1296. The rich but unfortified burgh of Berwick made some resistance. It was taken by storm (March 30th), and the male inhabitants were slaughtered without mercy. The town was then rebuilt, in effect as a *bastide*, to be colonised by English burgesses and to form the headquarters of an English administration in Scotland. On April 27th the main Scottish army, composed largely of inexperienced cavalry, was easily defeated at Dunbar, and many Scots leaders were taken prisoner. Ten weeks later, in the churchyard of Stracathro near Brechin, John Balliol surrendered his kingship to Edward I.[2] Already his regalia, along with the bulk of the royal records of Scotland, had been taken from Edinburgh Castle to London, leaving only certain Exchequer records essential to the new government. Balliol also was taken south, as a state prisoner.

During July and August the English king proceeded slowly and impressively into the country north of the Mounth, reaching Elgin, the northern limit of his stay, on July 26th, and returning to Berwick by way of Perth. At Scone, outside Perth, he removed the ancient stone on which the Scottish kings had been enthroned since time

---

[1] Richardson and Sayles, *op. cit.* 304, n. 5.

[2] The trimming, possibly heraldic, of Balliol's surcoat or tabard was stripped from him on this occasion, giving rise to his later nickname of " Toom Tabard ", " empty surcoat ".

immemorial. It was taken to Westminster and placed in the shrine of St. Edward the Confessor. A harder loss for the Scots to bear was the king's seizure at Edinburgh of the " Black Rood " of Saint Margaret, the most precious relic in the country. (Unlike the Stone of Destiny it was later restored, only to be lost finally by the Scots in 1346 at the disastrous battle of Neville's Cross.) Finally, in 1296, Edward received the individual homages and oaths of fealty of over two thousand Scotsmen, from earls to lesser freeholders, from bishops to rectors of parish churches. After this massive display of power Edward believed that Scotland had been safely as well as easily conquered. In his view the kingdom had been abolished : Scotland was now equivalent to North Wales, an outlying part of his own realm. It had its own administration, separate from that of England but entirely English. The now ageing Earl Warenne was nominally in control, and tried to govern Scotland from his estates in Yorkshire. The purse-strings and real power were held by Hugh Cressingham, an Exchequer clerk. At this point Robert Brus, the competitor's son, is said by the later Scottish chroniclers to have lodged a vain claim to the throne. Edward's crushing answer, as they report it, certainly sounds characteristic : " Have I nothing else to do but win kingdoms for you ? "

Apart from the sack of Berwick Scotland in 1296 had suffered not conquest but shock. Organised resistance on a national scale was out of the question, but in the early months of 1297 sporadic acts of revolt were reported from Moray in the north, where an attempt was later made to seize Urquhart castle near Inverness, to Clydesdale in the south, where in May the English sheriff of Lanark, William Hazlerig, was slain by William Wallace. Wallace and his band crossed the country to Perth ; here they surprised and nearly captured William Ormsby the Justiciar while he was holding court. The new Scots leader who had thus made his dramatic entry upon the scene was a younger son of Malcolm Wallace, the knightly tenant of Elderslie near Paisley, part of the great Renfrew fief held by the Stewart. Wallace had not sworn fealty to Edward I in 1296, and throughout a career which has rightly made him one of the immortals of Scottish history he never swerved from the cause of independence.

The lead given by Wallace and others was quickly followed by men of more exalted rank. Bishop Wishart of Glasgow, James the

Stewart, the younger Robert Brus (to whom Edward I had restored the earldom of Carrick), and William, lord of Douglas, joined to raise a force in the south-west during June. At Irvine (Ayrshire) they were confronted by a superior English army and gave in without a struggle. It would be wrong, however, to suppose that in the resistance movement the baronage proved spineless and ineffective. In praising Wallace for his steadfastness we must remember that if he had submitted he would have been shown no mercy. By contrast, in the early stages of the war, the prelates and lay magnates had lands to lose but not life. They might, and several did, perform greater service to their country by following what seems to us a dishonourable policy of alternate submission and rebellion. The statement found in many histories that the barons were half-hearted because they held lands in England as well as in Scotland is a generalisation whose truth has never been proved in detail and which would probably not stand up to critical examination. There were, of course, a number of great magnates, almost all laymen, who sincerely supported Edward I and fought on his side more or less steadily throughout the war of independence. But they were by no means all men who had estates south of the border.

At all events, the submission of Irvine did not make Wishart and the rest loyal to Edward I, while from the outset the resistance of 1297 had one brilliant leader of undoubtedly baronial rank. The revolt in the north in the early months of 1297 had been led by Andrew Moray, whose father and uncle, both prisoners in England, were respectively lords of Petty near Inverness and Bothwell in Clydesdale. Andrew Moray had been so far successful that by September all castles held for Edward beyond the Mounth had fallen to the Scots. There had also been risings in Mar, Angus, and Fife. By joining forces north of the Forth, Andrew Moray and William Wallace truly became, as they styled themselves, " leaders of the army of Scotland ".

The army of Scotland had yet to win a major battle. It was largely composed of infantry, and prior to Courtrai no one with military experience would have rated highly the chances of infantry against heavy-armed cavalry, especially where (as at Maes Moydog) there was close support from archers. It cannot be stated too emphatically that on the English side nobody took the Scots revolt seriously. The king, so preoccupied with his Flanders expedition that he could barely attend to the protest of the earls, scarcely gave Scotland a thought. Warenne and Cressingham knew better, but not much better. They marshalled a useful cavalry army and a corps of Welsh foot, and reached Stirling on September 10th. The Forth was spanned here by a narrow wooden bridge, built near the southern tip of a great horseshoe loop in the river. Moray and Wallace had drawn up their men well north of the bridge, in such a way that both flanks were protected by the river, while at their back rose the wooded heights of the Abbey Craig, and beyond that again the higher slopes of the Ochils. Warenne would have been well-advised not to have crossed the bridge, wide enough for only two or three horsemen abreast, but to have guarded it and taken his main force through the Fords of Frew, a mile or so up river. But according to one account this plan was rejected by Cressingham on grounds of economy. Money was short and no time must be lost. So the English knights began to cross. When half were over, the Scots attacked them at the bridge end, cutting the enemy in two. Havoc was caused among both van and rearguard. The unarmoured Welsh swam the river to safety, but the cavalry were cut down or drowned. Warenne barely escaped to Berwick. Cressingham was killed, his skin was flayed from his body and pieces of it were sent through Scotland as grisly tokens of the victory. Andrew Moray was wounded, it seems fatally, for he died soon afterwards. But at once Wallace, still acting in Moray's name and his own, and taking the style of guardian of the realm for John Balliol, led his army into the northern counties of England and raided there with much destruction.

The nucleus of a second and greater English army was collected in the winter of 1297-8. The king returned home in March, 1298, and showed his determination to be finally rid of the Scottish problem by immediately transferring the administration from Westminster to York. The Exchequer and Common Law Courts remained at York until the end of 1304. The army took the field in July, 1298. It consisted of some 12,000 infantry, of whom over 10,000 were Welsh, together with perhaps 2,000 cavalry, half recruited from those who owed service by their tenure but served for pay, half supplied by the earls, who in this campaign showed for once a high degree of unity in their support of the king. It was probably the largest organised force ever to have invaded Scotland up to that time. It had reached Liston, a few miles west of Edinburgh, by July 15th, when shortage of stores, poor morale and a threatened mutiny among the Welsh nearly caused a withdrawal.

William Wallace still commanded the Scots, although by now he had been joined by several of the great magnates, among them the Stewart and his brother John. Their best course would have been to retire northward, burning the country behind them, and waiting till the enemy was exhausted. But the memory of Stirling Bridge and the rumour of an imminent English withdrawal seem to have made the Scots over-confident. They decided to pit a largely inexperienced army of spearmen, with a few archers from Selkirk Forest and some cavalry of poor quality, against veteran campaigners of the Welsh wars. Even so, the battle, fought a little to the east of the village of Falkirk (July 22nd), proved no easy victory for the invaders.

On the Scottish side, horse, foot, and bowmen were quite unco-ordinated. The cavalry fled almost at once. The archers from the Forest, under John Stewart, formed isolated, vulnerable groups, and from their commander downwards were killed almost to a man. Wallace had arranged his main body according to the antique Germanic fashion in four great " schiltroms ", densely packed circles of spears impossible for cavalry alone to penetrate. A reliable contemporary account tells us that Wallace addressed his men in the homely English tongue : " I have brought you to the ring: hop if ye can." [1] Against this stout-hearted but ill-equipped army the king could deploy several thousand archers and some hundreds of crossbowmen. Their hail of arrows and bolts pierced the schiltroms from above, and enabled the cavalry to move in and break them up. The tactics of combining cavalry with archers in open battle, as used at Maes Moydog, were thus repeated at Falkirk with notable success.

It was one thing to lead an army into Scotland and win a battle ; it was quite another to hold the land in permanent subjection. Geography told heavily against an Edwardian conquest. There were but two points of entry from the south, the eastern march, involving a long approach through Northumberland, and the western march, nearer to the more southerly English bases but owing to boggy ground impracticable for a large army save by difficult fords

[1] W. Rishanger, *Chronica*, ed. H. T. Riley, 187.

across the tidal Solway Firth. Naval support was useful, but Edward I could not blockade Scotland like North Wales. By garrisoning Berwick, Roxburgh, Jedburgh, Edinburgh, and other castles, he could, it is true, repeat in Lothian the system by which the Welsh were successfully overawed. But control of Lothian counted for little if the country north of Forth were not subdued. There, the key castles, unlike those of Lothian, were but posting stations along an extended and highly vulnerable line of communication.[1]

In fact Scotland was less conquered after Falkirk than ever. Edward I burned Perth and St. Andrews, and returned to England through the south-west. But except for a few southern castles in English hands, the country was back under native Scottish rule. Wallace resigned his command after Falkirk, presumably because a man of his relatively humble rank could justify a position of the highest authority only by winning battles, and defeat had to some extent discredited him. He went to the continent to get assurances of French and, probably, papal support. At home his place was taken by two magnate guardians, Robert Brus, Earl of Carrick, and John Comyn, son of the Black Comyn (a prisoner in England since 1296) and known, like his grandfather, as " the Red ". Since the submission of Irvine, Brus had come out more and more positively against Edward I. He was holding the west country when Wallace lost Falkirk, and shortly afterwards he burned the town of Ayr to prevent it being of use to the English. As guardian he now came into the forefront of the struggle, and it may be that he already aimed to succeed where his grandfather the competitor had failed. The election of Comyn, on the other hand, meant preserving the cause of Balliol, in whose name Moray and Wallace had professedly fought.

In 1299 Brus and Comyn were joined in the guardianship by the new Bishop of St. Andrews, Fraser's successor, William Lamberton, elected under Wallace's influence in 1297 and consecrated by Pope Boniface VIII a year later. Lamberton was outstanding both for firmness of character and statesmanship. As far as possible he seems to have moderated between Brus and Comyn, though to judge from what happened later he inclined to Brus's side, and his appointment as bishop had, indeed, been the subject of a protest by one of Comyn's kinsmen, William Comyn, an influential member of the St. Andrews clergy. However this may be, it is a fact that during the next ten

[1] See the map on p. 389.

years the rivalry of Brus and Comyn grew into an irreconcilable feud and replaced both English invasion and English occupation as the governing factor of Scottish history.

From 1299 to 1304 the guardians tried as far as possible to carry on the normal administration of the country. Sheriffs and bailiffs were appointed in the shires; parliaments were convened, perhaps more regularly than our evidence will allow us to say for certain.[1] But Brus would not co-operate with Comyn, and his place as guardian was taken first by Ingram de Umfraville, a kinsman of the Earl of Angus, then by John de Soules, lord of Liddesdale. Militarily speaking, the Scots at least held their own. Edward I's summer campaigns in 1300 and 1301 were failures, and though he wintered at Linlithgow from 1301 to 1302, it was to no purpose, except as an opportunity for Master James of St. George to perform one of his last services to the king by building the new " peel " of Linlithgow. Early in the following year (February 24th, 1303) an English cavalry force under John Segrave, the king's lieutenant in Scotland, was worsted at Roslin, south of Edinburgh. John Comyn led his troop of horse during the night from Biggar in upper Clydesdale and took the Englishmen by surprise. Comyn shared this exploit with Simon Fraser, whose family had for over a century held the hereditary sheriffdom of Peebles. Fraser emerges in this period as a staunch supporter of the struggle for independence.

On the diplomatic side also, the Scots had some success for a time. In 1300, Pope Boniface VIII declared openly in their favour, claiming Scotland, much to Edward I's indignation, as a papal fief. What the Scots feared above all was a breach in their alliance with the King of France. They were relatively safe so long as the French refused to make permanent terms with Edward unless the Scots were included in the peace. But in 1303 the blow fell. Four years earlier, Philip IV had praised the Scots

" for the constancy of perfect faithfulness which they had shown towards the illustrious King of Scotland and the vigour of proven courage which they had manfully displayed in the defence of their native land against injustice ".[2]

A very different tune was sung in his negotiations with England

[1] Richardson and Sayles, *Scot. Hist. Rev.*, xxv (1928), 315-17.
[2] J. Bain, *Calendar of Scottish Documents*, ii. 536 (translated and abridged). For the correct dating of this letter in 1299, see E. M. Barron, *The Scottish War of Independence* (1934), 132-6.

(1302-3), after the defeat of Courtrai. The treaty of Paris of May, 1303, left the Scots to fend for themselves, and left Edward I free to concentrate all his forces on the conquest of Scotland. The extent to which Scots resistance had been weakened by the feud of Brus and Comyn was now made painfully clear. By April, 1302, Brus had submitted to the English king. In the absence of certain evidence, his action is most reasonably, though not very creditably, explained by frustrated ambition. If Scottish freedom could be saved only with Balliol nominally and the Comyns actually in power, then Brus, believing in his own right to the throne, would not help to save it at all. Yet without Brus the Comyns—the guardian, John the Red, and his kinsman John, Earl of Buchan—proved helpless in the face of a full-scale English offensive.

Edward invaded Scotland for the last time in May, 1303. Little was left to chance. Three floating bridges, prefabricated at Lynn, were brought north by the fleet so that the army could cross the Firth of Forth directly into Fife. There was no organised resistance. In the late summer, the king penetrated the country as far as Kinloss, at the mouth of the River Findhorn in Moray. He returned in October and wintered at Dunfermline Abbey. In February, 1304, the Red Comyn came into the king's peace at Strathord, near Perth. Other leaders surrendered at this time, including the Stewart, John de Soules, the Earl of Buchan, and the bishops of St. Andrews and Glasgow. Some had but newly returned from a long and fruitless embassy to the court of Philip IV. The king's terms stipulated for varying periods of exile, but on the whole they were not severe. Simon Fraser still held out, and (though no man knew where) William Wallace, for whose capture the king offered large rewards. It seemed that apart from Fraser and Wallace Scottish resistance was confined to the garrison of Stirling castle. Elaborate siege was laid to Stirling, a dozen of the very latest engines being used. The operation was watched by the queen and her ladies from a specially made window, and there was in addition a great concourse of earls, barons and knights, including lords from Ireland and Gascony. The defenders endured the siege for three months (May-July) before surrendering. They numbered about fifty, for the most part obscure men from southern Scotland and Perthshire. There were two knights among them, both members of the Oliphant family. They were all taken to various English castles to be closely guarded.

Early in the next year Wallace was captured. It is said that one of his servants betrayed him, in or near Glasgow, to a bailiff of John Stewart, otherwise known as John of Menteith, who since March 20th, 1304, had been the Constable of Dumbarton Castle. John Stewart was a younger son of Walter Stewart, Earl of Menteith, and although he had fought against the English at various times, he came into King Edward's peace early in 1304 and must evidently have been regarded by the king as exceptionally trustworthy, for he was one of the very few Scotsmen to be put in charge of an important castle. He repaid this trust, and became infamous to the later Scots chroniclers, by handing Wallace over to the king. Wallace, proclaiming to the last that he had never owed allegiance to Edward I, was condemned as a traitor on August 23rd, dragged by a horse from Westminster to the Tower and Smithfield (more than four miles), and then hanged and quartered.

It was King Edward's conviction that he had now conquered Scotland finally. In 1305, after careful consultation with the leading Scottish magnates, he drew up an ordinance for the future government of the country. Four principal royal officers were appointed, Lieutenant, Chancellor, Chamberlain, and Comptroller. Power was vested in these offices, which were held by John of Brittany [1] and three Englishmen respectively. There was, however, to be a largely Scottish council to advise and assist, and Brus and the two Comyns were nominated to it. There were to be four pairs of justiciars, one each for Lothian, Galloway, and Scotland south and north of the Mounth respectively, each pair consisting of an Englishman and a Scotsman. The key castles were to remain in English hands save for Dumbarton, held by John Stewart, and Kildrummy in Aberdeenshire, in charge of Brus. The strategic importance of Lothian and Berwick was of course crucial, and this whole district remained under English control. Elsewhere, however, the sheriffdoms seem to have been given mainly to Scots. The law of Scotland, defined as the Laws of King David together with amendments made by later kings, was to stand ; but henceforth statutes enacted by the King of England might, if appropriate, be applied to Scotland. The " Laws of the Scots and Brets ", i.e. the antique customs with regard to wergild which apparently still prevailed in Galloway, were to be abolished.

[1] Now holding the English earldom of Richmond.

The Ordinance of 1305, tidy and statesmanlike as it was, took no account of the depth of hostility in Scotland to English rule, nor, as soon became clear, of a change of front on the part of Robert Brus. It seems likely that Brus had never in his heart abandoned his claim to the throne. While the Comyns were in the ascendant, he preferred to take the English part. In a final estimate, we should set against this selfishness the fact that in 1306, when Scotland seemed to be finally vanquished, Brus brought to life once more the spirit of Moray and Wallace and the garrison of Stirling. It is sometimes said that he did so as it were by accident. On February 10th, 1306, he came to a meeting with the Red Comyn in the Franciscan church at Dumfries. According to the story put out by Edward I shortly afterwards, which may well be substantially correct, Brus proposed rebellion to Comyn, who threatened to tell the king. Weapons were drawn and John Comyn himself was stabbed to death.

This sudden act of violence is made to account for the whole of Brus's subsequent career, his bid for the Crown, his patience in adversity, his systematic reduction of English-held fortresses, his vigorous and prudent rule as king. The explanation must be dismissed as inadequate. It fails to notice the signs of Brus's impending revolt in 1305, and above all the speed with which after Comyn's murder he collected about him a sizeable body of magnates and had himself enthroned at Scone on March 27th in the presence and with the full support of Bishop Lamberton. The Comyns of course had become his mortal enemies ; but the Church leaders, Simon Fraser, several earls, knights and other gentry came out at once in his support.

The coup nearly failed, and had Edward I been a younger man might well have failed altogether. The Earl of Pembroke, the English military commander in Scotland, defeated Brus and his following at Methven, near Perth, on June 20th. The new king was forced to flee his kingdom. He took refuge no one knows where, perhaps in northern Ireland, perhaps in Orkney or elsewhere in the dominions of the King of Norway, his brother-in-law's brother. Before his return, Edward had struck ruthlessly at those of his adherents upon whom he could lay hands. The bishops of St. Andrews and Glasgow were imprisoned in irons. Laymen—among them Simon Fraser and the Earl of Atholl—were hanged and quartered in London and elsewhere. One of Brus's sisters and the Countess of Buchan were placed in cages specially built in the castles of Roxburgh and Berwick. The countess was treated in this way because, as sister and sole available representative of the Earl of Fife, she had performed the earl's traditional function of placing the new King of Scotland on the seat of royalty at Scone.

At the same time, the old King of England gathered all his resources for a last onslaught upon the Scots. Illness kept him at Lanercost Priory near Carlisle for most of the winter of 1306-7. In February Brus landed in Carrick and a few months later won a victory at Loudoun in Ayrshire. In the northern parts, where there were few English troops, revolt was imminent. The preaching friars were going about the country repeating a prophecy of Merlin " which said that after the death of Le Roy Coveytous the people of Scotland and the Britons, by which they mean the Welsh, would rise together and have sovereign power and live in harmony to the end of the world ".[1]

King Edward died at Burgh-by-Sands on July 7th. In the course of the next seven years all his work in Scotland had been undone by Robert Brus. Brus struck first at the Comyns, knowing that independence could no longer be achieved in unity. The Earl of Buchan was defeated at Inverurie (? December 24th, 1307), and immediately afterwards the province of Buchan was laid waste with great ferocity. The subjugation of Galloway by the king's brother Edward (1308-9) formed a corollary to the Buchan campaign, for the extreme south-west was Balliol and Comyn territory. The king's strategic sense is evident in his expedition, so successful that it soon became legendary, against the men of Argyll (1308), whose lord, John of Lorne, supported Edward of England. The final task was to recapture the castles held by English or pro-English constables and garrisons. In many ways this was Robert I's greatest achievement. His methodical reduction of Inverness, Forfar, Dundee, and Perth (1307-January, 1313) brought the country north of Tay securely under his control, and enabled him to carry the war in earnest into Lothian. By a remarkable combination of patience and daring, Linlithgow, Roxburgh, and finally Edinburgh itself were all

[1] In 1241 a writer at the Scots abbey of Melrose noted that the Welsh, after the death of Llywelyn the Great, were compelled to have their lawsuits decided in London by the English, and thought that this fulfilled another of Merlin's prophecies.

in Scottish hands by March, 1314. There remained only the crucially important castle of Stirling, whose Constable, through the foolish chivalry of Edward Brus, had been given twelve months' respite at midsummer 1313 and had agreed to surrender at the end of that term if he were not relieved by the King of England.

The famous challenge of Stirling brought forth an impressive response from Edward II, who deserves to be remembered for this when his other actions speak only of ineptitude and failure. He led an immense army into Scotland by the eastern march, reaching Edinburgh on June 21st, with but three days to spare. The King of Scots had had plenty of time to marshal all his forces, but it should be borne in mind that he had never yet won a major battle, while it was 600 years since the Scots had defeated an army commanded by an English king. Yet in Robert Brus they had the first king for centuries to combine military skill with courage and determination ; their morale was high ; and their position, guarding the north bank of the Bannock Burn, three miles south of Stirling, could not have been better chosen.

It is a curious fact that the site of the actual engagement, one of the relatively few decisive battles in the history of Britain, is not certainly known. " From the available evidence, it is impossible to construct a complete picture of the Battle of Bannockburn." [1] Edward II's army arrived in front of the Scots position on Sunday, June 23rd. It seems that two minor engagements were fought that day, in both of which the English were worsted. Before nightfall the main body of Edward's army crossed the burn in the flat carse beside the River Forth and camped there for the night. Although this movement brought them in contact with Stirling Castle, their position was perilous in the extreme unless the Scots could be thrown back immediately. This the English cavalry counted upon doing. But instead, on midsummer morning, King Robert boldly resolved to advance from the higher ground down on to the carse. Without any support from archers, the English cavalry charged the Scots

[1] J. D. Mackie, *Scot. Hist. Rev.*, xxix (1950), 210. The modern literature on Bannockburn is as voluminous as the primary sources are scanty. The account given here follows W. M. Mackenzie, *The Battle of Bannockburn* (1913), as reviewed and modified by T. F. Tout, *History*, v (1920). For a full statement of the " traditional " account of the battle, with an excellent map, see T. Miller, *The Site of the Battle of Bannockburn* (Historical Association Leaflet, 1931).

schiltroms, now much better armed and armoured than at Falkirk, and fell back with great slaughter. Their withdrawal became a rout. Men and horses floundered in the pools beside the Bannock. The English wagons, laden with stores and equipment, were too great a temptation for the Scots to resist, a fact which proved the saving of many English lives. King Edward, who had fought bravely, rode to Stirling. He was refused entry to the castle, and not without great risk turned eastward and made for the coast at Dunbar, where he found a ship to carry him to safety. The invaders' defeat was complete and decisive. Bannockburn made possible the later medieval Scottish kingdom, and must remain Brus's justification, not, indeed, for Comyn's murder, but for having wrested from the Comyns the leadership in the struggle for independence.

Something should be said in conclusion on the causes of the war and reasons for English failure. The principal cause, Edward I's determination to vindicate what he believed to be his right in Scotland, has been made apparent in the narrative of events. We may reasonably acquit Edward of the charge of planning the conquest of Scotland from the moment of the child Queen Margaret's death. Until the last ten years of his reign, all the evidence goes to show that Scotland formed a very insignificant item on his political agenda. The earliest English campaigns in Scotland, in 1296 and 1297, had meant an unwelcome diversion of precious time and resources which the king would sooner have used against Philip IV. But he misjudged Scottish feeling and underrated the country's capacity for resistance. In stubbornly persisting with his military effort he created a bitter antagonism between the two countries which endured for centuries.

Among the reasons for the failure of the Edwardian attempt facts of geography have already been mentioned. To these we should add the enormous expense, coming on top of the cost of war in Wales and France, and also the constitutional crisis, grave enough during Edward I's last years, crippling during the reign of his son. But undoubtedly the chief reason was the cohesion and resiliency of a majority of the inhabitants of Scotland. It is broadly true to say that two hypotheses have been put forward by modern historians to explain the strength of Scottish resistance. On the first view, Scotland in 1290 was already largely anglicised, save in the highlands, which from a military and political standpoint counted for little. A union of the Crowns would have been acceptable, but Edward I went too far and too fast by insisting on hearing appeals. Even so, the Scottish magnates would have had little objection to English rule, but the oppression of English agents after 1296 drove the common folk under Wallace to resistance. Brus took up the challenge only because the quite unforeseen murder of Comyn made him desperate. The second view, propounded by Dr. E. M. Barron,[1] may fairly be called racial or cultural. According to his view, a fundamental distinction must be drawn between Lothian and the rest of Scotland. Apart from Lothian, which was Teutonic (i.e. English), the rest of the country was homogeneous because it was Celtic. It was therefore bound at the outset to be opposed to English rule. In confirmation of this, evidence is marshalled to show that in the earlier stages of the war, right down to 1308 and after, " Celtic Scotland " bore almost the whole brunt of the fighting, while Lothian, being English by race and therefore not disposed to be anti-English in political sympathies, played little part at all.

The chief weakness of both these views seems to be that they take far too little account of the steady process by which, for almost two centuries prior to 1286, the monarchy and the Church had both imposed and induced a very large measure of unity in the kingdom of Scotland. The racial or cultural theory in particular minimises the extent to which the whole of Scotland, outside the extreme north and west, had been subject to intensive feudal settlement, involving both native families and incomers in large numbers, giving numerous families of importance (e.g. the Comyns, Morays, and Oliphants) estates and interest in many widely separated parts of the realm. Scores of men fought for the guardians and for Brus whose ancestors had been enfeoffed in Scotland by earlier kings. It was to the Scottish monarchy that these men owed knight-service or serjeanty for their lands, and it was according to the Laws of King David and well-established Scottish custom that they were wont to receive and dispense justice. Moreover, while it is an extremely valuable part of Dr. Barron's study that he has clearly shown the importance of the north of Scotland from beginning to end of the war, to speak of

---

[1] *The Scottish War of Independence* (2nd edn. 1934). I regret to have to differ on this important point of interpretation from the conclusions of a study to which this chapter is much indebted.

Lothian's part as insignificant is to do an injustice to the men of Berwick and the heroic garrison of Stirling, who were not northerners and included Lothian men. The Stewart, who held important fiefs in Lothian, Bishop Fraser and Simon Fraser of Tweeddale, John de Soules of Liddesdale, Bishop Lamberton, whose family took their name from Lamberton in Berwickshire, all gave notable or out-standing service in the cause of independence. Moreover, and this cannot be emphasised too strongly, the English hold over Lothian from 1296 to *c.* 1313 was so tight that its inhabitants lacked the freedom to resist, enjoyed and well used by the people north of Forth. For its part, the first view greatly underrates the importance of the clergy individually and the Church corporately, not merely during the war, for there the facts speak for themselves, but more significantly in forming the concept of a united Scottish realm in the generations before 1286.

In consequence, the view offered here cannot follow either of these accepted interpretations. It would suggest rather that Scotland, including Lothian but excluding the far western highlands and the isles, was relatively homogeneous in 1290, but that the homogeneity was not racial or linguistic but feudal and governmental. at was expressed most clearly in the habit of a common feudal Illegiance to a strong monarchy, and in the observance of a substantial body of accepted law and custom.

APPENDIX I

CONTEMPORARY RULERS

1. *Kings of France*

Philip I	1060-1108
Louis VI	1108-37
Louis VII	1137-80
Philip II Augustus	1180-1223
Louis VIII	1223-6
Louis IX	1226-70
Philip III	1270-85
Philip IV	1285-1314

2. *Holy Roman Emperors*

Henry IV	1056-1106
Henry V	1106-25
Lothair II	1125-37
Conrad III	1138-52
Frederick I Barbarossa . . .	1152-90
Henry VI	1190-7
Philip (of Swabia)	1198-1208
Otto IV (of Brunswick) . . .	1208-18
Frederick II	1218-50
Conrad IV ⎫ . . .	⎧ 1250-4
William of Holland ⎬ Interregnum .	⎨ 1247-56
Richard (of Cornwall) ⎭ . . .	⎩ 1257-72
Rudolf (of Hapsburg) . . .	1273-91
Adolf (of Nassau)	1292-8
Albert (of Hapsburg) . . .	1298-1308
Henry VII (of Luxemburg) . .	1308-13
Lewis IV (of Bavaria) . . .	1314-47

3. *Counts of Flanders*

Baldwin V	1036-67
Baldwin VI	1067-70
Arnulf III	1070-1
Robert I	1071-93
Robert II	1093-1111
Baldwin VII	1111-19
Charles I	1119-27
William " Clito "	1127-8
Thierri	1128-68
Philip	1168-91
Margaret of Alsace with Baldwin VIII .	1191-4
Baldwin IX	1194-1206
Joan with	
(1) Ferrand of Portugal ⎫	
(2) Thomas of Savoy ⎬ . .	1206-44
Margaret II	1244-80
Guy of Dampierre	1280-1305
Robert III	1305-22

4. *Counts and Kings of Sicily*

Roger I (Count)	1072-1101
Roger II (Count to 1130, then King) . .	1101-54
William I	1154-66
William II	1166-89
Tancred	1189-94
William III	1194
Henry VI (Emperor ; see (2) above) . .	1194-7
Frederick II (Emperor)	1197-1250
Conrad IV (Emperor)	1250-4
Conradin	1254-8
Manfred	1258-66
Charles of Anjou	1266-85
Peter of Aragon [1]	1282-5
James of Aragon	1285-95
Frederick of Aragon	1296-1337

[1] Disputed throne with preceding.

Appendix I

5. Kings of Norway

Harold III " Hardrada "	1047-66
Olaf III	1066-93
Magnus III " Bareleg "	1093-1103
Civil War and Disputed Succession	
Magnus V	1162-84
Sverre	1184-1202
Hakon III	1202-4
Guthorm	1204
Ingi II	1204-17
Hakon IV	1217-63
Magnus IV or VI	1263-80
Eric II	1280-99
Hakon V	1299-1319

APPENDIX II

1. *Archbishops of Canterbury*

Stigand	1052-70 (deposed)
Lanfranc	1070-89
Anselm	1093-1109
Ralph	1114-22
William of Corbeil	1123-36
Theobald	1139-61
Thomas Becket	1162-70
Richard of Dover	1174-84
Baldwin	1185-90
Hubert Walter	1193-1205
Stephen Langton	1207-28
Richard le Grant	1229-31
Edmund Rich	1234-40
Boniface of Savoy	1245-70
Robert Kilwardby	1273-8
John Pecham	1279-92
Robert Winchelsey	1294-1313

2. *Popes*

Alexander II	1061-73
Gregory VII	1073-85
Victor III	1086-7
Urban II	1088-99
Paschal II	1099-1118
Gelasius II	1118-19
Calixtus II	1119-24
Honorius II	1124-30
Innocent II	1130-43
Celestine II	1143-4
Lucius II	1144-5
Eugenius II	1145-53
Anastasius IV	1153-4

Adrian IV	. . . . . .	1154-9
Alexander III	. . . . . .	1159-81
Lucius III	. . . . . .	1181-5
Urban III	. . . . . .	1185-7
Gregory VIII	. . . . . .	1187
Clement III	. . . . . .	1187-91
Celestine III	. . . . . .	1191-8
Innocent III	. . . . . .	1198-1216
Honorius III	. . . . . .	1216-27
Gregory IX	. . . . . .	1227-41
Celestine IV	. . . . . .	1241
Innocent IV	. . . . . .	1243-54
Alexander IV	. . . . . .	1254-61
Urban IV	. . . . . .	1261-4
Clement IV	. . . . . .	1265-8
Gregory X	. . . . . .	1271-6
Innocent V	. . . . . .	1276
Adrian V	. . . . . .	1276
John XXI	. . . . . .	1276-7
Nicholas III	. . . . . .	1277-80
Martin IV	. . . . . .	1281-5
Honorius IV	. . . . . .	1285-7
Nicholas IV	. . . . . .	1288-92
Celestine V	. . . . . .	1294
Boniface VIII	. . . . . .	1294-1303
Benedict XI	. . . . . .	1303-4
Clement V	. . . . . .	1305-14

APPENDIX III

I. Rulers of England
A. The English Line
B. The Norman Line
C. The Angevin Line

II. Rulers of Scotland

III. Rulers of Wales
A. The Line of Gwynedd
B. The Line of Deheubarth

(I) RULERS OF ENGLAND. *(Kings of England shown in capitals)*

A. THE ENGLISH LINE

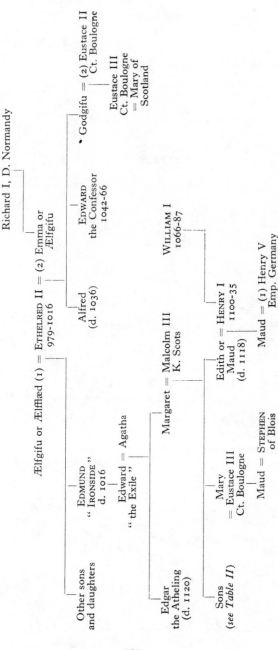

B. THE NORMAN LINE

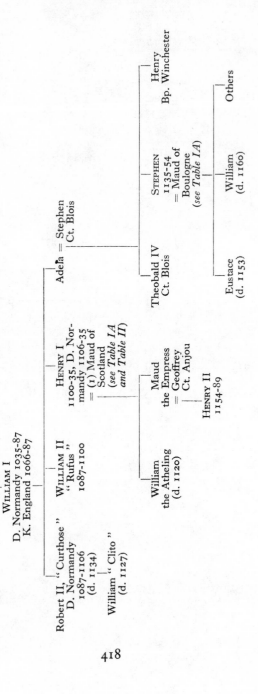

418

HENRY II = Eleanor
"Plantagenet" | D. Aquitaine
D. Normandy
Ct. Anjou
K. England
1154-89

Henry
"the young king"
(d. 1183)

Maud
= Henry the Lion,
D. Saxony
(d. 1189)

Otto IV (Welf)
Emp. of Germany
(d. 1218)

RICHARD I
1189-99
= Berengaria
of Navarre

Geoffrey
(d. 1186)
= Constance
Cts. Brittany

Arthur
(d. 1203)

JOHN, 1199-1216
= (1) Isabel or (2) Hawise
Cts. Gloucester
= (1) Isabel of Angoulême (2) = Hugh X (Lusignan)
Ct. La Marche

Eleanor
= Alfonso IX
K. Castile

Joan
= (1) William II K. Sicily
= (2) Raymond VI Ct. Toulouse

Isabel
= Frederick II (Hohenstaufen)
Emp. Germany

Joan
(d. 1238)
= Alexander II K. Scots

Henry
Ct. La Marche

William de Valence
lord of Pembroke

Guy

Geoffrey

Aymer
Bp-elect
Winchester

Eleanor = (1) William Marshal
E. Pembroke
= (2) Simon de Montfort
E. Leicester

Henry

Simon

Guy

Eleanor =
Llywelyn ap Gruffydd,
P. Wales

HENRY III
1216-72
= Eleanor, dau. of Raymond Berenger
Ct. Provence

Richard
E. Cornwall
Emp. of Germany
1254-72

Eleanor (d. 1241)

Henry of Almain
(d. 1270)

Edmund
E. Cornwall

Beatrice
= John,
D. Brittany

Margaret
(d. 1283)
= Alexander III
K. Scots (see Table II)

Edmund of Lancaster
"Crouchback"
= (1) Aveline, Cts. Aumale
= (2) Blanche, dau. of Robert, Ct. Artois
(s. Louis VIII, K. France)

Whence the earls and dukes of Lancaster

EDWARD I
1272-1307
= (1) Eleanor, dau. of Alfonso X, K. Castile
= (2) Margaret dau. Philip III K. France

Two sons and two daus.
(d. young)

Joan
= Gilbert
E. Gloucester

Margaret

Alphonso
(d. 1284)

Berengaria
(d. in infancy)

Elizabeth
= Humphrey
E. Hereford

EDWARD II
("Edward of Carnarvon"
1307-1327
(P. of Wales and E. Chester 1301)

Two daus.
(d. young)

Thomas of Brotherton,
E. Norfolk

Edmund of Woodstock

Eleanor
(d. young)

(II) RULERS OF SCOTLAND

(*Kings of Scotland shown in capitals*)

MALCOLM II

```
                                    ? dau. = Finlaech
                                             Mormaer of Moray
                                             │
                                    MACBETH = (2) Gruoch (1) = Gillacomgan
                                    1040-57                     Mormaer of
                                                                Moray
                                             LULACH "the simple"
                                             1057-8
```

Crinan = Bethoc
Abbot of Dunkeld

Duncan I
1034-40

Ingibjorg (1) = MALCOLM III = (2) Margaret
                "Canmore"   g-dau. of
                1058-93   Edmund
                                 Ironside
                                 (*see Table IA*)

DONALD
"Bán"
1093-4
1094-7

DUNCAN II
(d. 1094)
William
The Line of
MacWilliam

Edward
(d. 1093)

Edmund

Ethelred
Abbot of
Dunkeld

EDGAR
1097-1107

ALEXANDER I
1107-24
= Sibylla, illeg. dau.
of Henry I, K. England

Edith or
Maud
= Henry I,
K. England

DAVID I, 1124-53
= Maud, dau. of
Judith wid. of
Waltheof,
E. Huntingdon

Mary
= Eustace III
Ct. Boulogne

Henry,
E. Northumberland
(d. 1152)

Ada, dau. = Henry,
of William II
E. Warenne

David
E. Huntingdon
1185-1219

Ada = Florence Ct. Holland

WILLIAM I
"the Lion"
1165-1214
= Ermengarde of
Beaumont

Margaret
= Hubert de
Burgh,
E. Kent

John of
Scotland
E. Huntingdon
1219-37

Margaret
= Alan, lord
of Galloway

Isabel
= Robert
Brus

Ada =
Henry
Hastings

MALCOLM IV
"the Maiden"
1153-65

Joan = (1) ALEXANDER II (2) = Mary,
dau. of John   dau. of
K. England   Enguerrand
                           lord of Coucy

ALEXANDER III (2) = Yolande,
1249-86   dau.
                   Ct. Dreux

Margaret = (1) ALEXANDER III,
dau. Henry III,
K. England

Dervorguilla
lady of Galloway
= John Balliol

JOHN
1292-6

Robert Brus
"the Competitor"
(d. 1295)

Henry
Hastings

Margaret
= Eric II,
K. Norway

Alexander
d. 1284

Robert Brus
E. Carrick
(d. 1304)

John Hastings
Competitor 1291-2

MARGARET
"the Maid of Norway"
1286-90

ROBERT I
1306-29

(III) RULERS OF WALES

A. The Line of Gwynedd

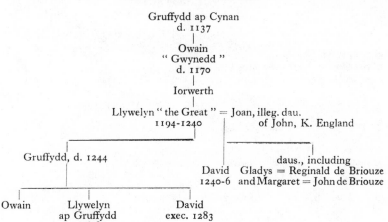

Gruffydd ap Cynan
d. 1137

Owain
" Gwynedd "
d. 1170

Iorwerth

Llywelyn " the Great " = Joan, illeg. dau.
1194-1240   of John, K. England

Gruffydd, d. 1244

David   Gladys = Reginald de Briouze
1240-6   and Margaret = John de Briouze

daus., including

Owain   Llywelyn   David
           ap Gruffydd   exec. 1283
           1246-82

B. The Line of Deheubarth

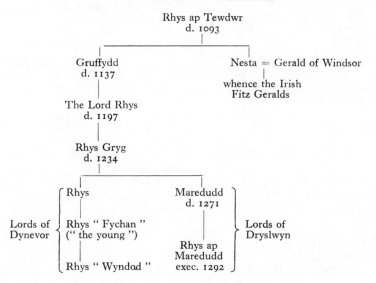

Rhys ap Tewdwr
d. 1093

Gruffydd   Nesta = Gerald of Windsor
d. 1137
                   whence the Irish
The Lord Rhys   Fitz Geralds
d. 1197

Rhys Gryg
d. 1234

Lords of   ⎧ Rhys   Maredudd ⎫ Lords of
Dynevor   ⎨   d. 1271 ⎬ Dryslwyn
           ⎪ Rhys " Fychan "   ⎪
           ⎪ (" the young ")   ⎪
           ⎪   Rhys ap ⎪
           ⎩ Rhys " Wyndod " Maredudd ⎭
                         exec. 1292

421

BIBLIOGRAPHY

NOTE.—The date of publication is given only at the first occurrence of the title of a book in the bibliography.

[Fr.] and [Ger.] before a title indicate that the work is available only in a French or German edition respectively.

Part I

Anglo-Saxon Chronicle, transl. G. N. GARMONSWAY, 1953.
BARLOW, F., *The Feudal Kingdom of England, 1042-1216*, 1954.
BLAIR, P. H., *An Introduction to Anglo-Saxon England*, 1956.
CAM, HELEN, *England before Elizabeth*, 2nd edn. 1952.
Cambridge Medieval History (1911-36), Vol. III (1924), chap. xv (W. J. CORBETT).
CHAMBERS, R. W., *England before the Norman Conquest*, 1926.
CHAMBERS, R. W., *The Exeter Book of Old English Poetry*, 1933.
FOWKE, F. R., *The Bayeux Tapestry*, 1898.
FREEMAN, E. A., *The Norman Conquest* (6 vols.), 1867-79.
FREEMAN, E. A., *William the Conqueror*, 1894.
HARMER, FLORENCE, *Anglo-Saxon Writs*, 1952.
HODGKIN, T., *The Political History of England*, Vol. I (1920).
JOLLIFFE, J. E. A., *Constitutional History of Medieval England*, 1937.
MACLAGAN, SIR ERIC, *The Bayeux Tapestry*, 1943.
MAITLAND, F. W., *Domesday Book and Beyond*, 1897, reprinted, Fontana Library, 1960.
OMAN, SIR CHARLES, *England before the Norman Conquest*, 1910, 9th edn. 1949.
ROBERTSON, AGNES, *The Laws of the Kings of England from Edmund to Henry I*, 1925.
ROBERTSON, AGNES, *Anglo-Saxon Charters*, 1939.
SEEBOHM, F., *The English Village Community*, 4th edn. 1905, reprinted 1915.
STENTON, SIR FRANK, *Anglo-Saxon England*, 2nd edn. 1947.
STENTON, SIR FRANK, *William the Conqueror*, 1908; new edition, 1967.
STENTON, SIR FRANK (Ed.), *The Bayeux Tapestry*, 1957.
VINOGRADOFF, SIR PAUL, *English Society in the XIth century*, 1908.
WHITELOCK, DOROTHY, *Anglo-Saxon Wills*, 1930.
WHITELOCK, DOROTHY, *The Beginnings of English Society*, 1952.
WHITELOCK, DOROTHY, *English Historical Documents, c. 500-1042*, 1955.

Part II

(Chapters iv, v and vii)

ADAMS, G. B., *The Political History of England*, Vol. II, 1905.
ARMITAGE, ELLA, *Early Norman Castles of the British Isles*, 1912.
BARLOW, F., *The Feudal Kingdom of England*.
BROOKE, C. N. L., *From Alfred to Henry III*, 1961.
BROOKE, Z. N., *The English Church and the Papacy from the Conquest to the reign of King John*, 1931.
Cambridge Medieval History, Vol. III (1924), chap. xviii (SIR P. VINOGRADOFF) ; Vol. V (1926), chaps. xv, xvi (W. J. CORBETT).

CHEW, HELENA, *English ecclesiastical tenants-in-chief and knight-service*, 1932.
DARBY, H. C. (and others), *The Domesday Geography of England* (in progress): *Eastern England*, 1952 ; *Midland England*, 1954 (with I. B. TERRETT).
DAVID, C. W., *Robert Curthose*, 1920.
DAVIS, H. W. C., *England under the Normans and Angevins, 1066-1272*, 1905, 13th edn. 1949.
DOUGLAS, D. C. and G. W. GREENAWAY, *English Historical Documents, 1042-1189*, 1953.
FREEMAN, E. A., *The Norman Conquest.*
FREEMAN, E. A., *William the Conqueror.*
FREEMAN, E. A., *The Reign of William Rufus*, 2 vols., 1882.
GALBRAITH, V. H., *Studies in the Public Records* (Chap. Four), 1948.
GANSHOF, F. L., *Feudalism* (transl. P. Grierson, 1952).
HASKINS, C. H., *Norman Institutions*, 1918.
HASKINS, C. H., *The Normans in European History*, 1919.
KNOWLES, D. (ed. and transl.), *The Monastic Constitutions of Lanfranc*, 1951.
LLOYD, SIR JOHN, *The History of Wales from the earliest times to the Edwardian Conquest*, 2 vols., 1911 ; 3rd edn. 1939, reprinted 1948.
MACDONALD, A. J., *Lanfranc*, 1926.
MORRIS, W. A., *The Frankpledge System*, 1910.
MORRIS, W. A., *The Medieval English Sheriff to 1300*, 1927.
POOLE, A. L., *From Domesday Book to Magna Carta*, 1951, 2nd edn. 1955.
POOLE, R. L., *The Exchequer in the XIIth Century*, 1912.
POTTER, K. R. (ed. and transl., with notes by R. A. B. Mynors and A. L. Poole), *Gesta Stephani*, 1955.
RAMSAY, SIR JAMES, *The Foundations of England*, Vol. II, 1066-1154, 1898.
RÖSSLER, O. [Ger.], *Kaiserin Mathilde*, 1897.
ROUND, J. H., *Geoffrey de Mandeville*, 1892.
ROUND, J. H., *Feudal England*, 1895.
STENTON, SIR FRANK, *William the Conqueror.*
STENTON, SIR FRANK, *The First Century of English Feudalism, 1066-1166*, 2nd edn. 1961.
STENTON, SIR FRANK, *Anglo-Saxon England* (Chaps. xvi-xviii and epilogue).

Part II

(Chapter vi)

GENERAL

BARNARD, F. P., *Companion to English History, The Middle Ages*, 1902.
BOASE, T. S. R., *English Art, 1100-1216* (Vol. III of the Oxford History of English Art), 1953.
BORENIUS, T. and E. W. TRISTRAM, *English Medieval Painting*, 1927.
BROWN, G. BALDWIN, *The Arts in Early England*, 7 vols., 1903-37.
CLAPHAM, SIR ALFRED, *English Romanesque Architecture after the Conquest*, 1934.
COULTON, G. G., *Social Life in Britain from the Conquest to the Reformation*, 1918.
COULTON, G. G., *Medieval Panorama*, 1938, new edn. 1947.

COULTON, G. G., *Life in the Middle Ages*, 2nd edn. 1928, reprinted 1 vol., 1954.
EVANS, JOAN, *A History of Jewellery, 1100-1870*, 1953.
GARDNER, A., *English Medieval Sculpture*, 1935, revised edn. 1951.
HASKINS, C. H., *The Renaissance of the XIIth Century*, 1927.
HASKINS, C. H., *Studies in Medieval Culture*, 1929.
HASKINS, C. H., *Studies in the History of Medieval Science*, 1924.
PRIOR, E. S. and A. GARDNER, *An Account of Medieval Figure-sculpture in England*, 1912.
SALZMAN, L. F., *Building in England down to 1540*, 1952.
SOUTHERN, R. W., *The Making of the Middle Ages*, 1953.
STENTON, DORIS, *English Society in the Early Middle Ages*, 1951.
TRISTRAM, E. W., *English Medieval Wall-painting*, 1944.
WADDELL, HELEN, *The Wandering Scholars*, 6th edn. 1926.
WARD, A. W. and A. R. WALLER (eds.), *Cambridge History of English Literature*, Vol. I (1907).

(i) RELIGION, CHURCH AND CLERGY

BOHMER, H. [Ger.], *Kirche und Staat in England und in der Normandie*, 1899.
BROOKE, Z. N., *The English Church and the Papacy from the Conquest to the reign of King John*.
Cambridge Medieval History, Vol. V, Chap. xx (A. HAMILTON-THOMPSON).
CHURCH, R. W., *St. Anselm*, 1870.
CLAYTON, J., *St. Anselm*, 1933.
COLVIN, H. M., *The White Canons in England*, 1951.
COULTON, G. G., *Five Centuries of Religion*, 4 vols., 1927-50, esp. Vol. I.
DICKINSON, J. C., *The Origins of the Austin Canons and their introduction into England*, 1950.
FOREVILLE, RAYMONDE [Fr.], *L'église et la royauté en Angleterre sous Henri II Plantagenet*, 1943.
GRAHAM, ROSE, *St. Gilbert of Sempringham*, 1901.
GRAHAM, ROSE, *English Ecclesiastical Studies*, 1929.
GRAHAM, ROSE, *An Essay on the English Monasteries*, 1939.
HILL, G., *The English Dioceses*, 1900.
HUTTON, W. H., *Thomas Becket, Archbishop of Canterbury*, 1926.
JAMES, M. R., *Abbeys*, 1926.
KNOWLES, D., *The Monastic Order in England*, 1940, reprinted 1949.
KNOWLES, D., *The Episcopal colleagues of Archbishop Thomas Becket*, 1951.
KNOWLES, D. and R. N. HADCOCK, *Medieval Religious Houses, England and Wales*, 1953.
LEES, B. A., *Records of the Templars in England in the XIIth Century*, 1935.
MAKOWER, F., *Constitutional History of the Church of England*, 1895.
Ordnance Survey, *Map of Monastic Britain* (2 sheets, 1950).
POWICKE, SIR MAURICE, *The Christian Life in the Middle Ages*, 1935.
POWICKE, SIR MAURICE (ed. and transl.), *The Life of Ailred of Rievaulx by Walter Daniel*, 1950.
RADFORD, L. B., *Thomas of London*, 1894.
RULE, M., *The Life and Times of Anselm*, 2 vols., 1883.
SALTMAN, A., *Theobald, Archbishop of Canterbury*, 1956.
STEPHENS, W. R. W., *The English Church, 1066-1272*, 1901.
THOMPSON, MARGARET, *The Carthusian Order in England*, 1930.

(ii) THE CLASSES OF SOCIETY

ADLER, M., *Jews of Medieval England*, 1939.
BENNETT, H. S., *Life on the English Manor*, 1937.
BERESFORD, M., *The Lost Villages of England*, 1954.
Cambridge Economic History, Vol. I (1942), Chap. vii, § 7 (NELLIE NEILSON) ; Vol. II (1952).
COULTON, G. G., *The Medieval Village*.
DOUGLAS, D. C., *The Social Structure of Medieval East Anglia*, 1927.
DOUGLAS, D. C. and G. W. GREENAWAY, *English Historical Documents*, *1042-1189*.
GROSS, C., *The Gild Merchant*, 2 vols., 1890.
JACOBS, J., *The Jews of Angevin England*, 1893.
LAPSLEY, G., *Boldon Book*, in *Victoria History of the County of Durham*, Vol. I (1905), pp. 259-341.
LENNARD, R., *Rural England 1086-1135*, 1959.
LIPSON, E., *Economic History of England*, Vol. I, 7th edn. 1937.
ORWIN, C. S. and C. S., *The Open Fields*, 2nd edn. 1954.
PAGE, W., *London : its origin and early development*, 1923.
POOLE, A. L., *The Obligations of Society in the XIIth and XIIIth Centuries*, 1946.
ROTH, C., *History of the Jews in England*, 1941.
ROUND, J. H., *The Commune of London* (1899), Chap. xi.
SALZMAN, L. F., *English Industries of the Middle Ages*, 1913.
SALZMAN, L. F., *English Trade in the Middle Ages*, 1931.
SEEBOHM, F., *The English Village Community*.
STENTON, SIR FRANK, H. E. BUTLER, M. B. HONEYBOURNE, and E. JEFFRIES DAVIES, *Norman London*, 1934.
STEPHENSON, C., *Borough and Town*, 1933.
TAIT, J., *The Medieval English Borough*, 1936.
VINOGRADOFF, SIR PAUL, *Villeinage in England*, 1892.
VINOGRADOFF, SIR PAUL, *Growth of the Manor*, 2nd edn. 1911.
(The Bibliography for Chapters viii and ix will be found below, under Part IV, Chapter xv.)

Part III

ADAMS, G. B., *The Political History of England*, Vol. II.
BARLOW, F., *The Feudal Kingdom of England*.
BOUSSARD, J. [Fr.] *Le gouvernement d'Henri II Plantagenet*, 1956.
BROOKE, Z. N., *The English Church and the Papacy from the Conquest to the reign of King John*.
Cambridge Medieval History, Vol. V (1926), Chap. xvii (D. M. STENTON) ; Vol. VI (1929), Chaps. vii and ix (SIR MAURICE POWICKE).
CARTELLIERI, A. [Ger.], *Philipp II August*, 4 vols., 1899-1921.
CHRIMES, S. B., *An Introduction to the administrative history of Medieval England*, 1952.
CURTIS, E., *History of Medieval Ireland*, 2nd edn. 1938.
DAVIS, H. W. C., *England under the Normans and Angevins*.
DOUGLAS, D. C. and G. W. GREENAWAY, *English Historical Documents*, *1042-1189*.
ELLIS, C., *Hubert de Burgh*, 1952.
FOREVILLE, R. [Fr.], *L'église et la royauté en Angleterre sous Henri II Plantagenet*.

Bibliography

GIRALDUS CAMBRENSIS (Gerald of Barry or Gerald of Wales), *De rebus a se gestis* (Autobiography), ed. and transl. H. E. Butler, 1937.

GOEBEL, J., *Felony and Misdemeanor*, Vol. I, 1937.

JAMES, M. R. (ed. and transl.), *Walter Map's " De Nugis Curialium "* (Cymmrodorion Society Record Series, Vol. IX), 1923.

JOHNSON, C. (ed. and transl.), *The Course of the Exchequer by Richard, son of Nigel (Dialogus de Scaccario)*, 1950.

JOLLIFFE, J. E. A., *Constitutional History of Medieval England*.

JOLLIFFE, J. E. A., *Angevin Kingship*, 1955.

KNOWLES, D., *The Episcopal Colleagues of Archbishop Thomas Becket*.

LANDON, L., *Itinerary of Richard I*, 1935.

MCKECHNIE, W. S., *Magna Carta*, 2nd edn. 1914.

MAITLAND, F. W., *Roman Canon Law in the Church of England*, 1898.

MALDEN, H. E. (ed.), *Magna Carta Commemoration Essays*, 1917.

MITCHELL, S. K., *Studies in Taxation under John and Henry III*, 1914.

NORGATE, KATE, *England under the Angevin Kings*, 2 vols., 1887.

NORGATE, KATE, *Richard the Lion-heart*, 1924.

NORGATE, KATE, *John Lackland*, 1902.

ORPEN, G. H., *Ireland under the Normans, 1169-1216*, 4 vols., 1911.

PAINTER, S., *The Reign of King John*, 1949.

PAINTER, S., *William Marshal*, 1933.

PETIT-DUTAILLIS, C., *Feudal Monarchy in France and England* (transl. E. D. Hunt), 1936.

POLLOCK, SIR FREDERICK and F. W. MAITLAND, *The History of English Law before the time of Edward I*, 2nd edn., 2 vols., 1911.

POOLE, A. L., *From Domesday Book to Magna Carta*.

POOLE, R. L., *The Exchequer in the XIIth Century*.

POWICKE, SIR MAURICE, *The Loss of Normandy*, 1913.

RAMSAY, SIR JAMES, *The Angevin Empire, 1154-1216*, 1903.

SALZMAN, L. F., *Henry II*, 1917.

STUBBS, W., *Historical Introductions to the Rolls Series* (ed. A. Hassall), 1902, esp. pp. 89-172.

STUBBS, W., *Select Charters* (9th edn., revised by H. W. C. Davis, 1913, reprinted 1946).

TOUT, T. F., *Chapters in the administrative history of Medieval England*, Vol. I (1920).

TUPPER, F. and M. B. OGLE (ed. and transl.), *Master Walter Map's Book " De Nugis Curialium "* (Courtiers' Trifles), 1924.

WARREN, W. L., *King John*, 1961.

Part IV

(Chapter xiv)

BUTLER, H. E. (ed. and transl.), GIRALDUS CAMBRENSIS (Gerald of Barry or Gerald of Wales), *De rebus a se gestis* (Autobiography).

DAVIES, J. C. (ed.), *The Welsh Assize Roll, 1277-1284*, 1940.

EDWARDS, J. G., *Calendar of Ancient Correspondence concerning Wales*, 1935.

EDWARDS, J. G. (ed.), *Littere Wallie*, 1940.

LLOYD, SIR JOHN, *The History of Wales from the earliest times to the Edwardian Conquest*, 2 vols., 3rd edn. 1939.

Bibliography

Chapter xv

(The Bibliography for Part II, Chapters viii and ix, is included here.)

ANDERSON, A. O., *Scottish Annals from English Chroniclers*, 1908.
ANDERSON, A. O., *Early Sources of Scottish History, 500-1286*, 2 vols., 1922.
ARMITAGE, ELLA, *Early Norman Castles of the British Isles.*
BARROW, G. W. S., *The Acts of Malcolm IV, 1153-1165*, 1960.
BROWN, P. HUME, *History of Scotland*, Vol. I, 1899.
BRYCE, W. M., *The Scottish Grey Friars*, 2 vols., 1909.
Cambridge Medieval History, Vol. VII (1932), Chap. xix (C. S. TERRY).
DICKINSON, W. C., *Scotland from the earliest times to 1603*, 1961.
DICKINSON, W. C., G. DONALDSON, and ISABEL MILNE (eds.), *A Source Book of Scottish History*, Vol. I, 1952, 2nd edn. 1958.
DOWDEN, J., *The Medieval Church in Scotland*, 1910.
EASSON, D. E., *Medieval Religious Houses, Scotland*, 1957.
FRANKLIN, T. B., *A History of Scottish Farming*, 1952.
GRANT, ISABEL, *The Social and Economic Development of Scotland before 1603*, 1931.
HAILES, SIR DAVID DALRYMPLE, LORD, *Annals of Scotland*, 3 vols., 3rd edn. 1819.
INNES, C., *Sketches of early Scotch History*, 1861.
INNES, C., *Scotch Legal Antiquities*, 1872.
LANG, A., *A History of Scotland*, Vol. I, 1900.
LAWRIE, SIR ARCHIBALD, *Early Scottish Charters*, 1905.
LAWRIE, SIR ARCHIBALD, *Annals of the reigns of Malcolm and William, Kings of Scotland*, 1910.
MACEWEN, A., *History of the Church of Scotland*, Vol. I, 1913.
MACKENZIE, AGNES, *A History of Scotland*, 6 vols., 1935-42, esp. Vols. I (1938) and II (1935).
MACKENZIE, W. M., *The Mediæval Castle in Scotland*, 1927.
MACKENZIE, W. M., *The Scottish Burghs*, 1949.
RAIT, SIR ROBERT, *A History of Scotland*, 1929.
RAIT, SIR ROBERT, *The Making of Scotland*, 2nd edn. 1929.
RITCHIE, R. L. G., *The Normans in Scotland*, 1954.
SKENE, W. F., *Celtic Scotland*, 2nd edn., 3 vols., 1886-7.
THOMSON, J. M., *The Public Records of Scotland*, 1922.

Part V

(Chapters xvi and xvii)

GENERAL

CAM, HELEN, *Liberties and Communities in Medieval England*, 1944.
Cambridge Medieval History, Vol. VI (1929), Chap. viii (E. F. JACOB); Chap. ix (SIR MAURICE POWICKE); Vol. VII (1932), Chap. xiv (HILDA JOHNSTONE).
DAVIS, H. W. C., *England under the Normans and Angevins.*
JOLLIFFE, J. E. A., *Constitutional History of Medieval England.*
LUNT, W. E., *Financial Relations of the Papacy with England to 1327*, 1939.
POWICKE, SIR MAURICE, *King Henry III and the Lord Edward*, 2 vols., 1947.
POWICKE, SIR MAURICE, *The Thirteenth Century*, 1953.
RAMSAY, SIR JAMES, *The Dawn of the Constitution*, 1908.
SAYLES, G. O., *The Medieval Foundations of England*, 1948.

THOMPSON, FAITH, *The First Century of Magna Carta*, 1925.
TOUT, T. F., *The Political History of England, 1216-1377*, 2nd edn. 1920.
WILKINSON, B., *Constitutional History of England*, Vol. I (1216-1307), 1948.

(Chapter xvi)

BÉMONT, C., *Simon de Montfort*, 1884 (transl. E. F. Jacob, 1930).
BLAAUW, W., *The Barons' War*, 2nd edn. 1871.
DENHOLM-YOUNG, N., *Richard of Cornwall*, 1947.
JACOB, E. F., *Studies in the period of Baronial Reform and Rebellion*, 1925.
MITCHELL, S. K., *Studies in Taxation under John and Henry III*.
NORGATE, KATE, *The Minority of Henry III*, 1912.
PROTHERO, SIR GEORGE, *The Life of Simon de Montfort*, 1877.
TREHARNE, R. F., *The Baronial Plan of Reform, 1258-63*, 1932.

(Chapter xvii)

CAM, HELEN, *The Hundred and the Hundred Rolls*, 1930.
GRAS, N. S. B., *The Early English Customs System*, 1918.
HASKINS, C. L., *The Statute of York and the interest of the Commons*, 1935.
MCILWAIN, C. H., *The High Court of Parliament and its supremacy*, 1910.
MCKISACK, MAY, *Representation of English Boroughs in the Middle Ages*, 1932.
MAITLAND, F. W. (ed., with introduction), *Records of the Parliament of 1305* (*The " Memoranda de Parliamento "*), 1893.
MITCHELL, S. K., *Taxation in Medieval England*, 1951.
PASQUET, D., *An Essay on the Origins of the House of Commons* (transl. R. G. D. Laffan, with notes by G. Lapsley), 1925.
PLUCKNETT, T. F. T., *The Legislation of Edward I*, 1949.
POLLARD, A. F., *The Evolution of Parliament*, 2nd edn. 1926.
RICHARDSON, H. G. and G. O. SAYLES, *The Irish Parliament in the Middle Ages*, 1952.
SAYLES, G. O., *The Medieval Foundations of England*, Chap. xxvii.
WILLARD, J. F., *Parliamentary Taxes on Personal Property, 1290-1334*, 1924.

Part V

(Chapter xviii)
GENERAL

(See titles given above, under Chapter vi, General.)
EVANS, JOAN, *English Art, 1307-1461* (Vol. V of the Oxford History of English Art), 1949.
HARVEY, J., *Gothic England*, 1947.
HARVEY, J., *English Medieval Architects*, 1954.
HARVEY, J. and H. FELTON, *The English Cathedrals*, 1950.

(i) THE CHURCH FROM LANGTON TO WINCHELSEY

CALLUS, D. (ed.), *Robert Grosseteste*, 1953.
Cambridge Medieval History, Vol. VI, Chap. xxi (A. G. LITTLE).
CHURCHILL, IRENE, *Canterbury Administration*, 2 vols., 1933.
COULTON, G. G., *Five Centuries of Religion*, esp. Vols. II and III.

CROMBIE, A. C., *Robert Grosseteste and the Origins of Experimental Science, 1100-1700*, 1953.

DOUIE, DECIMA, *Archbishop Pecham*, 1951.

EDWARDS, KATHLEEN, *The English Secular Cathedrals in the Middle Ages*, 1949.

GALBRAITH, GEORGINA, *The Constitution of the Dominican Order*, 1925.

GIBBS, MARION and JANE LANG, *Bishops and Reform, 1215-1272*, 1932.

GRAHAM, ROSE, *English Ecclesiastical Studies*.

HINNEBUSCH, W. A., *The Early English Friars Preachers*, 1951.

HUTTON, E., *The Franciscans in England*, 1926.

JAMES, M. R., *Abbeys*.

JARRETT, B., *The English Dominicans*, 1921.

KNOWLES, D., *The Religious Orders in England*, Vol. I, 1948.

LITTLE, A. G., *Studies in English Franciscan History*, 1917.

LITTLE, A. G., *Franciscan papers, lists and documents*, 1943.

MOORMAN, J. R. H., *Church Life in England in the XIIIth Century*, 1945.

POWER, EILEEN, *Medieval English Nunneries*, 1922.

RASHDALL, H., *The Universities of Europe in the Middle Ages*. A new edition by Sir Maurice Powicke and A. B. Emden, 3 vols., 1936 (esp. Vol. III).

SHARP, D. E., *Franciscan Philosophy at Oxford in the XIIIth Century*, 1930.

STEVENSON, F. S., *Robert Grosseteste*, 1899.

WOOD, SUSAN, *English Monasteries and their patrons in the XIIIth Century*, 1955.

(ii) CHANGES IN COUNTRY AND TOWN

(See titles given above under Part II, Chapter vi.)

ADDY, S. O., *Church and Manor*, 1913.

BENNETT, H. S., *Life on the English Manor*.

Cambridge Economic History, Vol. I (1942), Chap. vii, § 7 (NELLIE NEILSON) ; Vol. II (1952).

DENHOLM-YOUNG, N., *Seignorial Administration in England*, 1937.

GROSS, C., *The Gild Merchant*.

HENLEY, WALTER OF, see LAMOND, E.

HOMANS, G. C., *English Villagers of the XIIIth Century*, 1942.

LAMOND, E. (ed. and transl.), *Walter of Henley's Husbandry*, 1890.

LEVETT, ADA, *Studies in Manorial History*, 1938.

PLUCKNETT, T. F. T., *The Mediæval Bailiff*, 1954.

SMITH, R. A. L., *Canterbury Cathedral Priory*, 1943.

TAIT, J., *The Medieval English Borough*.

Part VI

(Chapter xix)

EDWARDS, J. G., *Edward I's Castle-building in Wales*, The Sir John Rhys Memorial Lecture for 1944, reprinted from the *Proceedings of the British Academy*, Vol. XXXII.

LLOYD, SIR JOHN, *History of Wales*, Chap. xx.

MORRIS, J. E., *The Welsh Wars of Edward I*, 1901.

REES, W., *South Wales and the March, 1284-1415*, 1924.

WATERS, W. H., *The Edwardian Settlement of North Wales in its administrative and legal aspects, 1284-1343*, 1935.

Bibliography

(Chapter xx)

(See titles given above under Part V, Chapter xvii.)
LODGE, ELEANOR, *Gascony under English Rule*, 1926.
POWICKE, SIR MAURICE, *The Thirteenth Century*, Chaps. vii and xiv.

(Chapter xxi)

(For general works, see titles given above under Part IV, Chapter xv.)
BARRON, E. M., *The Scottish War of Independence*, 2nd edn. 1934.
FERGUSSON, JAMES, *William Wallace, Guardian of Scotland*, revised edn. 1948.
MACKENZIE, W. M., *Battle of Bannockburn*, 1913.
MAXWELL, SIR HERBERT, *Robert the Bruce*, 1897.
MILLER, T., *The Site of the Battle of Bannockburn*, 1931.
MORRIS, J. E., *Welsh Wars of Edward I*, Chap. viii.
MORRIS, J. E., *Bannockburn*, 1914.

INDEX

Figures in italics refer to the pages of genealogical tables.

Index

Philip II, " Augustus ", King of France (1180-1223), 175-6, 177, 181, 184, 185, 186, 187, 188, 189, 204, 208, 263 ; on crusade, 178, 182, 183

Philip III, King of France, 370

Philip IV, " The Fair ", King of France (1285-1314), 370, 373, 374, 375, 377, 379, 384, 396, 402, 403

Philip of Alsace, Count of Flanders, 172, 173

Pipe Roll, 76, 200-1

Plessis, John du, Earl of Warwick (d. 1263), 271

Plessy, Hugh de, 339

Poitou, 167-8, 187, 189, 190, 274

Pontigny, Cistercian abbey of, 152, 153

Pont l'Evêque, Roger of, Archbishop of York (1154-81), 121, 152, 154

Poole, Dr. A. L., *quoted*, 71

Poore, Richard, Bishop of Chichester (1215-17), Salisbury (1217-28), Durham (1228-37), 314 and n, 318, 319, 348

Portsmouth, 189

Powicke, Sir Maurice, *quoted*, 268, 293, 307, 358, 370

Powys, 41, 213, 217, 218, 222, 350

Premonstratensian Order, 106

Presentment, jury of, 156-7

Preston (E. Lothian), 235

Prise, under Edward I, 306, 382, 384, 385 ; of wine, 198 ; *see also* purveyance

Provisions of Oxford (1258), 269-71, 275, 276

Provisions of Westminster (1259), 272-3, 276, 283

Puiset, Hugh du, Bishop of Durham (1153-95), 179, 180

Purveyance, royal right of, 306 ; *see also* Prise

Queensferry (Fife and Midlothian), 130

Quia Emptores, see Statutes

Quinci, Saer de, Earl of Winchester (1207-19), 189 n, 247, 257

Quo Waranto enquiries, 284-6 ; *see also* Statutes

Radnor, 214, 216 ; Radnorshire, 213

Ralf, Earl of East Anglia, 40

Ramsay, Peter, Bishop of Aberdeen (1247-57), 241

Ramsey (Hunts), Benedictine abbey of, 119

Reading (Berks), Benedictine abbey of, 102, 108 ; church council at (1279), 320

Reform Movement and Programme (1258), 269-80, 301

Regenbald, chancellor, 29

Reichersberg, Gerhoh of, 153

Remigius, Bishop of Lincoln (1072-92), 61, 347

Rere Cross on Stainmore, boundary mark, 127

Reyns, Henry de, architect of Westminster Abbey, 284

Rheims Cathedral, 284

Rhodri, son of Owain Gwynedd, 213

Rhos (N. Wales), 352, 355

Rhufoniog (N. Wales), 352, 355

Rhys ap Gruffydd, Prince of South Wales (" the Lord Rhys "), 170, 212, 217, *421*

Rhys ap Maredudd, Lord of Ystrad Tywi (d. 1292), 351, 352, 355, 359, *421*

Rhys ap Tewdwr, Prince of South Wales, 41, *421*

Richard I, King of England (1189-99), 99, 192, *419* ; as Duke of Aquitaine, 168, 172, 175, 176 ; England in his absence, 178-81 ; his leadership of the Third Crusade (1190-2), 182-4 ; his relations with Philip Augustus, 177-8, 184-6 ; his death, 186

Richard, Earl of Cornwall, King of Germany (d. 1272), 264, 277, 294, 301, *419* ; marries Sanchia of Provence, 265 n

Richard, Bishop of St. Andrews (1165-78), 236

Richard the mason, 347

Richmond (Yorks, N.R.), earls of, *see* Alan, John

Rievaulx (Yorks, N.R.), Cistercian abbey of, 105

Ripon (Yorks, N.R.), 120

Rivaux, Peter des, royal administrator, 260, 261, 262

Rivenhall (Essex), 96

Robert I (Brus), King of Scots (1306-29) as Earl of Carrick, 308, 309, 392, 396, 398, 401, 402, 403 ; as Guardian of Scotland, 401-2 ; supports Edward I, 403-4 ; made king at Scone (1306), 405 ; as king, 406, 407, 408, 409, *420*

Robert of Jumièges, Archbishop of Canterbury (1051-70), 33, 57

Robert, Abbot of Molesme, afterwards abbot of Citeaux, 104

Robert, Bishop of St. Andrews (d. 1159), 139

447